T0298481

Collaborative Policing

Police, Academics, Professionals,
and Communities Working Together for Education,
Training, and Program Implementation

Advances in Police Theory and Practice Series

Series Editor: Dilip K. Das

Collaborative Policing

Police, Academics, Professionals,
and Communities Working Together for Education,
Training, and Program Implementation

Edited by

Peter C. Kratcoski
Kent State University
Kent, Ohio, USA

Maximilian Edelbacher
Austrian Federal Police (Retired)
Austria

CRC Press
Taylor & Francis Group
Boca Raton London New York

CRC Press is an imprint of the
Taylor & Francis Group, an **informa** business

CRC Press
Taylor & Francis Group
6000 Broken Sound Parkway NW, Suite 300
Boca Raton, FL 33487-2742

First issued in paperback 2019

© 2016 by Taylor & Francis Group, LLC
CRC Press is an imprint of Taylor & Francis Group, an Informa business

No claim to original U.S. Government works

ISBN-13: 978-1-4822-5140-1 (hbk)
ISBN-13: 978-0-367-87041-6 (pbk)

Visit the Taylor & Francis Web site at
http://www.taylorandfrancis.com

and the CRC Press Web site at
http://www.crcpress.com

This book is dedicated to Lucille Dunn Kratcoski and Edith Edelbacher. The assistance and support they gave us during the entire time we worked on this book is much appreciated.

Contents

Section I

POLICE AND ACADEMIC COLLABORATION IN RESEARCH, EDUCATION, AND TRAINING

Section II

COLLABORATION AMONG THE POLICE, PROFESSIONAL PRACTITIONERS, AND THE COMMUNITY IN THE CRIMINAL JUSTICE PROCESS AND IN CRIME PREVENTION PROGRAMS

Series Editor's Preface

While literature on police and allied subjects is growing exponentially, its impact on day-to-day policing remains negligible. The two worlds of policing—research and practice—remain disconnected even though cooperation between them is growing. A major reason is that the two groups speak in different languages. The research work is published in hard-to-access journals and is presented in a manner that is difficult to comprehend for a lay person. On the contrary, the police practitioners tend not to mix with researchers and remain secretive about their work. Consequently, there is little dialog between the two and almost no attempt to enrich one another. Dialog across the globe, among researchers and practitioners situated in different continents, is of course even more limited.

I attempted to address this problem by starting the IPES, www.ipes.info, where a common platform has brought the two together. IPES is now in its 21st year. The annual meetings which constitute the major annual events of the organization have been hosted in all parts of the world. Several publications have come out of these deliberations, and a new collaborative community of scholars and police officers has been created with membership running into several hundreds.

Another attempt was to begin a new journal, *Police Practice and Research: An International Journal*, PPR, which would offer a platform to practitioners to share their work and experiences. PPR would be completing its 16th year in 2015. The fact that PPR which began with four issues a year, expanded into five issues in its fourth year, and is presently issued six times a year is certainly evidence enough of the growing collaboration between police research and practice.

Clearly, these attempts, despite their success, remain limited. Conferences and journal publications do help create a body of knowledge and an association of police activists but cannot address substantial issues in depth. The limitations of time and space preclude larger discussions and more authoritative expositions that can provide stronger and broader linkages between the two worlds.

It is this realization of the increasing dialog between police research and practice that has encouraged many of us—my close colleagues and I connected closely with IPES and PPR across the world—to conceive and implement a new attempt in this direction. This led to the book series,

"Advances in Police Theory and Practice," which seeks to attract writers from all over the world. Further, the attempt is to find practitioner contributors. The objective is to position the series as a serious contribution to our knowledge of the police force as well as to improve police practices. The series strives not only to describe the best and successful police practices at work but also to challenge current paradigms and break new ground in preparing the police for the twenty-first century. It seeks comparative analyses that highlights achievements in the distant parts of the world as well as encourages an in-depth examination of specific problems confronting a particular police force.

Collaborative Policing: Police, Academics, Professionals, and Communities Working Together for Education, Training, Research, and Program Implementation focuses on the ways knowledge obtained from education, training, and scientific research is being used by police practitioners and other professionals working in the justice system to assist them in the completion of their work. In the past, police administrators did not view academics' research findings on the causes of crime, citizens' satisfaction with the police, and suggested models for police management as important for police administration and for on-the-job performance of the rank and file of the police force. However, as police administrators and officers began to collaborate with academics and professional practitioners on research projects, they came to recognize the value of the information produced and incorporated it into police training and program implementation. The chapters in this book reveal that police education, training, and practices are now closely tied to collaboration between police, academics, professional practitioners, and community agencies, and such collaboration is described and evaluated.

It is hoped that through this series, it will be possible to accelerate the process of knowledge building about policing and also bridge the gap between the two worlds—the world of police research and police practice. This is an invitation to police scholars and practitioners across the world to join this venture.

Dilip K. Das, PhD
Founding President
International Police Executive Symposium, IPES, www.ipes.info

Founding Editor-in-Chief
Police Practice and Research: An International Journal,
PPR, www.tandf.co.uk/journals

Foreword

The theory and practice of collaboration among academics, the police, and communities are more diverse and difficult to implement than the idea and policy envisioned for a variety of reasons. Collaboration, or partnerships for working together, promises more effective protection and prevention of crimes and disorders. For those involved, the outcome can be improved training, learning, and integration of the different knowledge possessed by the partners and better relations among them. Hopefully, they will come to understand the assumptions, biases, and strengths of each other's occupational, group-based, and private cultures, and that they will also use more creative approaches and policies to negotiate and overcome the practical and organizational obstacles that assuredly will complicate any attempts at working together in harmony and with mutual respect.

Working together involves many practical challenges, from the most mundane issues on how to schedule meetings to the "who will pay for what" part of the collaboration. From the sharing of the information possessed by each partner to the creation of the negotiating processes and the ironing out of the inevitable difference in opinions and preferences when people with different life experiences come together to decide on what should be done will present challenges to the participating parties.

Working together only "works" if the psychological preconditions that are the foundations for effective and peaceful collaboration are present. Partners have to be willing to trust each other and to overcome, forget, and/or compromise their own organizational and private interests. That trust has to be earned, and it has to be reenforced continually by the manner in which this collaboration is organized and carried out.

The postulated consequences of collaboration are worthwhile goals, no doubt of that, but only if collaboration is properly implemented. Collaboration looks good in theory and in policy plans, but it is also a practical activity. A crucial issue is the partners' equality of participation in designing, organizing, implementing, and assessing the effects of specific collaborations. For example, following the basic issues around which the sections of this book are organized, will the knowledge possessed by each partner be valued and used equally by all, or will the police, academics, or communities assert priority of their knowledge over that of the other partners? Will the selection of topics, teachers, and teaching styles at police academies and in collaborative adult learning programs be controlled by the police or be opened for discussion and compromise, allowing input by the other partners? Will the selection and definition of problem areas meriting crime prevention programs be open to influence by the views of the community and the other partners, and how will differences of opinion be negotiated and resolved?

Some rough parity or equality among diverse opinions exists. Collaborations will flounder if partners see their views, knowledge, and preferences relegated to subordinate status. Why should they bother if others will treat these views with benign neglect? Collaboration, therefore, requires that the partners involved seriously take a look at and value what others know, want, and need and, equally important and more difficult, engage in some self-reflection about their knowledge and why it should be accepted or should dominate the design and implementation of the collaborative work. Partners have to be able to say to each other, with genuine belief, "You have some good ideas there."

I would argue that the police believe that their knowledge acquired through training, experience, and personal hunches is more valuable to their work and its perceived dangers, challenges, and frequent tawdriness. They often view academic knowledge and advice as "impractical, abstract, and not actionable" within the realities of their work. At best, academic knowledge can validate and influence what the police want to do in any case, but it should not determine policing policies. The police tend to view the community largely as a helper rather than as a partner. The community's additional eyes and ears supply information but should not be enabled to do anything that imitates police work. The police naturally see themselves as the lead agency. The challenge is how policing can be improved to achieve security, crime control, social order, and community well-being through collaboration. Collaboration is about what they do every day.

Academics, in turn, have a different perspective on their knowledge than do the police and communities, and they tend to value their own knowledge as more accurate, scientific, and theoretical. Academics tend to believe that their knowledge is essential for the planning and designing of programs if these programs are to work and not be a waste of time and resources. Crime and disorder problems cannot be solved by a hit-or-miss approach to policing policies based on inertia and traditions and on "let's see what works." Academic and theoretical knowledge will improve the design, implementation, efficiency, and effectiveness of policies and, of course, academics are the experts in evaluating whether policies and programs have achieved the desired impacts. Conducting research is part of their daily work.

Communities know best what problems they fear and want to be taken care of, even though many of those problems are not policing issues—that is, problems that can be solved by legal and legitimate police actions.

But a community's views are seen as essentially parochial and not based on universal notions of what problems matter theoretically and practically. Community views do not always fit the preferences of the police on how to conduct their work nor do they always fit the views of academics that they understand what really matters in keeping a community or society safe and stable.

In short, collaboration, to be useful and to enhance the effectiveness and justice of police work, requires extensive information sharing and acceptance of different knowledge based on trust. Collaboration on paper and as policy goals will not work unless all three partners believe that their specialized knowledge, once combined and synthesized, provides a better basis for police and social actions that serve the public good.

The chapters in this book present genuinely comparative, theoretically informed, and experience-based collaborative programs to appraise and analyze the specific practical, theoretical, and psychological challenges of working together and the creative means to overcome those challenges.

Otwin Marenin
Department of Criminal Justice and Criminology
Washington State University

Preface

The sociological and psychological study of deviance and criminology has a long tradition in Europe and in the United States. However, in the United States, it was not until the 1950s that several universities began offering specific courses in criminal justice and in police studies. In the United States, the implementation of police studies, criminology, and other justice studies programs were stimulated by federal grants from the Law Enforcement Assistance Administration. These early criminal justice degree programs tended to be technical in nature (almost training courses) and were often ridiculed by the faculty of other well-entrenched academic departments. In turn, police administrators at that time generally did not consider education received at a university to be very useful in preparing an officer for police work.

The research and writings of established academics helped stimulate interest in the development of criminal justice as a respectable academic discipline as well as an area for study and research that can provide useful information to the police and others who have the responsibility for protecting and servicing the community in addition to preventing crime. As educators, researchers, and practitioners began to collaborate, they gained knowledge of and appreciation for the significant contributions each could make in developing quality programs in training, education, and research.

As a young sociologist trying to determine what would be a fruitful area to develop for his special topic of research and writing, Peter C. Kratcoski presented a paper on law enforcement and criminal justice education at an international conference of the American Society of Criminology held in Caracas, Venezuela, in the early 1970s. The section in which his paper was presented was chaired by Gerhart Mueller, a well-known scholar in these fields. This experience of having the opportunity to interact with and be encouraged by Dr. Mueller and other prominent academics who attended that conference led Kratcoski to follow a career development path that focused on teaching and research in criminal justice.

Maximilian Edelbacher's exposure to the subject matter was quite different from that of Kratcoski. Having developed a career with the Austrian Federal Police and eventually assumed the position of head of the Major Crimes Bureau, he was not oriented toward exploring theories of crime causation that seemed to have no immediate practical importance (i.e., that did not help in the investigation of crime). However, after meeting and interacting with Dilip K. Das, who was collecting data for a book he was writing on comparative criminal justice systems, Edelbacher began to gain an understanding and appreciation of the work of academics and how it contributes to the work of the police. This experience stimulated him to become involved in criminal justice professional organizations and to collaborate with academics in research as well as in writing.

The two editors of this book first met at a professional conference. Having similar interests in criminal justice topics, they began to collaborate on research and writing. Over a number of years, they have presented papers at professional meetings and have coauthored books, chapters in books, and journal articles. They also became very involved in the International Police Executive Symposium, an organization founded by Dilip K. Das.

The relationship among the police, academics, and professionals who provide services to victims of crime and to criminal offenders has not always been cooperative. However, as academics and professional practitioners—such as psychologists, social workers, and counselors—became directly involved in criminal justice agencies, and as police practitioners became more directly involved in higher education and research, an understanding and appreciation of each other's activities gradually developed. This resulted in the types of collaboration that are the focus of this book.

The academic and professional credentials of the authors who have contributed to this volume and the scope and importance of their work reveal that criminal justice practitioners and academics have formed strong collaborative relationships throughout the world, and that this collaboration has produced levels of information that are extremely important to crime control, the welfare of victims of crime, and to communities in the twenty-first century. We have every expectation that this type of collaboration will continue and increase in the future.

Peter C. Kratcoski
Maximilian Edelbacher

Acknowledgments

Police, academic, and community cooperation and collaboration in research and training and in community matters such as crime prevention have been discussed at a number of criminal justice and law enforcement professional meetings. In addition, many articles on this subject have been written and published in professional journals. The focus of the 10th International Police Executive Symposium, held in Antalya, Turkey, in 2002, was on Police Education and Training in a Global Society and two special issues of *Police Practice and Research,* published in 2011 and 2012, were devoted to articles that pertained to various aspects of police, academic, and community cooperation in research, training, education, crime prevention, and programming.

Thus, when Dilip K. Das, founding president of the International Police Executive Symposium and editor in chief of *Police Practice and Research* discussed the idea of producing a book on police, academic, and community cooperation and collaboration for the *Advances in Police Theory and Practice Series* of which he is the series editor, the coeditors of this book, who had completed research and publications on the subject, submitted a proposal to the justice editor of CRC Press, Carolyn Spence. This book would not have been possible without the endorsement and assistance of Dilip and Carolyn, and we deeply appreciate their support.

We wish to also express thanks to the many police and professional practitioners who took time from their busy schedules to either write a chapter for this book or be interviewed by the editors to contribute their knowledge to this undertaking. Many of the selections were either solely written by police or professional practitioners or by such practitioners in collaboration with academics.

Finally, we wish to give our thanks to Lucille Kratcoski, who edited portions of this book, and to the CRC Press/Taylor & Francis Group for their assistance and guidance during the production phase.

Peter C. Kratcoski
Maximilian Edelbacher

Editors

Peter C. Kratcoski earned a PhD in sociology from the Pennsylvania State University, University Park, Pennsylvania, an MA in sociology from the University of Notre Dame, Notre Dame, Indiana, and a BA in sociology from King's College, Wilkes-Barre, Pennsylvania. He was selected for several post-doctoral grants by the National Science Foundation. He taught at the College of St. Thomas, St. Paul, Minnesota, and at the Pennsylvania State University before assuming the position of assistant professor of sociology at Kent State University in 1969. He retired as professor of criminal justice studies and chairman of the Department of Criminal Justice Studies at Kent State in 1997 where he is currently a professor emeritus and adjunct professor. He has published many books, chapters in books, and journal articles in the areas of juvenile delinquency, juvenile justice, international policing, and crime prevention. He is a member of the International Police Executive Symposium, the Society for Police and Criminal Psychology, and the Academy of Criminal Justice Sciences.

Maximilian Edelbacher was born in 1944 in Vienna, Austria. He graduated from the University of Vienna (Mag), Wien, Austria, and as Hofrat of the Federal Police of Austria. He served as the chief of the Major Crime Bureau, an international expert for the Council of Europe, OSCE, and UNO. He also chaired the Austrian Antifraud Insurance Bureau and lectured at several universities, including the Vienna University of Economics and Business Administration, Danube University Krems, and the Vienna University Department of Sociology. Edelbacher was appointed as special investigator of the AVUS Group on White Collar Crime Cases, as vice president of the Vienna Liaison Office of the Academic Council on the United Nations, and as director of International Police Executive Symposium (IPES). He is the author of a number of books and journal articles.

Contributors

Jansen Ang is senior principal psychologist, assistant director, Police Psychological Services Division (PPSD) and current deputy director of the Home Team Behavioural Sciences Centre, Ministry of Home Affairs, Government of Singapore. He is also the deputy commanding officer and chief psychologist of the Crisis Negotiation Unit within the Special Operations Command of the Singapore Police Force where he works on selecting, training, and developing a cadre of crisis negotiators.

Mr. Ang holds a masters in forensic psychology. His professional experiences involve developing psychological profiles for various offenses. He is also an assistant professor (adjunct) in the School of Humanities and Social Sciences at Nanyang Technological University where he teaches the psychology of crisis stress management. As part of his work on leadership development, he is a mentor with the Police Command and Staff Course and also lectures on the Home Team Senior Command and Staff Course. For his work in expanding the mental health and resilience capabilities of the Home Team and in developing the concept of red teaming in operations, he was awarded the Home Team Achievement Award.

József Boda is former director general of the Coordination Centre Against Organized Crime, National Police of Hungary. Major General Boda received his PhD from Miklos Zrinyi National Defense University. He also completed education and training at the Lajos Kossuth Military Academy, the FBI National Academy, and the University Doctor Miklos Zrinyi War College.

During his long service with the Hungarian National Police, he has served as director general of the Special Service for the National Security of Hungary (SSNS), director general of the International Training and Civilian Crisis Management Center of the Ministry of Justice and Law Enforcement, director of the International Training Center of the Ministry of Interior and later the Ministry of Justice and Law Enforcement, director of the International Law Enforcement Academy, and deputy commander of the Police Special Forces Hungarian Defense Forces. In addition Dr. Boda has served on United Nations peacekeeping operations in Cambodia, Mozambique, Bosnia and Herzegovina, and Georgia.

JoAnne Brewster earned her PhD in experimental psychology from McMaster University, Hamilton, Ontario, Canada, and she did her retraining in clinical psychology at the University of Virginia, Charlottesville, Virginia. She has worked in community mental health and was in private practice for many years before joining the faculty at James Madison University, Harrisonburg, Virginia, where she is a professor in the Department of Graduate Psychology. She teaches abnormal psychology, forensic psychology, and police psychology. Her current practice consists solely of work with police departments. She is the secretary of the Society for Police and Criminal Psychology (SPCP). She is board certified in police and public safety psychology by the American Board of Police and Public Safety Psychology (ABPPSP) and is past-president of the American Academy of Police and Public Safety Psychology (AAPPSP). She represents the AAPPSP on the Council of Organizations in Police Psychology (COPP).

Edward Chafe has been employed as a police officer with the Ontario Provincial Police for 28 years. In 1990, he was assigned to the Criminal Investigations Unit as a detective constable. In 1995, he was transferred to General Headquarters to serve in the Violent Crime Linkage Analysis System. In 1997, he was promoted to detective sergeant and transferred within the Behavioural Science Section to the Threat Assessment Unit as the unit manager. In 2002, he was transferred to the Criminal Profiling Unit and was accepted into the International Criminal Investigative Analysis Fellowship (ICIAF) Understudy Program. He completed the program in 2005 and is currently a fellow within the program. Detective Sergeant Chafe has extensive experience and training in behavioral science concepts as well as management of incidents where there is a potential for targeted violence. His primary function as a criminal profiler is to provide investigative support and training pertaining to criminal investigative analysis to personnel of the Ontario Provincial Police, as well as to other law enforcement and criminal justice agencies.

Peter I. Collins obtained his masters in applied criminology from the University of Ottawa, Ottawa, Ontario, Canada, his medical degree from McMaster University, Hamilton, Ontario, Canada, and he completed his post-graduate medical training in psychiatry and forensic psychiatry at the University of Toronto. He is a psychiatrist with the Criminal Behaviour Analysis Unit of the Behavioural Sciences and Analysis Section, Ontario Provincial Police. His clinical appointment is with the Complex Mental Illness Program at the Centre for Addiction and Mental Health; he is an associate professor in the Division of Forensic Psychiatry at the University of Toronto and an associate clinical professor with the Department of Psychiatry and Behavioural Neurosciences at McMaster University. Dr. Collins is an authority on violent crime and has worked with, and instructed, numerous criminal justice agencies in Canada, the United States, the Caribbean, Central America and South America, Europe, South Africa, southwest Asia, Micronesia, and in Australia including the FBI, the U.S. Department of Homeland Security, INTERPOL, and EUROPOL.

He is also the consulting forensic psychiatrist to the Royal Canadian Mounted Police "O" Division Integrated National Security Enforcement Team (INSET), and since 1992, he has been a member of the negotiation team of the Toronto Police Service Emergency Task Force. In addition, he consults with the Behavioral Analysis Unit of the U.S. Marshals Service, the Investigative Psychology Unit of the South African Police, the Profiling Unit of the Florida Department of Law Enforcement, and the Behavioural Science Section of the Calgary Police Service. He is also a co-investigator with the Health Adaptation Research on Trauma (HART) Lab, University of Toronto at Mississauga, and a consulting editor for the *Journal of Threat Assessment and Management*, published by the American Psychological Association. He was elected a member of the International Criminal Investigative Analysis Fellowship in 1997.

Gary Cordner is a professor emeritus in the Department of Criminal Justice at Kutztown University, Kutztown, Pennsylvania. He currently serves as senior research associate at the Police Foundation. He served as a commissioner with the Commission on Accreditation for Law Enforcement Agencies, and he was the co-principal investigator on the National Police Research Platform. Previously, he was a dean and professor in the College of Justice and Social Policy at Eastern Kentucky University, editor of the *American Journal of Police* and *Police Quarterly*, and a police officer and police chief in Maryland. He is past-president of the Academy of Criminal Justice Sciences and author of the textbook *Police Administration* (8th edition, Elsevier, 2013). His PhD is from Michigan State University, East Lansing, Michigan.

Jon D. Cromer is a senior special agent, a board-certified psychological criminal profiler, and an International Criminal Investigative Analysis Fellowship (ICIAF) fellow with the Virginia State Police, Bureau of Criminal Investigation Violent Crimes Unit. He holds a BS in criminal justice from Radford University, Radford, Virginia, 1990, and is presently pursuing a masters in applied psychology at James Madison University, Harrisonburg, Virginia. He also serves as vice chair of the National Advisory Board for the FBI's Violent Criminal Apprehension Program (VICAP). Agent Cromer routinely provides instruction to law enforcement officers, medical professionals, prosecutors, and to students at various academic institutions. The majority of his career has been devoted to the investigation of death, missing persons, and sexually motivated crimes. Although his primary duties are in the western district of Virginia, he routinely consults on the behavioral aspects of violent crime throughout the United States.

Eugene R. D. Deisinger earned his doctorate in psychology from Iowa State University. He is a licensed psychologist, a certified health service provider in psychology and, until his retirement, a certified law enforcement officer.

Until his retirement in 2014, Dr. Deisinger also served as Deputy Chief of Police and Director of Threat Management Services for Virginia Tech. As executive officer for the Virginia Tech Police Department, he provided leadership for law enforcement operations to support a safe and secure campus environment. In addition to his police command responsibilities, Dr. Deisinger also managed the university's multi-disciplinary threat management functions.

Dr. Deisinger currently is a managing partner and co-founder of SIGMA Threat Management Associates, a professional services firm involving internationally recognized experts in psychology and behavior, law, organizational development, security and law enforcement. SIGMA provides training and consulting services to a broad range of clients worldwide, including educational institutions, governmental agencies, security and protective services, corporations, and public figures. SIGMA helps clients evaluate threatening circumstances, manage situations, mitigate risk for violence, and enhance their safety and well-being.

Angela Wyatt Eke received her BS (with honors) from the University of Toronto, Toronto, Canada, and completed her graduate studies in psychology at York University, Toronto. She has worked with the Behavioral Sciences and Analysis Services of the Ontario Provincial Police (OPP) since 1997 and is the coordinator of research within the Criminal Behavior Analysis Unit. Dr. Eke's areas of research include offender crime scene behavior and risk assessment with a focus on intimate partner violence and child pornography. In addition to publishing and providing training in these areas, Angela consults for various services and government agencies. She is a reviewer for a number of journals and is on the editorial board of the *Journal of Family Violence*. Dr. Eke was named OPP civilian of the year in 2005. In 2014, she received the Commissioner's Coin for Leadership. Dr. Eke is an adjunct faculty member at Laurentian University and teaches an undergraduate forensic psychology course.

John A. Eterno, PhD, is the chairperson and associate dean and director of the graduate program in criminal justice at Molloy College, Rockville Centre, New York. He is a retired captain with the New York City Police Department. He is the author and coauthor of many peer-reviewed journal articles that have appeared in *Criminal Law Bulletin, Women and Criminal Justice, Policing: An International Journal of Police Strategies and Management, Professional Issues in Criminal Justice,* and in the *International Journal of Police Science and Management.* His books include *Policing within the Law* (Praeger, 2003); *Police Practices in a Global Perspective,* with Dilip K. Das (Rowman & Littlefield, 2010); *The Crime Numbers Game: Management by Manipulation* (CRC Press/Taylor & Francis Group, 2012);

The New York City Police Department: The Impact of Its Policies and Practices (CRC Press/Taylor & Francis Group, 2015); *The Detective Handbook*, with Cliff Roberson (CRC Press/Taylor & Francis Group, 2015); and *Global Issues in Contemporary Policing*, with Dilip K. Das and Mintie Das (CRC Press/Taylor & Francis Group, 2015).

Jana Grekul was granted a Doctorate in Philosophy (Sociology) from the University of Alberta, Edmonton, Alberta, Canada in 2002. Dr. Grekul is an associate professor of sociology and director of the bachelor of arts in criminology program at the University of Alberta. Her research interests include aboriginal street and prison gangs, correctional policy, the eugenics movement in Alberta, and impaired and risky driving behaviors and the community and police response to these behaviors.

Majeed Khader is the senior consulting psychologist and deputy director of the Police Psychological Services Division (PPSD), Singapore Police Force. Dr. Khader also serves as the concurrent director, Home Team Behavioural Sciences Centre, Ministry of Home Affairs, Government of Singapore. Dr. Khader is the chief psychologist with the Singapore Police Force. He holds an MS in forensic psychology from the University of Leicester, Leicester, UK, and a PhD in psychology from the University of Aberdeen, Scotland. Dr. Khader has overseen the development of psychological services in the areas of stress, counseling, resilience, personnel selection, leadership, crisis negotiations, profiling, and crisis psychology in law enforcement settings. He is presently an adjunct assistant professor at National Training University (NTU), where he teaches forensic psychology. He is a registered psychologist with the Singapore Psychological Society. He is presently Asian Director for the Society of Police and Criminal Psychology (USA).

Diong Siew Maan graduated from the National University of Singapore, Singapore, with a master's degree in social science (psychology) with a strong focus in the area of health psychology. She is currently the principal psychologist with the Singapore Civil Defence Force, leading a team of psychologists, counselors, and uniformed officers to provide psychological resilience and crisis management programs. She has developed and enhanced several new programs which include selection framework to select fire and emergency rescue officers, counselling and crisis management system, as well as peer support program for the organization.

Concurrently, Siew Maan is also the deputy director of the Operations and Leadership Psychology Branch with the Home Team Behavioural Sciences, Ministry of Home Affairs. In her capacity, Siew Maan has developed selection exercises and framework to help the ministry select high potential law enforcement and emergency rescue officers. These selection exercises include the use of psychometric tests as well as assessment center methodology.

Prior to her current appointment, Siew Maan has accumulated more than 10 years of experience as a psychologist with the Singapore Police Force. She was involved in providing counseling and crisis intervention to police officers and leaders. She has coordinated several psychological operations to monitor and assess the police officers' morale during major operations and was also involved in supporting an overseas police humanitarian operation during the Asian Tsunami in 2006. She has also conducted research into police suicides as well as studies in police resilience. In addition, Siew Maan has served as a psychologist with the Singapore Police Force Crisis Negotiation Unit and had worked alongside with negotiators to manage hostage and suicide incidents.

Otwin Marenin is a professor in the criminal justice program at Washington State University, Pullman, Washington. He received his BS degree from Northern Arizona University, Flagstaff, Arizona, and his MA and PhD degrees (in comparative politics) from UCLA, Los Angeles, California. He has taught at Ahmadu Bello University and the University of Benin in Nigeria and the Universities of Baltimore, California, Colorado, and Alaska–Fairbanks in the United States. His research and publications have focused on policing systems in Native American communities in the United States and in communities in Africa, especially Nigeria. More recently, he has done research and written on developments in international policing, police in UN peacekeeping operations, transnational police assistance programs, and on efforts to reform the policing systems in failed, transitional, and developing states. His recent publications include *Policing Change, Changing Police: International Perspectives* (Garland Press, 1996); *Transforming the Police in Central and Eastern Europe*, with Marina Caparini (LIT Verlag, Munster, Germany, 2002); *Challenges of Policing Democracies*, with Dilip K. Das (Gordon and Breach Science Publishers, 2000); and *Borders and Security Governance: Managing Borders in a Globalized World*, with Marina Caparini (LIT Verlag, Munster, Germany, 2006).

Gilbert Norden was born in Vienna and studied sociology and economics at the University of Vienna, Wien, Austria. Dr. Norden was granted a degree in sociology and economics (Magister rer.soc.oec.) in 1978 from the University of Vienna, Austria, and the doctorate in sociology and economics (rer.soc.oec) in 1984 from the University of Vienna. He has worked at the Institute of Sociology at the University of Vienna since 1981. In 1995, he became an assistant professor. He has written a number of publications about the sociology of police and has lectured on sociology at the Education

Centre of the Gendarmerie, later the Security Academy, in Modling, later Traiskirchen (Lower Austria). He currently conducts a seminar in policing at the Vienna University together with Maximilian Edelbacher, Josef Horl, and Simone Jungwirth.

Craig Paterson is a principal lecturer in the Department of Law, Criminology, and Community Justice at the Sheffield Hallam University, Sheffield, UK. He received his PhD from Brunel University, Uxbridge, UK, in 2006, and also holds degrees from Keele University and Portsmouth University. His current research agenda focuses on restorative policing, police education, and the role of surveillance technologies within criminal justice. His research appears in numerous journals, including the *British Journal of Community Justice* (2011) and *Criminology and Criminal Justice* (2012). Dr. Patterson is also the author of *Understanding the Electronic Monitoring of Offenders* (VDM Verlag, 2009) and *Policing and Criminology*, with Ed Pollock (Sage, 2011).

Pamela Patrick is a psychologist with Australia's Ministry of Home Affairs. She graduated from the University of Queensland, St Lucia, Australia, with a honors degree. Her work involves research on human trafficking, specifically qualitative research to understand the victimology of sex trafficked individuals. She is also involved in work undertaken by the Operations and Leadership Psychology Branch of the Home Team Behavioural Sciences Centre of the Home Team Academy. Her key areas of focus include the assessment, training, and development of law enforcement officers.

Karen Rich is an associate professor in the School of Social Work and Administrative Studies, Marywood University, Scranton, Pennsylvania. Dr. Rich received an MSW from Wurzweiler School of Social Work, Yeshiva University, New York, and a PhD from the State University of New York at Albany. She is a clinician, educator, speaker, and researcher specializing in sexual assault victimization. She has investigated the police response to sexual victimization, campus rape, secondary victimization, interdisciplinary collaboration, and survivors with disabilities. She is a leading member of several local, national, and international organizations concerned with trauma and recovery.

Cynthia C. Shain received a Diplome practique d'etudes francais (Diploma of French Studies) from the Centre International d'Etudes Francais, Universite d' Angers, France, a Bachelor of Arts (Humanities), from the Bellarmine University, Louisville, Kentucky, and a master of science degree (Loss Prevention and Safety), from Eastern Kentucky University, Richmond, Kentucky, in 1997. She is the associate director of the Southern Police Institute,

Department of Justice Administration, at the University of Louisville, Louisville, Kentucky, and director of the Kentucky Regional Community Policing Institute. She is a retired police executive with 24 years of law enforcement experience with the Louisville Police Department. She serves as cochair of the International Association of Women Police International Scholarship Committee and is a member of INTERPOL's Expert Group on Police Training, the immediate past chair of the International Association of Chiefs of Police Training, and is the immediate past chair of the International Association of Chiefs of Police International Managers of Police and College Training (IMPACT) section. She is a member of Southern Police Institute (SPI) faculty for the administrative officers' course, and presents papers and lectures nationally and internationally on a variety of topics relating to democratic policing issues, including community policing, major event planning, police leadership, and the advancement of women in law enforcement.

Susanne Strand received her university diploma in mathematics, in 2001, master of science in psychology, in 2002, both from Vaxjo University, Sweden, and PhD in health sciences from Mid Sweden University, Sweden, in 2006. Currently, she is an adjunct associate professor of criminology at the Centre for Forensic Behavioral Sciences at Swinburne University of Technology in Melborne, Australia. She researches risk of violence in different contexts, with applied criminology as the academic base. The focus of her research is on risk assessment and risk management in three different areas—domestic violence, stalking, and honor-related violence. Her research is to a large extent conducted in collaboration with practitioners from the police and those involved with forensic psychiatric care in Sweden. Gender is the focus of her studies; women and men are studied from the perspectives of victims as well as from that of perpetrators. She collaborates with the Centre for Forensic Behavioral Sciences in Melbourne, Australia, in her research on stalking and with researchers at Simon Fraser University in Vancouver, Canada, and in her research on domestic violence. Ms. Strand's research has shown that structured checklists for assessment of risk are an effective method for use by the police in the correctional setting and in forensic psychiatric care while working with management of risk for violence.

Eunice Tan is senior psychologist and assistant director of the Operations and Leadership Branch, Home Team Behavioural Sciences Centre, Ministry of Home Affairs, Government of Singapore, and she is also the assistant director of the Operations and Leadership Psychology Branch at the Home Team Behavioural Sciences Centre based at the Home Team Academy. Her work involves the selection, assessment, training, and development of law enforcement leaders. She has also been involved in the research and development of the Home Team Crisis Leadership Competency Framework (HTCLCF), as well as the Home Team Command Leadership Framework (CS Framework). Ms. Tan holds a master's degree in investigative and forensic psychology, and she is also a member of the Society of Police and Criminal Psychology (SPCP).

Birentha Dhevi Thiagaraja is a psychologist with the Operations and Leadership Psychology Branch of the Home Team Behavioural Sciences Centre (HTBSC), Ministry of Home Affairs, Government of Singapore. Ms. Dhevi graduated from the National University of Singapore with a bachelor's degree in psychology and is currently pursuing her postgraduation in MSc I/O and business psychology at University College, London. She has played an integral role in the design and implementation of HTBSC's first Scholarship Assessment Centre to attract talent to the different Home Team agencies. In addition, she has worked on command leadership research developing the Home Team Command Leadership Framework (C5 Framework).

Laura Thue received her MA in criminology from Simon Fraser University, Canada, in 1996, and PhD in sociology from the University of Alberta, Edmonton, Canada, in 2003. Currently, she is a senior research coordinator in the Office of Traffic Safety, Edmonton. Dr. Thue's research interests include the relationship between risky driving and criminal behavior, the impact of traffic enforcement on reducing collisions and crime, and traffic safety culture.

Minoru Yokoyama completed his BA in law and his MA in criminal law and sociology at Chuo University, Tokyo, Japan, where he also finished a doctoral course. He is a professor emeritus and former dean of the faculty of law and a former vice-president of Kokugakuin University, Tokyo, Japan. He is a former second vice-president of the Research Committee for the Sociology of Deviance and Social Control of the International Sociological Association. He is the president of the Japanese Association of Social Problems, a former president of the Japanese Association of Sociological Criminology, and the president of the Tokyo Study Group of Sociological Criminology. He is a member of the Presidium of the General Assembly of the Asian Criminological Society. He worked as a vice chair of the Local Arrangement Committee, 16th World Congress, International Society for Criminology, held in August 2011. He has presented numerous papers at national and international conferences and symposia, and has published many articles in professional journals.

Prologue

Police–Academic Collaboration from a Police Administrator's Perspective

Police and academic collaboration is a very valuable tool that not only accelerates the progress but also enhances the quality of the work and extends the repertoire of the partners.

Academic collaboration is beneficial to police services in increasing the breadth of their knowledge and in their learning different approaches to solving a problem. This tool is being increasingly utilized successfully in developed countries.

Unfortunately, police services sometimes have neglected this valuable tool. It is time that police leaders and academics address this weakness. Individual and institutional collaboration must be emphasized, encouraged, and brought to a level where it can impact and improve the quality, resources, and capabilities of both parties. A police culture that fosters partnership and cooperation has more benefits that improve quality service as well as accelerate progress.

The effectiveness of police services depends on their collaboration with academics. Sharing specialized knowledge, techniques, and expertise is the engine that speeds up the progress and the success of the police and that gives life to new ideas and to scientific breakthroughs for academics. The presence of established channels that allow effective communication, stable partnerships, and large networks between police services and academics enables the flow of critical information among them. Such networking and cooperation are extremely valuable for sharing information on new approaches and resources but also for acquiring specialized and new expertise (DAWN 2009).

Police and academic collaborations are imperative for the development of police education and training. Even when police universities and colleges are running smoothly, they need feedback from operational police practitioners to improve the quality of their teaching and learning. Sharing specialized knowledge, techniques, equipment, and expertise between police and academics is needed not only to improve the quality and to enhance the progress of the work but is often a necessity because of rapidly changing information technology.

In recent decades, development of information technology in police work and education has made possible the production of very specialized and complex pieces of equipment that are expensive to purchase and that require highly specialized professionals to operate them correctly. For example, to equip a modern forensic laboratory with the proper instruments is not only a financial challenge but requires an academic, scientific knowledge. It is true for both police and academics that, in addition to needing common facilities such as computers and access to the Internet, specific and complex laboratory equipment is essential for carrying out police work and for conducting scientific research.

These investments require long-term planning and additional funding to cover the cost of operating, maintaining, repairing, and updating equipment. Some specialized equipment requires a team of specialists who not only should have expertise in operating it successfully but who also should have the scientific abilities to find the right answers to significant questions that advance the knowledge base for those who work in the criminal justice system.

Police and academics can work together to bring about new ways of thinking and acting within police services using a research approach. Even small changes in police services are significant, and meaningful collaborations require both police and academic researchers to define themselves as actors with fluid identities and modes of intervention. The personality one brings to joint research endeavors is an essential transmission mode to ensure enduring change and influence (Roberg et al. 2014).

The literature on police subjects is growing rapidly, and its impact on day-to-day policing is also increasing. The two worlds of policing practice and research are moving closer and closer, year by year, despite the fact that sometimes the two groups speak different languages. With the help of international, regional, and local organizations, the two groups can exchange dialogue and learn from each other. International conferences, police journals, and various other publications do help provide more knowledge, and several associations of police activists do address contemporary and future policing issues. Police administrators and academics are spending more time engaging in deep discussions and in more expositions that can provide stronger and broader linkages between the two worlds. It is this realization of the increasing dialogue between police practice and research that encouraged many of us around the world to conceive and implement new ideas in this direction. Publishing books on policing issues is one way of accomplishing this.

To understand the importance of cooperation between practitioners and researchers, we need to go back to police history and recall Sir Robert Peel, the nineteenth-century British home secretary influential in passing the Metropolitan Police Act, which established the world's first recognizable local police department. Peel envisioned a police service comprised of citizens who were paid by the community to devote full-time attention to preventing crime and disorder. To support this vision—which was unique for nineteenth-century London—Peel established the following principles of policing:

1. The basic mission for which police exist is to prevent crime and disorder.
2. The ability of the police to perform their duties depends on public approval of police actions.
3. The police must secure the willing cooperation of the public in voluntary observance of the law to be able to secure and respect of the public.
4. The degree of cooperation that can be secured from the public diminishes, proportionately, with the need to use physical force.
5. Police seek and preserve public favor not by catering to public opinion but by constantly demonstrating absolutely impartial service to the law.
6. Police use physical force to the extent necessary to secure observance of the law or to restore order only when the exercise of persuasion, advice, and warning is found to be insufficient to achieve police objectives.
7. Police at all times should maintain a relationship with the public that gives reality to the historic tradition that the police are the public and the public are the police. The police are the only members of the public who are paid to give full-time attention to duties that are incumbent on every citizen in the interest of the community's welfare.
8. Police should always direct their actions toward their functions and never appear to usurp the powers of the judiciary.
9. The test of police efficiency is the absence of crime and disorder, not the visible evidence of police actions in dealing with it (*New York Times*, 2014).

Research indicates that no single set of policing principles attributed to Peel can be definitively shown as originating with him. The research findings indicate that "Peel's principles," as they are generally presented today, were actually invented by authors of twentieth-century policing textbooks. However, the fact that the principles cannot be traced directly to Peel does not necessarily make them fiction; nor does it mean they have no relevance for aspiring police administrators and leaders (Lentz and Chaires 2007).

Policing philosophies, strategies, and operations may change over time, but the basic principles of policing—to protect and serve—remain constant.

The person considered one of the founders of modern policing was August Vollmer, who served as chief of police in Berkeley, California, from 1902 to 1932. In the early 1920s, Vollmer initiated the use of the police car as a patrol device and the two-way radio as a means for rapidly answering calls for service. He also introduced the polygraph as an investigative tool and helped establish college-level courses for police officers. Vollmer also promoted the use of other forensic science technologies, such as fingerprinting, as well as crime laboratories. Moreover, he strongly advocated professionalism in policing. Chief August Vollmer of Berkeley, California, was subsequently appointed professor of police administration at the University of Chicago. Vollmer's innovations were shared with police agencies around the world (Bennett 2010).

Today, each police agency's executives, in conjunction with citizens and elected political and community leaders, must decide what policing principles and strategies to incorporate into their mission. Most agencies across the country mix traditional policing with community- and problem-oriented policing, some statistical policing, intelligence-based policing, and strategic policing to prepare for the future. In addition to demonstrating greater flexibility with regard to strategy, the police have also entered a time of transition in terms of how they and others perceive their level of professionalism. To carry out effective law enforcement activities, we need the scientific support from academics.

From a police administrator's point of view, the education and training of law enforcement officers is a key component for the ability of the policing agency to accomplish its goals. Modern policing, intelligence-based policing, and the effective fight against organized crime require well-trained and educated police officers. They should be able to use modern information technologies and equipment. This is not possible without the support of academic researchers.

Leadership versus Management and Supervision

Another area for cooperation between police leaders and researchers is in the art of leadership. Today every member of a police agency has the opportunity and responsibility to become a leader. Managers and supervisors can and should be leaders, but management and supervision are not synonymous with leadership. Managers direct subordinates in the completion of tasks. Supervisors oversee subordinates' work and provide guidance. Leaders influence and motivate others. Managers and supervisors thus focus on directing and maintaining current operations, while leaders guide growth and change with an eye toward the future. Anyone can take steps to cultivate leadership abilities, including knowing where one's organization is headed strategically and regularly communicating the organization's mission, values, and goals to others.

This book is a very good example of the cooperation that exists between these two parties. Among the authors we can find well-known researchers and internationally recognized police leaders and practitioners.

Major General József Boda PhD
Director General
Special Service for National Security

References

Bennett, C. (2010). Legendary lawman August Vollmer. *Law Enforcement Product News*. http://www.officer.com/10232661/legendary-lawman-august-vollmer. Retrieved on July 2, 2014.

DAWN. (2009). Benefits of academics and research collaboration. http://www.dawn.com/news/506880/benefits-of-academic-and-research-collaboration. Retrieved on July 1, 2014.

Lentz, S. and Chaires, R. (2007). The invention of Peel's Principles: A study of policing "textbook history". *Journal of Criminal Justice* (35)1: 69–79.

New York Times. (2014). *Sir Robert Peel's nine principles of policing*. http://www.nytimes.com/2014/04/16/nyregion/sir-robert-peels-nine-principles-of-policing.html. Retrieved on May 30, 2015.

Roberg, R., Novak, K., Cordner, G. and Smith, B. (2014). *Police and society*, 6th edition. Oxford: Oxford University Press. https://global.oup.com/user/product/police-and-society-9780199300884?cc=&lang=en. Retrieved on July 12, 2014.

Police and Academic Collaboration in Research, Education, and Training

I

The chapters found in Section I, written by police practitioners, university professors, and professional practitioners (including psychologists, sociologists, and research consultants) are based on their research, training, or consulting experiences.

In Chapter I, Kratcoski presents an overview of the ways police practitioners have collaborated with academics, professional practitioners, and community residents in research projects pertaining to police matters, educational and training programs, and in the implementation of programs. It is noted that many of these collaborative relationships have a long history and that the relationships have not always been positive; this is due to suspicion about the motives and purposes of the collaboration as well as to a lack of conviction on the part of police administrators that the academics, with the exception of those scientists who developed methods for the investigation of crimes, could make any positive contributions to the improvement of police effectiveness. In the past, police relationships with the public were often outright hostile and were expressed with a "we against them" mentality. However, in recent years, the relationships among the police, community, and private practitioners have become strong, as demonstrated by the numerous collaborative projects in training, education, research, and program implementation mentioned in the various chapters included in this book.

In Chapter 2, Strand discusses how the members of a large police department and academic researchers collaborated in developing an instrument to assess the risk for women who were victims of domestic violence of being victimized again by the same offenders. This risk assessment is useful in assisting the judges responsible for deciding on such issues as the need to incarcerate offenders, on which court orders regarding visitation rights would be appropriate, or—if no contact orders are warranted—on decisions about how to administer other rules regulating the behavior of the offenders.

In Chapter 3, Cordner and Shain reflect on the major factors that have led to changes in police education and training in the United States and in other countries around the world. An important police and academic collaboration trend in the United States is for policing position candidates to have completed the basic police training course before applying for such positions. The basic training is now provided by universities or by privately administered training academies. Another trend in police education and training involves changes in the curriculum so that it focuses on preparing officers for police work in a global society.

In Chapter 4, Thiagaraja, Khader, Ang, Maan, Tan, and Patrick provide information on Singapore's Ministry of Home Affairs' training program, which is used to prepare police, fire, border security, corrections, internal security, and narcotic officers in command positions to be effective and efficient in these positions. The training is geared toward preparing commanders in five competencies, including command thinking, command teams, command partners, command expertise, and command character. The training framework also focuses on developing communications, information, and strategies for collaborating with other Singapore agencies.

In Chapter 5, Deisinger describes how law enforcement agencies, campus security, and the community cooperate in providing security for a large public university. Based on many years of research, a systematic approach to assessing threatening situations has been implemented. This plan has been adopted by a number of universities in the United States.

In Chapter 6, Yokoyama presents an overview of how various security agencies, the mass media, and the public collaborated in responding to the tsunami and earthquakes that hit Japan in 2011. In order for rescue efforts to be successful, with the minimum amount of loss of life property and the maximum crime prevention, a united effort on the part of all public and private agencies was required.

In Chapter 7, Paterson provides a comparative review of the role higher education plays in police education and training in the United States, European Union, Australia, and India.

In several of the countries included in the analysis, there was more emphasis on service-professional development in the educational and training of the police than in the past. In addition, those police officers who completed a higher education degree tended to have a greater knowledge and appreciation of the values and lifestyles of peoples of other cultures, particularly minority groups and immigrants.

In Chapter 8, Kratcoski, Edelbacher, and Eterno discuss the importance of experiential education in the preparation of students for careers in policing and other justice-related professions. These learning experiences are gained through field trips, internships, workshops, and team taught courses in which one of the instructors is a police practitioner. Having an experienced police officer team teaching with a professor tends to give the students an understanding of the theories relating to crime causation and the administration of the justice system and also provides an opportunity for the students to obtain insight into the "realities" of police work and how the theories are applied. As criminal justice education has become more focused on international crime and comparative justice systems, it is becoming more common for students to travel to other counties to study their systems.

In Chapter 9, Norden, a senior professor of sociology teaching at the University of Vienna, reflects on his teaching experiences with Austrian police officers. Striking a balance between the theoretical and applied aspects presents a real challenge to the instructor. The methods used to try to make the theoretical material relevant to the officers are discussed in this chapter.

Introduction

Police–Academic and Professional Practitioner Collaboration in Research, Education, Training, and Programming

1

PETER C. KRATCOSKI
Kent State University
Kent, Ohio, USA

Contents

Introduction: Collaborative Policing

Before gaining employment in any occupation, it is essential to first obtain the knowledge needed to perform the tasks that are to be completed by those employed. The more basic the job, the less knowledge needed for the person who is employed in that position. For example, we tend to categorize work into unskilled, semi-skilled, skilled, technical, and professional, with the amount of knowledge required increasing as one moves from the unskilled to the professional category. For some jobs, such as a spot on an assembly line, a few hours of instruction is all that is needed to become skillful at a job where the operations are repetitive. However, skilled work involving the use of highly technical instruments may take years of education and training before the person becomes competent. The same is true for the professional occupations.

Sources of Knowledge

What is knowledge? *Webster's New Collegiate Dictionary* (1970, 639) offers a number of definitions of knowledge. The one most appropriate for this chapter is "the fact or condition of knowing something with familiarity gained through experience or association." Regarding the sources of our knowledge, we realize that information (knowledge) can come from many sources, including personal experiences, parents, teachers, political and religious leaders, books, mass media, and scientific research. The possession of knowledge can be very useful. Much of the knowledge we have obtained from our family, friends, and from our early education, including that information relating to our culture and moral values, is used to make decisions about everyday living. We do not generally question whether the information is true; we accept it at face value. However, when preparing for employment—depending on the type of work— the knowledge base must be grounded on more than experiences. The formal education and training required for those who wish to assume various positions, particularly those considered professional, is considerable. This knowledge base is grounded in empirical facts, and it is possible to determine, through research, if the information is true (valid).

The Development of Police–Academic Collaboration in Education, Training, and Research in the United States

Much of the knowledge used in current policing has its origins many years ago. For example, research on causes of crime, characteristics of criminal types, the geographic distribution of crime, and the tools used in criminal investigation, such as fingerprinting, were developed many years ago by academics and scientists who at the time they were completing their research did not envision how the findings would be useful in police work. Those who enter police work, regardless of the positions they hold in the organizations, quickly realize that, on the one hand, there are basic skills that one develops related to communications, interpersonal relations, observation, and the ability to make quick decisions and take decisive action that do not change and that are useful throughout one's career. On the other hand, many aspects of the job can change very quickly, including the use of new technical equipment and the methods for detecting crime. The police officer of today, either basic patrol or administrator, must constantly be upgrading his or her skills through education and training.

Former South Australia Police Commissioner Mal Hyde (Baker 2011, 7) noted that, "Policing is a profession where some things change and some things remain the same. The dynamics of policing, the problem of policing, and what policing is all about don't change because it is a mixture of the behavior of people (innate human behavior that might vary because of different cultures) and then also the way authority interplays with the behavior." However, Commissioner Hyde does emphasize that some things in police work do change. He noted that some crime problems change. New crimes are added to the criminal code, such as those related to the Internet that involve fraud, stealing, laundering money, and distribution of pornography. Laws relating to environmental crimes and various types of international crimes such as trafficking in drugs, weapons, and humans have resulted in the need for international cooperation in the enforcement of these laws as well as a recognition that the techniques used by the criminals to commit these crimes have become more sophisticated. There is a need to develop and use modern technological tools, including communications, to combat such crimes. In comparison with the past, the administration of a modern police agency has become more complex. To be efficient and effective, current administrators must be knowledgeable in their disciplines and must be surrounded by a staff trained in such areas as business, budgeting, personal relations, communications, strategic planning, and research.

The chapters selected for this book on collaborative policing focus on how knowledge obtained from education, training, and scientific research pertains to current police practices. Neyroud (2011) notes that, in the past, police administrators and rank-and-file police officers were not impressed by the contributions academics made to police practices that were based on scientific research, the causes of crime, citizens' satisfaction with the police, models for police management, and on other matters. Generally, police administrators did not think findings provided by academics were important sources of information that could be used to assist in administration and on-the-job performance. Interviews with regular officers on the usefulness of scientific research in police practice were likely to elicit such responses as "experience is the best teacher," "research does not provide answers to the types of problems a police officer faces on a daily basis," "the findings from the research are too difficult to understand," "the research findings are not available when needed," or "research is not applicable to our situations because there are too many exceptions."

Police administrators also observed that academic researchers were generally the persons most likely to benefit from their findings because, regardless of the benefits to the police, the publication of the research in professional journals enhanced the reputation of the academic. In short, many police officers contended that experience is still the best preparation for effective police work, in both administration and operations.

The chapters in this book on the collaboration of the police with academics, professional practitioners, and with members of the community regarding higher education, training, research, and program implementation challenge many of the claims that such sources of knowledge are of little value to police practices. In fact, a number of the chapters were coauthored by academics and police practitioners. Several new areas are highlighted in this book pertaining to how education, training, and research enhance the effectiveness of police work and how the research findings of academics and professional practitioners (such as psychologists, social workers, and even those in the medical professions) are beneficial to both practitioners and academics. Kratcoski (2012, 303) notes that the relationship among education, training, research, and police practices is a very complex matter and that it is constantly changing. In the United States and in many countries throughout the world, the number of universities offering degrees in justice studies has continued to increase. In addition, the focus of both long-entrenched and new programs has become more theoretical and research-oriented.

Higher Education and Police Work

In the United States, formal education beyond the high school level is still not required for employment for the majority of municipal and state policing agencies (Kratcoski 2011, 6–7). Generally, the federal policing and investigative agencies in the United States do require the minimum of a bachelor's degree for an entry level position. There is a trend for state and local law enforcement agencies to require at least a two-year associate degree as the minimum educational requirement for a uniformed position with a police department. It is more common in many European countries and elsewhere to require a higher education degree for either entry level positions or supervisory level positions. A large proportion of applicants for policing positions that do not require a higher education degree as a prerequisite for employment have completed some higher education in criminal justice subjects, and many have baccalaureate or advanced degrees. In addition, police practitioners in general have more formal education than in the past, and many former police administrators now hold important positions in universities as professors and/or researchers. This blending of formal education and practical experience has led to an increased appreciation of how a relationship between practitioners and academics can be mutually beneficial.

The in-depth analysis of the police practitioner–academic researcher relationship provided in the chapters in this book reveals that many factors can affect this relationship, including the purpose or goals for completing the research, whether administrators or academics initiated the research, how the research is being funded, whether the research is conducted in-house or by an external researcher, the level of support and cooperation provided by police administrators, the political or social environment in which when the research is being completed, and so forth.

The Evolution of Police–Academic Cooperation in Police Education and Training

During the 1930s (see Kratcoski and Kempf 1995, 609), most large city police departments discarded the "spoils system" as the basis for hiring police officers and instituted knowledge-based employment practices. During this police reform period, civil service examinations and minimum education standards were introduced. Kratcoski (2012) note that attempts to create professionalism in U.S. law enforcement through collaborative efforts of police administrators and academics date back to the early 1900s, beginning with the University of California at Berkeley's program in criminology. These efforts were expanded considerably through the creation of the Law Enforcement Assistance Administration (LEAA) by the Omnibus Crime Control and Safe Streets Act (1967).

This act resulted in the establishment of the National Institute of Justice, which became the research and evaluation arm of the U.S. Department of Justice. The LEAA provided grants to educational institutions to develop degree programs in criminal justice and law enforcement as well as grants to individuals who were either already employed in police work or who were interested in pursuing careers in law enforcement or a related justice occupation.

The new higher education programs varied in their goals and quality. Generally, the distinction between education and training was not clear and, in many law enforcement academic programs, the head or chair of the program was selected more on the basis of law enforcement experience than on academic credentials.

A survey of police administrators completed by Eastman (1972, 80) revealed that police administrators were generally in agreement that individuals with law enforcement degrees were better candidates for employment than those with a liberal arts or social science background.

Eastman also found that the majority of respondents from policing agencies believed that law enforcement experience should be a prerequisite for teaching law enforcement courses in colleges and universities.

Newman (1975, 8) disagrees with the contention that higher education degree programs geared toward preparing students for policing positions should emphasize the practical over the theoretical and took the position that academics from a variety of physical and social sciences must become more involved in the education and training of students seeking careers in criminal justice occupations. Newman contended that, regardless of the obstacles, a partnership between academics and criminal justice personnel must be established because, "In a variety of areas, universities have been the focal point for the accumulation of specific knowledge and skills developed to apply rational approaches to major sets of problems." Newman, who was employed as the coordinator of the Law Enforcement and Correctional Services Program at Pennsylvania State University, and many others—including Gerhard O.W. Mueller, pioneered the movement toward the integration of academic education and practical experience in criminal justice occupations. In his introduction to *Education for Crime Prevention and Control* (1975, v), Mueller envisioned a tremendous increase in the collaboration between academics and practitioners in education, training, and research. He stated that, "The search for solutions to America's crime problems is on. The emphasis is clearly on education. There will be many future research projects and action programs in the field of criminology education."

Tenney (1971, 78) analyzed the curriculum of new criminal justice and law enforcement higher education programs that were funded by development grants from the Office of Law Enforcement Assistance. He categorized these new programs into three distinct types: training, professional, and social science. Tenney found profound differences in the direction, academic standards, and credentials of the personnel employed as instructors in the criminal justice programs. As expected, the training programs focused on teaching the skills needed to maintain the traditional military organizational model that is followed by police groups. The curriculum was designed to instill the development of mechanical skills, the application of rules, and the mastery of equipment. The social science programs, on the contrary, usually present the study of political institutions, including those in the criminal justice system, from a general theoretical perspective. Tenney (1971, 79) found that two-year associate degree programs were predominately oriented toward the training model, while the bachelor degree programs, especially those housed in sociology and political science departments, tended to emphasize theory, research, and analysis of social and political subjects relating to criminal justice. Kratcoski (1975), using Tenney's classification model, surveyed the faculty of the colleges and universities listed in the *1970 Law Enforcement Education Directory* as offering baccalaureate or master's degrees in criminology, law enforcement, or corrections. There were 55 colleges and universities listed in the directory. The majority of these programs were recently established and were independent of other departments such as sociology and political science. More than 50% of the respondents teaching in these programs had a PhD, a Juris Doctor (JD), or a medical degree, less than 10% had academic credentials below a master's degree, and more than 80% of the professors had prior experience in a criminal justice occupation. The vast majority of the respondents stated that the predominant emphasis of the program in which they taught was on general education in the criminal justice field rather than on specific training in the development of skills needed to perform in criminal justice occupations (Kratcoski 1975, 83). The majority of the respondents also believed that a general education in the social sciences was the best preparation for criminal justice occupations but observed that a good program should also provide opportunities for students to engage in some type of field experience, such as an internship, during their course of study. Part-time faculty members placed much more emphasis on the development of skills (training), while full-time faculty members were more likely to emphasize theory and research as critical components of a good criminal justice degree program (Kratcoski 1975, 85).

When comparing the number of higher education degree programs located in colleges and universities in the United States during the 1970s with the number operating in the early part of the twenty-first century, we find that the number of programs increased by more than 75%. More than 200 criminal justice programs were being offered at the bachelor's, master's, or doctoral level in 2005 (Finckenauer 2005, 413). By providing grants to individuals and higher education institutions, the U.S. government played a large role in determining the direction of education and training for police officers. Since the initiation of these new degree programs in the 1970s, thousands of college-educated police officers assumed positions in local, state, and federal policing agencies, and a number of these officers assumed high level positions in policing agencies. It is difficult to measure the impact university-educated police officers have had on the content and focus of the present-day training of police officers. Generally, research has shown that the importance of having a college education is not necessarily related to being better prepared to perform the tasks expected of a police officer. However, just by being in the university environment, by interacting with people from different cultures, and by having different values leads to developing more ethical and positive attitudes toward minorities, as well as to becoming more culturally aware (Roberg and Bonn 2004).

The debate over whether the appropriate focus for a viable criminal justice education should be a general theoretical and research orientation or be based on practical training still exists, even though the distinction between training and education has become somewhat blurred. In the United States, the number of degree programs in criminal justice has continued to increase. In addition, police training institutes, research institutes, and other educational features (such as having a police practitioner and an academic serve as team instructors for specialized courses, such as crime mapping or statistical analysis of crime data) are found in universities and colleges. Marenin (2007, 170) notes that the focus of police training in democratic societies has become more theoretical, more community-oriented, and more respectful of human rights.

In summary, police–academic collaboration in education, training, and research is more extensive today than at any other time period. Even basic police training programs have been significantly altered to reflect the new methods of criminal justice investigation, and emphasis is placed on human relations, victims, and community involvement in crime prevention. Kratcoski (2012, 302) notes that, "Police education and training must prepare officers to react to crowd management, disasters, and medical emergencies, and it must also prepare officers on how best to use crime prevention techniques and how to enlist community cooperation in crime prevention activities."

Collaboration in Police Education and Training in Other Countries

The annual meeting of the International Police Executive Symposium on education and training for police was held in Antalya, Turkey in 2002. At this meeting, representatives from throughout the world presented papers on police education and training. It was determined that, to be effective, police education and training must be skill-based and grounded in theory and research. Kratcoski notes that, "The great increase in incidents of terrorism, suicide bombings, and attacks on civilians in public places, internal civil disturbances, and transnational criminal activities has increased the importance of police training and education for quick response and effective action when such events occur, and also for effective intelligence gathering and infiltration of suspected terrorist and subversive groups to deter or reduce the possibilities of harm to the general public" (Kratcoski 2011, 18–19).

Types of Education and Training

When comparing the education and training provided for police in the United States with that provided in many countries in Europe, Asia, and Africa, one finds many similarities as well as some differences. The influence of the United States and England is apparent in the training models used in many countries. Typically, police training consists of a basic program for new recruits, in-service training for officers to upgrade skills, and various types of advanced training for those who need to develop the special skills needed to perform in the units to which they are assigned. Generally, basic training includes class lectures and field work on the types of information and skills a police officer needs to be effective on the job. Included in the training are academic topics such as laws, criminal codes, communications, human relations, crisis intervention, and how to handle crowds. Skill-based training generally is provided through lectures and "hands-on" experience in investigations, accidents, securing crime scenes, collection and preservation of evidence, driving skills, traffic tactics, use of force, use of firearms, fingerprinting, physical fitness, defense tactics, use of radar, interviewing, interrogation, and report writing (Kratcoski 2007, 10).

The advanced specialized training provided to police officers in many countries is determined by the specific purpose of the training. For example, those officers selected for leadership positions might be sent to complete a higher education program, either at a public university or at an academy under the auspices of the U.S. Department of Justice. Senior officers selected for supervisory or administrative positions would likely receive training in leadership, management, and public relations (Kratcoski 2007, 11).

Administration of Police Training

In the United States, there are several ways for a person interested in becoming a police officer to obtain the basic training required. The large majority of policing agencies are municipal; that is, they have jurisdiction over a specific city, town, or village. The sheriff's office generally has jurisdiction over a county, and such agencies as state police and state highway patrols have statewide jurisdiction. Most federal law enforcement agencies, with the exception of the Federal Bureau of Investigation, have special functions to perform. Their duties in regard to the investigation and apprehension of criminals are limited to those types of crimes falling under their jurisdictions.

The larger municipal and county policing agencies, as well as state and federal agencies, administer their own police academies. An individual will not have the opportunity to enroll in those academies unless he or she has been selected for a position with the police agency. The Federal Law Enforcement Training Center, located in Glynco, Georgia, serves as the basic training center for a number of federal law enforcement agencies and also offers many advanced training courses.

In many states, another basic training opportunity open for those interested in becoming a police officer is to attend a privately owned training academy.

These privately owned academies are accredited by state agencies, and the training provided must adhere to the subjects and hours required by the state. Those who complete these programs are not guaranteed a position with a policing agency; generally, they must pass a standardized state-administered examination before becoming eligible to assume a sworn officer position.

In addition to the avenues for obtaining basic training mentioned earlier, many colleges and universities in the United States either offer police basic training in a special program or integrate that training within the requirements for a higher education degree. The former is more typical because a distinction is made in the curriculum between education and training.

In contrast to the United States, the large majority of countries throughout the world have national police forces, with directives and policies coming from their department. The basic training mandated, in terms of content and amount of training, is standardized throughout the country. Training centers, located in various parts of the country, are also administrated by the state. In some countries, universities have been created specifically to educate police officers who are expected to fill higher level positions in the national police organization (Kratcoski 2007).

Police Training for a Global Society

Cordner and Shain (2011) state that the most important factor affecting police education and training throughout the world is globalization. They note that, in the past, police training was nationally focused but, "Today, police trainers fly around the world to deliver their courses. Organizations like Interpol, Europol, the U.S. International Criminal Investigative Training Assistance Program (ICITAP), and the International Association of Chiefs of Police play a growing role in the provision of training, and training content centers more and more on global issues such as transnational crime" (281–282). Much of the training curriculum dealing with transnational crimes is focused on preparing police officers in the use of modern technology for investigating and apprehending those involved in cybercrimes, financial crimes, and organized crimes—such as trafficking in drugs, weapons, and humans.

Internationally, the transmission of knowledge pertaining to police education and training is reflected in the adoption of organizational models and policing strategies developed in one country by other nations. Salgado (2013) notes that, regardless of the location and size of the police agency and the culture of the people, the universality of the functions of the police remains the same. The results of Salgado's research show that the most important goals of the police organizations of the two cities studied, Tokyo and The Hague, were achieved even though the Tokyo police organization was centralized and The Hague police organization was decentralized. De Benedetto (2013) notes that police organizations throughout the world are being forced to develop new management models because they are experiencing reductions in personnel, funding, and in other resources. He also suggested that police administrators can adopt organizational models developed for private enterprise even though private corporations and businesses are profit-oriented and police agencies are nonprofit service agencies.

The Impact of Higher Education on Police Work

The number of higher education institutions in the United States offering degrees in criminology or criminal justice or degrees in sociology and political science with a justice-law focus exceeds several thousand. However, the value of obtaining a higher education degree as general background preparation for police work in the United States is still being debated because, with the exception of federal policing agencies, a higher education degree is not required for entry into most U.S. police departments. In addition, those agencies that do require a degree usually do not specify criminal justice as the only degree acceptable and will generally allow any social sciences degree. Paterson (2011, 288) notes that, since the 1960s, the U.S. government has played a large role in determining the direction of education and training for police officers by providing funding for officers who wish to attend universities as well as providing funding for colleges and universities to develop new degree programs in law and criminal justice. These new degree programs were initiated beginning in the 1970s and continue to the present. Thousands of college-educated officers have assumed positions in local, state, and federal policing agencies, and many of these officers have assumed high level positions in policing agencies. The impact these university-educated officers have had on the direction of police training is not certain. Roberg and Bonn (2004) concluded that the overall experience of being in a university setting and interacting with people from different cultures, many of whom with different values, led to the police officers in their study developing more ethical and positive attitudes toward minorities as well as to their becoming more culturally aware.

Importance of Higher Education for Police in Europe and Other Continents

Paterson (2011) described the difficulties encountered by the European Union (EU) in trying to integrate the police officer education and training programs of the 27 member states. In 1999, the Bologna Declaration was instrumental in furthering the transfer of knowledge to students by promoting internationally compatible learning modules throughout EU university programs. The European Police Academy was established in 2005. Paterson (2011, 290) notes that, "The demands made upon European Police forces for a much broader focus on police management, policing strategies and ethics has resulted in a proliferation of police studies degrees." In addition, the strategies of police leaders in the EU member nations appear to embrace community policing and to place much more emphasis on human relations.

Research findings on the impact higher education has on police performance in countries throughout the world reveal that, in order to interpret the likely outcome, it is necessary to have a good understanding of a country's cultural values, its political system (whether the country is under a dictatorship or is a democracy), its economic stability, and the level of corruption among its political leaders. Marenin (2005) contended that the main benefit democratic societies with an educated police force receive are having police who are professional, accountable, and who are considered legitimate by the public. As a result, the citizenry has more confidence in the police.

Summary of Police Education and Training

In the final analysis, it is quite evident that the collaborative programs between the institutions for higher education and training and the policing establishments that have commenced in the United States and most other countries throughout the world will continue. In addition, there is considerable evidence to support the notion that many other cooperative ventures will be instituted. As in the past, the structure and content of the education and training programs will change to meet the needs of current societies. Police education and training must be integrated, ongoing, and based on theory and research. In addition, formal classroom learning must be combined with direct experience opportunities for the officers being trained. There will be a constant need to adapt to ever-changing crime problems and to the methods used to control and prevent crimes. Education and training must prepare officers for critical thinking and for how to make important decisions (Kratcoski 2012, 304).

Although future needs have been identified, the question of which model of education and training for police officers can best meet these needs still remains. White and Heslop (2012), commenting on the connections among education, learning, and professional performance for the training of the police constabulary in the United Kingom, contend that, even though training will continue to be theoretical and classroom-based, there will be a mandate to move toward a more vocational and competence-based model. They recommend that police education and training be based on a professional model that includes theoretical and practical knowledge.

Adopting this model should lead to police officers understanding why they are taking the actions they have been trained to take and realizing that there are often several different ways to accomplish the same goal.

Academics and Police Collaborating in Research and Program Development

Ancient Greek and Roman philosophers, speculating on the causes of crime, concluded that humans have free will and can make rational choices. The methods that can be used to maintain social control center on finding the means to motivate the individual not to commit crimes because of the fear of the punishment if caught. When science and pseudoscience entered into the picture during the eighteenth and nineteenth centuries, two distinct schools of thought emerged—"nature" and "nurture." On the one side were those who were trained in the biological sciences—including medicine, such as Ceasare Lombroso (Southerland and Cressey, 1974), who used science to establish characteristics of criminals. Lombroso claimed that most criminal behavior is essentially grounded in biological factors and that these inherent factors manifest themselves in recognizable physical traits of the "born criminal," such as shape of head, amount of body hair, and length of arms.

In contrast, Ceasare Beccaria (1738–1794) attempted to apply science to his theories of crime by searching for the social, economic, and psychological factors that might motivate a person to commit a crime. He also promoted the idea that punishment can be an effective deterrent to criminal behavior if the punishment administered to the convicted criminal is just, not excessive, and is administered soon after the conviction of the crime. In contrast, researchers of the nurture school (social scientists) looked for the causes of criminal behavior in the physical and social environment.

The early European social philosophers—such as Durkheim, Toennies, Cooley, Ward, and Sorokin—and American sociologists—such as Small, Sutherland, and a number of sociologists at the University of Chicago [Clifford Shaw (1929), (Shaw and McKay, 1942)]—completed a considerable amount of research that was essentially "crime mapping," seeking to demonstrate that the distribution of crime and delinquency in the city was directly related to the physical and social characteristics of neighborhoods. Frederick Thrasher (1927) completed research on the number, types, and locations of gangs in the city of Chicago.

Many academic research projects focus exclusively on police behavior or, more specifically, police misbehavior. Research completed by Chevigny (1969) on police misuse of force, by Reiss (1970) on police brutality, and by Roebuck and Barker (1974) on police corruption, did not generally lead to ongoing cooperative relations between the academics and the police agencies in which the research was conducted. However, with the creation of the LEAA by Congress in 1969, considerable funds became available to academics to complete scientific research that not only had theoretical implications but practical implications as well. The results led to changes in police practices and to an improvement in police performance. The Kansas City Police Patrol Experiment, in which different models were used to assign officers to patrol neighborhoods, challenged some of the customary ways of thinking about the importance of police patrols in preventing crime. A San Diego study revealed that having two officers in a patrol car is generally not any safer or more effective than having one person in the patrol car. Research on how foot patrols can be useful in crime prevention and in developing positive community relations epitomizes the beginning of the collaborative relationship between the academic community and policing agencies that exists at the present time. The research completed by Reiss (1971) on police and community relations helped to pave the way for the introduction of community policing in the United States.

Currently, in the United States and in many other countries around the world, police agencies are collaborating with public and private institutions of higher education, as well as with various private professional and business organizations in providing a variety of services to police organizations. For example, developing instruments for the psychological screening of candidates for police positions, providing technological training for operating communication systems, giving technical assistance in crime labs, consulting on implementation of new programs, and completing evaluation research are a few of the areas for which private and public agencies provide assistance to police agencies. In the past, academics interested in conducting research in police agencies had to "jump through hoops" to even open up the door to discuss a research proposal with a high level police administrator. Now, researchers are in high demand, particularly if they are providing a needed service, such as the evaluation of a new state or federally funded program when the funding agency has specified that an independent evaluation of the program's outcomes must be completed.

In addition to collaborating with academic, professional, and private researchers, police administrators are known to adopt management models and leadership styles that were developed in the private sector and that are used by profit-making industrial and business enterprises. For example, Silverman (1999, 82) notes that when Commissioner William Bratton was preparing the way for the introduction of the Compstat management model for the New York City Police Department. According to Silverman (1999, 98), "The name Compstat arose from "Compare Stats," a computer file name, and not, as is commonly thought, from the abbreviated version of "computer statistics. The concept of "reengineering" was constantly used in management terminology. According to Eterno (2003, 15), Compstat attempts to control police behavior by focusing, to a great extent on the power of the higher-ranking officers and in particular the C.O. of a precinct. De Benedetto (2013) showed how a management model that was initially developed by the Harvard Business School for private enterprise can be used by police organizations. The important components of the model include measuring quantifiable outcomes and performance, collecting and analyzing data, and using the data collected to improve individual performance as well as collective performance of the police agency. Yung et al. (2013) demonstrated how higher education for police officers is relevant in Hong Kong, a city of protest.

Academic–Police Collaboration in Research

The proliferation of research projects in which academics and police agencies or individual police officers have collaborated are too numerous to mention in this chapter. Several noteworthy trends are apparent. They include:

- An increasing number of publications pertaining to research on policing matters in which at least one of the authors is a police practitioner
- An increasing amount of international comparative research on policing agencies
- Changes in the quality of the research, reflecting the fact that those police practitioners who engage in research have developed research skills comparable to those of academics

Guillaume et al. (2012) compared the number of articles in the journal, *Police Practice and Research*, since it was first established in 2001 to the present, either singularly authored or coauthored with an academic to the number of articles authored or coauthored by a police practitioner. They found that, although the small proportion of the articles authored by a police practitioner remained stable over the years, the proportion of articles coauthored by an academic *and* a practitioner increased significantly. This finding gives credence to the assertion that collaborative research by police practitioners and academics has increased.

The evidence is clear that police administrators and practitioners have become more aware of the importance of research and of how research findings can be useful in the performance of their policing tasks. It is also evident that many police officers have become sufficiently prepared to complete research as a result of their higher educational training as well as to understand the theory and methodology being used by an outside researcher. However, this is not to say that the problems relating to academic–police collaboration in research have been entirely eliminated. Many police administrators are still reluctant to have "outsiders" coming into their agency and having access to the information needed to complete their research. In addition, there are often communication problems and suspicions about the purpose or goals of the research. If the research findings are not positive, the administration may question the value of the research or may refuse to accept the findings. This might be particularly important in program evaluation. It is difficult for a police administrator who has invested a great deal of money, personnel, and resources in a program to accept research findings that indicate that program is ineffective in producing the outcomes desired. Most of the academic–police collaborative research is applied; that is, the research is undertaken for the purpose of using the knowledge gained to make decisions on policing matters such as implementing a new organization model, making changes in the deployment of personnel, or improving police relations with the citizenry.

From the very beginning, the importance of having everyone who takes part in collaborative research understand the purpose, methodology, and professional ethics relating to scientific research is critical. If the police administrator involved in initiating the research has a basic understanding of the scientific method, major sources of potential problems relating to the exchange of knowledge can be avoided. Henry and Mackenzie (2012) examine how research can enhance knowledge transfer and exchange in a project involving implementing a Scottish community policing model. They note that when the Scottish community model was changed from having one officer assigned to one beat to having several officers working as a team assigned to several beats, research was needed to determine if the new model was effective. They concluded that, in order to insure that the reason for the change would be understood by the officers who would be involved in the changes, it was necessary to communicate to everyone right at the beginning of the implementation process the reasons for the changes and the theory underlying the assumptions about the likely outcomes. Henry and Mackenzie use the concept of "knowledge exchange" to emphasize the fact that the communication between the administrators and the rank-and-file officers had to be two-way, with the officers having an opportunity to express their ideas and concerns.

Steinhelder et al. (2012) surveyed police practitioners and police researchers to determine if there were differences in philosophical beliefs and other factors between the academics and police practitioners that would interfere with the establishment of positive communications. The authors concluded that the differences in operating philosophies between academics and police that made it difficult for them to collaborate on productive research may have been based on faulty assumptions on the part of the police and the academics completing the research. The erroneous assumptions may have been based on stereotypes grounded in past beliefs and research findings.

Many academics currently engaging in research on police matters are former police administrators who hold advanced degrees in criminal justice or related disciplines. These former police administrators now employed in academia have become aware of the importance of research. Many of them not only are competent to complete scientific research but also have the knowledge to determine if the research findings are valid. Although law enforcement and academics may differ significantly in their operating philosophies, these differences need not prevent productive research partnerships. Even though differences in the philosophies and the goals of the police and academics may exist, these differences need not prohibit collaborative research projects that result in mutually valued research.

Although all of the indicators show that collaboration between the police and academics will continue and expand, there are still questions to be answered and issues to be addressed. Such matters as the usefulness of the research for police administrators and the manner in which police administrators are made aware of research findings must be considered. For example, in a survey of police decision makers, researchers found that 75% of police administrators claimed to have used criminal justice research findings in the performance of their jobs. However, the authors could not establish whether awareness of the research findings contributed to the decisions made by police administrators and if the research findings had an impact on the operations of the department. The researchers concluded that police administrators were more likely to obtain their knowledge from police- or justice-oriented journals as opposed to the professional journals in which academic research generally is published.

Types of Research and Validity

Academic researchers as well as police practitioners engage in many types of research, including descriptive, exploratory, and explanatory research. The technical skills needed to complete routine reports, such as compiling the information for the Uniform Crime Report, can be easily developed. However, learning the process for completing qualitative and quantitative research projects, in which the researchers are attempting to determine the cause of changes in situations relating to police work, is more difficult to master. Determining the reasons for drastic increases or decreases in a city's crime rate, predicting outcomes when a new program is implemented, or assessing the effects of a significant change in the organizational structure of a department are matters that call for careful and more sophisticated research analysis, and considerable knowledge of research techniques is needed. In addition, the same set of data may be interpreted in different ways and often even the experts are not able to determine which interpretation of the information obtained is correct. For example, New York City experienced a drastic decline in all types of crime after COMPSTAT was put into operation in the 1990s. The mass media, politicians, and the police commissioner highlighted these changes as proof that the COMPSTAT model was working. However, some researchers were quick to point out that crimes were decreasing drastically in other cities throughout the country because of improvements in the economy, low unemployment, a lower proportion of the population in the young age category, and other socioeconomic factors, and they declared that these were the main reasons for the decline in crime in New York City. Silverman (1999, 5) completed a thorough analysis of the research on factors other than COMPSTAT that might explain the dramatic decline of crime in New York City and found that socioeconomic factors did not appear to significantly explain the drastic decrease in crime that was experienced after the introduction of COMPSTAT. Therefore, he concluded that COMPSTAT *was* a significant factor in the decline of crime in New York City.

Police–Professional Collaboration

Nonacademic professionals, such as psychologists, social workers, victim advocates, and other behavioral scientists who collaborate with the police, generally provide specific services to police departments. In many of the larger departments, psychologists are either a permanent part of the noncommissioned staff or have ongoing contracts with the department. Their roles may vary from administering personality tests given to candidates being considered from employment to interviewing and providing counseling to officers under extreme stress who are experiencing emotional problems or "burnout." Psychologists may be assigned to be present and assist in hostage situations, to profile serial killers and potential terrorist groups, or to provide on-the-spot counseling and support to victims of crimes, particularly in cases of sexual violence or when the victim is a child. Police and social workers collaborate in a number of ways in situations pertaining to victims of crime. Police and social worker teamwork in responding to domestic violence is well established and, in many jurisdictions, a team consisting of a police officer, a social worker, a medical doctor, and a prosecutor work together on cases of child physical or sexual abuse.

Police–Community Collaboration

In Europe, accounts of citizen involvement in crime prevention and law enforcement have been recorded for centuries. Kratcoski and Dukes (1995, 7) note that the responsibility for providing security and service to communities in the colonial period and in the early history of the United States was shared by private citizens and government officials. Beginning with the organization of a professional police force in London and later in major British cities in the early nineteenth century, developing good relationships with the community and providing service to the residents became one of the foundation principles of the modern police organization. This approach was also adopted in the establishment of formal police departments in U.S. cities (Kratcoski and Walker 1978, 98).

Wiatrowski (1995, 78) notes that the evolution of the professional model broke that cooperative bond between the police and the community through the emphasis on calling 911, the utilization of motorized patrols, and the largely reactive nature of the police function in the community. In the late 1970s, police became more isolated from the community, and in some areas of the larger cities—especially those with large minority populations, police and citizen relations became outright hostile. This was particularly true in those cities in which the crime rate was increasing and where the citizens had little confidence in the ability of the police to prevent crime and to protect the citizenry from being victimized.

Community policing and several variations of its basic model were implemented in many cities with the sole purpose of trying to prevent crime and to establish positive relationships with those residents most vulnerable to becoming victims of crime. Regardless of the specific structure of the community policing model adopted by policing agencies, Silverman (1995, 36) notes that, "An even more fundamental change in policing values and behaviors is captured in community policing's emphasis on joint police-public cooperation in the determination and resolution of community problems and issues."

Many of the initial community policing programs implemented in cities throughout the United States have been discarded or have been replaced with variations of the original programs. Nevertheless, the notion of police community cooperation and interaction on crime prevention has continued to be emphasized. In addition, community policing, based on principles established in the early development of formally organized police departments, has spread to many countries in Europe and to other continents.

Currently, citizens are able to communicate with the police and to assist them in many areas in addition to neighborhood crime watch and crime prevention programs. Those who have access to and mastery of electronic communications equipment are encouraged to use it to report erratic drivers, to look for missing children, to report accidents, fires, or motorists in need of assistance, and to report suspected criminal behavior or the sighting of wanted fugitives.

Concluding Remarks

The chapters presented in this book pertain to the ways academics and practitioners collaborate in providing the education, training, and knowledge obtained from research that will be useful to on-the-street police officers, as well as to administrators of police agencies. Although a positive relationship between the police practitioners and private professional practitioners, such as physical scientists and psychologists, has existed for a long time in areas such as forensics and mental health counseling, collaboration with the general academic community, particularly in the area of research, has often been rocky and mired in suspicions about the motives of academic researchers as well as in doubts about the benefits police organizations receive from the research. However, as interaction between police administrators and academics has increased, often as a result of the police practitioners being enrolled in higher education degree programs, police administrators have gained more knowledge of the scientific research process and an appreciation of the benefits scientific research can provide to policing agencies. This is not suggesting that the problems that existed regarding communications, acceptance of common goals, and suspicions about motives for the research have disappeared. There are still many academics who collaborate with police agencies on research projects solely for the purpose of advancing their own careers. Likewise, some police administrators still believe that research can provide instant solutions to policing problems and become very critical when research findings do not provide the answers they expect. Thus, we should think of collaboration among police, academics, professional practitioners, and the community as being an ongoing, developing process that, in the long run, can be improved, with mutual benefits for all participants. More research is needed pertaining to the benefits of the research for individual practitioners, the motivation for completing research, what type of research designs—including data collection techniques—are most likely to provide the type of information that is most useful to police practitioners, and what factors inhibit the implementation of recommendations based on the findings of research. Such factors could include government policies, community resistance, lack of resources, police administrative policies, or political pressure.

References

Baker, D. (2011). Interview with Commissioner Mal Hyde. In *Trends in policing*, Vol. 3, O. Marenin and D. Das, eds. Baca Raton, FL: CRC Press, pp. 1–22.

Chevigny, P. (1969). *Police power.* New York: Vintage Books.

Cordner, G., and C. Shane. (2011). The changing landscape of police education and training. *Police Practice and Research*, 12(4), 281–285.

De Benedetto, R. (2013). Best practices in police performance measurement and management. Paper presented at the Annual Meeting of the International Police Executive Symposium, Budapest, Hungary, Durkheim, E.

Eastman, E. M. (1972). *Police education in American colleges and universities: A search for excellence.* Washington, DC: U.S. Department of Health, Education, and Welfare.

Eterno, J. (2003). *Policing within the law: A case study of the New York City Police Department*. Westport, CT: Praeger.

Finckenauer, J. (2005). The quest for quality in criminal justice education. *Justice Quarterly*, 22, 413–426.

Guillaume, P., A. Sidebottom, and N. Tilley. (2012). On police and university collaborations: A problem-oriented policing case study. *Police Practice and Research*, 13(4), 389–401.

Henry, A., and S. Mackenzie. (2012). Brokering communities of practice: A model of knowledge exchange and academic–practitioner collaboration developed in the context of community policing. *Police Practice and Research*, 13(4), 315–328.

Kratcoski, P. (1975). The integration of social sciences into the fields of criminology, law enforcement, and corrections. In *Education for crime prevention and control*, R. J. McLean, ed. Springfield, IL: Charles C. Thomas, pp. 77–88.

Kratcoski, P. (2007). The challenges of police education and training in a global society. In *Police education and training in a global society*, P. Kratcoski and D. Das, eds. Lanham, MD: Lexington Books, pp. 3–21.

Kratcoski, P. (2011). The challenges of police education and training in a global society 2002. In *Police education and training in a global society*, paperback edition, P. C. Kratcoski and D. K. Das, eds. New York: Lexington Books, pp. 3–21.

Kratcoski, P. (2012). Editorial comments. *Police Practices and Research*, 13(4), 302–305.

Kratcoski, P., and D. Dukes. (1995). Perspectives on community policing. In *Issues in community policing*, P. Kratcoski, ed. Cincinnati, OH: Anderson Publishing, pp. 5–20.

Kratcoski, P., and K. Kempf. (1995). Police reform. In *Encyclopedia of police science*, 2nd ed., W.G. Bailey, ed. New York: Garland Publishing, pp. 609–613.

Kratcoski, P., and D. Walker. (1978). *Criminal justice in America: Process and Issues*. Glenview, IL: Scott, Foresman and Company.

Marenin, O. (2005). Building a global police studies community. *Police Quarterly*, 8(1), 99–136.

Marenin, O. (2007). Police training for democracy (United States of America). In *Police education and training*, P. C. Kratcoski and D. K. Das, eds. Lanham, MD: Lexington Books, pp. 169–182.

Mueller, G. O. W. (1975). Introduction. In *Education for crime prevention and control*, R. J. McLean, ed. Springfield, IL: Charles C. Thomas.

Newman, C. O. (1975). The university and the criminal justice system: Partners for a science of criminology. In *Education for crime prevention and control*, R. J. McLean, ed. Springfield, IL: Charles C. Thomas: 5–10.

Neyroud, P. (2011). *Review of police leadership and training*. London, UK: Home Office.

Paterson, C. (2011). Adding value? A review of the international literature on the role of higher education in police training and education. *Police Practice and Research*, 12(4), 286–297.

Reiss, A. (1970). Police brutality-answers to key questions. In *Crime, criminology and contemporary society*, R. D. Knudten, ed. Homewood, IL: Dorsey Press, pp. 233–236.

Reiss, A. (1971). *The police and the public*. New Haven, CT: Yale University Press.

Roberg, R., and S. Bonn. (2004). Higher education and policing: Where are we now? *Policing: An International Journal of Police Strategies and Management*, 27 (4), 469–486.

Roebuck, J., and T. Barker. (1974). A typology of police corruption. *Social Problems*, 21, 423–436.

Salgado, J. (2013). A tale of two cities' police departments: Community oriented policing in The Hague and Tokyo. Paper presented at the Annual Meeting of the International Police executive Symposium, Budapest, Hungary.

Shaw, C. (1929). *Delinquent areas*. Chicago, IL: University of Chicago Press.

Shaw, C., and H. McKay. (1942). *Juvenile delinquency and urban areas*. Chicago, IL: University of Chicago Press.

Silverman, E. (1995). Community policing: The implementation gap. In *Issues in community policing*, P. Kratcoski and D. Dukes, eds. Cincinnati, OH: Anderson, pp. 35–50.

Silverman, E. (1999). *NYPD battles crime*. Boston: Northeastern University Press.

Southerland, E., and D. Cressey. (1974). *Criminology*. Philadelphia, PA: Lippincott.

Steinhelder, B., T. Wuestewald, R. E. Boyatzis, and P. Kroutter. (2012). In search of a methodology of collaboration: Understanding researcher–practitioner philosophical differences in policing. *Police Practice and Research*, 13, 357–374.

Tenney, C. (1971). *Higher education programs in law enforcement and criminal justice*. Washington, DC: U.S. Government Printing Office.

Thrasher, F. (1927). *The gang*. Chicago, IL: University of Chicago Press.

U.S. President's Commission on Law Enforcement and Administration of Justice. (1967). *Task force: Police*. Washington, DC: U.S. Government Printing Office.

White, D., and R. Heslop. (2012). Escaluating, legitimizing or accessorizing? Alternative conceptions of professional training in U.K. higher education: A comparative study of teacher, nurse and police officer educators. *Police Practices and Research*, 13(4), 342–356.

Wiatrowski, M. (1995). Community policing in Delray Beach. In *Issues in community policing*, P. Kratcoski and D. Dukes, eds. Cincinnati, OH: Anderson, pp. 69–84.

Woolf, H. B., ed. (1970). *Webster's New Collegiate Dictionary*, 8th ed. New York: Merriman-Webster, p. 639.

Yung, W., S. Chau, and A. Chi-Wai. (2013). Higher education for policing in the city of protest-Hong Kong. Unpublished paper presented at the Annual Meeting of the International Police executive Symposium, Budapest, Hungary, August 4–9, 2013.

Risk Assessment and Risk Management

2

How the Police Work Together with Researchers to Protect Victims in Cases of Intimate Partner Violence, Stalking, and Honor-Based Violence

SUSANNE STRAND
Swinburne University of Technology
Australia

Contents

Introduction

Risk assessment and risk management are the basis on which the work for protection of the victims of threats and violence rests. Cases of threats and violence committed toward a family member or someone that is close to the victim are difficult to work with because the relationship between the victim and the perpetrator can be very strong. To prevent further victimization, it is important to understand these difficulties in order to construct the best case-by-case risk management plan with the most effective protective actions. This chapter will focus on the outcome of developmental work done during the last decade by the Swedish police, together with a group of researchers, on risk assessment and risk management in the areas of intimate partner violence, stalking-related violence, and honor-related violence.

Intimate partner violence (IPV) is defined in terms of actual, attempted, or threatened physical harm of a current or former intimate partner (Kropp et al. 2005). A World Health Organization study (WHO 2005) has shown that the worldwide prevalence of IPV as a lifetime risk is 15–71%. Other studies have revealed similar results. In Western societies, the lifetime risk for IPV is about 30% (Tjaden and Thoennes 2000; Lundgren et al. 2001; Thompson et al. 2006). All kinds of violence are represented, such as physical violence (with murder as the most severe consequence), sexual violence, and psychological violence. The perpetrators of IPV often exhibit controlling behavior such as calling the victim several times a day and getting upset if the victim cannot explain where she has been and with whom; ultimately, the victim is isolated from her friends and family. The perpetrator's behavior can alternate from good to bad, which makes it even more difficult for the victim to report the perpetrator and to take protective action. IPV is a public health problem, and many countries have prioritized working toward finding better strategies to reduce the violence. Finding methods and models that will increase possibilities for police, health care workers, social services, and other agencies to work together to protect victims from further victimization is of utmost importance.

As a lifetime risk, the prevalence of *stalking*, defined as repeatedly harassing a person in such a way that the victim becomes concerned or scared (Mullen et al. 2009), is approximately 15% in Western societies (Australian Bureau of Statistics 2006; BRÅ 2006; Finney 2006; Baum et al. 2009). Relationship-based stalking accounts for about 50% of stalking cases in the general population. Stalking cases can be divided into those who stalk an ex-intimate partner and those who stalk non-ex-intimates such as a former friend, an acquaintance, or a stranger (Purcell et al. 2002; Dressing et al. 2005; Baum et al. 2009). However, a Swedish study showed that, of the cases reported to the police, as many as 76% involved ex-intimate partner-related stalking (Belfrage and Strand 2009). Common stalking behaviors are unwanted communication (such as intrusive phone calls or e-mails) or contact such as loitering, surveillance, following and approaching the victim. Physical violence occurs in about 50% of ex-intimate partner stalking cases compared with 10–25% of non-ex-intimate partners. It is more common for a stalker to behave violently toward someone they know, such as a family member or a friend (Purcell et al. 2002; McEwan et al. 2009). The impact of stalking on victims is severe even if no violence is present; the fear and worry about what will happen next limits stalking victims from freely living their lives. Victims change their lives in order to avoid a stalker as much as they can, and psychological stress is often present. There is a need for society to better understand the harm stalkers do to their victims in order to better protect and help victims to cope with stalking situations. There is an obvious need for more knowledge about the risk from different types of stalkers and about the protective actions that can be taken in order to prevent further stalking.

Honor-based violence is defined as any *actual, attempted, or threatened physical harm, including forced marriages, with honor as the motive* (Kropp et al. 2013, 1). It is difficult to measure in terms of lifetime risk in different countries because the motive of the violence not always has been defined specifically as honor based but more often as domestic violence. However, according to United Nations' estimates, approximately 5000 women lose their lives in honor-related killings each year (UNFPA 2000). An honor killing, which can be defined as the murder of a family member who has seriously violated societal norms and thereby is perceived to have brought shame upon the family, is the most extreme form of honor-related violence; it is based on the idea that honor is restored after this killing is performed. To some extent, honor-based violence is also a form of domestic violence; the difference is that the motive behind honor-based crimes is focused on how a family's honor is perceived to be affected by a person's actions and that the violence can be collectively performed. Examples of actions performed by a family member that are perceived as disgracing the family could be meeting a boyfriend/girlfriend without the family's approval, wanting a divorce, or preventing an arranged marriage. Adolescent behavior, such as not obeying parents or dressing in inappropriate ways according to cultural norms, can be seen as shaming the family. These acts do not always need to be proven; a bad reputation can be just as shameful as the act itself. Teenage girls are more exposed to honor-related violence because a family's honor to a large extent depends on that family's ability to control the sexuality of young female family members. For example, it is very important that a young girl is a virgin when she gets married. Older women, men, and boys are also at risk if they perform acts considered as dishonoring the family.

Honor-related violence is not linked to or expressed by any specific religion, culture, ethnic group, or any particular country, but it can be practiced within any of these groups. It is important to remember that this type of violence is carried out in many different regions of the world, and that it may be more anchored to a cultural perspective, a gender perspective, and an intersectional perspective than to specific groups (NCK 2010). Honor-based violence cannot be generalized to specific groups or countries; it is considerably more complex than that.

Risk Assessment of Violence

In order to prevent violence and to protect victims with appropriate safety measures, the police need to make a viable risk management plan. By accurately assessing the risk of violence, the possibility of making a successful risk management plan increases. The police need to be knowledgeable about both the specific area of violence to be assessed (e.g., domestic violence) and the different methods that can be used to assess the risk for violence within the specific context. Awareness of the underlying motive in a case is one of the key issues to consider when making a risk assessment; this is the basis for risk management. There are several different methods and models to work with when it comes to assessing risk for violence in different contexts, and it is crucial that the police have knowledge about which methods work successfully in order to use the best methods available. When the police work closely with researchers that can evaluate the methods used, knowledge increases not only for the specific officers but also for the police organization within which they work.

The research literature describes three different approaches for risk assessment—clinical, actuarial, and structured professional judgment; several different risk assessment methods and instruments can be found within these approaches (Webster and Hucker 2007; Otto and Douglas 2010).

The *clinical approach* was the first to be used to assess risk for violence. The research field of assessing risk for violence started in the mid-twentieth century. Studies were conducted within the prison system and within psychiatric care because risk assessments were used by courts and by parole boards upon the release of mentally disturbed patients and prisoners. The assessments were solely based on the clinician's own intuitive judgment about the risk factors for a specific person. The outcome was a yes or no answer to the question: Is this person dangerous? The knowledge and experience that the assessor had were the basis for the risk assessment. In many cases, this method was successful because the clinician often knew his patient and thereby knew what risk factors they exhibited. On the other hand, patients unknown by clinicians were far more difficult to assess, and the assessment outcomes were poor.

Steadman and Cocozza (1974) concluded, in their four- to five-year follow-up study of violent recidivism in released prisoners with a history of mental illness, that the risk assessments these prisoners received were correct in only one out of three cases. The problem was that the clinicians had to a large extent assessed the prisoners as dangerous, but the results showed that only 15% of the prisoners recidivated into new violent crimes. The risk assessments were based mainly upon the diagnosis of the prisoner's mental illness, which turned out to be insufficient information for a valid risk assessment.

The *actuarial approach* was developed as the next generation of risk assessment. The risk for violence still needed to be assessed for courts and parole boards, and the judicial system now demanded better validity. In the 1980s, Monahan conducted important research on predicting violence, which can be said to be the origins of the actuarial approach (Monahan and Steadman 1994). He was concerned that the knowledge about risk assessment was limited and also that there were few discussions on what risk assessment actually would be used for. Monahan asked for more studies using risk assessment methods that relied more upon actuarial techniques—studies performed in different settings that also considered short-term risks. The actuarial methods that were developed were based on more static risk factors (i.e., statistics helped in building these instruments). Factors that were important for predicting the risk for violence were combined and then weighted with statistical methods. The problem had been that the risk factors were not empirically founded but were more a list of factors that the specific clinician or researcher found important. Most of the risk factors were historical static factors (i.e., risk factors that cannot be changed for the better). Using the actuarial approach meant that the risk factors were measurable in a much better way than before; reliability increased substantially with this approach as did validity. The typical actuarial instrument consists of several, often historical, risk factors that are scored on a specific scale, which can be the same for all factors or can be different for individual items. The assessor adds the score of the risk factors into a total score. The total score is the risk assessed for the offender. This means that the overall risk is assessed more as a probability rather than as at risk or not.

This way of developing risk assessment created many instruments that were valid in the environment for which they were created, but they had a tendency to fail outside that context. Although there were some promising results, there was still more to be done. False positive assessments were still a problem. One of the reasons was that the instruments were static (i.e., there was no room for decreasing the risk). Another problem was that risk assessment results based on the actuarial approach were not always valid for individuals because they were based on group statistics. Monahan's request for new research using the actuarial approach was, however, a great improvement over the clinical approach. The research conducted was now methodologically superior to earlier studies, and the results were much better. The short-term predictions were now correct in 50% of the cases; these were better results than before but still were not satisfactory (Monahan and Steadman 1994).

Webster and colleagues developed the *structured professional judgment* (SPJ) approach in the 1990s. The SPJ approach combines the clinical approach and the actuarial approach; the instruments use checklists with the most important, evidenced-based risk factors that are both static and dynamic. These checklists are the basis for making an overall risk judgment without cutoffs or categories for risk but those that are determined from present risk factors and other considerations for the specific individual being assessed. The outcome predicts the overall risk level—low, moderate, or high. The researchers wanted to create a method to assess risk that was evidenced-based as well as clinically relevant, and they also wanted to assess the possibility of developing risk management that would decrease the risk. The result was the Historical Clinical Risk-20 (HCR-20), a checklist that combines the more static actuarial risk factors with the dynamic clinical risk factors (Webster et al. 1997). It consists of three different parts: ten historical items, five clinical items, and five risk management factors. All risk factors were assessed on a three-point scale: the risk factor was present (*yes*), the risk factor was present to some degree (*to some extent*), and the risk factor was not present (*no*). The overall risk was then assessed based on the amount of risk factors as well as on the clinical judgment (i.e., if you have all the risk factors, you were most likely to be at high risk; if you have only a few, you were more likely to be at low risk). But in between there were no cutoffs or categories that decided the probability of risk or categorized the risk. The assessor needed to use his own knowledge and experience now to assess the overall risk based upon which factors were present for an individual and how they affected the risk. Four out of five assessments were correct. Research showed that both the reliability and validity increased and that the most important factors impacting violent recidivism were the dynamic risk factors (Strand et al. 1999). The HCR-20 has become the state-of-the-art assessment instrument and is used worldwide when assessing risk for general violence. The third version of the HCR-20, the HCR-20V3, was recently developed and released (Historical Clinical Risk-20 Version 3; Douglas et al. 2013). However, it is not explicitly created to target specific violence such as domestic or sexual violence. Therefore, specific risk assessment instruments have been developed within the SPJ approach in order to better determine risk factors that are specific for certain types of violence. This has increased the validity and the reliability of this approach. Because the SPJ approach works well in many areas, risk assessment method development still follows this approach (Otto and Douglas 2010).

The reason for undertaking risk assessments for violence has changed with the SPJ approach—from predicting violence to preventing violence—where the outcome of the risk assessment serves as the basis for creating a risk management plan that will reduce the risk for violence and thereby protect potential victims from further harm.

Risk Assessment Instruments Used by the Police

The three instruments described in this section are all checklists developed within the SPJ approach by undertaking a systematic literature review of the existing research for the specific area of concern, as well as by doing a review of existing standards of practice, codes of ethics, and legal principles that exist for the specific field. These instruments also have the same working procedure when assessing risk. The first step is to gather information by interviews and file reviews. It is most beneficial for the assessors to conduct individual semi-structured interviews with the perpetrator and with the victim. If that is not possible, it is even more important that those who have interrogated the offender and the victim have gathered the information needed for the risk assessment and that they have documented it properly. The second step is to assess the specific risk factors one by one on a three-point scale: "yes" (coded Y) means that the risk factor is present; "to some extent" (coded $?$) means that the risk factor is present to some degree; and "no" (coded N) means that the risk factor is not present. If there is no information available, the risk factor can be assessed as missing. When the individual risk factors are assessed, other considerations can be noted (i.e., if there is anything specific about this case that has not yet been taken into consideration for the assessment, such as if the offender has access to a weapon). Then the assessors need to go through the checklist and make an overall risk judgment on a three-level scale—low (L), moderate (M), or high (H)—based on the results as though no protective actions were undertaken. When this is done, the risk management plan needs to be developed, which means that the assessor must outline possible scenarios and what the assessed risk means specifically. From that a risk management plan is completed that incorporates the most effective protective actions for the victim.

Many different professionals, such as the police, can use these instruments since they were not specifically designed for psychiatric care or for the prison system (such as the HCR-20). One common denominator is that these instruments were developed in a way so that nonclinicians can perform the assessment. Although an instrument such as the HCR-20 assesses the risk that the perpetrator will be violent again toward anyone, these three instruments assess the risk for violence toward a specific victim. As outlined in the following sections, the Brief Spousal Assault Form for the Evaluation of Risk (B-Safer) (Kropp et al. 2010a), the Stalking Assessment and Management (SAM) checklist (Kropp et al. 2010b), and the Patriarch (Kropp et al. 2013) consider risk factors for the perpetrator and also have victim vulnerability factors. This difference is important because the risk management plan will be completed for the victim; whereas, in psychiatric care, the risk assessment is the basis for a treatment plan for the offender. The only protective action that the police can work with includes the perpetrator is to serve him with a restraining or take him into custody order with different kinds of restrictions; all other protective actions involve the victim's situation. Within the prison system or while in psychiatric care, the offender needs to follow the treatment plan that is set up for him in order to reduce the risk for violence to such a degree that he will be released into the community.

Changes have been made in risk assessment instruments when researchers have worked with police to develop risk assessment methods, and new versions have been developed as part of that work. These new versions have replaced all those used previously. The versions described in this chapter were those used for the specific research presented.

The Brief Spousal Assault Form for the Evaluation of Risk (B-SAFER)

The B-SAFER (Kropp et al. 2010a) is an evidenced-based checklist constructed to assess the risk for further IPV. It is based on the SPJ approach and was designed to be used by nonclinicians such as the police, prison system officers, and social services. The B-SAFER (Kropp et al. 2008), or the screening version of the Spousal Assault Risk Assessment (SARA:SV) guide, was developed as a shorter version of the SARA (Kropp et al. 1994, 1995, 1999) in order to be better suited for use by the police. The number of risk factors was changed from 20 to 10; there were five risk factors related to the type of IPV (e.g., violence, threats of violence, escalation, violation of court orders, and violent attitudes) and five risk factors focusing on the perpetrator's psychosocial adjustment (general criminality and intimate relationship problems as well as problems with employment, substance use, and mental health issues). An additional five victim vulnerability factors were added to better assess the risk of further victimization of a specific individual who had been previously victimized by a specific offender. These new vulnerability factors (inconsistent behavior, negative attitude and extreme fear of the perpetrator, inadequate access to resources, unsafe living situation, or having personal problems) are also important factors to assess in order to find the most effective safety plan. The risk factors are coded as present, present to some extent, or not present for both the current and past situations. Other considerations may be taken into account, such as the presence of extreme jealousy or access to weapons. The next step is to assess the overall risk as low, moderate, or high for acute risk (within four weeks) and the risk for severe/lethal violence. Then the risk management plan is created based upon the results; protective actions should be suggested based on different scenarios related to the specific case.

Risk assessments for IPV have been carried out by the police in Sweden since 1999, and the work has progressed from being developmental to being more intense and more research oriented during the last decade (see Belfrage and Strand 2002, 2003, 2008, 2012). Studies on female perpetrators of domestic violence have also been carried out in the same way as with male perpetrators, with results showing that there are more similarities than differences between male and female perpetrators concerning risk factors for violence (Storey and Strand 2012).

Guidelines for Stalking Assessment and Management (SAM)

The SAM (Kropp et al. 2007, 2010b) checklist is an evidence-based risk assessment method that uses the SPJ approach for assessing the risk of stalking and stalking violence (Kropp et al. 2007, 2010b). The SAM risk factors are divided into three categories: (1) the nature of the stalking, which includes ten risk factors that describe the stalking behaviors for the current stalking situation and past stalking incidents (e.g., communication and contacts with the victim, violence, escalation); (2) perpetrator risk factors, including ten factors concerning the perpetrator's background and adjustment to society (e.g., angry, obsessive, and irrational behavior as well as antisocial behaviors such as other criminality and substance abuse); and (3) ten victim vulnerability factors designed to describe the victim's situation (e.g., inconsistent behaviors and attitude, unsafe living situation, and concerns related to others dependent on the victim). After assessing the 30 items as present, present to some extent, or not present for the current and the past situations, other considerations can be taken into account such as specific obsessions or having access to weapons. The next step is to assess the overall low, moderate, or high risk of stalking, the risk for violence, and/or the risk for severe/lethal violence. Then the risk management plan for a specific individual is developed based on the results where protective actions will be created and on the suggestions from different scenarios for the specific case.

The Patriarch

The Patriarch (Belfrage 2005, 2009; Kropp et al. 2013) is an evidence-based risk assessment method predicated on the SPJ approach for assessing the risk of honor-based violence (Belfrage 2005, 2009; Kropp et al. 2013). It has been used for several years in Sweden as an aid for law enforcement and social authorities in cases where a risk of honor-based violence has been suspected. The instrument has been under testing, and the final official version has been developed just recently (Kropp et al. 2013). The developmental versions were used as examples for this chapter because these versions were the methods the police used when collecting data for research projects in 2009–2014. The Patriarch version used was a two-part checklist. The first part consisted of ten risk factors such as the presence of serious violent threats, thoughts, acts, and specific honor-based violent acts as well as risk factors such as escalation, attitudes, degree of insult, origin from area with known sub-cultural values, lack of cultural integration, and personal problems. The second part consisted of the same five factors concerning the victim's vulnerability as in the B-SAFER. When each risk factor and victim vulnerability factor was assessed as present, present to some extent, or not present, other considerations could be noted (e.g., was there more than one victim and were there more perpetrators). Then, overall risk was assessed as low, moderate, or high for three different situations: the acute risk (near future—approximately four weeks), the risk of exposure in the longer term, and the risk of serious/deadly violence, regardless of when it might occur. When this assessment was completed, a risk management plan with specific scenarios and suggestions for the most effective protective actions was created and then acted upon.

For honored-related violence, where protective actions are to a large extent protective living actions (because many of the victims are adolescents), contacts with social service agencies may be required. Because the whole family can be involved as well as other victims and more perpetrators, collaboration with multiple agencies is necessary for both the investigation and the protection of the victim (Belfrage and Strand 2010; Belfrage et al. 2012b). This makes the creation of strategies and methods that can work and be understood by different professions even more important. A common methodology will significantly increase the possibility for a smoothly functioning collaboration in the community.

Police Working with Structured Professional Checklists

In 2002, the Swedish government initiated a statement of intent to counter domestic violence in Sweden (Swedish Government Official Reports, SOU 2002). National routines with structured violence risk assessment methods were to be implemented by Swedish authorities in order to better manage cases of IPV. In the past decade, the Swedish police have worked with risk of violence in several areas, and a particular focus has been on cases involving IPV. Evaluations in Sweden have shown that risk assessment methods based on the SPJ approach work well for the Swedish police for both assessing risk for partner violence as well as risk for general violence (Belfrage and Strand 2002, 2003, 2008, 2012; Belfrage et al. 2012c; Mellgren et al. 2012). Using risk assessments to make a risk management plan, the results showed that the higher the risk was assessed, the more protective actions were taken to reduce the risk of repeated victimization. Risk assessment instruments such as the B-SAFER, the SAM, and the Patriarch were designed to be used by different agencies such as the police, prison systems, social services, psychiatric services, and so forth. It is important to find methods that can be used and understood across organizations when the problems of these crimes are complex and most often involve whole families. This means that several different authorities have to decide on the kind of protective actions that can be implicated, especially when it comes to honor-related violence (Belfrage et al. 2012b). The Swedish National Council for Crime Prevention (BRÅ 2012) showed in its 2012 study that when the risk assessment was done with the Patriarch, more protective measures were given to the victim compared to those whose cases were not assessed with the Patriarch.

Risk Assessment and Management Performed by the Police

Risk assessments conducted by the police have several steps and involve different police officers, depending on the type of risk analysis that is needed. When a crime is reported, an initial risk assessment is done by the first police officer that meets the victim, with the purpose of assessing the acute risk in order to determine whether or not protective action is needed immediately. The person who makes the initial risk assessment is also responsible for informing the victim support coordinator if there is a risk of threat or violence and if an additional structured risk assessment needs to be done. This first assessment primarily is a clinical assessment performed based upon the knowledge and experience of the police officer on-site. This initial risk assessment also serves as the basis for the risk analysis done later. This is a crucial step because most of the information gathered in the case relies upon what the responding officer reports.

The next step is to perform a structured risk assessment with the appropriate instrument for the specific case (i.e., using the B-SAFER for IPV cases). The outcome of the risk assessment determines the risk management planning (where the decision to initiate or continue with already taken protective actions will be taken). If the assessed risk is elevated, the case can be given priority, and the victim support coordinator will make arrangements for and be responsible for the victim's safety by providing adequate support and protection measures.

If the risk for severe violence is elevated, a more comprehensive risk assessment can be undertaken since the risk management plan may need lots of protective measures and coordination with other agencies. Cases assessed as high risk for serious/lethal violence will be prioritized. As a protective action, the victim can be kept safe by a security team, which then will be in charge of the implementation of the risk management plan together with the victim support coordinator.

Risk Management and Protective Actions

A risk management plan contains the protective actions that will be offered to the victim and how they will be performed and followed up. These actions are determined by the results of the risk assessment for the specific case. There are guidelines approved by the Swedish National Police on how to work with victims and on protective measures. The protective actions can be of short or long term, depending on the case. Both supportive and/or more offensive protective actions can be taken for the victim, depending on the situation. One of the most common protective actions is a safety talk to inform and motivate the victim to take part in the suggested protective actions, to continue to pursue the criminal charge, and to participate in the investigation against the alleged perpetrator. The safety talk can help victims to better understand the risks to which they are exposed and what they can do to protect themselves. Another protective action that is common for female victims of relational violence is to help them to contact a women's shelter where they can get additional support and make protective living arrangements, if necessary. If there are children in the relationship, social services will also be contacted as a mandatory procedure. In Sweden, a noncontact order (also known as a restraining order) is applied for and decided upon by the district attorney. This means that the police can make a suggestion to apply for a noncontact order in the risk management plan, but they cannot be sure that the victim will have the non-contact order granted. This process complicates the protection of the victim; therefore, it is even more important that there is cooperation between the police and the district attorney. A specific study on restraining orders showed that they can prevent domestic violence, specifically in cases where domestic violence was the only criminal behavior of the perpetrator (Strand 2012).

If the victim needs to be relocated, protected living arrangements can be offered. This means that the victim will be placed at a safe house with a secret address, and only a few persons will know where the victim is. In cases with extreme risk for violence, bodyguards can be an option to protect the victim. The kind of protective actions that can be offered to the victim are based on the outcome of the risk assessment, the local conditions, the possibility of collaboration with other agencies or organizations, the resources, and on the duration of the protection. It is also important that the victim will cooperate with both the criminal investigation and the suggested protective actions in order to reduce the risk of re-victimization. Offering the victim a support person who can help explain the legal process and who can offer encouragement throughout the whole process can help the victim to continue to cooperate with the police.

Working with protective actions for victims affected by crime from related parties is difficult and can sometimes be very resource intensive.

When resources are limited, it is of great importance to assess the degree of risk for re-victimization in order to better prioritize and apply the most effective protective actions. Severe violence, such as honor-related violence that is reported to the police, becomes a public prosecution case, which means that the prosecution cannot be withdrawn by the victim; the investigation will continue even if the victim takes back the accusation and refuses to cooperate. It will be much more difficult though for the district attorney to get the offender convicted for the alleged crime if there is no witness statement. The results from a study by the Swedish National Council for Crime Prevention (BRÅ 2012) showed that, in those cases where honor was a motive for the crime that was reported, four out of ten women at some stage in the investigation did not want to participate anymore. It then becomes difficult to proceed, and the police would be more likely to close down the investigation. The reason many girls and young women do not want to participate or wish to discontinue their involvement in police investigations is often because they have a close relationship and strong emotional ties to the perpetrator. Schyttler and Linell (2008) showed in their study on honor-based violence that it may be difficult for a young woman to continue to cooperate with the investigation when her family does not confirm the alleged violence or when the woman has contacted the family during the investigation. If she is at risk from the family or is being subjected to indirect or direct pressure from family members, the likelihood of the victim taking back her testimony increases.

Researchers Working with the Police

Academics and police officers have collaborated on risk assessment and risk management of IPV, stalking, and on honor-based violence with the aim of validating risk assessment methods for the Swedish police to use. Research and developmental projects have been conducted in collaboration with the Swedish police for more than a decade. The projects were mainly carried out with participants working together, where the practitioners were carrying out the risk assessments and the risk management planning, and the researchers were in charge of the scientific process of collecting the data and of the follow-up processes. The police funded the practitioner's caseloads as part of their day-to-day work, while the researchers were not employed by the police but by the university. Grants from the Crime Victim Compensation and Support Authority and Mid Sweden University have to a large extent funded the research reported in this chapter.

In cases where the plaintiff has been the victim of a crime of IPV, stalking, or with honor as the motive, comprehensive studies of risk assessment and risk management planning were performed using assessment instruments such as the B-SAFER, the SAM, and the Patriarch. The research was partially based on registry studies with data collected from police files. During the time period 1999–2014, research and developmental projects were carried out within regular activities of the police county in Stockholm, Kalmar, Västernorrland, and Jämtland. Included criteria for the studies were that the risk assessments would be based on police reports where the motive for the crime was IPV, stalking, or honor related, and that the material of the cases would be large enough in size to be followed up. Several projects have been carried out with an almost identical setup. This approach has facilitated the work and the possibility of merging data between projects and comparing results. The first step was always to find a contact person for the project. Usually this has been the victim support coordinator or someone working with victim support at the specific police district. Based on discussions with the contact person and other key staff, a research plan was set up. In addition to the research plan, a schedule for education of the police officers involved was also set up for each project. The education was part of the research project because one of the requirements for using the risk assessment instruments is that the assessors are educated and trained in using the specific instrument. The education was not limited only to those police officers involved in the research but was available to everyone for whom the police wanted it to be offered. Therefore, the education was also a contribution to the police as a way of reproducing the results of the research in the organization.

Collection of Data

Data collection for the studies was done mainly by the police but also by the researchers. A specific research document containing background factors, the outcome of the risk assessment instrument, a list of protective actions taken, and a follow-up sheet was produced for each study. The follow-up contained data on the outcome of the initial index crime in terms of legal sanctions and data on recidivism into any new crimes, violent and nonviolent. The police were responsible for completing and encoding the data for all the alleged perpetrators that met the inclusion criterion. The researchers were available to help upon request from the police. All the data from the research documents was decoded into a data file using the software SPSS.

Results from a Study on IPV Assessed with the B-SAFER

This is a summary of the results from a study that has been published by Belfrage and Strand (2012). Two hundred and sixteen assessments of male offenders of IPV with a mean age of 38 years (SD = 11, R = 19–74) were performed with the B-SAFER by 82 police officers from May 2005 to January 2007 in Stockholm. The follow-up ranged from 28 to 48 months. The alleged index crimes were assault (59%), illegal threat (17%), violation of a woman's integrity (17%), rape (2%), attempted murder (2%), and other crimes such as insult, arson, or invasion of privacy (3%). Forty-six percent (100) of the perpetrators were convicted for the crime for which they were charged and 28% (60) were sentenced to prison.

The results from the assessment showed that the risk factors were present to a large extent in this group. The three-point scale was translated into numbers (i.e., $Y=2$, $?=1$, and $N=0$). The mean value was 1.11 (SD=0.83) per risk factor ($R = 0.20–1.46$); for the victim vulnerability factors, the mean value was 0.81 (SD=0.83) per factor ($R=0.54–1.05$). Missing values varied from 2–32% for the current situation and from 7–49% for the past, where the risk factor "mental health problems" had the most missing data. For the victim vulnerability factors, the missing data was found to vary from 4–20%, where the factor "personal problems" had the most missing data. The overall risk for the acute situation was assessed as low for 25% of the cases, as moderate for 36%, and as high for 39% of the cases. For the risk of severe/fatal violence, the risk was assessed as low for 54% of the cases, moderate for 32%, and high for 14% of the cases.

The protective actions were summarized into low and high interventions. Low intervention included mandatory actions such as filing a search for weapon access, contacting social services if children were present, and helping victims contact a women's shelter. High intervention included more offensive protective actions such as initiating a noncontact order, alarm packages, and protected living; 32% received a low intervention, while 68% received a high intervention. Correlation with the overall risk assessment was good for acute risk (tau-b=0.30, $p < 0.001$) and for risk of severe/lethal violence (tau-b=0.25, $p < 0.001$).

Forty-two percent (90) of the victims were re-victimized by the same perpetrator, and the most common re-offenses were assault and threats. Twenty-eight (31%) of those who reoffended had a no-contact order toward the victim; there was a 46% recidivism rate among those who were granted a noncontact order. Among those who recidivated (90), there was a significant difference in the level of risk assessed; 60% were assessed with low risk, 30% with moderate risk, and 10% with high risk (chi-2[2] = 32.99 $p < 0.001$). Because there was a relationship between high risk and high intervention, the interpretation of this result was that high intervention had a positive effect and prevented re-victimization.

Results from a Study on Stalking Assessed with the SAM

This is a summary of the results from a study that has been published by Belfrage and Strand (2009) of 153 assessments of male stalking offenders with a mean age of 40 years ($R=14–68$) that were performed with the SAM by 41 police officers from May 2005 to December 2006 in the police counties Stockholm and Kalmar. No follow-up was conducted for this study. Seventy-six percent of the offenders stalked an ex-intimate partner, while 14% stalked an acquaintance, and 10% stalked a stranger. The alleged index crimes were harassment (47%), illegal threat (29%), assault (9%), and other crimes such as breaking and entering, and violation of a noncontact order (15%). Twenty-two percent of the perpetrators had a noncontact order in place at the time of the most current stalking episode. The duration of the stalking ranged from a few days to 20 years. Approximately 50% of the offenders had stalked their victim for up to six months, and 25% continued to stalk their victim for more than 18 months.

The results of the assessment made with the SAM showed that the risk factors for the nature of the stalking were fully or partially present in 16–90% of the cases. The perpetrator risk factors were present or partially present in up to 64% of the cases, and victim vulnerability factors were found to be present or partially present in up to 53% of the cases. Missing values varied from 1–16% for the 20 risk factors of the perpetrator; for the victim vulnerability factors, the missing data was found to vary from 1–4%. The risk factor with the most missing values was "intimate relationship problems."

The overall risk assessed for continued stalking was low for 9% of the cases, moderate for 31%, and high for 59% of the cases. The risk of violence was assessed as low for 44% of the cases, moderate for 44%, and high for 12%. The risk of severe/fatal violence was assessed as low for 82% of the cases, moderate for 16%, and high for 2% of the cases.

A significant correlation between the nature of the stalking and the overall risk for stalking was found for eight out of ten risk factors, for violence in eight out of ten risk factors, and for severe/fatal violence in five out of ten risk factors. A significant correlation between the perpetrator risk factors and the overall risk for stalking was eight out of ten risk factors; for violence, it was nine out of ten risk factors; and for severe/fatal violence it was nine out of ten risk factors. A significant correlation between the victim vulnerability factors and the overall risk for stalking was found for seven out of ten factors, for violence in ten out of ten factors, and for severe/fatal violence in seven out of ten factors.

Results from a Study on Honor-Related Violence Assessed with the Patriarch

Ninety-six assessments on 91 female and 5 male victims with a mean age of 24 years (SD = 9, R = 14–57) were made with the Patriarch during the period from October 24, 2008, to April 27, 2012, in Stockholm, the police county of Stockholm. The follow-up ranged from 9 to 49 months, with a mean of 28 months (SD = 9). The relationship between the victims and the main suspected perpetrator was either a partner/ex-partner (31%) or a close relative (69%). Forty-three percent of the cases involved a woman who was or who had been in a relationship with a man, while 57% of the cases involved young women and men. In all cases except one, the victim had either emigrated from another country, was born in another country, or had parents that were immigrants from another country. The most common countries of origin for the victims and the suspected perpetrators were Iraq (30%), Turkey (14%), and Iran (11%). Forty-four percent of the victims came from other countries, primarily in the Middle East or Africa. The most common offenses were assault (34%), physical abuse (34%), and violation of a woman's integrity (14%). Two cases were reported as preparation for murder. In six of the ten cases, the victim cooperated in the criminal investigation (64%). Nearly one in four (23%) discontinued the participation; and in every tenth case (12%), the victim refused to participate in the criminal investigation. Twenty-two percent of the cases were prosecuted in court, and 16% of the offenders were sentenced in the district court. This corresponds to 71% of those who were prosecuted; 16% of the total sample. The victim participated in the investigation in 12 (86%) of the 15 cases that resulted in a conviction.

The results of the assessment made with the Patriarch showed that the risk factors were fully present in 10–74% of the cases; 10–29% of the victim vulnerability factors were also present. In 6–39% of the cases, the coding for the risk factors and 19–23% of the victim vulnerability factors was missing. Most difficult to assess were the risk factors about past honor-related violence and if there were any previous marriage agreements as part of the tradition; there was no information available in 37% and 39% of these cases, respectively. The overall risk for the acute situation was assessed as low in 30% of the cases, as moderate risk for 31%, and as high risk for 30%. For severe/lethal violence, it was almost the same for low risk (30%), moderate risk (34%), and high risk (24%). There was a strong correlation among the assessed risks; that is, if the acute risk was considered low risk, so was the assessed risk for lethal violence (tau-b = 0.67, p < 0.001).

Additional protective actions were suggested for 50% of the victims based upon the Patriarch risk assessment. A total of 91 (95%) of the victims received some form of protective action; 54% had a safety talk, 25% had a support person, 74% had contact with social services, and 50% were transported to a safety house for protected living.

Thirty-two percent of the victims were re-victimized with honor as the motive for the initial victimization.

Discussion

Assessing the risk and protecting individuals who are subjected to violence from a person with whom they have or have had a strong relationship is a complex problem. Study results showed that the police performed risk assessments on offenders with severe criminality, including elements of threats and violence, and that many risk factors were present. Even though the index crimes were severe, convicting the perpetrators for the alleged crime was difficult. Of the IPV perpetrators, 46% were sentenced for the crimes they committed; in this sample, the recidivism rate was 42%. For the perpetrators of honor-based violence, 16% were sentenced, and the recidivism rate was 32%. If the perpetrator is not convicted for his or her crime, it makes it even more difficult to protect the victim and to get the victim to collaborate with the police. Of those cases in which perpetrators were convicted for an honor-based crime, the victims had collaborated with the police in 86% of the cases. It is very important to get the victims to cooperate with the criminal investigation and for them to take the suggested protective actions.

Risk factors were present to a large extent for all the assessment instruments—but especially for the Patriarch assessments. The large amount of missing data for risk factors might be a result of how the police assess whether or not a risk factor is missing rather than whether the risk factor is really not present. The results showed that risk factors concerning mental health problems and relational problems were the most difficult ones to assess, and there was a large amount of missing data for all three instruments. Missing data is an accepted outcome for some of the risk factors because it can be difficult to obtain all the information needed for a risk assessment. However, if too many risk factors are missing, the validity of the risk assessment will decrease. One way to get more information is to create routines regarding risk assessments for all the police officers that will take part in the initial interrogations. This might be the only opportunity to interview the perpetrator. Therefore, it is important that all the questions for the risk assessments are asked and reported. Educating a large proportion of the police about IPV, stalking, and honor-based violence with a specific focus on mental health issues can be one step toward increasing the validity of the risk assessments since it is crucial to obtain the right information.

The results from the overall risk assessment showed that, for the acute situation, the risk was elevated for 70–75% of cases. The risk for continued stalking was elevated for 91%, which makes sense because many victims report crimes to which they recently had been exposed. The risk for violence was elevated for approximately half of the cases and was assessed as high for 12% of the stalkers, 14% of the IPV cases, and 24% of the honor-based cases. This implies that these groups of victims have a great need for protection and that the assessment instruments can help the police prioritize allocation of resources.

The results show that the structured professional checklists work well as tools for the police to use to assess the risk for IPV, stalking, and honor-based violence, and that these checklists help them with risk management.

The more risk factors present on the checklist, the higher the risk. The higher the risk of violence, the more protective actions are suggested in the risk management plan. Although many protective actions have been taken for victims, the research to date cannot identify which protective actions work well and are effective in preventing further victimization. More research needs to be done in the area of risk management.

The recidivism rate is still high for these kinds of crimes. Recidivism also occurs to some extent for those who were assessed as low risk, implying that not enough protective actions were taken. However, this is a complex issue that cannot solely be simplified into results based on group statistics. There will always be cases where victims are extremely difficult to protect, and there will also be cases where the risk is very low and the victim does not need any obvious protective action. When conducting research on the group level, one must keep in mind that the results are not applicable per se on the individual level, which is the core of the SPJ approach.

The results from working with the police have shown that the combination of the researchers' work and the police experiences increased the possibility of continuing developmental work and of implementing the results into the organization's operations.

Limitations

When studies are conducted as a part of the regular activities in an organization, the design of the research will generally have some limitations. However, the benefits outweigh the disadvantages. One such limitation is that studies that are based solely on information from police records may contain a variety of sources of error depending on what is reported and documented in the files. Another likely source of error is that a large proportion of all crimes involving close relationships between the offender and the victim never will be reported to the police at all and thus will be missed in the follow-up from police records. Obtaining a more comprehensive picture of repeated victimization requires studies where interviews are conducted with both the victim and the perpetrator. However, this means much more voluminous research than a registry study. Another limitation raised by researchers is about the problem of the validity of the follow-up studies that measure various risk factors and their relationship to repeated victimization based on complaints of victimization without regard to the protective actions taken. A measure of repeated reported vulnerability can, however, provide indications of police opportunities to improve the situation of women who come to their attention. In other words, investigating the relationship among risk analysis, protection, and actual relapse leading to a renewed contact with the police will be a good way to validate the work of risk assessment and risk management as shown in this chapter.

Another limitation of the data is that the present studies were based on secondary data (i.e., someone else performed the risk assessment and recorded the information). Different persons who conducted the risk assessments have different training and experience, which may influence the outcome. The studies contain collected material from several different police counties, which may have different procedures for how they responded to the situations even if they have the same basic instructions, and that may have affected the outcome—a factor that needs to be considered. The limitations presented here must be considered, and they restrict the ability to generalize the results.

Conclusion

The outcome of the close collaboration between academics and the police showed that the police have learned about structured risk assessment methods, which now are a part of their everyday work. Researchers are working closely with the police in providing education for police officers who are working with risk assessments and risk management in their daily duties as a result of this collaboration. This research helps the practitioners to use evidence-based methods, which will improve their work in supporting and protecting victims of crimes. This also improves the quality of the research because researchers and practitioners are working together with the same goal—that of preventing violence from occurring.

References

Australian Bureau of Statistics. (2006). *Personal safety survey, Australia, 2005.* Canberra: ABS.

Baum, K., Catalano, S., Rand, M., et al. (2009). *Stalking victimization in the United States. National Crime Victimisation Survey.* Washington, DC: US Department of Justice, Office of Justice Programs.

Belfrage, H. (2005). *Patriark. bedömning av risk för patriarkalt våld med hedern som motiv. Användarmanual* [Patriarch. Assessment of Risk for Honour Based Violence. User manual]. Sundsvall: Rättspsykiatriska Regionkliniken.

Belfrage, H. (2009). *Patriark. bedömning av risk för patriarkalt våld med hedern som motiv. Användarmanual* [Patriarch. Assessment of Risk for Honour Based Violence. User manual]. Sundsvall: Rättspsykiatriska Regionkliniken.

Belfrage, H. (2012). *Patriark. bedömning av risk för patriarkalt våld med hedern som motiv. Användarmanual* [Patriarch. Assessment of Risk for Honour Based Violence. User manual]. Sundsvall: Rättspsykiatriska Regionkliniken.

Belfrage, H., & Strand, S. (2002). *Polisiär bedömning av risk för upprepat partnervåld. Resultat av ett års arbete med strukturerade riskbedömningar enligt SARA i Kalmar, Kronoberg och Blekinge län* [Police assessment of repeated intimate partner violence. The results of one year work with structured risk assessment with SARA in Kalmar, Kronoberg and Blekinge County]. Sundsvall: Rättspsykiatriska Regionkliniken.

Belfrage, H., & Strand, S. (2003). *Utveckling av ett riskinstrument för polisiär bedömning av risk för upprepat partnervåld (SARA:PV). Slutrapport från ett utvecklingsprojekt i Kalmar, Kronoberg och Blekinge län* [Development of a risk assessment instrument for the police in assessing risk of repeated intimate partner violence. Final report from a one-year development work in Kalmar, Kronoberg and Blekinge County]. Sundsvall: Rättspsykiatriska Regionkliniken.

Belfrage, H., & Strand, S. (2008). Structured spousal violence risk assessment: Combining risk factors and victim vulnerability factors. *International Journal of Forensic Mental Health Services, 7*(1), 39–46.

Belfrage, H., & Strand, S. (2009). Validation of the stalking assessment and management checklist (SAM) in law enforcement: A prospective study of 153 cases of stalking in two Swedish police counties. *International Journal of Police Science and Management, 11*(1), 67–76. DOI: 10.1350/ijps.2009.11.1.110.

Belfrage, H., & Strand, S. (2010). *Strukturerad bedömning av risker vid hot och trakasserier med hedersrelaterad bakgrund. Ett utvecklingsprojekt i Polismyndigheten Stockholms län om polisiär riskbedömning och riskhantering* [Structured risk assessment of threats and harassments with honor related background. A development project concerning police risk assessment and risk management in police authorizes Stockholm County]. Sundsvall: Rättspsykiatriska Regionkliniken och Mittuniversitetet.

Belfrage, H., & Strand, S. (2012). Measuring the outcome of structured spousal violence risk assessments using the B-SAFER: Risk in relation to recidivism and intervention. *Behavioral Sciences and the Law, 30*(4), 420–430.

Belfrage, H., Strand, S., Ekman, L., & Hasselborg, A.-K. (2012b). The PATRIARCH. Six years experiences from the use of a checklist for the assessment of risk for patriarchal violence with honor as motive. *International Journal of Police Science and Management, 14*(1), 20–29.

Belfrage, H., Strand, S., & Hasselborg, A.-K. (2012c). *"SARA-MODELLEN" Strukturerade vs. ostrukturerade riskbedömningar vid polisanmält partnervåld. Implementering och utvärdering av införandet av strukturerade riskbedömningar för partnervåldsrelaterad brottslighet som en arbetsmetod hos polismyndigheterna i Västernorrland och Jämtland* ["SARA-MODEL" Structured vs. unstructured risk assessment of police reported interpersonal violence. Implementation and evaluation of the introduction of structured risk assessment for intimate partner violence as a method of working at the police authorities in Västernorrland and Jämtland]. Umeå: Brottsoffermyndigheten.

BRÅ, Swedish National Council for Crime Prevention. (2006). *Stalking in Sweden. Prevalence and prevention.* Stockholm: Swedish National Council for Crime Prevention.

BRÅ, Swedish National Council for Crime Prevention. (2012). *Polisens utredningar av hedersrelaterat Rapport 2012:1.* Stockholm: Swedish National Council for Crime Prevention.

Douglas, K. S., Hart, S. D., Webster, C. D., & Belfrage, H. (2013). *HCR-20. Assessing risk for violence. Version 3.* Burnaby, BC: Mental Health, Law, & Policy Institute, Simon Fraser University.

Dressing, H., Kuehner, C., & Gass, P. (2005). Lifetime prevalence and impact of stalking in a European population: Epidemiological data from a middle-sized German city. *British Journal of Psychiatry, 187*, 168–172.

Finney, A. (2006). *Domestic violence, sexual assault and stalking: Findings from the 2004/05 British Crime Survey. Home Office Online Report 12/06.* London: Home Office.

Kropp, P. R., Belfrage, H., & Hart, S. D. (2013). *Assessment of Risk for Honour Based Violence (Patriarch). User manual.* Vancouver, BC: ProActive ReSolutions. Swedish translation by Belfrage, H. Bedömning av risk för hedersrelaterat våld (PATRIARK). www.evidensbaseradkrim.se

Kropp, P. R., Hart, S. D., & Belfrage, H. (2005). *Brief spousal assault form for the evaluation of risk (B-SAFER), Version 2: User manual.* Vancouver, BC: Proactive Resolutions.

Kropp, P. R., Hart, S. D., & Belfrage, H. (2008). *Bedömning av risk för upprepat partnervåld (SARA:SV) Version 2:* Användarmanual. Sundsvall, Sweden: Rättspsykiatriska regionkliniken, Landstinget Västernorrland. Swedish translation of; Kropp, P. R., Hart, S. D., & Belfrage, H. (2008). *Brief spousal assault form for the evaluation of risk (B-SAFER): User manual.* Vancouver, BC: Proactive Resolutions.

Kropp, P. R., Hart, S. D., & Belfrage, H. (2010a). *Brief spousal assault form for the evaluation of risk (B-SAFER), Version 2: User manual.* Vancouver, BC: Proactive Resolutions.

Kropp, P. R., Hart, S. D., & Lyon, D. R. (2010b). *Stalking assessment and management.* Vancouver, BC: Proactive Resolutions.

Kropp, P. R., Hart, S. D., & Lyon, D. R. (2007). *Stalking assessment and management.* Vancouver, BC: Proactive Resolutions.

Kropp, P. R., Hart, S. D., Webster, C. D., et al. (1994). *Manual for the spousal assault risk assessment guide.* Vancouver, BC: British Columbia Institute on Family Violence.

Kropp, P. R., Hart, S. D., Webster, C. D., et al. (1995). *Manual for the spousal assault risk assessment guide.* Vancouver, BC: British Columbia Institute on Family Violence.

Kropp, P. R., Hart, S. D., Webster, C. D., et al. (1999). *Manual for the spousal assault risk assessment guide.* Vancouver, BC: British Columbia Institute on Family Violence.

Lundgren, E., Heimer, G., Westerstrand, J., & Kalliokoski, A.-M. (2001). *Slagen dam. Mäns våld mot kvinnor i jämställda Sverige—en omfångsundersökning.* Stockholm: Fritzes Offentliga Publikationer.

McEwan, T. E., Mullen, P. E., MacKenzie, R., et al. (2009). Violence in stalking situations. *Psychological Medicine, 39*, 1469–1478.

Mellgren, C., Svalin, K., Levander, S., & Torstensen Levander, M. (2012). *Riskanalys i polisverksamhet. En utvärdering av polisens arbete med riskanalys för våld på individnivå: Skånemodellen och Check 10+. FoURapport 2012:3.* Malmö Högskola: Fakulteten för hälsa och samhälle.

Monahan, J., & Steadman, J. H. (1994). *Violence and mental disorder. Developments in risk assessment.* Chicago, IL: University of Chicago.

Mullen, P. E., Pathé, M., & Purcell, R. (2009). *Stalkers and their victims.* 2nd edn. New York: Cambridge University Press.

NCK (Nationellt centrum för kvinnofrid). (2010). *Hedersrelaterat våld och förtryck—en kunskaps- och forskningsöversikt. Rapport 2010:1.* Uppsala: Nationellt centrum för kvinnofrid.

Otto, R. K., & Douglas, K. S. (2010). *Handbook of violence risk assessment. International perspectives on forensic mental health.* London: Taylor & Francis.

Purcell, R., Pathé, M., & Mullen, P. E. (2002). The prevalence and nature of stalking in the Australian community. *Australian and New Zealand Journal of Psychiatry, 36,* 114–120.

Schyttler, A., & Linell, H. (2008). *Hedersrelaterade traditioner i en svensk kontext—en studie av omhändertagna flickor.* Stockholm: Forsknings—och utbildningsenheten för socialtjänstens individ—och familjeomsorg i nordvästra Stockholm.

Steadman, H. J., & Cocozza, J. J. (1974). *Careers of the criminally insane: Excessive social control of deviance.* Lexington, KY: Lexington Books.

Storey, J., & Strand, S. (2012). The characteristics and violence risk management of women arrested by the police for intimate partner violence. *European Journal of Criminology, 9*(6), 636–651.

Strand, S. (2012). Using a restraining order as a protective risk management strategy to prevent intimate partner violence. *International Journal of Police Practice and Research, 13,* 254–266.

Strand, S., Belfrage, H., Fransson, G., & Levander, S. (1999). Clinical and risk management factors in risk prediction of mentally disordered offenders—More important than historical data? A retrospective study of 40 mentally disordered offenders assessed with the HCR-20 violence risk assessment scheme. *Legal and Criminological Psychology, 4,* 67–76.

Swedish Government Official Reports, SOU. (2002). *Nationell handlingsplan mot våld i nära relationer* [A national statement of intent to counter domestic violence], SOU 2002:71. Stockholm: Justitiedepartementet [Ministry of Justice].

Thompson, R. S., Bonomi, A. E., Anderson, M., et al. (2006). Intimate partner violence: Prevalence, types, and chronicity in adult women. *American Journal of Preventive Medicine, 30,* 447–457.

Tjaden, P., & Thoennes, N. (2000). *Full report of the prevalence, incidence and consequences of violence against women (Rep. No. NCJ 183781).* Washington, DC: U.S. Department of Justice.

UNFPA—United Nations Population Fund. (2000). *The state of world population 2000. Lives together, worlds apart. men and women in a time of change.* Available at http://www.unfpa.org/sites/default/files/pub-pdf/swp2000_eng.pdf. Retrieved on January 19, 2014.

Webster, C. D., Douglas, K. S., Eaves, D., & Hart, S. D. (1997). *HCR-20 Assessing risk for violence. Version 2.* Vancouver, BC: Simon Fraser University and Forensic Psychiatric Services Commission of British Columbia.

Webster, C. D., & Hucker, S. J. (2007). *Violence risk: Assessment and management.* West Sussex, England: Wiley.

World Health Organization. (2005). *WHO multi-country study on women's health and domestic violence against women: Summary report of initial results on prevalence, health outcomes and women's responses.* Geneva: WHO.

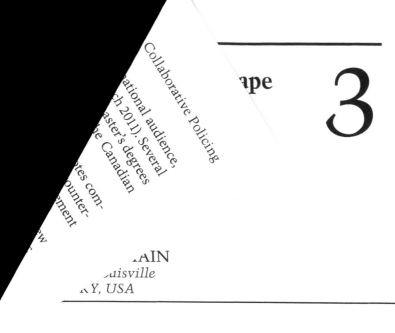

Collaborative Policing

...ape   3

...AIN
..uisville
.. Y, USA

Contents

Introduction

Police education and training are in transition around the world. Here are just a few examples of recent developments:

- In the United States, it is increasingly common for individuals to "pay their own way" through the police academy and then seek police employment. This represents a major change from just 20 to 30 years ago, when nearly every police agency hired new recruits first and then put them through the academy at the agency's expense.
- A massive national review of the structure and operation of policing in the United Kingdom recommended shifting the responsibility for police training from the police service itself over to colleges and universities (Neyroud 2011). The review suggested that entry level education and training be modeled after the partnership between the New South Wales police in Australia and Charles Sturt University (The Scottish Institute of Police Research 2011).
- The Scottish Institute of Police Research (SIPR), in cooperation with the Scottish Police College, offers a postgraduate diploma/master

of science degree in policing studies for an inter...
delivered primarily online (Institute of Police Resear...
UK universities and consortia are similarly offering m...
in policing and law enforcement in hybrid format (T...
Police Sector Council 2011).

- CEPOL, the European Police College, develops and prom...
  mon curricula on a variety of important topics, such as ...
  terrorism, domestic violence, and civilian crisis manag...
  (European Police College 2011).
- The Canadian Police Sector Council completed a national revi...
  of police tasks and training in order to map curricula to job-specifi...
  competencies.
- INTERPOL has expanded its training services, offering courses, an
  online Global Learning Centre, and the *International Police Training
  Journal* (Interpol 2011).
- The Commission on Accreditation for Law Enforcement Agencies
  (CALEA) revised its Public Safety Training Academy accreditation
  program to focus it more on instructional system design in order
  to encourage police academies to put greater emphasis on needs
  assessment, course development, and on course evaluation (Panel
  to Draft Police-University Bill 2014; CALEA 2011).
- Several countries have recently announced the establishment of new
  police universities, including South Africa and India (UNISA 2014).

Underlying these recent developments are a number of longer term trends.
Police education and training expanded greatly all around the world during the
twentieth century and were seen as cornerstones of police professionalization
and modernization (Kelling and Moore 1988). Within police agencies, training came to be regarded as a very important component of police administration with significant impacts on individual performance and organizational
change. From the outside, training was often seen as a means for correcting
police misconduct and for reforming the entire police institution. In the international arena, police training has been used to upgrade technical police skills
and as a vehicle to help export community policing, human rights, rule of
law, and democratization to developing, post-Soviet, and post-conflict nations
(Brogden 2005; Bayley and Perito 2010).

Current Issues and Trends

In the early twenty-first century, two of the most powerful factors
affecting police education and training are globalization and the current
economic downturn. Not too long ago, policing was almost entirely

a local and/or national endeavor, and police training was exclusively intranational. Today, though, police trainers fly around the world to deliver their courses. Organizations such as INTERPOL, Europol, the U.S. Bureau of International Law Enforcement Affairs (INL), the U.S. International Criminal Investigative Training Assistance Program (ICITAP), and the International Association of Chiefs of Police (IACP) play a growing role in the provision of training, and training content focuses more and more on global issues such as transnational crime (i.e., illicit drug trafficking, financial crimes, terrorism, and human trafficking). Regionalization can be observed as well: Brazil and Colombia offer police training to other countries in Central and South America, while South Africa provides police training throughout its continent. Since 1995, the U.S. Department of State has established International Law Enforcement Academies (ILEAs) on five continents with the goal of bringing together local law enforcement officers from participating countries to reduce crime, combat terrorism, increase cooperation, and to share in knowledge and training. The authors of this chapter both sit on the Executive Committee of International Managers of Police Academy and College Training (IMPACT), a section of the IACP, and have witnessed growing international participation and cooperation firsthand.

Education and training cost money, though. Particularly in the last five years, diminished resources may have led to reductions or postponements of police training in many countries. In the United Kingdom, much of the impetus for the recent national review of policing has been driven by the economy; the proposed shifting of some police training responsibility from the police service to colleges and universities may be seen as shifting the cost of training onto individuals rather than onto the government. This trend is in full swing in many U.S. states, where individuals pay their own way to attend the basic police academy and then go in search of police employment. At the Southern Police Institute (SPI), a 60-year-old U.S. university-based organization specializing in police management and executive development, police supervisors and commanding officers are increasingly paying the tuition out of their own pockets to attend long- and short-term training courses that may enhance their chances for promotion to higher ranks within their own agencies or make them more competitive in police executive searches.* Also, there is more and more interest in delivering continuing police education and training via distance learning, particularly using video and online courses. It can be anticipated that police training will increasingly be subjected to much more rigorous cost-benefit analysis than in the past, with an eye toward eliminating unnecessary training and making all training as efficient as possible.

---

* This phenomenon is not exclusive to the United States. See Kordaczuk-Was and Sosnowski (2011).

Increased scrutiny of police education and training, driven by tight fiscal conditions, will hopefully lead to a more scientific approach to training and to healthy examination of current systems and courses. Some of the more important issues likely to surface include:

- What is the proper distinction between police education and police training?
- What are the responsibilities of individuals (as opposed to the police) in obtaining both initial and ongoing police education/training?
- What institutions (police, universities, others) are best suited to provide police education and police training?
- What methods of instruction are most effective for delivering police education and training?
- In what substantive areas are police education and training currently in need of improvement?

Police Education in the Twenty-First Century

Structures for police education vary widely around the world. Some countries, particularly in Europe and Asia, have long had specialized police colleges or universities that offer higher education to aspiring police officers—and by "officers" what is generally meant is commissioned officers, the equivalent of lieutenants or inspectors, not bottom level, noncommissioned personnel (sergeants and below). Students typically spend three to four years completing an undergraduate university degree in law or police science, taking courses with other police officer candidates, and perhaps spending summers "in the field" learning practical policing skills. Upon graduation they become junior lieutenants/inspectors. These systems are very similar to the models used by the military in the United States and other countries, with separate entry schemes for commissioned and noncommissioned personnel.

Countries with police systems derived from the British model, including the United States, have traditionally taken a different approach in which all "sworn" police personnel begin at the bottom rank,* regardless of their level of education. Specialized police universities generally do not exist in these countries. Those police aspirants who choose to obtain higher education before starting their careers, and those police personnel who decide to take university courses while employed, attend "ordinary" colleges and universities along with students pursuing various types of careers and studies. Those interested in

---

* In the British model all police start as constables, and the highest rank is Chief Constable. In the United States, the bottom rank is usually police officer or patrol officer, and the highest rank is Police Chief. In U.S. sheriff departments, the bottom rank is deputy sheriff and the highest rank is Sheriff.

policing may have the opportunity to obtain their degrees in criminal justice or criminology; but even when pursuing those degrees, they take the majority of their courses in "general education" subjects related to liberal arts and social sciences, enrolling in classes alongside the general population of students. In other words, police education in these countries is usually integrated with the wider system of higher education not separated or specialized just for police.

There is a third model that combines features of the two already described. Some countries do not have separate police universities, but they still provide the opportunity for university-educated individuals to enter the police at advanced rank, often on the basis of competitive testing. Interestingly, the United Kingdom has announced that it will begin utilizing this scheme on a limited basis with direct entry to the rank of superintendent (College of Policing 2014). This represents a break from nearly 200 years of tradition and has generated a great deal of consternation.

Different structures and systems aside, several basic questions would seem to have universal relevance: How much higher education should bottom-rank police personnel have, and what should the nature of that education be? What institutions are best suited to provide that education? How much education should police managers and police executives have and what type?

The importance and feasibility of higher education for bottom-rank police personnel has long been debated in the United States. Progressive police reformers began advocating college education for police in the early 1900s (Carte 1973), and a prominent national commission in the 1970s established an ambitious formal goal that by 1982 every officer should have a bachelor's degree (National Advisory Commission 1973). However, the current situation more than 30 years later is that only about one-third of U.S. police have a four-year undergraduate degree (Taylor et al. 2005). A separate commission in the 1970s strongly recommended the broad liberal arts/social science model for police higher education, rather than a technical or occupational approach (Sherman and the National Advisory Commission on Higher Education for Police Officers 1978). Since that time, undergraduate degree programs in criminal justice have flourished throughout the country, most of them reflecting the liberal arts/social science orientation. Significantly, there have been many studies over the last 30 to 40 years attempting to measure differences between college-educated and non-college-educated police, with largely inconsistent results (Worden 1990). In the absence of compelling evidence that higher education produces better police performance, the debates have mostly revolved around philosophical, cultural, and financial issues.

In a recent international review of the contribution of higher education to policing, Paterson (2011) found that studies of the impact of higher education on police officers have tended to yield mixed evidence in regard to effects on behavior and performance but generally positive effects on attitudes and beliefs. Shifting to a broader perspective, he found convincing evidence that higher education contributes to the crucial policing dimensions of professionalism, accountability, and legitimacy. He concluded that "Higher education promotes creativity and critical thinking ahead of control and [has] the potential to counteract the cultural instincts of criminal justice institutions through flexible value-systems that are more suited to the demands of community-oriented policing and an enhanced focus on ethical and professional behavior" (294). Notwithstanding these benefits, though, he also observed that many countries lack an evidence base for their particular police education schemes. In other words, they undoubtedly believe that their police education systems "work" but do not have any scientific evidence to support their optimistic beliefs.

Beginning early in the twenty-first century, the national government in the United Kingdom began promoting two-year "foundation degrees" for police, primarily for two reasons—to increase educational levels of police recruits and to expose them to the broadening and liberalizing influences of the university experience. Ironically, Heslop's (2011) study of the Initial Police Learning and Development Programme (IPLDP) at one British university revealed unintended consequences of a negative sort. New police officers working on foundation degrees were treated poorly by their university instructors, their practical knowledge and experience were dismissed in the classroom, and they were physically and socially isolated from other students and other aspects of campus life. This reform approach to police education, intended in large part to counteract the legendary corrosive effects of the police culture (Chan 1997), fell prey instead to an equally corrosive academic culture (Waddington 1999).

Heslop's UK study illustrates that traditional general purpose universities may not be inherently better than special-purpose universities when it comes to providing aspiring or in-service police with the kinds of broadening influences on professionalism, accountability, legitimacy, creativity, critical thinking, and ethics mentioned earlier by Paterson. A similar note of caution is sounded by Bayley (2011), who observed that, even though academics have been in the forefront in criticizing police organizations as "rigid, unreflective, ineffective, wasteful, unaccountable, bureaucratized, self-serving, and hide-bound … in several respects universities, American ones at least, may be even less rational than the police, despite their pretensions to intellectual superiority, rationality, and selfless service" (313).

We have even less evidence about the effectiveness of different structures for educating police managers and executives around the world. The U.S. system is quite fragmented and ad hoc. Many aspiring police leaders obtain master's degrees on their own from local or online universities, typically in criminal justice or public administration, but there is no national curriculum or lead institution for anything other than short courses (Cordner 2010). In the United Kingdom, senior and strategic command courses offered at Bramshill provided a unifying educational foundation for police leaders for many years, but the

Bramshill center is being closed with its functions assumed by others, including the new College of Policing. It remains to be seen whether any of the new policing master's degrees mentioned earlier will gain enough traction to become the expected route for police leadership education in the United Kingdom.

As with police education in general, there are strong debates about the best form and content of police leadership education. Some argue that management is management and leadership is leadership; therefore, police executives should study the more venerable fields of public and business administration. A competing argument is that the main focus of policing, crime and disorder, is so distinct from what other types of organizations confront that police leaders need to study those problems in depth, which tends to point toward graduate education in criminology and criminal justice. A third argument is that we now have voluminous research and literature about policing and police organizations, such that aspiring police executives should master the body of knowledge specific to their "business" and their complex organizational environment, not the business of running schools or factories or hi-tech start-ups. In principle, these are all worthy arguments— what is lacking is any evidence that it makes any difference.

Police Training in the Twenty-First Century

Before we turn our attention to police training, as contrasted with police education, it should be conceded that the distinction between education and training is not precise or clear-cut. It is sometimes explained that training teaches "how" whereas education teaches "why." This helps distinguish firearms and emergency driving training from urban sociology and gender studies, but if one delves into community policing, problem solving, ethics, diversity, or a host of other topics that police need to study, it quickly becomes apparent that the how and the why are intermingled. Moreover, students in higher education typically learn statistics, which is a "how," while police trainees study the Constitution, which is much more about "why." Suffice it to say that the distinction between education and training is often rather inexact and artificial.

On the surface, at least, police training has changed substantially over the last few decades. In the United States, the length of police recruit training (the police academy) has increased, on average, about 50% since 1990, and the average length of field training (which follows the academy) has more than doubled. The total length of introductory training (police academy plus field training) for the average law enforcement agency in 2007 was 922 hours, or 23 weeks (Reaves 2010, 12). For agencies serving populations of one million or more, the average length was significantly longer at 1700 hours, or 42 weeks.

Although training has gotten longer, the overall impact of police recruit training is debated, and there is a lack of consensus on how best to conduct it. In regard to the effectiveness of basic police training, police academies certainly ensure knowledge and skill acquisition by administering tests that trainees must pass before they graduate. One point of debate, however, is whether the police academy does enough to teach recruits how to actually do the job, that is, how to integrate and apply knowledge and skills in order to handle situations correctly, solve problems, and satisfy the public (Bayley and Bittner 1984; Himelfarb 1997). To that end, there has been some degree of adoption of adult learning and problem-centered approaches within police academies over the last two decades, but the extent of real change is unknown. The COPS Office has supported and promoted problem-based learning (PBL) and the police training officer (PTO) model as alternatives to traditional field training (COPS Office 2004; Cleveland 2006) (Police Society for Problem Based Learning 2014), but it does not seem that most police academies and field training programs have adopted these approaches to any significant degree.

One study of police academy training using PBL yielded promising results. Werth (2011) reported that trainees and staff consistently evaluated the new scheme positively, citing improvements in learning, technical skill development, decision making, and problem solving. The study was particularly valuable because it identified a host of lessons learned from the evolving implementation of full-scale PBL into ten consecutive police academy classes. Werth also identified four important challenges associated with this innovative approach to training: (1) PBL costs more than lecturing; (2) PBL requires more commitment from training staff than traditional approaches; (3) some students resist PBL's requirement that they take an active role in their own learning; and (4) some training staff resist PBL's reliance on student-directed learning. These challenges reflect the fact that learning is hard work—trainers and trainees tend to revert to the lecture/note-taking format, unless they are pushed, because it is both familiar and easier, although often not as effective as more active learning methods.

Another recent study reviewed the available evidence on the effectiveness of a very traditional and basic component of police training, firearms training. This is a very technical, skills-based, hands-on aspect of police training, one that we might expect to be very scientifically based because it is obviously such an important aspect of policing, with significant negative consequences if poorly performed. As Morrison and Garner (2011) point out, though, police firearms training in the United States is based more on tradition, professional judgment, and the predilections of individual firearms instructors than on any universal standards or scientific evidence about what works best. Certainly, such training has changed substantially over the past decades, undoubtedly for the better, with more emphasis on training in all kinds of conditions, training in realistic scenarios, and training to make better "shoot/don't shoot" decisions. But if one looks for studies that have evaluated the effectiveness of different methods and alternatives in firearms training, they are few. Also, the authors point out that few police agencies seem to systematically examine their own shooting incidents as a means of assessing training effectiveness and identifying new training requirements. It is possible that this situation is unique to the United States, with its highly fragmented policing and police training systems, but our suspicion is that it is more common than that.

The other main question related to the impact of police training, besides effectiveness in knowledge and skill acquisition, is the role that the police academy plays in socializing new employees to the organization, the occupation, and the police culture. Early studies emphasized the role that the police academy played in the socialization and indoctrination of recruits into the traditional police culture (Van Maanen 1973). However, it has also been noted that the police academy is sometimes expected to play a reform or change role (i.e., it is expected to produce new kinds of employees who will perform their duties differently than their predecessors). Furthermore, when this is the expectation, it has sometimes been observed that recruits, after they graduate from the police academy, have difficulty resisting the influence of their more veteran peers in the police culture, gradually rejecting the reform values and philosophy promoted by the training academy in favor of the traditional values of the police work group (Haarr 2001). One factor that complicates this even further is that, in the United States, the vast majority of police agencies are too small to operate their own police academies; therefore, they send their recruits (if they are not already trained) to regional or state academies (Reaves 2009). These smaller police agencies do not have very much control over whether "their" police academy merely reproduces traditional police culture or, alternatively, prepares officers to do things differently.

In regard to the way in which police academy training is conducted in the United States, besides the issues mentioned here associated with adult learning and problem-centered approaches, the main controversy surrounds stress versus nonstress training. An early experiment by Assistant Sheriff Howard H. Earle (1973) in the Los Angeles County Sheriff's Department Academy still seems relevant for modern day policing. Earle found that "Non-stress trained subjects performed at a significantly higher level in the areas of field performance, job satisfaction, and performance acceptability by persons served" (145). Higher levels of performance in these areas are qualities that can lead to better community-oriented police officers—with better skills in problem solving and building collaborative relationships with community stakeholders (COPS 2013).

Nationally, police academies are closely split (53% to 47%) on whether they lean toward the stress model, based on military training, or the non-stress model, which more closely resembles an academic setting. Because state police agencies and larger local law enforcement agencies tend to favor the stress model, and they hire more new officers each year, 61% of new recruits attend an academy that leans more toward the stress model than the non-stress model (Reaves 2009). Supporters of the stress training model tend to emphasize its role in weeding out trainees who lack discipline and toughness, but its methods are clearly in conflict with what we know about how people actually learn (Berg 1990; Cleveland 2006). In the near future, one would hope to see some new experimental studies comparing the effectiveness of these two quite different models of entry level police training. This would be a perfect opportunity to contribute to more evidence-based police administration (Weisburd and Neyroud 2011).

Conclusion

Contemporary developments and modern trends seem to demonstrate ongoing innovation in the world of police education and training but also significant challenges. We assume that pressure on police organizations to utilize more and more cost-effective operational and administrative methods will continue to increase (Gascon and Fogelsong 2010). This fact of modern life seems destined to place police education and training under ever greater scrutiny. Given how much importance is placed on education and training within policing, and how expensive they can be, it seems advisable that police leaders and researchers should begin placing more emphasis on developing scientific evidence about what works in this sphere of the policing business. Although much effort has been devoted over the past 40 years toward developing evidence-based police operational methods, the same cannot be said for police administrative methods, including training (Skogan and Frydl 2004). Now would be a very good time to start.

References

Bayley, D. (2011). Et tu brute: Are police agencies managed better or worse than police agencies? *Police Practice & Research: An International Journal* 12(4): 313–316.

Bayley, D. & Bittner, E. (1984). Learning the skills of policing. *Law and Contemporary Problems* 47(4): 35–59.

Bayley, D. & Perito, R. (2010). *The police in war: Fighting insurgency, terrorism, and violent crime.* Boulder, CO: Lynne Rienner Publishers.

Berg, B. (1990). First day at the police academy: Stress-reaction training as a screening-out technique. *Journal of Contemporary Criminal Justice* 6: 89–105.

Brogden, M. (2005). 'Horses for courses' and 'thin blue lines': Community policing in transitional society. *Police Quarterly* 8(1): 64–98.

CALEA. (2011). *Public safety training academy accreditation.* Gainsville, VA. http://www.calea.org/content/public-safety-training-academy-accreditation. Retrieved on June 15, 2014.

Carte, G. (1973). August Vollmer and the origins of police professionalism. *Journal of Police Science and Administration* 1: 274–281.

CEPOL. (2011). European Police College: Training and learning: Commom curriculaBram Skill. http://www.cepol.europa.eu/index.pgp?id=common-curricula. Retrieved on June 15, 2014.

Chan, J. (1997). *Changing police culture: Policing in a multicultural society.* Cambridge: Cambridge University Press.

Cleveland, G. (2006). Using problem-based learning in police training. *The Police Chief* 73. Online at http://www.policechiefmagazine.org/magazine/index.cfm?fuseaction=display_arch&article_id=1051&issue_id=112006. Retrieved on June 15, 2014.

College of Policing. (2014). http://www.college.police.uk/. Accessed June 18, 2014.

COPS. (2013). http://cops.usdoj.gov/html/dispatch/06-2013/preparing_officers_for_a_community_oriented_department.asp

COPS Office. (2004). *PTO: An overview and introduction.* Washington, DC: COPS Office.

Cordner, G. (2010). The U.S. needs a national police university. In Frost, N., Freilich, J. & Clear, T. eds., *Contemporary issues in criminal justice policy: Policy proposals from the American Society of Criminology Conference.* Belmont, CA: Wadsworth/Cengage, pp. 279–287.

Earle, H. (1973). *Police recruit training stress vs. non-stress: A revolution in law enforcement career programs.* Springfield, IL: Charles C. Thomas, p. 145.

Gascon, G. & Fogelsong, T. (2010). Making policing more affordable: Managing costs and measuring value in policing. In *New perspectives in policing.* Washington, DC: National Institute of Justice.

Haarr, R. (2001). The making of a community police officer: The impact of basic training and occupational socialization on police recruits. *Police Quarterly* 4: 420–433.

Heslop, R. (2011). Reproducing police culture in a British university: Findings from an exploratory case study of police foundation degrees. *Police Practice & Research: An International Journal* 12(4): 298–312.

Himelfarb, F. (1997). RCMP learning and renewal: Building on strengths. In Thurman, Q. & McGarrell, E., eds., *Community policing in a rural setting.* Cincinnati, OH: Anderson Publishing, pp. 33–39.

Interpol. (2011). International police training journal. http://www.interpol.int/Public/ICPO/corefunctions/Ejpurna.asp. Retrieved on June 12, 2014.

Kelling, G. & Moore, M. (1988). The evolving strategy of policing. In *Perspectives on policing.* Washington, DC: National Institute of Justice.

Kordaczuk-Was, M. & Sosnowski, S. (2011). Police in-service training and self-education in Poland. *Police Practice & Research: An International Journal* 12(4): 317–324.

Morrison, G. & Garner, T. (2011). Latitude in deadly force training: Progress or problem? *Police Practice and Research: An International Journal* 12(4): 341–361.

National Advisory Commission on Criminal Justice Standards and Goals. (1973). *Report on police.* Washington, DC: Government Printing Office.

Neyroud, P. (2011). *Review of police leadership and training.* London, UK: Home Office.

Panel to draft police-university bill. (2014). http://timesofindia.indiatimes. com/city/thiruvananthapuram/Panel-to-draft-police-university-bill/ articlesshow/31589646.cms. Retrieved on July 2, 2014.

Paterson, C. (2011). Adding value? A review of the international literature on the role of higher education in police training and education. *Police Practice & Research: An International Journal* 12(4): 286–297.

Police Sector Council. (2011). Policing competency framework, Ottawa, Canada. http://www.policecouncil.ca/pages/hr2.html. Retrieved on April 2, 2011.

Police Society for Problem Based Learning. (2014). Mission statement. http://www. pspbl.org/about/mission-statement/. Retrieved on July 1, 2014.

Reaves, B. (2009). *State and local law enforcement training academies, 2006.* Washington, DC: Bureau of Justice Statistics.

Reaves, B. (2010). *Local police departments, 2007.* Washington, DC: Bureau of Justice Statistics.

Sherman, L. and the National Advisory Commission on Higher Education for Police Officers. (1978). *The quality of police education.* San Francisco, CA: Jossey-Bass.

SIPR. (2011). The SIPR postgraduate diploma/MSc in policing studies. Dundee. http:// www.sipr.ac.uk/courses/postgraduate_diploma.php. Retrieved on April 22, 2011.

Skogan, W. & Frydl, K., eds. (2004). *Fairness and effectiveness in policing: The evidence.* Washington, DC: National Academies Press.

Taylor, B., Kubu, B., Fridell, L., Rees, C., Jordan, T. & Cheney, J. (2005). *The cop crunch: Identifying strategies for dealing with the recruiting and hiring crisis in law enforcement.* Washington, DC: Police Executive Research Forum.

UNISA. (2014). *Academics are keen to affect the policing sector.* http://www.unisa. ac.za/news/index.php/2014/02/unisa-academics-are-keen-to-affect-the- policing-sector/. Retrieved on July 3, 2014.

Van Maanen, J. (1973). Observations on the making of policemen. *Human Organization* 32: 407–418.

Waddington, P. A. J. (1999). Police (canteen) sub-culture. *British Journal of Criminology* 39(2): 287–309.

Weisburd, D. and Neyroud, P. (2011). Police science: Toward a new paradigm. In *New perspectives in policing.* Washington, DC: National Institute of Justice.

Werth, E. (2011). Scenario training in police academies: Developing students' higher- level thinking skills. *Police Practice & Research: An International Journal* 12(4): 325–340.

Worden, R. (1990). A badge and a baccalaureate: Policies, hypotheses, and further evidence. *Justice Quarterly* 7: 565–592.

A Command Leadership Framework for Law Enforcement, Safety, and Security Commanders in Singapore

4

BIRENTHA DHEVI THIAGARAJA,
MAJEED KHADER, JANSEN ANG,
DIONG SIEW MAAN,
EUNICE TAN, AND
PAMELA PATRICK*
Home Team Behavioural Sciences Centre
Home Team Academy
Ministry of Home Affairs
Government of Singapore, Singapore

Contents

---

* The views expressed in this chapter are that of the authors' only and do not represent directly or imply any official policy position or view of the Home Team Academy or Ministry of Home Affairs, Singapore.

Introduction

Singapore: The Red Dot

Singapore is an island as well as a country, but perhaps it is best described as a city-state; it is one of few such entities in the world. The smallest country in Southeast Asia, Singapore is usually depicted on world maps as a red dot located at the tip of the Malay Peninsula. The main island has a total land area of 716.1 km², and one can easily travel across the island in a span of 30 to 40 minutes. Home to slightly more than five million, the density ratio is estimated at 7540 km². The city features a vibrant mix of high-rise buildings, heritage rich locales, and landscaped gardens. From its humble origins as a fishing village, Singapore has experienced phenomenal economic growth and now commands a presence in the global arena. It continues to thrive as a commerce hub with an estimated gross domestic product per capita of US$51,709. This cosmopolitan city has also strived to achieve world standards in fields such as transportation with its award-winning airport and seaport. This city-state's multiracial makeup creates a harmonious blend of culture, cuisine, arts, and architecture. Singapore's diverse demographics consist of four major ethnic groups: the Chinese (the majority), Malays, Indians, and Eurasians; English is the main language of instruction and the medium of communication.

The Singapore Home Team—Law Enforcement in the City-State

The "Home Team" concept was initiated in 1995 and refers to all law enforcement and emergency response agencies under Singapore's Ministry of Home Affairs. The Singapore Police Force, Singapore Civil Defence Force (fire and ambulance services), Singapore Prisons Service (corrections), Immigration and Checkpoints Authority (border control), Central Narcotics Bureau, and Internal Security Department make up the Home Team. These different organizations have their own unique operational missions, roles, and responsibilities.

However, under the Home Team umbrella, they are seen as a collective partnership working together as one team to coordinate efforts to fulfill the ministry's overall mission, which is to ensure a "safe and secure Singapore." In this way, despite the multiplicity of purpose, the various agencies are united by one shared mission. The Home Team concept is probably unique as far as organizational collaborations are concerned. It may be the first of its kind, and this is probably possible because of the nation's small size. It is hoped that this concept drives the importance of departments working together. By increasing interaction and cooperation among departments, the Home Team concept hopes to strengthen the overall safety and security measures put in place to safeguard Singapore and its people.

The Home Team departments (HTDs) are paramilitary in nature, and their operations are based on hierarchical organizational structures. Within these hierarchical organizational structures are varying levels of command—each associated with a particular rank and an accompanying command authority and responsibility. Because command forms the central tenet of how leadership is exercised within the Home Team, there is a need to ensure that a set of leadership competencies is present to guide the selection, assessment, and development of Home Team command leaders. This chapter describes how a Home Team Command Leadership framework was developed in Singapore.

Overview of the Home Team Command Leadership Research

The Home Team Command Leadership framework was developed from three years of research undertaken by the Home Team Behavioural Sciences Centre (a research and training component of the Home Team), in close partnership with representatives from the various HTDs. Research data was collected in three key phases: (1) 71 subject matter expert interviews, (2) focus group discussions with 120 officers, and (3) opinion surveys administered to 1105 officers. Details on each of these research phases are described in the section "Voices from Above and Below—Research Methodology."

Command: Introductory Definition and Concepts

Command and Control—The Paradigm Shift

What exactly is "command" and how does control relate to command? Despite the common usage of these terms, many operational commanders do not fully appreciate their meanings and connotations. The word "command" has its roots in the Latin word, *mandare* (which means power), and in the fifteenth-century Old French word *comand* (which means control and authority). In modern definitions of command, power and authority continue to feature as central tenets of the term. However, the understanding of control in relation to command has undergone a paradigm shift in the last decade.

Command refers to the "who" (or the human actor) in command and control (referred to here as C2) and is the creative expression of the human will to accomplish the organization's mission. That is, only humans can command; command and control machines and paraphernalia do not. Indeed, it is only humans who possess the capability to demonstrate cognitive skills (including creativity) that can overcome novel and complicated problems in operating terrains. In addition, accepting accountability, demonstrating dedication, and motivating others are all demonstrations of human actors in the C2 equation.

Control, on the other hand, refers to the "what" in C2 and to the structures and processes devised by command to enable it. Some examples of these include personnel, facilities, equipment, policies, standard operating procedures (SOPs), and rules of engagement (ROEs). A commander uses these structures and policies to plan, direct, and to coordinate resources to accomplish the organization's mission.

Another way of looking at this is to consider all of these factors as an ecosystem of command (in the sense that there are many interdependencies among the human actors at various levels of command, the processes and systems they work with, and how these affect one another) (Alberts and Hayes 2006).

Command in Military and Law Enforcement

Command in Military Context

In military literature, command refers to the authority that a commander lawfully exercises over his/her subordinates. This authority may be legal powers or a mandate given to a commander, which can be used to punish subordinates when they fail to execute given orders (McCann and Pigeau 2000, 2001). Command also assumes that the organization is structured as a hierarchy, which creates a *chain of command* (i.e., a line of authority along which orders are passed on from officers of higher ranks to those of lower ranks) and corresponding command responsibility. Commanders hold a specific position or rank within this chain of command (i.e., a higher rank than subordinate officers).

Command in Law Enforcement Context

Due to similarity in roles and functions, the term commander began to be used in paramilitary organizations, including law enforcement agencies.

However, unlike in the military, command does not feature prominently within a law enforcement context. This does not mean that the concept of command is absent in law enforcement but rather that command principles are interwoven more subtly within these organizations. This is evident in how law enforcement agencies throughout the world continue to establish lines of authority and communication according to the chain of command principle (Bennet and Hess 2007). In addition, commanders within law enforcement organizations—like their military counterparts—have sanctioned legal powers to exact obedience from their subordinates.

Command Lexicon—Dictionary of Command Terms

Research findings reveal a vocabulary of command related terms that provide insight into the roles and responsibilities of a commander as well as to the environment within which he/she operates. Some of these command terms are outlined in Table 4.1.

Coining the Term Command Leadership

Command, Leadership, and Management—Knowing the Difference

Having examined the concept of command, it is important to understand how it is different from leadership and management. *Command* refers to the legal powers or mandate given to a commander to exact compliance from subordinates, and it is tied to a specific position or rank. *Leadership* refers to an individual's ability to influence subordinates to perform their roles willingly and may not be tied to a specific rank or position (i.e., no legal powers). *Management*, on the other hand, refers to a leader's ability to plan, organize, and manage resources within his/her span of control. These three concepts are highlighted in Figure 4.1.

Given the clear distinction between command and leadership, it is theoretically possible for a commander to get his/her subordinates to carry out orders using the legal or mandated powers or authority given to him/her without exercising the qualities of effective leadership such as influence, energy, motivation, or effective team building. However, in reality, a commander usually exercises leadership because failure to do so may result in negative consequences such as poor morale of subordinates and subsequent declines in their work performance. In addition, management forms a large part of a commander's responsibilities and necessitates that the commander exercise corporate governance on issues such as human resources, finance, and logistics (Baker 2011).

Table 4.1 Command Lexicon

Command Term	Meaning
Command Responsibility	A commander is responsible for accomplishing the mission assigned to his/her. As part of this responsibility, a commander has accountability for overseeing and ensuring the effective and ethical performance of his/her subordinates. As such, the commander can only delegate his authority but not his responsibility. This means that a commander may not always be in control of a situation but has to remain accountable at all times; this is known as the "burden of command" (Doty and Doty 2012). As such, commanders have the responsibility of ensuring that their subordinates are trained and can operate independently and ethically in the absence of the commander.
Command Intent	Command intent refers to the articulation of a desired end-state or outcomes to ensure mission success (Shattuck 2000). As part of mission-oriented command, commanders need to clearly communicate mission intention, rules of engagement, and other key considerations to their subordinates.
Command Presence	Command presence refers to how a commander presents himself/herself to subordinates and how this impacts the subordinates. At a micro level, it comprises how a commander carries himself/herself—his/her body language, tone of voice, the way he/she stands, and the degree of eye contact made (Wollert 2012). At a macro level, it is the sense of confidence and perceived control over situations that the commander instills in his/her subordinates.
Command Climate	Command climate is the climate of a unit, and it includes operational readiness, morale, discipline, leadership, training, and understanding of the operating atmosphere and values. An ideal command climate is one in which the commander articulates the core values of the unit and sets the moral/ethical overtone through character-based leadership (i.e., serving as a good role model/demonstrating desired behaviors), which inspires subordinates to adhere to the standards set in place (Doty and Gelineau 2008).
Command Philosophy	Command philosophy refers to a set of beliefs, values, and principles that influence and guide a commander (Garner and Peterson 2012). Command philosophy is unique to each commander and should stem from self-reflection and personal interpretation of leadership. Ideally, it should also incorporate the organization's values to bring about alignment between the values of the commander and those of the organization.

Figure 4.1 Command, leadership, and management. (Adapted from Chan, K., et al. (2011). *Military leadership in the 21st century: Science and practice.* Singapore: Cengage Learning, pp. 1–14.)

The term *command leadership* denotes a leader who occupies a position of command and who exercises both leadership and management as part of his/her command responsibilities. This term highlights the importance of a commander exercising command as well as leadership to direct subordinates and to fulfill an organization's mission.

Command Leaders—Leaders with Dual Functions

Command leaders have both routine roles and roles undertaken in times of crisis. The nature of law enforcement entails elements of uncertainty, risk, and danger. This poses significant challenges for a commander during a crisis, when he/she needs to direct his/her subordinates to act in life-or-death situations. Command authority (or mandate) therefore serves the function of driving subordinates into action during a crisis when there may be limited time to influence, motivate, or energize officers to act. However, police commanders do not always operate in crisis mode and, during routine operations, it may not suffice for a commander to lead solely using his/her command authority or mandate.

During routine operations, a commander has the responsibility of ensuring that his organization operates effectively on a day-to-day basis. Commanders have a great number of officers and resources under their direct charge (i.e., a large span of control). A commander's sphere of influence also extends up and down the chain of command by virtue of his/her position within the organizational hierarchy, whereby he/she serves as a conduit between senior leaders and ground officers (Bennet and Hess 2007; Baker 2011). Commanders play a critical role in facilitating communication and in aligning higher directions from senior leadership with actions taken by ground officers. As such, commanders have to gain buy-in from their men and must invest sufficient time and energy to influence and motivate them.

The C5 Framework—Competencies for Home Team Commanders

Why Home Team Commanders? Research Background

Our research findings suggests that effective command is determined by a number of factors, especially a commander's effectiveness in routine as well as crisis operations. As shown in Figure 4.2, a commander operates primarily during routine operations, at which time, in addition to carrying out the core duties of the department, he/she also takes measures to prevent and plan for appropriate responses to crisis situations. When a crisis occurs, a commander needs to move swiftly into crisis mitigation mode. During the post-crisis period, a commander must study the lessons learned during the crisis (i.e., feedback loop) to enhance routine preparations and to ensure better crisis leadership performance in the future.

Situated above strategic leaders and below operational officers in the chain of command, commanders also play a unique role in aligning directions given from senior leadership with actions by ground officers to achieve mission success. In addition, by virtue of being ground commanders, they are also better able to monitor the pulse of the organization by picking up signals (e.g., satisfaction/discontent/imminent threats) and relaying these up through the hierarchy. On the other hand, commanders are more privy to the strategic intent of senior leaders and in a better position to translate management directives into operational deliverables for their officers on the ground.

Given the vital role commanders play in ensuring optimal functioning of the various departments and the Home Team as a whole, it is important

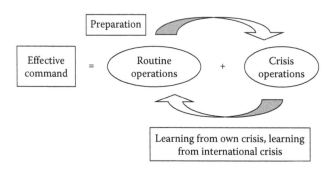

Figure 4.2 Commanders during routine and crisis operations.

that the right persons are selected for these positions. In addition, these persons should be continually assessed to ensure sustained performance; they should be developed through training and other initiatives that hone their ability to command and lead effectively. Recognizing this need, in 2010, Singapore's Ministry of Home Affairs tasked the Home Team Behavioural Sciences Centre with developing a Home Team Command Leadership Competency Framework. This framework's purpose was to guide the selection, assessment, training, and development of current and future Home Team commanders.

Unlike existing department-specific leadership frameworks that articulated competencies for leaders of all ranks and levels of each department, the Home Team Command Leadership framework was to be nuanced in its nomenclature to capture higher order attributes, skills, and qualities that a commander needs to possess. Furthermore, it was hoped that this research project would bring about enhanced understanding of command and its relation to leadership so as to create shared awareness and a common language of what command leadership constituted across the various HTDs.

Voices from Above and Below—Research Methodology

From the onset, it was expected that competencies generated through this research would overlap significantly with those articulated by the existing leadership framework. However, the unique nature of command positions (e.g., serving as a conduit between senior and ground officers) and the need to exercise dual functions of command as well as leadership meant that general leadership competencies might not be sufficiently nuanced for the needs of commanders. With this premise in mind, the research team embarked on a three-year qualitative and quantitative study. Representatives from the various HTDs also came on board to aid the core research team in data collection and in providing input on the unique operating principles underlying their respective departments.

The first step undertaken by the research team was to complete a literature review to understand command and related concepts. The research team also looked at the local and international leadership framework for military, law enforcement, corrections, and fire services. After key constructs of command leadership were identified, a detailed interview protocol was developed and 71 subject matter experts (SMEs) were interviewed. These SMEs were comprised of existing and former command leaders (as well as select senior management). They shared their views on command and what it takes to be an effective commander. In addition, they provided personal accounts of their leadership experiences in command positions.

In the next stage, the research team was interested in hearing the views of ground officers. They conducted structured focus group discussions (FGDs) with 120 officers selected from across the various HTDs. These FGDs, in addition to validating the findings from the SME interviews, also generated rich narratives and stories of effective and ineffective command leadership. A preliminary command leadership framework was generated after all of the FGDs were completed.

Finally, in order to further ratify this preliminary framework, the competencies and their underlying facets were designed as an opinion survey made up of 64 items. A total of 1105 Home Team officers took part in this survey and rated each of the items on a seven-point Likert scale (1 = not important; 7 = very important). Results indicated how important participants thought a particular competency was for a commander to demonstrate effective command leadership. In this way, the perceptions of ground officers were compared with the views of senior leaders and commanders (i.e., job incumbents). The results revealed that there was consensus across the ranks on what it takes to be an effective command leader. Therefore, the competency framework was finalized.

The C5 Framework—Home Team Command Leadership Competencies

Our research findings suggested that a set of command leadership competencies could be derived and clustered into five domains: command thinking, command teams, command partnerships, command expertise, and command character. For ease of recall and to ensure buy-in, the term "C5" was used to refer to the set of competencies. This was also similar to other command related terms that were in use—for example, command and control (C2); command, control, and communications (C3); and command, control, communications, and computers (C4).

The complete set of 15 command leadership competencies in the C5 framework is captured in Figure 4.3. It is beyond the scope of this chapter to outline each of these competencies in detail. However, some highlights of this framework include incorporating Home Team (i.e., joint operations) elements to emphasize the importance of working beyond silos (e.g., C3.2), nuancing the competencies to capture higher order leadership competencies such as critical thinking (e.g., C1.3), and highlighting the operating environment and the actors with whom the commander needs to interact (e.g., the concept of a command ecosystem captured in C3.1).

Command Character—Bedrock of Command Leadership

Moving away from skills traditionally highlighted by leadership frameworks (e.g., domain expertise, decision making, and team building), the C5

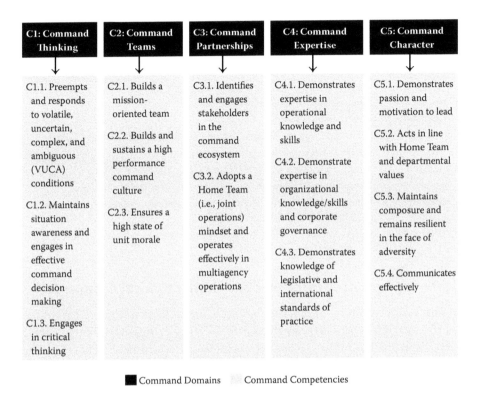

C1: Command Thinking	C2: Command Teams	C3: Command Partnerships	C4: Command Expertise	C5: Command Character
C1.1. Preempts and responds to volatile, uncertain, complex, and ambiguous (VUCA) conditions	C2.1. Builds a mission-oriented team	C3.1. Identifies and engages stakeholders in the command ecosystem	C4.1. Demonstrates expertise in operational knowledge and skills	C5.1. Demonstrates passion and motivation to lead
C1.2. Maintains situation awareness and engages in effective command decision making	C2.2. Builds and sustains a high performance command culture	C3.2. Adopts a Home Team (i.e., joint operations) mindset and operates effectively in multiagency operations	C4.2. Demonstrate expertise in organizational knowledge/skills and corporate governance	C5.2. Acts in line with Home Team and departmental values
C1.3. Engages in critical thinking	C2.3. Ensures a high state of unit morale		C4.3. Demonstrates knowledge of legislative and international standards of practice	C5.3. Maintains composure and remains resilient in the face of adversity
				C5.4. Communicates effectively

■ Command Domains ▦ Command Competencies

Figure 4.3 The C5 command leadership framework.

framework hopes to highlight qualities such as passion for leadership, leading with values, and resilience in adversity. All of these qualities are captured in the fifth domain of command character. Research has shown that character-based leadership enables enforcement of discipline, sets standards for performance, and builds trust and cohesion. This brings about a positive command climate (characterized by high morale), which ensures that personnel within the organization sustain high performance. In this way, the personal qualities and character of a commander have significant implications for the organization and its people.

Officers who took part in the opinion surveys endorsed character-based leadership as well. When ratings of perceived importance were analyzed across the five command domains, all six HTDs rated the command character domain as the highest. This suggests that across the Home Team competencies associated with character are deemed most important for effective command leadership. An analysis of the 64 items in the opinion survey also revealed similar findings with seven out of the top 10 (highly rated) items belonging to the command character domain (see Table 4.2).

Table 4.2 Support for Character-Based Leadership

Domain	Top Ten Items
Character	1. Conducts self with high levels of discipline
Thinking	2. Demonstrates effective thinking
Character	3. Demonstrates leadership by example
Character	4. Shows passion to lead
Character	5. Commands respect of his/her officers (carries self with pride and dignity)
Character	6. Demonstrates departmental core values
Expertise	7. Demonstrates professional expertise
Thinking	8. Engages in effective response to uncertain and complex problems
Character	9. Remains calm and collected in the face of crisis (personal, departmental, or national) and leads with resilience
Character	10. Able to communicate his/her goals to promote shared understanding in the unit/department/division

Different Operating Principles but Similar Critical Competencies

As part of the opinion survey, officers were asked to rank the top three (out of 15) competencies that they perceived as being critical for allowing their department commanders to demonstrate effective command leadership. The results revealed that, despite the different operating principles and cultures of the various HTDs, critical competencies for effective command leadership were similar across the departments. In fact, the situation awareness and decision-making competency (C1.2) was consistently ranked as the top competency across all six HTDs. Communicating effectively (C5.4) and ensuring high state of unit morale (C2.3) came out as the second and third most highly ranked command leadership competencies across departments. This does not mean there were no differences in ranking. For example, the fire services department ranked resilience and ability to maintain composure (C5.3) as one of its top three competencies. However, by and large, there were more similarities than differences across the departments.

What Accounts for the Similarities in Rankings?

One hypothesis for the similarities in rankings is the need for similar skill sets for all commanders despite differences in their respective departments. For example, all commanders face a large span of control (i.e., a leader's ability to maintain situation awareness of and to manage multiple resources). As personnel and other resources (e.g., equipment, facilities, procedures, systems) are added to the organization, the cognitive load of a commander increases exponentially; thus, maintaining situation awareness becomes more challenging. Unintended consequences such as stress may follow, and high levels of stress have the potential to degrade the cognitive processes, including decision making, of the commanders. The ability to maintain situation awareness is critical for commanders. This may explain why situation awareness and decision making (C1.2) were ranked as the most important command leadership competencies across all the HTDs.

Application and Future Directions of the C5 Framework

Training and Development Initiatives for Senior Commanders

The completed C5 framework is currently used for Home Team training and development. These initiatives are primarily targeted at senior commanders who attend leadership milestone courses such as the Home Team Senior Command and Staff Course (HTSCSC). This six-week intensive training program was developed for leaders at the superintendent/lieutenant colonel level who have recently assumed or who are about to assume positions of command. As part of this training, the C5 framework is taught over a three-and-a-half-day period. A variety of training methodologies—including case study discussions, leadership games, tabletop exercises, reflection exercises, and group work (in line with adult learning principles)—are used to provide participants with optimal learning conditions. Based on our research finding that character-related competencies are deemed most critical to the success of a commander, the C5 training emphasizes character as the cornerstone of command leadership development.

In addition, the research team has worked out behavioral indicators for each of the C5 competencies, articulating how commanders should demonstrate these competencies in addition to merely highlighting which competencies are important. These indicators are currently being translated into practical tips, which will be featured in the form of a *C5 Handbook*. This handbook will be used as a training aid in all C5 instruction and will highlight command concepts, the C5 framework, and also will offer practical suggestions to commanders for displaying the stated competencies.

Future Directions

The Home Team Command Leadership framework, or C5 framework, continues to be a work in progress. The research team hopes to obtain feedback from commanders in order to identify existing gaps and to bridge them with further research and inquiry. One of the key limitations of the current research is that the C5 competencies were derived based on the officers' *perceptions* of what they deemed to be essential competencies for effective command leadership. Future research needs to assess the C5 competencies' predictive validity in being able to determine an individual's future command leadership performance. In addition, the C5 framework will be mapped on existing models of leadership to determine how it fits in the overall leadership literature.

Conclusion

In conclusion, the C5 framework was developed *by* the Home Team *for* the Home Team. It is a pioneering effort highlighting leadership that is unique to positions of command and is the first Home Team level framework targeted at command leaders that articulates competencies.

Acknowledgments

The Home Team Behavioural Sciences Centre would like to thank the following officers who formed the working group of the Home Team Command Leadership project. This group, known as the C5 working group,* was comprised of two subgroups: (1) the resource group and (2) the research group. The resource subgroup provided critical input on their departments' existing leadership framework and training initiatives. The research group assisted the core research team in data collection throughout the various phases of research.

THE C5 COMMAND LEADERSHIP WORKING GROUP
A. PRINCIPAL INVESTIGATORS
Dr. Majeed Khader Senior Consultant Psychologist Deputy Director, Police Psychological Services Division (PPSD), Singapore Police Force Concurrent Director, Home Team Behavioural Sciences Centre
Mr. Jansen Ang Senior Principal Psychologist Assistant Director, Police Psychological Services Division (PPSD) Concurrent Deputy Director, Home Team Behavioural Sciences Centre
Ms. Diong Siew Maan Principal Psychologist Commander, Emergency Behavioural Sciences Centre (EBSC), Singapore Civil Defence Force Concurrent Deputy Director, Operations and Leadership Psychology Branch, Home Team Behavioural Sciences Centre
Ms. Eunice Tan Senior Psychologist Assistant Director, Operations and Leadership Psychology Branch Home Team Behavioural Sciences Centre

Continued

* Designation of working group members are reflected as stated at the time of the research.

(LEAD RESEARCHER)
Ms. Birentha Dhevi
Psychologist
Operations and Leadership Psychology Branch
Home Team Behavioural Science Centre

Ms. Pamela Patrick
Psychologist
Operations and Leadership Psychology Branch
Home Team Behavioural Sciences Centre

B. RESOURCE GROUP MEMBERS

Superintendent Bridget Goh
Commanding Officer (Advanced Training Centre)
Singapore Police Force

Lieutenant Colonel Abdul Razak
Commander (3rd CD Division)
Singapore Civil Defence Force

Superintendent Michael Neo
Deputy Director (Supervision)
Central Narcotics Bureau

Ms. Joyce How
Deputy Director (Training)
Ministry of Home Affairs

Ms. Jasmine Bok
Deputy Director (Talent Development HRD)
Ministry of Home Affairs

Deputy Superintendent Lee Kong Wee
Senior Assistant Director (Training and Development)
Singapore Prison Service

Assistant Commissioner Evelyn Wu
Senior Deputy Director (ICA Training School)
Immigration and Checkpoints Authority

C. RESEARCH GROUP MEMBERS

Ms. Ho Hui Fen,
Senior Psychologist
Singapore Police Force

Ms. Khoo Yan Leen
Psychologist
Singapore Police Force

Continued

Ms. Poh Li Li
Principal Psychologist
Central Narcotics Bureau

Ms. Leung Chi Ching
Manager (Operational Research)
Singapore Prison Service

Captain Ellena Quek
Senior Instructor (CDA)
Singapore Civil Defence Force

Ms. Goh Seow Hoon
Senior Executive (OD Branch)
Immigration and Checkpoints Authority

Ms. Daphne Ng
Staff Officer (Training)
Ministry of Home Affairs

Ms. Karen Fu
Psychologist
Home Team Behavioural Sciences Centre

References

Alberts, D. S., & Hayes, R. E. (2006). *Understanding command and control.* Washington, DC: Command and Control Research Program.

Baker, T. E. (2011). *Effective police leadership: Moving beyond management* (3rd Ed.). New York: Looseleaf Law Publications, pp. 48–69.

Bennet, W., & Hess, K. (2007). *Management and supervision in law enforcement* (5th Ed.). Canada: Thomson-Wadsworth Publication, Toronto, Canada, pp. 16–23.

Chan, K., Soh, S., & Ramaya, R. (2011). *Military leadership in the 21st century: Science and practice.* Singapore: Cengage Learning, pp. 1–14.

Doty, J., & Doty, C. (2012). Command responsibility and accountability. *Military Review* 92: 35–38.

Doty, J., & Gelineau, J. (2008). Command climate. *Army* 58(7): 22.

Garner, H. C., & Peterson, J. S. (2012). Developing an effective command philosophy. *Military Review* 92: 75–81.

McCann, C., & Pigeau, R. (Eds.). (2000). *Human in command: Exploring the modern military experience.* New York: Kluwer Academic.

McCann, C., & Pigeau, R. (2001). Re-conceptualizing command and control. *Canadian Military Journal* 2: 53–64.

Shattuck, L. G. (2000). Communicating intent and imparting presence. *Military Review* 80: 66–72.

Wollert, T. N. (2012). Command presence what is it? Why is it important? How do we measure it? *ILEETA Journal* 2(2): 20–23.

Threat Assessment and Management

5

A Collaborative Approach to Mitigating Risk for Targeted Violence

EUGENE R. D. DEISINGER
*Managing Partner, Sigma Threat
Management Associates
Blacksburg, VA, USA*

Contents

Introduction

During the past two decades, several communities have suffered incidents of targeted violence in educational settings. Incidents such as those at Columbine, Virginia Tech, Northern Illinois, Chardon, and Newtown have become reference points for our perceptions of violence within education.

As communities and professionals seek to understand what occurred in order to prevent this type of violence from happening again, so too do potential perpetrators seek tactical insights in order to maximize carnage.

In reaction, law enforcement agencies have helped schools and campuses enhance physical security and emergency preparedness. Many law enforcement agencies have also strengthened their own training protocols for responding to situations involving "active shooters" and other ongoing threats. These efforts are designed to confront and neutralize an active threat as quickly as possible in order to reduce casualties.

Although these are appropriate and necessary considerations in responding to and minimizing damage from mass casualty incidents, they are not sufficient to prevent and mitigate harm as fully as possible. The occurrence of a catastrophic incident can lead to a narrowed focus on the issues that appear relevant to that crisis but which may not be reflective of the totality of lessons learned from incidents across time and locations. Although the public tends to focus on mass shootings as defining violence concerns, the range of issues is broader in scope and effect (Braga et al. 2014). We have learned that violence is a complex issue with many and varied causes and contributing factors. Therefore, no single method or entity is likely to have a marked impact on the reduction of such a complex phenomenon. Reducing violence will require involvement and intervention across a range of disciplines (American Psychological Association 2013). Effective strategies involve comprehensive and collaborative efforts (e.g., between law enforcement and school/campus personnel) to address all aspects of prevention, planning, mitigation, response, and recovery for the range of violence that can impact upon a community (U.S. Department of Education et al. 2013).

Collaborative Policing

There is increasing acknowledgment that crime and violence are not unidimensional problems that will be effectively addressed by law enforcement alone, but rather that comprehensive partnerships will be necessary in achieving more effective and long-lasting benefits (Aden 2013; Duffee et al. 2006; Ederheimer 2013; Friedmann and Cannon 2007; Mayer and Erickson 2011; McCampbell 2010; Trinkle and Miller 2013; Wolf 2012). Collaborative policing is an engagement-oriented approach that helps to enhance the relationship between law enforcement and the community they serve. Community engagement builds support, trust, and cooperation from and with the community, and it is instrumental in identifying gaps or underserved populations (Aden 2013).

Collaborative policing approaches share similar principles and strategies with public health approaches that emphasize multidisciplinary collaboration and problem solving to address complex health care issues (Dahlberg and Mercy 2009; Markovic 2012). A robust public health approach involves multiple elements including surveillance (identifying and understanding the problem); control (containing the problem); coordination (managing multiple partners, strategies, and resources to maximize control of the problem); and communication (engagement and interaction to facilitate the process; Wolf 2012). Community oriented or collaborative policing models incorporate a similar process that is often referred to as the scanning, analysis, response, assessment (SARA) model, which is used to strengthen partnerships and solve problems (McCampbell 2010). In both the public health and collaborative policing models, there is a strong emphasis on collaboration. However, the approach is not only to involve the community with identifying and reporting concerns but to engage with the community as an active and ongoing part of addressing those concerns.

Like collaborative policing approaches, public health models can serve to react to existing concerns, but they are also designed to incorporate preventative and proactive strategies to minimize future harm. This involves a shift in prioritization of efforts from reactive to proactive, with a greater emphasis on prevention and mitigation of risk (Wolf 2012). In addition to a shift in priorities in addressing problems of violence and crime, collaborative policing approaches (like public health approaches) involve a range of performance measures including, but not limited to, the reduction of crime and violence (Federal Law Enforcement Training Centers and Johns Hopkins University 2013). In addition to violence reduction, comprehensive programs measure and evaluate changes in reporting of concerns, community engagement and input, collaboration, quality of life, fear, climate, respect, connectedness, confidence, competence of service providers, and in other related factors (Sulkowski and Lazarus 2011; Wolf 2012).

Collaborative policing models have been utilized effectively in: enhancing responses and services to persons with mental illness (Council of State Governments Justice Center 2008), reducing school violence (International Association of Chiefs of Police 2009), improving prevention of campus violence (Major Cities Chiefs Association 2009; Sulkowski et al. 2011; Richard 2013), enhancing strategies to counter violent extremism (International Association of Chiefs of Police 2012; Stanek 2013), improved strategies to reduce mass casualty violence (Federal Law Enforcement Training Centers and Johns Hopkins University 2013; Paparazzo et al. 2013), reducing family violence and increasing victim participation in prosecution (Lansdowne and Gwinn 2013), and intervention in cases of stalking (National Center for Victims of Crime 2002) and bullying (Virginia Board of Education 2013). Collaborative policing approaches, such as the SMART Policing Initiative, an intelligent approach that employs pro-active strategies to providing security and preventing an escalation of violence and disorder during those situations when violence and disorder erupts which emphasizes collaboration and engagement with a range of community partners, have shown positive results in reducing gun violence in a number of communities (Braga et al. 2014).

Threat Assessment and Management

Threat assessment and management is a systematic process that guides practitioners in their efforts to identify, assess, and manage cases where there is a risk for violence or the escalation of harm (Meloy et al. 2013). Threat assessment (or threat management) is used to facilitate early identification and intervention strategies that prevent violence (where possible) and mitigate risk for harm or significant disruption. Although originally formalized for use in protective intelligence operations (e.g., U.S. Secret Service), the last two decades have seen broader implementation across a variety of sectors including: primary and secondary education, institutions of higher education, workplaces, houses of worship, and military and other governmental agencies (Deisinger et al. 2013). There is a growing emphasis on intelligence-led policing that similarly emphasizes collaboration and coordination to facilitate a process of gathering, organizing, analyzing, and using intelligence to guide operational decisions (U.S. Department of Justice 2007).

As different sectors and organizations have implemented threat management processes, there has often been a significant emphasis on the utilization of multidisciplinary teams. A multi- or interdisciplinary process is crucial for successful operation of violence prevention approaches; however, the appointment of a multidisciplinary team (although necessary) is not sufficient. As in other aspects of collaborative policing, collaboration (i.e., multidisciplinary teams) is an important component. However, so too is the development, implementation, and operation of a systematic approach to problem solving for the prevention and mitigation of risk.

Deisinger et al. (2013) summarized the essential elements for an effective threat management program in which organizations must have a systematic process that:

- Utilizes an effective and relevant multidisciplinary approach that is designed to identify and mitigate all threats
- Enables centralized awareness of, and response to, developing concerns through active outreach programs and consultations
- Facilitates a thorough and contextual assessment
- Implements proactive and integrated case management strategies

- Monitors, reassesses, and manages cases on a longitudinal basis
- Conducts all practices in accordance with relevant laws, policies, and standards of practice
- Adapts to evolving challenges and changing needs over time.

Multidisciplinary Approach to Address All Threats

Although there are a range of potential configurations for team membership, the critical aspect is that the members are connected with key components of the organization that allow them to maximize awareness about concerns that may be developing in (otherwise) disconnected areas of the organization, but that also provide skills, resources, intervention, and monitoring capabilities that no one area would likely possess (Deisinger et al. 2008). Key organizational membership typically involves professionals from management, human resources, security/law enforcement, mental health, and legal services. However, there may be additional core members that help the organization address and respond to identified concerns, or the team may seek out ad hoc consultation from organizational or community members with specific sources of information or with specialized skills not held by members of the core team.

In the aftermath of mass casualty events at schools and campuses, there is often a focus on students as subjects who may pose a threat of violence. Although several mass shootings have involved student perpetrators, it is important to note that not all violence (in schools and on campuses) is perpetrated by students, and that mass shootings do not represent the range of violence that impacts on educational settings (Deisinger et al. 2008, 2013; Drysdale et al. 2010). In a study of targeted violence impacting upon institutions of higher education, Drysdale et al. (2010) found that approximately 60% of the perpetrators were students. Of those; however, two-thirds were currently enrolled, but one-third were formerly enrolled. Similarly, 11% of perpetrators were employees (i.e., faculty or staff), but only 6% were currently employed, and 5% were formerly employed. Beyond those internal constituents, the study found that 20% of perpetrators were indirectly affiliated with the campus (i.e., were in relationships with students or employees or were vendors/contractors providing services on campus). Finally, the study noted that 9% of perpetrators had no affiliation with the campus that had been impacted upon. Although there is certainly a need to implement processes to facilitate early identification and intervention with internal constituents, effective programs recognize a broader range of potential threats (Deisinger et al. 2013).

Enables Centralized Awareness

Effective threat management processes provide for a centralized entity that is multidisciplinary in nature and is authorized to be a central point of coordination for receiving, analyzing, and responding to concerns that may pose a threat to the educational setting. To facilitate that centralized awareness, team members should recognize the factors that can inhibit reporting and involvement from community members.

There has been much research on the "bystander effect" (i.e., where persons have knowledge of safety concerns but do not get involved) and how to better facilitate those bystanders' involvement in the safety and well-being of their community. The U.S. Department of Education and the U.S. Secret Service conducted an analysis of bystander issues related to school violence (Pollack et al. 2008) and identified several challenges related to bystander issues as well as strategies to address those challenges. Effective teams will incorporate such bystander intervention principles to maximize community engagement with the process (Deisinger et al. 2008). Bystander intervention approaches emphasize that the safety and well-being of the community is a shared responsibility of all members. Community members all have the responsibility to not only report concerns (to the centralized process) but to be part of the response to the concern—to the extent that is appropriate—based on their skill level and role within the community (International Association of Chiefs of Police 2009).

An essential aspect of such engagement (and overcoming so-called "information silos") is an active outreach program that builds awareness and provides training for early identification, referral, and intervention with safety concerns. Incorporating lessons learned from the bystander intervention research, those outreach and training programs help community members recognize behaviors that may pose a concern, understand where and how to report and consult about concerns, understand that those consultations are wanted even if there turns out not to be any significant concern, and trust that appropriate actions will be taken and understand the range of response that may be appropriate. Given that educational settings experience ongoing turnover within their internal communities, outreach and awareness efforts will need to be ongoing endeavors (Aden 2013; Deisinger et al. 2008).

Contextual Assessment

As noted earlier, violence is a complex and multifaceted problem on the community level and with regard to individual cases where violence is a concern (American Psychological Association 2013). Violence and other significantly disruptive behaviors are understood as a product of an interaction among four factors: the subject who may be at risk for taking violent action, the vulnerabilities of the target(s) of such actions, an environment that facilitates or permits violence or does not discourage it, and precipitating events that may trigger escalations in behavior. Deisinger and colleagues reference this as the subject, target, environment, and precipitant (STEP) model for a holistic and contextual assessment (Deisinger et al. 2008, 2013). Effective teams strive to understand identified concerns in the context (time, place, and circumstances) in which they are occurring.

Implements Proactive and Integrated Case Management Strategies

Based on observations and information obtained through the reporting and assessment processes, the threat assessment team develops a multidimensional and integrated strategy to address the concerns identified (Meloy and Hoffman 2013). For example, using the STEP model (Deisinger et al. 2013), teams identify strategies to de-escalate, contain, or control the behavior of the subject of concern; to decrease vulnerabilities of the identified target(s); to modify the physical and cultural environment to discourage escalation and support safety; and to prepare for and (where possible) mitigate against anticipated precipitating events that may trigger adverse reactions both acutely and over time. This active management continues until the case no longer poses a level of risk that necessitates such a level of coordinated intervention. Effective case management integrates interventions across the (relevant) domains.

Monitors and Reassesses on a Longitudinal Basis

In a meta-analysis of research on the effectiveness of a broad range of prevention programs, Nation et al. (2003) identified key elements of effective prevention strategies. Effective programs were comprehensive and systematic in their approach. They were collaborative and socioculturally relevant to the population(s) being served. They were appropriately timed, and services were delivered by well-trained staff using multiple and varied methods that were sustained over time. Finally, effective programs emphasized a process of continuous evaluation and improvement.

These findings emphasize the importance of sustained approaches that are monitored, evaluated, and adjusted over time to meet the needs of the situation. Threat assessment practitioners take the long view regarding their cases, developing not only interventions to address immediate and acute concerns but implementing long-term strategies to sustain their risk reduction efforts. Note that this can be a significant change in approach for organizations that have historically taken an approach that is crisis- or incident-based (i.e., designed only to address acute needs rather than to attempt to address underlying contributing factors that may evolve and resurface over time).

Conducts All Practices in Accordance with Relevant Laws, Policies, and Standards of Practice

There are a range of laws, regulations, and policies that may impact upon a given case and upon an organization's threat management process in general. Some of the areas of law that may be relevant include (but are not limited to) employment privacy laws, disability and public accommodations laws, employer liability and tort laws, health care records privacy laws and laws related to a duty to warn or protect, and freedom of information or open records laws that govern what records may or must be released to the public. In addition, members of the threat management team should be intimately familiar with their institutional policies related to campus safety and should ensure that team processes are in accord with those guidelines. Examples of policies related to threat management include workplace violence prevention, threat assessment and management, harassment and discrimination, crisis management, employee and student discipline, interim suspension, fitness for duty, weapons, and bomb threats.

Having access to a well-trained legal advisor in the formation and operation of a team can be very helpful because many aspects of law (impacting on workplace and school safety) can be rather complex and nuanced. Deisinger et al. (2013) summarized some of the relevant legal issues and cite a number of resources to help team members familiarize themselves with those issues.

Beyond the range of laws, regulations, and policies that may impact the specific actions of a threat management team, there is a growing body of literature related to the professional practice of threat assessment and management teams. There have been a number of local, state, regional, and national task forces that have reviewed school and campus safety and have recommended implementation of threat assessment and management teams (Deisinger et al. 2013).

Some states (e.g., Virginia, Illinois, and Connecticut) have enacted legislation that requires the development, implementation, and operation of threat assessment teams within educational settings. Even where they are not obligated under law, other state college systems (e.g., Iowa and North Carolina) may require implementation of threat assessment processes through system or institutional policy. Local and state educational and public safety officials should be aware of the statutory and policy requirements relevant to their setting.

Adapts to Evolving Challenges and Changing Needs

Educational settings face a number of challenges in supporting the safety and well-being of the school and campus. Over the past few years, a number of safety-related issues (i.e., targeted violence, bullying, sexual harassment, domestic violence, and others) have been recognized within educational settings, and multidisciplinary processes have often been implemented to address those concerns. However because those interventions are often a response to acute concerns, they may not be developed in a way that facilitates integration with each other. Ironically, as organizations have implemented approaches to address gaps in awareness of (and response to) concerns, they have often implemented compartmentalized and fragmented systems to address those concerns separately rather than collaboratively. The intervention processes have become silos in their own right! To counter that tendency, effective organizations ensure clarity in mission and roles of respective processes, look for shared linkages through membership and communication, and seek to integrate efforts as seamlessly as possible (Deisinger et al. 2013).

Threat assessment cases involve real or potential victimization. As a result, there is a strong emphasis on use of control-based strategies (e.g. discipline, suspension, administrative orders, court orders, criminal prosecution, termination or expulsion) in isolation rather than as part of an integrated case management plan. Team members are cautioned to never equate separation with safety and to recognize that, even when appropriately used, control-based strategies may serve as precipitating events leading to escalation of risk. This is not an admonishment against the use of control-based strategies (so long as they are not used in isolation) but rather a reminder that they can lead to escalations and for teams to consider contingencies when deploying such methods (Deisinger et al. 2013).

Over the past few years, with greater attention to safety concerns in educational settings, there has been a growth in the school and campus safety industry. This is largely a positive outcome because it provides for a range of approaches and types of expertise for schools and campuses to use as appropriate for their needs. However, it also can lead to a risk of using consultants with questionable expertise or methodologies to provide these services. Teams should carefully examine the background of potential consultants to ensure that they possess the relevant education, training, and applied experience to help teams address safety issues.

Operationalizing the Threat Assessment and Management Process

The previous section outlined several core elements of an effective threat management process from a strategic perspective. In addition to those strategic considerations, team members are guided by core principles developed through research and experience in the threat management field. This includes a foundational belief that, in many cases, prevention is possible but that violence is a complex and dynamic process that requires integrated and ongoing intervention to mitigate risk. Team members understand that threat assessment is about understanding behaviors rather than profiles, and that violence is the product of an interaction among multiple factors (e.g., the STEP model from Deisinger et al. 2008) that are incorporated into the assessment and management process. Teams strive to establish multiple reporting mechanisms to enhance early identification and intervention through an engaged community. Team members understand that these are complex situations, typically with incomplete (and sometimes biased information sources) so corroboration is critical. Team members sustain an inquisitive mind-set, seeking to understand if and how a situation poses a threat and not solely whether or not someone uttered a threat. Teams sustain safety as their primary focus and maximize their effectiveness through multiple, sustained, and coordinated efforts over time. These principles are touchstones for team members throughout the process to better support desired outcomes (Deisinger et al. 2008; McCampbell 2010).

Steps in the Threat Assessment and Management Process

This section provides a summary of the key steps in the threat assessment and management process, from a tactical or operational perspective, once a concerning subject or situation has been identified. This systematic process is designed to:

- Gather relevant information
- Assess situation in contextual manner
- Develop integrated case management plan
- Implement case management plan
- Monitor and reevaluate plan to ensure safety
- Follow up and refer as appropriate

Upon initial report of a concerning situation, the team should triage the case to determine whether that situation poses an imminent danger (Deisinger et al. 2008). When initial reports indicate an emergent situation, law enforcement agencies and security resources should be immediately notified to address and resolve the situation. Once the crisis is resolved, the team should review the situation to determine if there is any ongoing threat and (as appropriate) develop a case management plan to continue to mitigate that situation.

In the absence of an acute danger, once the team becomes aware of a concern, they must conduct a fair, objective, reasonable, and timely assessment (Deisinger et al. 2008). The team should review existing sources of information for the persons and settings involved. Teams check records and other sources that may already exist for information relevant to the situation. These sources may include a centralized threat management database of prior contacts with the subject, disciplinary records, criminal history, contacts with law enforcement that did not result in charges, performance evaluations, transcripts, and other information sources. The team should consider a range of persons that may serve as sources of information and monitoring about the subject of concern. The team should carefully weigh the risks and benefits from each of these potential contacts in considering not only who to interview, but when and in what setting as well as selecting the best person or role to gather the information or to conduct the interview (Deisinger et al. 2008).

Team members utilize their respective positions and sources to gather relevant information in each of these domains. The team considers the totality of the case information, incorporating key investigative questions (e.g., Deisinger et al. 2008, 2013) to determine whether the seriousness of and manner in which a subject of concern poses a threat to others or to the community.

When the situation necessitates intervention, the team will develop, implement, monitor, and (on an ongoing basis) review a case management plan to mitigate the threat(s) posed. The case management plan is based on an individualized and contextual understanding of the case, rather than on any proscriptive profile or formula. The team must consider not only the areas for intervention in the case but also the resources and mechanisms available to address those concerns.

Similar to the contextual assessment process, integrated case management plans incorporate coordinated interventions in each of the relevant domains of assessment outlined by Deisinger et al. (2008). An integrated case management plan involves relevant strategies to:

S De-escalate, contain, or control the *subject* who may take violent action

T Decrease vulnerabilities of the *target*

E Modify the physical and cultural *environment* to discourage violence or escalation

P *Prepare* for and/or mitigate precipitating events that may trigger adverse reactions

Strategies to de-escalate, contain, or control the subject of concern should utilize the least intrusive measures that are likely to help achieve those case management goals (Calhoun and Weston 2003). Examples of such strategies may include:

- Maintaining communication and engagement with the subject
- Involving an ally or trusted person to monitor and (where appropriate) to intervene with the subject of concern

- Assisting the subject in problem solving
- Facilitating access to services for assistance/support
- Referring for mental health evaluation and/or treatment
- Mandating psychological evaluation (where lawful and appropriate)
- Involuntary hospitalization for acute mental health assessment
- Confronting the subject and establishing expectations regarding behavior
- Control-based approaches (e.g., discipline, prosecution, termination, expulsion)

It is important to note that control-based strategies tend to be short-term interventions and may not address other key goals of moving the subject away from capacity for violence and disruption, connecting the subject with ongoing support resources, or monitoring the subject when they are no longer connected to the campus community. Where possible, teams should work diligently to sustain key relationships (with subjects, targets, and witnesses) as resources for information gathering and assessment, intervention, support, and for monitoring of the situation.

Many targets (or potential victims) have little experience in monitoring or addressing their personal safety. Team members can provide coaching regarding personal safety and can encourage targets to engage in a variety of interventions, including:

- Setting clear and reasonable limits with subject(s) engaged in unwanted contact or communication
- Avoiding/minimizing further contact with (or response to) subject's attempts to communicate
- Documenting subject's behaviors that cause concern and the impact of those behaviors
- Maintaining awareness of surroundings
- Varying routines
- Traveling in company of colleagues and friends
- Developing contingency plans for escape, shelter, and support
- Developing skills in personal defense
- Making referrals for support and assistance to deal with the stresses and impact of victimization

De Becker (1997) articulates the core needs of all victims when they are dealing with safety concerns. Victims want to know that safety professionals (including team members) care about them as people and not solely as "cases." They often want certainty for their safety, which no one can provide. Team members can, however, provide certainty about processes (i.e., what the team can and cannot provide to support the victim in enhancing his or her safety). Victims desire consistency in action that is supported by regular, timely, and meaningful communication between the safety professional and victim. When subjects engage in threatening behavior, it is all too easy to become solely focused on what the team should do to address the subject of concern and to lose sight of what it should do for the victim (and the larger community, where relevant).

Beyond the actions of the subject of concern, there are environmental, systemic, or cultural factors that impact upon a case. Environmental/systemic management strategies may include the following:

- Address systemic, policy, or procedural problems that have become ongoing precipitating events
- Implement prevention/intervention programs to address bullying, harassment, sexual assault, relationship violence, bias, and other behaviors that may have a bearing on the safety of those in the institutional environment
- Enhance campus climate by working toward a caring community
- Build a culture of care and consultation
- Support and expect timely accountability for inappropriate behavior
- Encourage early identification and intervention approaches
- Enhance conflict management skills
- Enhance supervisory skills
- Implement active and collaborative crime prevention programs through engaging the community

In practice, many precipitating events may not be preventable, and some may not be reasonably foreseeable. The team should strive to anticipate and plan for the impact of such precipitants so that a negative impact (on the subject, target, or community) can be mitigated where possible and to make plans to monitor those events as the case moves forward.

Threat cases generally remain open until the subject of concern no longer appears to pose a threat, which may be well after the point when criminal cases are closed or mental health services are concluded (Deisinger et al. 2008). If the team believes the person does still pose a threat, the team should continue to monitor the situation and modify the case management plan as needed for as long as the subject may still reasonably pose a threat.

Summary

Over the past several years, there has been increased attention to development, implementation, and operation of multidisciplinary approaches to prevent and mitigate violence risk within educational settings. These threat assessment and management approaches are consistent with collaborative policing and public health approaches that emphasize communication, collaboration, and coordination of multifaceted approaches. Increasingly, these integrated approaches are recognizing the value and need to engage the communities they are designed to serve. The safety and well-being of a community (and its individual members) is strengthened when community members (including service agencies) develop and sustain meaningful relationships, collaborate to maximize their respective abilities to identify and solve problems in a comprehensive and systematic manner, and communicate effectively and regularly to support relationships and problem solving. Threat assessment and management exemplifies the principles of collaborative policing and provides a means to reduce harm and to enhance the quality of life within our communities.

Select Resources

Association of Threat Assessment Professionals. (2006). *Risk assessment guideline elements for violence: Considerations for assessment the risk of future violent behavior.* Available at: http://www.downloads.workplaceviolencenews.com/rage-v.pdf

Fein, R. A. and Vossekuil, B. (1998). *Protective intelligence & threat assessment investigations: A guide for state and local law enforcement officials.* Available at: http://www.secretservice.gov/ntac/PI_Guide.pdf

Fein, R. A., Vossekuil, B., Pollack, W. S., Borum, R., Modzeleski, W. and Reddy, M. (2002). *Threat assessment in schools: A guide to managing threatening situations and to creating safe school climates.* Available at: http://www.secretservice.gov/ntac/ssi_guide.pdf

Randazzo, M. R. and Plummer, E. (2009). *Implementing behavioral threat assessment on campus: A Virginia Tech Demonstration Project.* Available at: http://www.threatassessment.vt.edu/Implementing_Behavioral_Threat_Assessment.pdf

U.S. Department of Defense and Defense Science Board. (2012). *Task force report: Predicting violent behavior.* Available at: http://www.acq.osd.mil/dsb/reports/PredictingViolentBehavior.pdf

U.S. Department of Justice Federal Bureau of Investigation. (2004). *Workplace violence: Issues in response.* Available at: http://www.fbi.gov/stats-services/publications/workplace-violence

U.S. Government. (2013). *Guide for developing high-quality emergency operations plans for houses of worship.* Available at: http://www.rems.ed.gov/docs/Developing_EOPs_for_Houses_of_Worship_FINAL.pdf

U.S. Government. (2013). *Guide for developing high-quality emergency operations plans for institutions of higher education.* Available at: http://www.rems.ed.gov/docs/REMS_IHE_Guide_508.pdf

U.S. Government. (2013). *Guide for developing high-quality school emergency operations plans.* Available at: http://www.rems.ed.gov/docs/REMS_K-12_Guide_508.pdf

U.S. Secret Service, U.S. Department of Education and Federal Bureau of Investigation. (2010). *Campus attacks: Targeted violence affecting institutions of higher education*. Available at: http://www.llis.dhs.gov/sites/default/files/campus-attacks.pdf

Vossekuil, B., Fein, R. A., Reddy, M., Borum, R. and Modzeleski, W. (2002). *The final report and findings of the safe school initiative: Implications for the prevention of school attacks in the United States*. Available at: http://www.secretservice.gov/ntac/ssi_finalreport.pdf

References

Aden, H. (2013). Inviting the community into the police strategic planning process. *The Police Chief*, October, pp. 28–31.

American Psychological Association. (2013). *Gun violence: Prediction, prevention, and policy*. Washington, DC: American Psychological Association.

Braga, A., Webster, D., White, M. D. and Saizow, H. (2014). *SMART approaches to reducing gun violence: Smart policing initiative spotlight on evidence-based strategies and impacts*. Washington, DC: US Department of Justice, Bureau of Justice Assistance.

Calhoun, F., and Weston, S. (2003). *Contemporary threat management: A guide for identifying, assessing, and managing individuals of violent intent*. San Diego, CA: Specialized Training Services.

Council of State Governments Justice Center. (2008). *Improving responses to people with mental illness: The essential elements of a specialized law enforcement-based program*. Washington, DC: US Department of Justice, Bureau of Justice Assistance.

Dahlberg, L. and Mercy, J. (2009). *The history of violence as a public health issue*. Atlanta, GA: Centers for Disease Control.

De Becker, G. (1997). *The gift of fear: And other survival signals that protect us from violence*. New York: Dell.

Deisinger, E., Marisa, R. D., Randazzo, M. and Nolan, J. (2013). Threat assessment and management in higher education: Enhancing the standard of care in the academy. In *International handbook of threat assessment*, J. R. Meloy and S. J. Hoffmann, eds. pp. 107–125. New York: Oxford University Press.

Deisinger, G., Randazzo, M., O'Neill, D. and Savage, J. (2008). *The handbook for campus threat assessment and management teams*. Stoneham, MA: TSG.

Drysdale, D., Modzeleski, W. and Simons, A. (2010). *Campus attacks: Targeted violence affecting institutions of higher education*. Washington, DC: U.S. Secret Service.

Duffee, D., Renauer, B., Scott, J., Chermak, S. and Garrell, E. (2006). *Community building measures: How police and neighborhood groups can measure their collaboration*. Washington, DC: US Department of Justice, National Institute of Justice, Final report for grant No. 97-IJ-CX-0052 Measuring the Community Interaction Variables in Community Policing.

Ederheimer, J. (2013). Partnerships and community policing. *The Police Chief*, October, pp. 20–21.

Federal Law Enforcement Training Centers and Johns Hopkins University. (2013). *Strategic approaches to information sharing: A report on the 2013 national summit on preventing multiple casualty violence.* Washington, DC: Office of Community Oriented Policing Services.

Friedmann, R. and Cannon, W. (2007). Homeland security and community policing: Competing or complementing public safety policies. *Journal of Homeland Security and Emergency Management,* 4(4): 1–20.

International Association of Chiefs of Police. (2009). *Guide for preventing and responding to school violence.* 2nd ed. Washington, DC: US Department of Justice, Bureau of Justice Assistance.

International Association of Chiefs of Police Committee on Terrorism Countering Violent Extremism Working Group. (2012). *Community outreach and engagement principles.* Washington, DC: IACP.

Lansdowne, B. and Gwinn, C. (2013). Lifesaving leadership to break the cycle of family violence: Partnerships between law enforcement and communities. *The Police Chief,* October, pp. 32–38.

Major Cities Chiefs Association. (2009). *Campus security guidelines: Recommended operational policies for local and campus law enforcement agencies.* Washington, DC: US Department of Justice, Bureau of Justice Assistance.

Markovic, J. (2012). Criminal justice and public health approaches to violent crime: Complementary perspectives. *Geography & Public Safety,* 3(2): 1–3.

Mayer, M. and Erickson, S. (2011). Changing today's law enforcement culture to face 21st-century threats. *Backgrounder,* No. 2566, pp. 1–6.

McCampbell, M. (2010). *The collaboration toolkit for community organizations: Effective strategies to partner with law enforcement.* Washington, DC: US Department of Justice, Community Oriented Policing Services.

Meloy, J. R., Hart, S. D. and Hoffmann, J. (2013). Threat assessment and threat management. In *International handbook of threat assessment,* pp. 3–17. New York: Oxford University Press.

Meloy, J. R. and Hoffmann, J. (Eds.) (2013). *International handbook of threat assessment.* London: Oxford University Press.

Nation, M., Crusto, C., Wandersman, A., Kumpfer, K., Erin Morriseey-Kane, S. and Davino, K. (2003). What works in prevention: Principles of effective prevention programs. *American Psychologist,* 58: 449–456.

National Center for Victims of Crime. (2002). *Creating an effective stalking protocol.* Washington, DC: US Department of Justice, Office of Community Oriented Policing Services.

Paparazzo, J., Eith, C. and Tocco, J. (2013). *Strategic approaches to preventing multiple casualty violence: Report on the national summit on multiple casualty shootings.* Washington, DC: U.S. Department of Justice, Office of Community Oriented Policing Services.

Pollack, W., Modzeleski, W. and Rooney, G. (2008). *Prior knowledge of potential school-based violence: Information students learn may prevent a targeted attack.* Washington, DC: U.S. Department of Education.

Richard, S., and Stanek, R. (2013). Countering violent extremism: A community partnership approach. *The Police Chief,* October, pp. 42–48.

Sulkowski, M. and Lazarus, P. (2011). Contemporary responses to violent attacks on college campuses. *Journal of School Violence,* 10(4): 338–354.

Trinkle, G. and Miller, T. (2013). Collaborative partnerships to solve community issues. *The Police Chief*, October, pp. 26–27.

U.S. Department of Education, Office of Elementary and Secondary Education and Office of Safe and Healthy Students. (2013). *Guide for developing high-quality school emergency operations plans*. U.S. Government Printing Office, Washington, DC, p. 2.

U.S. Department of Justice, Office of Justice Programs and Bureau of Justice Assistance. (2007). *Navigating your agency's path to intelligence-led policing*. Washington, DC: US Department of Justice.

Virginia Board of Education. (2013). *Model policy to address bullying in Virginia's schools*. Richmond, VA: Virginia Board of Education.

Wolf, R. (2012). *Law enforcement and public health: Sharing resources and strategies to make communities safer*. Washington, DC: US Department of Justice, Community Oriented Policing Services.

Cooperative Policing for Coping with Crisis Situations

6

Lessons from the Japanese Police Response to a Natural Disaster on March 11, 2011

MINORU YOKOYAMA
Emeritus Professor of
Kokugakuin University
Tokyo, Japan

Contents

Introduction: Development of Police Measures for Coping with Serious Disaster

After World War II, Japan was democratized following the example of the American model. However, through the enactment of the fundamental law,[*] the national government was gradually restored and able to take the initiative in coping with important issues throughout the country. The first step was the Nuclear Fundamental Law in 1955, which was enacted to introduce American procedures for using nuclear substances for peace.

In 1959, a large typhoon hit Mie, Aichi, and Gifu Prefectures; nearly 5000 persons were killed or found missing. The damage and loss was too much for a local government to cope with. In order to help prevent so many casualties and to restore communities damaged by severe disaster, the Fundamental Law on Disaster Countermeasures was enacted in 1961. Under this fundamental law, police developed measures to prevent and cope with similar disasters that might occur in the future.

Under the current Police Law, which was enacted in 1954, the National Public Safety Commission (NPSC) and the Prefecture Commission were established as administrative committee and counseling body responsible for supervising the National Police Agency and the prefecture police (Yokoyama 2001, 192). The National Police Agency (NPA) is responsible for three main tasks: (1) planning laws related to the police, police activity standards, and various police systems; (2) supporting activities of the prefecture police with "hardware" and "software"; and (3) coordinating activities of the prefecture police. Although the NPA does not have its own police force, it controls all prefecture police through personnel management and the subsidy from the national government.[†] Under the guidance of the NPA, prefecture police agencies have developed a system for coping with severe disasters, which has been improved with each occurrence. As explained in detail later in this chapter, this especially was true with the January 17, 1995, Hanshin Asaji Earthquake (magnitude 7.3) in which 6400 people died.

---

[*] Japan has 42 fundamental laws that are enacted through laws, rules, and manuals.
[†] All police officials above the rank of inspector are employed by the national government. In addition, elite officers directly employed by the national government occupy almost all important positions of authority within the prefecture police.

We had thought that our system for the prevention of damage caused by a large disaster was more than sufficient. However, it could not cope adequately with the catastrophe caused by the East Japan earthquake that occurred on March 11. Knowing that a natural disaster is beyond man's control, our system shifted from trying to completely prevent damages to reducing the amount of damage caused by a disaster through proper planning and the installation proper response mechanisms.

Establishment of the Security Headquarters for Coping with the East Japan Earthquake on March 11

The largest earthquake ever recorded in Japan, with a magnitude 9.0, occurred at 2:46 p.m. on March 11. A number of smaller earthquakes, or aftershocks, occurred for several months. Even Tokyo, Japan's capital city located about 375 km from the earthquake's epicenter, several casualties and much structural damage was reported due to the strong swing of the earthquake.

Immediately after the earthquake, the incident command system (established by the Fundamental Law on Disaster Countermeasures) began operation. Without directly receiving national government instruction, many public (including local governments and the police) and private sectors began coping with this catastrophe. The police incident command system was well prepared and functioning smoothly immediately after the earthquake occurred.[*] The NPA established the Security Headquarters to Cope with Disaster, which was chaired by a director of the Security Bureau (National Public Safety Commission and National Police Agency 2012, 19).

Four minutes after the quake, the national government established the Management Office to Cope with Disaster at the prime minister's office (White Paper on Disaster Prevention 2012, 24). At the same time, the prime minister gave directions to confirm the state of casualties and damages, ensure the safety of those persons affected by the disaster, continue evacuation from the disaster area, ensure lifelines, restore the damaged transportation system, and to provide accurate information to the people. Many organizations in the public and private sectors began assisting with these activities.

About 30 minutes after the first large earthquake, a large tsunami began to come ashore along the Pacific coastline. Many people watched the tsunami's arrival on live television broadcast from helicopters.[†] As this was the most disastrous catastrophe in Japan's modern history, the Emergency Headquarters to Cope with Disaster headed by the prime minister was set

---

[*] Concerning the measures taken to cope with the March 11 tsunami, see Yokoyama (2013).
[†] Most people affected by the tsunami could not view the television coverage due to power outages.

up for the first time since the enactment of the Fundamental Law on Disaster Countermeasures. At the same time, the NPA established the Emergency Security Headquarters to Cope with Disaster chaired by the director general. The Security Headquarters to Cope with Disaster was also set up at all prefecture police locations and headed by its director general. The highest level system set up for the police to cope with a disaster began to operate.

At 3:27 p.m., the tsunami hit Fukushima No. 1 Nuclear Electric Power Plant and caused all electric power to be lost in the plant. Due to the seriousness of the situation, a second meeting of the Emergent Headquarters to Cope with Disaster was held a short while later.

Prime Minister Naoto Kan focused on measures for preventing a severe accident at the nuclear plan. At that point, he did not have time to plan for the establishment of a support system for the people affected by the quake. It was not until March 20 that the secretariat for the Headquarters to Cope Specially with Support for the Life of Sufferers was established by the national government (Urushima 2012, 102). However, at the local level, many support services for quake victims were established.

Traffic Control by the Police in Big Cities such as Tokyo and Yokohama

At 4:57 p.m., at a press conference broadcast on live television, the Japanese prime minister appealed to the people to behave calmly. Although most people did not hear his appeal, they still behaved calmly and patiently. People working in big cities such as Tokyo and Yokohama continued to work until the end of the day even though they worried about their family and friends during the frequent aftershocks.[*]

After 5 p.m., many people began to return home. In Tokyo and its satellite cities, most trains and subways were not in operation due to power outages and safety checks being conducted to see whether the train and subway systems were damaged by the earthquake.[†] Thus, many people returned home by walking or riding a bus.

At a 5:39 p.m. press conference, the chief cabinet secretary appealed to people to stay in a safe place and not to return to their homes. However, his appeal was in vain. Many police were assigned to traffic control due to the huge number of vehicles and pedestrians on the roads. As most of

---

[*] Most telephone lines were busy because of the many people trying to dial out.
[†] A traffic jam continued until midnight. However, the Tokyo Metro began to run at about 10:30 p.m. after officials finished checking operation safety during the continuance of large-sized aftershocks.

the traffic signals were not in operation, police had to use hand signals at these street crossings.

The total number of police officers was not sufficient to control the terrible traffic jam of vehicles and huge confluence of pedestrians. However, pedestrians and drivers behaved well and rarely caused trouble. The police did not have to suppress any riots, which often can occur in other countries at the time of a large disaster.

Many organizations offered assistance to those walking home. For example, businesses and companies situated along a main road offered the use of toilets. One university offered accommodations for those who could walk no further.* In Tokyo and its satellite cities, order on the road was maintained in spite of the insufficient control by police officers. After this experience, the police—in cooperation with community organizations—endeavored to improve future traffic and crowd control at the time of an emergency or a big disaster.†

Activities of the Prefecture Police for Coping with the March 11 Catastrophe

Less than hour after the 9.0 magnitude quake occurred, ministers of the national government in charge of disaster prevention held the first meeting of Emergency Headquarters to Cope with Disaster. At the meeting, they decided to adopt the following fundamental policies to cope with this catastrophe (White Paper on Disaster Prevention 2012, 25):

1. To grasp the real situation by collecting information to carry out activities smoothly and cope with the disaster
2. To rescue victims first and foremost using such measures as dispatching the Self Defense Forces, the police, fighter fighting units, and medical teams
3. To restore the transportation system and lifelines, such as the supply line of food, clothes, water, electric power, natural gas, and gasoline
4. To establish the support system in public and private sectors all over Japan
5. To offer the people accurate information

---

* Kokugakuin University offered students, teachers, staff, neighbors, and pedestrians who gave up returning to their homes on foot classrooms to stay in overnight. The university also provided them with cookies and bottled water, which were available for the emergency.
† For example, the local government (including such agencies as the Shibuya Fire Fighting Station and Shibuya Police Station) has carried out mass disaster drills in which several universities asked students to participate.

Before this decision, prefecture polices in the area hit by the earthquake established the Security Headquarters to Cope with Disaster according to their own manual on how to cope with a serious disaster. For example, immediately after the first and largest earthquake, Yoshio Sato, a director in charge of security policing, entered a command room at Iwate Prefecture Police Headquarters and set up the Security Headquarters to Cope with Disaster (Iwate Prefecture Police 2013, 177). The Miyagi Prefecture Police Headquarters also set up at Security Headquarters at 2:49 p.m. (Takeuchi 2013, 40). All 24 police stations in Miyagi Prefecture established their own Security Headquarters to Cope with Disaster (Takeuchi 2012, 3). Of the 4200 police officers in Miyagi Prefecture, 3900 were assigned to cope with this disaster. As the plan on policing against natural disaster was revised in 2010, these assignments were performed smoothly. Following the plan, Miyagi Prefecture Police Headquarters established five bases to cope with the disaster, to which police officers were then assigned.*

The situation made it very difficult for the three prefectural police agencies to help those impacted by the disaster. Miyagi and Fukushima Prefecture, covering the area seriously damaged by the March 11 events, was greatly impacted by the earthquake and the tsunami—police buildings and equipment were damaged. Three damaged prefecture police departments had to perform their duties in damaged facilities while having lost lifelines such as electric power and water.

Three damaged prefecture police facilities did not have enough human resources available to cope with the disaster. Thus, they requested that the NPA dispatch the Wide-Area Emergency Rescue Corps, Wide-Area Police Aviation Corps, and Riot Police Communication Corps from other prefecture police departments.† The NPA directed 44 other prefecture police departments to dispatch these units and corps to the three damaged prefecture police departments. Soon afterward, about 700 police officers were dispatched from Tokyo Metropolitan Police and two Region Police units arrived in Miyagi in spite of the difficult traffic situations on the highways and roads.

---

* The riot police units affiliated with Miyagi Prefecture Police and the East North Region Police rushed to their bases (Takeuchi 2012, 3) where they were each assigned to specific damaged areas for rescue activities.
† At the time of the Hanshin Asaji Earthquake, many police officers affiliated with the riot corps were dispatched to the damaged areas from their prefecture police departments. However, they could not efficiently rescue people trapped in the destroyed buildings and houses because they did not have knowledge of proper rescue techniques, and they were not equipped with special rescue machines and instruments. On June 1, 1995, every prefecture police department set up a Wide-Area Emergency Rescue Corps. The member police officers of this unit learn special rescue techniques under the guidance of firefighting officers. When a large disaster occurs, they are dispatched with special machines and instruments for rescue.

Even after the rescue activities were completed, many ordinary police officers were dispatched to the three damaged prefecture police departments from all other prefectures to support those survivors who were living in temporary housing (Iwate Prefecture Police 2013, 147–175).

Police Activities Prior to the March 11 Tsunami

In Japan, many officers are in charge of responding to a disaster, such as police or firefighters. In addition, as supplemental manpower, community organizations such as volunteer firefighters and volunteer flood-fighters have formed. Thus, immediately after the first and largest earthquake, many officers and volunteers in charge of preventing a disaster drove their cars or emergency vehicles to the coast. After manually shutting a water gate and observing the situation along the seashore, they patrolled on the road, using megaphones to warn people to evacuate to higher ground.* While performing these heroic activities, some were killed or missing due to the unforeseen high waves of the tsunami. Twenty-five police officers were killed, and five were missing (National Public Safety Commission and National Police Agency 2012, 17); 253 volunteer firefighters were killed or missing in three damaged prefectures (Kanda and Suganuma 2011). A later analysis of the disaster suggests that this tragic loss may have been caused by the workers engaging in their routine activities according to the manual for disaster prevention.† However, surely it is difficult for any police officer to judge when they should stop doing their duty in order to protect their own life during a disaster. Most Japanese police officers may delay in the timing because they are earnest in the performance of their duty.

Collection and Delivery of Information by the Police

At the beginning of a disaster it is very important to collect data and to analyze it immediately. On March 11, Japan's Meteorological Agency failed to collect data and to analyze that data adequately because the earthquake observation equipment and the data retrieval system were seriously destroyed by the first (and largest) earthquake.

---

* Japan's Meteorological Agency issued the first warning based on an underestimation of the height of the tsunami, which resulted in many people not heeding the shouts for evacuation (Yokoyama 2013, 97). After the March 11 disaster, the police discussed ways to improve ways to notify people to evacuate during an emergency. The Tokyo Metropolitan Police decided that some police officers speak softly (like a disk jockey) to guide crowds (*Nihon Keizai Newspaper* on April 11, 2014).
† Although the manual is useful for coping with a disaster that is foreseen, people should not necessarily adhere to rules or manuals when confronted with an unexpected, large catastrophe.

Immediately after receiving the underestimated warning of the tsunami wave height, the municipal governments in those areas that might be hit by a tsunami transmitted this information to residents and shouted for their evacuation to a high place through their own radio communication systems for disaster prevention. The police also transmitted this warning via radio to police officers working along the seashore.* Although the first underestimated warning was later revised by the Meteorological Agency, many people—believing the first warning—might not have responded correctly and thus lost their lives.

The police collected information about damages suffered due to the earthquake and tsunami. Helicopters from three damaged prefecture police departments took off immediately after the first quake. Flying along the Pacific coastline, police officers videotaped live images of the seashore and towns being hit by the tsunami, which were broadcast to the prime minister's office, the NPA, the Security Headquarters of the three damaged prefecture police departments (White Paper on Police 2012, 8).

Due to the wide area damaged by the earthquake and tsunami, it was very difficult for the police to collect accurate information. Nearly all systems used to transmit information did not function properly due to the destruction of equipment by the strong swing of the tsunami and by power outages. Some rumors arose during these situations. One was that groups of foreign thieves were rampant in the areas damaged by the disaster (Takeuchi 2013, 45). Such rumors and incorrect information might disrupt police activities. However, in this instance, rumors seemed to be fewer in number than with previous disasters.†

Most Japanese people are familiar with the police emergency call system of dialing "110." Immediately after the largest earthquake on March 11, the number of emergency calls increased drastically, although few people could communicate by telephone at the areas damaged most seriously by this disaster. On March 11 and 12, police received many emergency calls for immediate rescue (Takeuchi 2013, 42). However, it was very hard to immediately dispatch police officers to respond to these emergency calls because of the chaotic situation.

---

* Since the supply of electric power stopped after the earthquake, most of the communication system did not work. In Iwate, only the battery-operated police radios and those powered by police department generators were operational (Iwate Prefecture Police 2013, 127). However, the total number of portable police radios was too small for police officers working along the shoreline that were outside a police car or a Koban (police box) to receive information about the large tsunami heading in their direction (Matsumoto 2012, 44).

† On September 1, 1923, a earthquake of magnitude 7.9 occurred offshore in Kanagawa Prefecture; some 105,000 persons were reported killed or missing. After the earthquake, a rumor spread that Koreans were rioting. The Japanese, believing the rumor, massacred many Koreans.

A few days later, the police received many calls from people seeking information about missing relatives. Police at the three damaged prefectures established a new calling system to respond to these inquiries and to consult with those trying to locate missing family members. In the Iwate Prefecture Police Headquarters, five lines for free dial calling to give out information about missing persons were established on March 13 (Iwate Prefecture Police 2013, 142). Twelve police officers answered calls, while three others worked to input data from the calls into a computer. However, the number of officers assigned to these tasks was too few to help all of those trying to obtain information about their relatives and friends. On March 16, there were 213,901 calls, of which the police could answer only 316. However, the police did contribute to confirmation of missing person reports through this exchange of information.

The police are obliged to transmit accurate information about a disaster to the people. However, it was very difficult for them to fulfill this obligation during and after the Great East Japan Earthquake. For example, according to protocol, the police are obligated to provide information on the total number of dead or injured persons by counting the number of individual victims. However, the number of persons killed or missing during this catastrophe was so large that the police could not get an accurate count of the number of individual victims. However, Naoto Takeuchi, the Director General of Miyagi Prefecture Police, wanted to provide some information on the large number of casualties. At a meeting at the Miyagi Prefecture Government Office, he stated that more than 10,000 appeared to have been killed or were missing as a result of the disaster (Takeuchi 2013, 42). His statement was reported by the news media and created large headlines, which contributed to the basic information distributed by the mass media to people all over the world.

Police Rescue Activities

Many officers and soldiers of the Self-Defense Forces were sent to the three damaged prefectures for rescue operations. On March 26 their total number reached to 107,000 (Cabinet Office 2011, 28). U.S. military forces stationed in Japan carried out a "Tomadachi (Friendship) Strategy." Under the strategy, more than 16,000 military personnel per day participated in the rescue activities with the use of 15 warships and 140 aircrafts (Cabinet Office 2011, 28). Japanese police also contributed to rescue efforts under the umbrella of the Self-Defense Forces. By the end of May 2011, 26,707 people had been rescued, of which 72.2%, 17.3%, 14.0%, and 1.3% were rescued by officers of the Ministry of Defense, the Fire and Disaster Management Agency, the police, and the Maritime Safety Agency, respectively (White Paper on Disaster Prevention 2011, 28). As time passed, rescue activities changed to searching for dead bodies under the debris.

Traffic Control by the Police

Immediately after the largest earthquake on March 11, the police began to collect information from the Ministry of Land, Infrastructure, Transport, and Tourism and the East Nippon Expressway Company about the condition of the primary roads in the northeast area of the main island. They judged that vehicles could operate on the main highways after some temporary pavement repairs were made. On March 12, the police designated the main highways used to travel to the three damaged prefectures as emergency traffic roads prescribed by the Fundamental Law on Measures to Cope with Disaster.

At the local level, the Iwate Prefecture Police assigned 12 main roads leading toward the seacoast as emergency traffic roads on March 11 (Iwate Prefecture Police 2013, 130). This early assignment was regarded as a favorable start by the NPA because it enabled emergency vehicles to reach the damaged areas quickly.

The police also began to issue identification markings for emergency vehicles. At the gate of an interchange with an emergent traffic road, the police checked drivers to determine if they had the identification marking that authorized them to use that road.* It was difficult for police officers at the checkpoints to dissuade drivers without proper identification from entering the road.† The assignment of emergent traffic roads was abolished on March 24, 2011, and up until that time, the police issued 163,208 emergency identification markings‡ (White Paper on Police 2012, 5).

Traffic was disrupted on many local roads after the largest earthquake on March 11. In the three damaged prefectures, a total of 692 signal posts were destroyed. Since many traffic signals did not work properly, police officers stationed at the main crossings on dusty roads in the central areas of big cities such as Sendai and Morioka had to direct traffic using hand signals.

---

* In Japan, there are many rules and regulations. Therefore, a private organization needs to establish a good relationship with the government in order to cope with an emergency. For example, Lawson, a large company that manages convenience stores under the franchise system, established a headquarters to cope with the disaster four minutes after the occurrence of the largest earthquake on March 11. At midnight on the same day, seven staff members drove from the headquarters to survey the situation at 911 branch stores in the areas severely damaged by the disaster (Yoshida 2013, 49). Since the company had established a good working relationship with the police, Lawson staff were permitted to drive into the damaged areas.

† Many of these drivers wanted to confirm whether or not their relatives were alive.

‡ Once the recovery efforts were running more smoothly, the scope of assigned high ways was reduced, and the markings were issued more flexibly to facilitate the transportation of such necessary goods as food and gasoline to the damaged areas.

Police Evacuation Guidance after the Nuclear Accident in Fukushima

At 3:27 p.m., on March 11, the high wave of a tsunami hit the Fukushima No. 1 Nuclear Electric Power Plant causing several electric power supply systems to stop completely. As a result, four nuclear reactors failed to cool, and officials feared the danger of leaking radiation from the melted reactors. Under the circumstances, the directors of Tokyo Electric Power Company (TEPCO) judged the situation to be an emergent accident (as prescribed by Article 10 of the Law on Special Measures Concerning Nuclear Emergency Preparedness).* At 3:42 p.m., they reported this situation to the Nuclear and Industrial Safety Agency.

As the national government became aware of the occurrence of a serious accident at Fukushima No. 1 Plant, the Management Office to Cope with Nuclear Accident was established at 4:36 p.m. in the prime minister's office. At 7:03 p.m. that evening, members of the Control Headquarters for Safety of Nuclear Power held a meeting at which they issued the Declaration on Nuclear Emergency prescribed by the Law on Special Measures Concerning Nuclear Emergency Preparedness. At 7:23 p.m., the third meeting of the Emergency Headquarters to Cope with Disaster was held. Finally, at 7:30 p.m., the minister of defense issued an order to dispatch troops from the Self-Defense Forces to cope with the disaster caused at the Fukushima No. 1 Plant.

Finally, at 11:23 p.m., the national government issued an evacuation order for people living within 3 km of the plant and an order to stay inside to all people living in the zone between 3 km and 10 km from the center of the disaster. By the request of the Ministry of Land and Transportation, 117 buses supplied by 11 companies were sent to the areas within the zone for evacuation of residents. Many police buses and vehicles also went to these areas. On the morning on March 12, about 50,000 residents living within the zone were asked by police officers (wearing nonflammable garments for protection) to board a bus immediately. These people were not given accurate information on the reasons for the evacuation or where they would be located after being evacuated. However, the police (in cooperation with Self-Defense Forces) assisted in the guidance activities for evacuating residents in. The first hydrogen explosion did not occur at the No. 1 reactor until 3:36 p.m. on March 12. At 6:25 p.m. that same day, the national government issued another evacuation order; all people living within 20 km of the Fukushima No. 1 Plant were ordered

---

* This law was enacted in 1999 after a critical accident at the JCO Company, during which 670 persons were exposed to leaking radiation, and two were killed.

to leave their homes. Fortunately, they were able to evacuate with the guidance of the police and the Self-Defense Forces before they were exposed to the leaking radioactive substances from the two explosions at the Fukushima No. 1 Plant (on March 14 and 15). After the evacuation had taken place, police established a gate to check all vehicles and pedestrians entering the areas that had been contaminated by high quantities of radiation. This contributed to preventing property crimes and theft in the areas from which residents had fled.[*]

Emergency Treatment of Suspects Confined in a Police Facility

On March 11, the police and the public prosecutors' office moved 356 suspects housed in a detention facility to a higher location in advance of the tsunami (National Public Safety Commission and National Police Agency 2012, 11). Although 28 suspects were confined at six police stations along the Pacific coastline in Miyagi and Iwate Prefecture, none of them were killed or missing.[†] A few days after the quake and tsunami, they were transferred to other police stations that did not suffer serious damage.

Search of Dead Bodies and the Completion of Forensic Autopsies after the Search

The Self-Defense Forces continued to carry out activities such as removing rubble, searching for bodies, and assisting victims until the end of August, 2011. The local police continue until to carry out special activities and to provide support for the victims of the disaster. For example, the police have continued to search for the bodies of missing persons, especially because Japanese culture demands that a dead person's body should be found if at all possible so that a funeral may take place.

The Miyagi Prefecture Police has a Special Squad for Searching Missing Persons affiliated with its headquarters to which 160 police officers belong

---

[*] Rescue efforts and the search for missing persons along the seashore were hindered by the serious radiation contamination in Fukushima Prefecture.

[†] Three suspects were confined at Kamaishi Police Station (Iwate Prefecture Police 2013, 180). According to regulations, the detained suspects should have been sent to Tono Police Station during the emergency. However, Yoshihiro Yamauchi, a police station official, deemed it impossible to send them to Tono. However, before the station was hit by the tsunami, the three suspects were taken up onto the roof for safety. Together with 26 police officers (including Yamauchi), they survived, although the high wave of the tsunami reached the building's second floor.

(*Asahi Newspaper* 2011).* A total of 15,791 bodies had been found by June 4, 2012 (White Paper on Police 2012, 13).

The three damaged prefecture police departments established a team for completing autopsies. Police officers who were member of this team were dispatched to such facilities as a public hall and a gymnasium where many dead bodied had been placed. They worked with police officers from other prefecture police departments to support the doctors and dentists who carried out the forensic autopsies.†

The police published some details about the recovered remains to help people searching for missing relatives identify the bodies. When family members of the missing visited the police for a consultation, the police treated them with kindness and compassion. Police officers working with the autopsy team behaved as social caseworkers would when delivering bodies to relatives. Speaking with so many of the bereaved was a difficult and emotional job for the police.‡

The bodies of many dead persons were so severely damaged, even having parts of their body missing, and their personal belongings were not found. It was difficult to establish the identity of the found bodies. Thus, Japanese police used such high techniques as DNA profiling to identify the bodies. According to the formal procedure, it takes a long time to identify the found body, since the cause of a death should be thoroughly investigated. However, in this unusual situation, in response to the request of Takeuchi, the director general of the Miyagi Prefecture Police, the National Police Agency was allowed to take the simplified procedure for identification of the dead bodies (Takeuchi 2012:13).

If it was not possible to identify a body, the police delivered it to the municipal government for cremation. This created major difficulties for the town and city municipal governments since their government buildings and the equipment were destroyed by the earthquake and the Tsunami. In addition, there remained few officers who understood the procedures for the cremations, as many police officers were victimized by the earthquake. Therefore, the police officers had to teach them about the procedures to follow for the cremation of bodies.§

---

* Thirteen members of this special squad together with fourteen police officers from Kesennuma Police Station searched for missing persons along the Rias seacoast on July 11, 2013 (*Nihon Keizai Shimbu* 2013).
† It was difficult for the police to locate doctors and dentists for the autopsies. Miyagi Prefecture Police only had about 40 medical doctors and 60 dentists that came, by the introduction of the Miyagi Prefecture Medical Association. to perform the autopsies (Takeuchi 2012,14).
‡ In Japan, people receive the high quality of service with the development of the service industry. Therefore, at the disaster on March 11 the police officers were obliged to take care of the bereaved kindly like a caseworker.
§ Municipal governments damaged by the disaster did not have enough officers available to assist with recovery efforts. Therefore, officers affiliated with various local governments were dispatched to offer assistance to those municipal governments impacted by the disaster.

Police Support of Victims

Survivors of the earthquake who had been evacuated from their homes or who were rescued were taken to temporary evacuation shelters set up in schools and other public buildings. Basic necessaries such as water, food, medications, natural gas, fuel, and gasoline were in short supply. Working with the Self-Defense Forces, the police assisted in bringing the necessary goods to the victims by trucks and helicopters. A few days after the quake, enough basic goods to meet the survivors' needs were donated by many people and supplied by governments and various organizations.

In Japan at this time, police officers perform duties similar to those of social workers in the community. In addition, a special police team helped to provide psychological support to sufferers. In Iwate Prefecture, the police organized a squad composed mainly of female police officers to support victims. Their task was to listen to the victims' concerns and to try to assure them that everything would be okay (Iwate Prefecture Police 2013, 113). Police even offered some recreational opportunities for the citizens affected by the quake. For example, the police brass band played music for at a temporary shelter (Iwate Prefecture Police 2013, 122–124). These activities helped the victims to recover from the psychological damage they experienced from the disaster on March 11.*

Later, the evacuated residents moved to temporary housing. Since they had been separated from their neighbors, they often felt lonely. In addition, the disaster had been a traumatic experience for many children. To support these victims, especially the children and senior citizens, the police officers patrolled the areas and visited these citizens in their temporary housing. These visits by police officers, especially the female officers, contributed greatly to easing the victims' worry and stress (White Paper on Police 2012, 18).

The police provided special services to support victims who had lost their driver's licenses. They quickly issued renewal licenses by using a special summary procedure. This was a very important service because the driver's license card is widely used for identification in Japan.

Community Policing for Crime Prevention

No serious rioting or plundering occurred in Japan immediately after the March 11 disaster (Abe 2013, 116–117). Nevertheless, the police strengthened crime prevention activities in the areas hardest hit by the March 11 disaster,

---

* In Japan, 25% of the popular was 65 or older. Many of these victims had little motivation to try to restore their old life. Building up the public morale also became an important task of the police.

especially near Fukushima No. 1 Plant where victims had been evacuated. Nearly 500 police officers (the Squad for Community Policing) patrolled these areas, as well as 210 police in cars and police officers from the three damaged prefecture police departments (White Paper on Police 2012, 16). In addition, private security companies from all over Japan sent many guards who volunteered to assist with crime prevention activities and to supplement the activities of the regular police officers.

Police were also assigned to protect dignitaries, such as the emperor and leading statesmen, who visited the damaged areas. These visits were important for the recovery. These individuals were able to gain a better understanding of the real situation in the damaged areas, and they were also able to provide hope and encouragement to the victims. Every time there was a visit, the police had to assign many officers for guard duty. Eventually, these visits were so frequent, and required so much police security that they interfered with the police performing services for the victims (Takeuchi 2012, 22).

About 6000 cashboxes were reported to the police as lost property in the damaged areas. The police tried to find the owners, and almost all of the money contained in the boxes was eventually returned (White Paper on Police 2012, 18). In cases where people found loose cash in the damaged areas, they reported it to the police (Iwate Prefecture Police 2013, 187). In Japan, even in ordinary situations, it is common for a person finding cash and valuables to report this to the police.

As a result of the tsunami, some dangerous substances were found in houses and other facilities, and these had to be removed or drained from the structures. Leaking fuel caused big fires in debris throughout the areas affected by the disaster. Firefighters, working police officers, could not always extinguish these fires. Guns that had been used for hunting were also carried away by the tsunami wave. However, these guns were damaged by the salty water and thus were no longer operative (Takeuchi 2012, 23). There were no official reports or information released about any crime committed using a weapon that had been lost in the disaster.

Investigation of Crimes after the March 11 Disaster

The Special Riot Squad for Investigation was also dispatched to the three damaged prefectures. Nearly 100 squad members were sent with 23 vehicles for investigation purposes (White Paper on Police 2012, 17). The Special Riot Squad arrested a total of 278 suspects for such offenses as theft and robbery during the period from March 13, 2011, to June 4, 2012.

In Japan, fraud and fraudulent business practices are rampant, although the number of conventional thefts have decreased.* Therefore, many prefecture polices issued warnings about possible frauds. On March 16, the first warning was issued by the Saitama Prefecture Police, which mentioned several possible fraud cases (*Asahi Newspaper* 2011). Some examples of some of the types of fraud associated with the disaster include an unemployed man was who was arrested on March 18 for fraudulently collecting donations for disaster victims (*Asahi Newspaper* 2011). On March 19, a man who said he was a director of an investment company was arrested for an attempted fraud; he had asked a 91-year-old woman to transfer her donation for victims to his bank account (*Asahi Newspaper* 2011).

Another type of a fraud discovered was the sale of a fake drug that was supposed to discharge radioactive substances from the body. The president of sales for a health foods company was arrested for a violation of the Pharmaceutical Affairs Law; he had sold a bottle of mineral water containing iodine as a drug that would discharge radioactive substances (*Asahi Newspaper* 2011). In all, the police had exposed 16 cases of fraudulent business practices and 70 cases of fraud by June 4, 2012 (White Paper on Police 2012, 17). In addition, the police watched the activities of Boryokudan, the Japanese mafia, to assure that it did not illegally benefit from the reconstruction projects in the damaged areas.†

Indictment for Professional Negligence Causing Death

Although Japanese living standards have been improved by the use of such highly developed technology as nuclear energy misuse has also resulted in great damage (Yokoyama 2007, 23). The police always investigate any incident when there is a suspicion that death and/or injury might have been caused by negligence. As a result of the March 11 disaster, many people were killed or missing; some of the casualties might have been the result of someone's negligence. However, there were too many casualties for police to investigate them for negligence; only in a few cases did the police

---

* In Japan, the purchasing power of older citizens has declined. Therefore, sale activities have become very competitive in which fraudulent business practices are very common. On the other hand, the number of more common types of thefts, such as pickpocketing and burglary, has declined.
† In the 1980s Boryokudan founded or bought many enterprises in such business areas as real estate, construction, and financial markets, in which some Boryokudan lieutenants work in secret as the executives (Yokoyama 1999, 143). Therefore, there was concern that Boryokudan might use their sub-enterprises for exploitation after the March 11 disaster.

start investigations after receiving a bill of indictment from victims and/ or the bereaved. However, they did not succeeded in proving the criminal accountability of the indicted persons.

Plan to Improve Measures to Cope with Future Large Disasters

In November 2011, the NPA established the Investigative Commission to Cope with Disaster, chaired by the assistant director general (National Public Safety Commission and National Police Agency 2012, 24). In addition, by January 2012, all prefecture police and organizations affiliated with the NPA had established the same commissions, which oversaw police activities related to the March 11 disaster and discussed measures for coping with large disasters in the future.

In December 2011, the national government revised the Fundamental Plan on Disaster Prevention. In the response to this revision, the NPSC and the NPA revised their Plan on Activities for Disaster Prevention the following March.[*] The revisions made for dealing with future crisis management issues are outlined in the following section.

Increase in Police Units and Rescue Corps Dispatched to Cope with Disaster

At the time of the March 11 earthquake, about 4700 police officers throughout Japan were affiliated with the Wide-Area Emergency Rescue Corps— approximately 2600 with the security unit, 1500 with the traffic unit, and 600 with the criminal identification unit (Matsumoto 2012, 40). Members of these rescue corps were dispatched after the quake, taking with them the necessary items they would need for living in the damaged areas. For example, the security unit carried enough food and a portable toilet so that they remain in a police vehicle for at least three days. Some 500 police officers affiliated with the Wide-Area Police Aviation Corps and 1200 affiliated with the Telecommunication Riot Police Corps were dispatched to three damaged prefectures.

However, after the events of March 11, both the NPSC and the NPA felt these numbers were not enough to cope with a future large disaster

---

[*] Under this revised plan, the recommended procedures for coping with a tsunami are mentioned separately from those dealing with a large earthquake. In addition, procedures to be used in the event of a large earthquake occurring along the eastern Pacific seacoast have been improved because many residents in Shizuoka and Aichi Prefecture may be affected and structures in that location likely will suffer serious damage.

similar to East Ocean Earthquake. Therefore, they decided to increase the total number of police officers affiliated with the criminal identification unit from 600 to 1500. In addition, the Security Corps for Emergency Disaster was established. About 3000 officers working with the riot police unit of the regional police are affiliated with this new corps (with the exception of those who are already members of the Wide-Area Emergency Rescue Corps). These officers are expected to work flexible shifts every a few days in damaged areas. The Wide-Area Emergency Rescue Corps, the Wide-Area Police Aviation Corps, and the Telecommunication Riot Police Corps together form Japan's Rapid Reaction Forces. Under the new plan, the Rapid Reaction Forces are required to carry more necessities for supporting themselves in areas hit by disasters.

The main members of the Rapid Reaction Corps planned to continue their jobs for about two weeks after the disaster. During this period, the police begin to assign ordinary police officers to a unit of the General Corps to work at the damaged areas after the withdrawal of the Rapid Reaction Corps. The General Forces are divided into eight units: (1) the special security unit for searching, (2) the special traffic unit for traffic control, (3) the special mobile patrol unit, (4) the special life security unit for consultation, (5) the special investigation riot police, (6) the support unit for supplying necessities and for receiving goods sent or donated from other places, (7) the unit to support jobs for identification, and (8) the unit to support telecommunications (White Paper on Police 2012, 27). Using this system, the prefecture police hit by a disaster can be supported for a long period by officers dispatched from all other unaffected prefecture police departments.

Improvement of Measures to Secure Job Continuity at Police Facilities Hit by Large Natural Disasters

In the event of a large natural disaster, the NPSC and the NPA foresee excessive damage in police facilities located in the affected region. To cope with such a situation, they plan to improve the measures taken at the police facilities in order to ensure adequate coverage of police activities on the national level and the prefectural level. On the national level, if the NPA's buildings are seriously damaged, the job NPA center would be moved to the Kanto Region Police Department or to the National Police Academy.* Necessities such as food, water, fuel, and medications would be stored at these facilities for use by the NPA in the event of an emergency.

* Under the new plan the National Police Academy is added, because the location of the Kanto Region Police is far from the center of Tokyo.

During an emergency situation, police officers working for the NPA would be housed in a dormitory easily accessible to an NPA building or to an alternative NPA job center. To receive accurate information about the disaster, the NPA will distribute portable police radio receivers to these officers. All prefecture police have been requested to establish similar measures. During the March 11 disaster, the Miyagi Prefecture Police did not have their own facility for supplying gasoline (Takeuchi 2012, 22). It would be desirable for all prefecture police to have this capability. The police have many mountain-top relay stations, but it was difficult for police officers to supply fuel to the stations (Iwate Prefecture Police 2013, 125). Moving forward, prefecture police are now required to have the necessary equipment to supply fuel easily to the station for a long period in case of emergencies.

Under the new system, police are expected to improve their activities for disaster prevention. We expect that quick implementation of the measures outlined for disaster prevention will be put in place because another big earthquake like the East Ocean Earthquake may occur in the near future.*

Conclusion

Japanese police encountered many unprecedented and severe difficulties during the disaster on March 11. However, because they had developed preparations for a large earthquake and tsunami after the 1995 Hanshin Awaji Earthquake, police were able to successfully undertake the necessary measures (based upon existing laws, rules, and manuals) for coping smoothly with the 2011 events, even though the scale of the earthquake and tsunami was unprecedentedly large, strong, and wide.

However, the police could not cope efficiently with the severe accident at the Fukushima No. 1 Nuclear Electric Power Plant. The government promoted policies and legislation for facilitating the industry of nuclear electric power, and ignored those who were opposed to increasing the use of this power. Government officials joined forces with the major power companies, and created a myth that nuclear electric power plants are absolutely safe (Yokoyama 2012). These companies insisted that the plant was completely equipped with facilities for a crisis such as the one that occurred with the Emergency Core Cooling System and that these facilities completely

---

* The Tokyo Metropolitan Government predicted that as many as 920,000 might be unable to return to their homes in case a big earthquake occurs in the near future. To cope with this difficulty, the Tokyo Metropolitan Assembly enacted the Ordinance on Persons with Difficulty in Returning to their Home for the first time in Japan, which was enforced on April 1, 2013 (*Mainichi Shimbu* 2013). Under this ordinance companies are encouraged to store enough necessities such as water and food for three days. To cover costs, the Tokyo Metropolitan Government offers a subsidy to companies.

conformed to the stringent legal requirements for safety. As the police believed in this myth, they did not have any plan or any idea how to cope with a severe accident at the Fukushima No. 1 Plant. At the national government's direction, they followed procedures for coping with accidents. However, because nothing had been planned in advance, these procedures were not effective. Having a proper plan in place prior to events taking place is very important for the police to effectively cope with a disaster.

The police incident command system functioned well after the earthquake on March 11. One reason is the division of jobs and the cooperation between the NPA and the prefecture police was well defined in advance. Another reason is the close working relationship between the NPA and top level of the prefecture police leadership; in fact, the main leaders of the prefecture police are dispatched from the NPA. Therefore, under the direction of the NPA, there was excellent cooperation between the unaffected prefecture police and the three damaged prefecture police departments.[*]

During an emergency, police leaders play an important role. In the Great East Japan Earthquake, having a general director for the three damaged prefecture police departments was a good solution, and Naoto Takeuchi did an excellent job.[†] Without a good director general, the police incident command system would not function well in a crisis.

Another reason why the damaged prefecture police departments functioned well was because of the positive relationship that they had been established previously with local governments and organizations in the community. For example, the Miyagi Prefecture Police assigned a high-ranking officer to the Miyagi Prefecture Government's liaison office to exchange information about the disaster. The Miyagi Prefecture Government gave permission for a large prefecture gymnasium to be used as a place to bring the bodies of the dead. Here, doctors and dentists from the Miyagi Prefecture Medical Association were able to efficiently carry out the forensic autopsies.

Cooperation between government and organizations all over the country is also important. For example, Miyagi Prefecture asked other

---

[*] The police must also deal with monetary issues if they perform extra work in connection a disaster. In the case of the March 11 earthquake and tsunami, a director-general of the Miyagi Prefecture Police asked the Miyagi Prefecture Government to increase salaries for police officers working to cope with the disaster, even though this type of salary increase usually is paid by the national government (Takeuchi 2012, 24). Another problem is paying for the salaries of police officers dispatched from another prefecture's police department. Since these salaries are paid by the dispatching department, it is financially difficult for a prefecture in a less prosperous area to send many police officers to offer assistance. The NPA has budgetary increases from the national government to support the poorer prefectures in these types of circumstances.

[†] Besides performing many jobs related to coping with the disaster, Takeuchi issued several messages of support in his own words to offer encouragement to police officers (Takeuchi 2012, 25).

prefectures to take remains for cremation because there were not enough facilities available. In response to this request, the Tokyo Metropolitan Government accepted 860 bodies for cremation.[*]

In conclusion, the lessons learned from this disaster can be applied throughout the world, and other countries can benefit from the experiences of Japanese police during the disaster on March 11, and use this information to help formulate their own plans for coping with such an emergency.

References

Abe, T. (2013). Mutual help and crimes at large earthquake disaster in East Japan. In Toyoji, S. (ed.). *Large disaster and crimes* [Japanese]. Kyoto: Horitsu-Bunka-sha, pp. 114–131.

Cabinet Office. (2011). White Paper on Disaster Prevention 2011 [Japanese]. Tokyo: Saeki Printing Company.

Iwate Prefecture Police, (editorial supervision). (2013). *Mission-evidences on March 11 from Iwate Prefecture police* [Japanese]. Morioka: Iwate Nippo-sha.

Kanda, S. and E. Suganuma. (2011). Prevent Volunteer Firefighters from Being Victimized. *Asahi Shimbun*, November 25, 2011 [Japanese].

Mainichi Shimbu. (2013). Ordinance on Persons with Difficulty in Returning to their Home. April 7, 2013 [Japanese].

Matsumoto, H. (2012). Large disaster and crisis management of police. In *Large-sized disaster and police response* [Japanese]. Division to Study Administration and Operation, the Association for the Study of Security Science, pp. 37–67.

National Public Safety Commission & National Police Agency. (2012). White Paper on Police 2012 [Japanese], Tokyo: Gyosei.

Nihon Keizai Shimbu. (2013). Search of Missing Persons by the Earthquake Disaster along Various Seacoasts. July 11, 2013 [Japanese].

Takeuchi, N. (2012). Looking back at police activities at Great east Japan earthquake disaster. In *Large-sized disaster and police response* [Japanese]. Division to Study Administration and Operation, the Association for the Study of Security Science, pp. 1–36.

Takeuchi, N. (2013). The disposition by police after Great east Japan earthquake disaster-from the view point of the director general of prefecture police. In *Security science review (Vol. XV, 2013)* [Japanese]. Tokyo: The Association for the Study of Securities Science, pp. 40–46.

Urushima, I. (2012). Crisis control of giant disaster-lesson from Great east Japan earthquake disaster. In *Large-sized disaster and police response* [Japanese]. Division to Study Administration and Operation, the Association for the Study of Security Science, pp. 97–115.

---

[*] At first, municipal governments in the damaged areas hesitated to deliver remains for cremation in Tokyo. A positive relationship existed with the local police. For this reason, the police were able to persuade these governments to deliver the remains to the Tokyo Metropolitan Government. This type of relationship between the police and the municipal government is very important during a disaster (Takeuchi 2012, 16).

Yokoyama, M. (1999). Trends of organized crime by Boryokudan in Japan. In Einstein, S. & Menachem, A. (eds.), *Organized crime: Uncertainties and dilemmas*. Chicago, IL: The Office of International Criminal Justice, The University of Illinois at Chicago, pp. 135–154.

Yokoyama, M. (2001). Analysis of Japanese police from the viewpoint of democracy. In Einstein, S. & Menachem A. (eds.), *Policing security and democracy: Theory and practice*. Huntsville, TX: The Office of International Criminal Justice, pp. 187–209.

Yokoyama, M. (2007). Criminalization under conservative public opinion in Japan. *Kokugakuin Journal of Law and Politics*, 44(4), 1–46.

Yokoyama, M. (2012). Serious concerns about Fukushima No. 1-The lack of information by TEPCO. In *Global security*, N. Seumenicht, ed. Hemer, Germany: Home Security UG, pp. 11–14.

Yokoyama, M. (2013). Are the measures to cope with large tsunami following after Great east Japan earthquake adequate? In Toyoji, S. (ed.), *Large disaster and crimes* [Japanese]. Kyoto: Horitsu-Bunka-sha, pp. 88–113.

Yoshida, K. (2013). Base for life security rooting in community. In *Security science review (Vol. XV, 2013)*, [Japanese]. Tokyo: The Association for the Study of Securities Science, pp. 46–52.

Higher Education, Police Training, and Police Reform

7

A Review of Police–Academic Educational Collaborations

CRAIG PATERSON
Sheffield Hallam University
Sheffield, UK

Contents

Introduction

A shift from police training toward police education has long been advocated by international scholars as a mechanism for broader police reform (Bayley and Bittner 1984; Roberg and Bonn 2004). This educational shift seeks to bring police and academic communities together to work toward collaboratively designed aims and learning outcomes that support the evolution of professional policing. Yet, policy implementation remains uneven due to sustained resistance across international jurisdictions from academics and police officers at all levels of their respective hierarchies. This resistance can take the form of cynicism from liberal academics about the possibility of reform within policing agencies as well as suspicions among police officers about the motives and abilities of those within academia. A clear evidence base outlining the "added value" of police and higher education collaborations for police education would go some way to addressing these cultural obstacles that resist change. The key question raised during this process is what "added value" do higher education institutions bring to police training and education. This chapter reviews the international literature on higher education, police training, and police education; draws out key themes for analysis; and identifies areas where higher education adds value to police training and education. The final section looks at the policy implications of these findings.

Police Reform and Higher Education

Research on policing has consistently demonstrated that operational police work is only partially guided by legal precepts and, instead, is influenced mainly by the extensive discretion of police officers in how they enforce the law (Bittner 1970; Manning 2005). The impact of individual police officer perspectives on everyday actions and behaviors is therefore experienced by the general public at the street level where operational policing is practiced. The historical roots of policing agencies—within the blue collar traditions of working class communities and the hierarchical organizational model of the military—has produced masculine and conservative occupational subcultures that err toward homogeneity and hierarchy ahead of diversity. For the majority of police history, the public (and especially offenders) have appeared at the bottom of this hierarchy—as those with the least knowledge about crime problems. The emergence of community policing as the dominant Western model of policing has, to varying degrees, inverted this hierarchy and re-situated communities as sources of knowledge for the police at all levels of the hierarchical structure. The dominant reform agenda of policing organizations across Western countries has subsequently revolved around the reemergence of community policing and a languorous cultural shift from "rules" to "values" (Paterson and Pollock 2013).

At the heart of this shift, there is a conflict between a reflective emphasis on the underpinning "values" of policing and a pragmatic emphasis on the commonsense "craft" of police work. Police education is central to the process of cultural change and reform with officers encouraged to question the established hierarchical order that generates police organizational knowledge and to seek answers from empowered communities. Whereas police training teaches officers how to deliver policing *to* the public, police education seeks to encourage more flexible values-based thinking from officers who actively engage *with* diverse communities. The absence of a police education program to support this cultural transition helps to explain the time lag between the introduction of community policing policy and its appearance within street-level policing (Cox 2011).

The impact of the global economic downturn has provided added impetus to ongoing demand for reform in the structure of police recruitment and training rather than the more commonplace crises in public confidence that are followed by calls for improvements in recruitment and training (Roberg and Bonn 2004; Holland 2007; Wimhurst and Ransley 2007). International debate already exists about the aims of practice-focused criminal justice degrees and the academic integrity of these qualifications. Critics have argued that the role of higher education is overly focused upon accreditation rather than education in criminal justice and policing (Farrell and Koch 1995) and that the motives of institutions relate to income rather than to educational standards. Therefore, a clear evidence base is required for those who advocate a more significant role for higher education in the initial and ongoing training of police officers as well as clarification of the specific attributes that these degrees enable undergraduates to develop. Put more succinctly, what is the educational goal? The rest of this chapter provides a review of international research to inform the debate about potential policy developments.

Methodology

This chapter provides a review of the literature found on the following eight electronic databases: Directory of Open Access Journals, Emerald Management Xtra, Google Scholar, Informaworld, JSTOR, Sage Journals Online, SpringerLink, and SwetsWise. The literature covers subjects such as criminology, psychology, education, criminal justice, and policing. The literature review is not exhaustive, and despite best intentions and rigorous examinations of bibliographies it has been impossible to include all relevant information. Most importantly, the literature review does not include research that has been conducted by police departments and not been made available to the public.

Police studies is dominated by Western scholars, and this means little reference to, or understanding of, other cultures is often demonstrated (India is an exception). English is the trading language of international policing debates, and this sidelines the substantial bodies of literature that have not been published in English from comparative debate. The multitude of different approaches to police training and education that exist across the globe can also mean that abstract generalizations have little comparative significance.

For this reason, this chapter focuses on the findings of English-language research from the United States, the European Union (EU), Australia, and India, with some supplementary commentary on other countries. This chapter does not attempt to provide a detailed evaluation of the objectives and content of police training and education across a multitude of jurisdictions. The countries that have been selected (aside from India which has been included for comparative distinction) demonstrate similarities in democratic structure, socioeconomic status, experiences of crime and globalization, plus the process of police professionalization.

The United States

There is an extensive body of research on the relationship between higher education and policing in the United States that has been built up over the last 40 years. From the late 1960s, onward, the U.S. government played a key role in funding criminal justice personnel's attendance at universities, and this encouraged the establishment of criminal justice programs for police officers. The rapid rise in the number of criminal justice courses raised questions about their quality and academic rigor, some of which remain today; but reductions in funding for criminal justice courses during the 1970s and 1980s ensured that only the stronger programs survived (Roberg and Bonn 2004).

Police personnel in the United States were initially reluctant to embrace the idea that a college education adds value to the training of police officers (Regoli 1976). This view came from a perceived gap between academic knowledge and the practical application of rules; on the academic side, mistrust was related to concerns that subjects such as criminal justice and policing were "intellectually shallow and conceptually narrow" (Sherman 1978). Critics of criminal justice degrees in the United States questioned their academic integrity and pointed to their rising popularity as an indication of "the willingness of higher education to surrender to market demands for relevant, practical courses that provided credentials" (Flanagan 2000, 2). Most scathingly, applied criminal justice degrees were referred to as descriptive introductions to the structure and function of criminal justice systems, thus compromising academic integrity in order to attract business (Williams and Robinson 2004).

Research evidence on the benefits of higher education for U.S. police officers is equivocal and can be split into two distinct bodies of literature. A body of research on the impact of higher education on police attitudes was built during the 1970s that demonstrated that university-educated police officers were less authoritarian than nonuniversity-educated police officers (Parker et al. 1976; Roberg 1978), less cynical (Regoli 1976), and that the higher the level of education attained, the more flexible the officers' value system became (Guller 1972). In particular, this evidence pointed to improved attitudes toward minority groups (Parker et al. 1976) as well as more ethical and professional behavior (Roberg and Bonn 2004). The research also made the important point that it was not criminology or criminal justice courses that cultivated this more ethical and culturally aware attitude but the overall university experience (Roberg 1978). Sherman (1978) argued that police education should be focused on new recruits and not on those already employed by police departments. This is due to the potential resistance that the occupational perspective of in-service police officers and police trainers could have on the impact of higher education teaching. Less conclusive evidence was provided on the impact of higher education upon police performance which is, at least partly, due to the nontheoretical nature of police studies, and the absence of agreement about how performance should be measured (Chapman 2012).

A second body of literature emerged during the 1990s that questioned the reforming zeal of the new university-educated police recruits. This literature pointed toward questionable attitudes toward female recruits (Austin and Hummer 1994), increasingly negative perceptions of the public (Ellis 1991), and reinstated questions about the value of higher education beyond the legitimacy and credibility provided to the police by accreditation. A recent comparative study by Owen and Wagner (2008) provided further support for this contention and indicated that criminal justice students demonstrated higher levels of authoritarianism than graduates from other disciplines. These research findings emulated those of Austin and O'Neill (1985) and Bjerregaard and Lord (2004) who questioned the value of education in influencing attitudes toward criminal justice ethics. The Owen and Wagner study also found that students in the earlier stages of a degree demonstrated higher levels of authoritarianism than those in the latter part of a degree; this has been supported by Hays et al. (2007) who identified a correlation between higher levels of education and an increasingly flexible value system.

It has been argued that the potential strengths of higher education are undermined in the United States by an absence of relevant benchmarks (Bufkin 2004) and a lack of clarity about the objectives of practice-focused degrees (Owen 2005). Yet, it is acknowledged that police officers who undertake criminal justice degrees gain great value from them (Chronister et al. 1982). Police officers in the United States reported that criminal justice degrees improved their knowledge of criminal justice as well as their ability to make sense of conceptual and managerial issues, though similar responses also came from police officers educated in other academic disciplines (Carlan 2007). Research also demonstrates that higher education has the ability to improve officer knowledge, skills, and problem-solving techniques and to utilize noncoercive strategies to resolve a situation (Chapman 2012). This improves police–citizen relations and police legitimacy (Paoline and Terrill 2007). The extensive literature on police education and training in the United States has had a significant influence on the police research agenda elsewhere in the world, although it retains critics— in particular Manning (2005), who accuses it of rampant empiricism and a general absence of explanatory value.

The European Union

Any attempt to identify common developments in police training and education across the EU undoubtedly encounters obstacles presented by the different social, political, and cultural contexts of the 28 member states. Police training and education in the EU is in the process of transition from systems that focus on experience, skills, and competencies to research-based collaborations with institutions that are tied into international networks (Jaschke 2010). In part, this transition has been driven by the 1999 Bologna Declaration, which encourages the reform of higher education systems in order to improve the transferability of knowledge, students, and lecturers around the EU. The Bologna process aims to promote university programs as internationally compatible learning modules, and this strategic objective is increasingly driven by the European Police Academy (CEPOL) that was formally established as an EU agency in 2005.

Pagon et al. (1996) differentiate developments in Europe from those in the United States by focusing on the police educational institutions that evolved out of police training institutions. Debate about the constitution of a police studies or police science discipline, as well as its role in the development of police education, has gathered pace in a number of European countries, most obviously Germany and the Netherlands (Jaschke and Neidhard 2007; Jaschke 2010). The demands made upon European police forces for a much broader focus on police management, policing strategies, and ethics has resulted in a proliferation of police studies degrees. The multi-agency focus required by the pluralization of policing at the local, national, and international levels has also made partnership work increasingly important. The police focus on professionalism emphasizes the importance of academic qualifications to undertake the police role and research to underpin policing strategies. This focus on academic understandings of developments in policing has resulted in the reform of police training programs and, in some cases, institutions. Police academies have gained university status in the Czech Republic, Lithuania, Greece, Slovakia, Norway, France, Spain, and Italy.

The shift to community policing in Northern Europe is being followed by similar reforms in police training and education that emphasize this change in strategy and that aim to improve the quality of policing. The Dutch use a dual system of education and training in order to facilitate links between theory and practice (Peeters 2010). Feltes's (2002) work in Germany emphasizes the importance of communication and conflict resolution skills alongside the traditional focus on the law for community-oriented police. Feltes also stresses the emphasis placed upon criminological theory within German institutions. Both Feltes (2002) and Peace (2006) indicate that the key to success is clear objectives, the identification of core curriculum content, and the adoption of an appropriate method to facilitate the transition from a law enforcement focus to a community focus. For example, the development of police studies in Germany was justified by the value it offered to the police and society to increase professionalism, develop a research-based approach to crime reduction, develop a portfolio of police programs for different levels, and to encourage a comparative approach that makes the most of developments in other countries (Jaschke and Neidhart 2007).

The proliferation of higher education courses in police studies across the United Kingdom has not, as yet, been met with equal enthusiasm in articulating the added value that these degrees provide to the Police Service, to students, and to the public. Peace (2006) and Heslop (2011) note the lack of fit between the community policing philosophy espoused by the UK government and the methodology employed in police training that has led to a lack of confidence in police studies and a theory–practice binary (Heslop 2011; White and Heslop 2012). As in the United States, Lee and Punch (2004) note that the value of higher education lies in a range of undergraduate courses that develop police officers' critical thinking skills and not just the police studies courses that have proliferated across the country.

Jaschke (2010, 303) acknowledges that policy developments in the EU are leading toward the establishment of a "modern police science," an integrative academic discipline that draws from a range of knowledge bases with the aim of enhancing police professionalism. This mixture of professionalization (underpinned by academic qualifications), research-based policing strategies and the reform of police training institutions is being implemented across Europe (Jaschke and Neidhart 2007). The police discipline adds value to police training by enabling senior police officers to make sense of developments in transnational crime, social exclusion, terrorism, public demand for transparency, and a shift to proactive intelligence led policing supported by an international research agenda. Yet, although research has demonstrated the value of higher education upon officer attitudes (Lee and Punch 2004), challenges remain in demonstrating the impact of higher education on behavior and police performance (Feltes 2002; Jaschke 2010) as well as the reproduction of negative facets of police culture within academic environments (Heslop 2011).

Australia

Two distinct models of police education emerged during the 1990s in Australia; one was based upon a traditional model of liberal education where students studied social science subjects, the other focused upon the professionalization of policing where universities and the police worked in partnership but the police controlled the development of the police discipline. This poses a problem for the relationship between higher education and policing with university-based educators having different perceptions about the aims of police education when compared to their police academy counterparts (Mahony and Prenzler 1996). A number of research studies came out of Australia during this period that highlighted minor improvements in attitudes and values of graduate recruits but, more worryingly, a clear and rapid deterioration of these attitudes and values during the early years of work (Cox 2011). Wimhurst and Ransley (2007) argue that the reasons for these findings and the lack of identified value of higher education to policing lies within the dominance of the professional policing model that has limited the impact of education on organizational reform.

As in the United States, the findings of the Australian literature on the added value of higher education for policing are mixed. The main objective of incorporating higher education into police education in Australia had been to improve public support for the police and to drive organizational reform in a police environment that was perceived to be conducive to corruption (Wimhurst and Ransley 2007). The introduction of the advanced certificate in policing in Queensland in 1991 was followed by significant improvements in public attitudes toward the police though the program itself was abandoned only three years later. This leaves a lack of clarity in the contribution of Australian studies with clear benefits identified for individual recruits but no clear empirical support for added value to the Police Service aside from an improvement in image and legitimacy (Wimhurst and Ransley 2007, 113). Cox (2011, 4) goes further and argues that the approach to training and education in Australia is intellectually redundant with a need to focus more on capability ahead of competence.

India

Police training in India has not encouraged police officers to engage with the humanities and the social sciences. Verma (2005), who is highly critical of India's police training, comments that calls for reform have generally been ignored. The value of the social sciences in India has been understood through its contribution to technical skills rather than a broader understanding of criminology. Khan and Unnithan (2008) note that the development of criminal justice education in India has been driven by the central government. They also comment on the lack of integration of academic criminology and criminal justice in both the United States and India. Research on the impact of higher education on police constables in India produced generally negative results and indicated that police officers who had been through higher education had more rigid value systems, were less interested in protecting the rights of citizens, and were indifferent toward legal boundaries (Scott et al. 2009). These findings contradict those from Western countries and highlight the limitations of perspectives that directly link higher education with improved police attitudes without an appreciation of the importance of sociocultural context when considering policy transfer from one jurisdiction to another. There are contradictory findings from other developing democracies with some evidence of improvements in police professionalism and legitimacy (Lino 2004), particularly as part of the process of political reform and the pursuit of democratic police legitimacy (Veic and Mraovic 2004).

Discussion

The themes in this section are drawn from Marenin's (2005, 109) requirements of democratic policing that emphasize the importance of professionalism, accountability, and legitimacy. These categories will be used to identify the "added value" higher education brings to police training and education. Policing in democratic societies takes place within a political landscape that acknowledges the importance of social justice, social cohesion, fairness, equity, and human rights. Bayley and Bittner (1984) argue that these values can be taught to police recruits. Roberg and Bonn (2004) take this further and state that education is necessary for the development of these values and the effective use of discretion that maintains both police performance and professionalism. Thus, there is a clear link among the professional use of discretion, understood as making appropriate situational judgments (Marenin 2004, 109), and the broader issues of public accountability and police legitimacy. These categories provide the framework for the following discussion.

Professionalism

The first category looks at three areas: organizational reform, training, and job satisfaction. First, higher education is most commonly incorporated into police training and education as part of the process of organizational reform. In Western democracies, organizational reform is geared toward community-oriented policing that embodies a core set of democratic values and a shift from a technical focus on competencies toward a more reflexive appreciation of the complexity of the police role, officer capability within changing contexts, and the importance of lifelong learning. This process mirrors long established developments in the fields of medicine, law, and social work. Schein's (1996) work on organizational culture points to the value of recruiting graduates who have the critical thinking skills to challenge managers. This is important in an environment where the constraints of occupational culture are widely documented and have an impact on public perceptions of the police (Hough et al. 2010). An academic education encourages flexibility in orientation to competing demands while also generating transferable skills that help individuals to develop competence in a number of areas (Jaschke and Neidhardt 2007).

Teaching officers how to operationalize their values and beliefs in a way that coexists with the different values and beliefs of other citizens is a formidably complex challenge, particularly in an organization that can resemble a paramilitary institution during times of social conflict (Waddington 1994). International evidence indicates that giving priority to an educational focus on critical thinking over an emphasis on control can aid the development of more flexible value systems suited to the demands of community-oriented policing (Paterson 2011; Paterson and Pollock 2013). This can benefit public confidence and perceptions of police accountability. Research demonstrates that university-educated police officers are less authoritarian than nonuniversity-educated police officers (Roberg and Bonn 2004), demonstrate improved attitudes toward minority groups (Chapman 2012), are less supportive of abuses of authority (Telep 2011), and take a more humanistic approach toward members of the public (Roberg and Bonn 2004).

Second, Conti and Nolan (2005) point to the similarities between police training structures and total institutions where recruits are separated from society to live a structured lifestyle that is geared toward identity transformation. Conti and Nolan argue that the focus within police training upon law enforcement runs contrary to the acknowledged goals set out in models of community policing. Thus, current police structure acts as an inhibitor to organizational reform and is unlikely to counteract the authoritarian tendencies that often provoke crises in policing. Here, the university environment potentially adds value to the training and education process. The didactic approach that has dominated police training for new recruits focuses upon law and procedure to the detriment of community-oriented, problem-solving skills that are learned through self-directed, interactive processes. To further development in this area, both Birzer (2003) and Peace (2006) advocate a dual strategy with teacher-centered tuition for programmed instruction related to law and procedure and humanistic, student-oriented strategies (andragogy) for the exploration of the affective issues related to community policing.

The ability to utilize the adult learning theory of andragogy (the theory that experience is the source of learning for adults) rather than traditional didactic models of teaching is central to the process of organizational reform. The theory of andragogy encourages collaboratively determined objectives between students and trainers that produce more positive learning outcomes. Peeters (2010) takes this further and advocates collaborative frameworks for police training and education with police institutions articulating the occupational requirements of different policing functions while educational institutions identify the curriculum and learning requirements that correspond to the occupational role.

Finally, there is substantial empirical support for improvements in job satisfaction through university study from the United States, Australia, and Europe. The most valued educational components are mind improvement, learning about law enforcement, leadership skills, and an appreciation of the complexity of social problems. Although some criminal justice graduates do not regard their degree as highly relevant to their policing duties, they recognize it is a platform for future employment (Carlan 2007). The UK literature highlights personal benefits to graduate police officers such as confidence, self-esteem, broadened outlooks, and greater tolerance that are also associated with enhanced professionalism (Lee and Punch 2004).

Accountability

It can be argued that university education helps develop skills that improve community orientation and local accountability. Community policing requires police officers to make decisions and solve problems (rather than incidents) using skills that can be developed as part of higher education courses. Research from the United States indicates that trainers focus on law enforcement functions that only take up approximately 10% of an officer's time (Palmiotto et al. 2000), a situation that Peace (2006) acknowledges is also evident in the United Kingdom. The educational literature on policing guides us toward a focus on community policing through the use of andragogical strategies that achieve deeper learning that remains with new recruits beyond the classroom and combats cultural issues. It can also be argued that this teaching strategy builds a more flexible value system that enables the police organization and individuals to change as society changes (Marenin 2004; Cox 2011).

The second area where higher education can improve accountability is in police officer attitudes and behavior. International research has shown that higher education can have a positive impact upon police behavior, particularly when it is combined with job experience (Roberg 1978; Paoline and Terrill 2007) to encourage the better use of discretion that improves public perception of police fairness (Roberg and Bonn 2004, 474). Understanding the value of higher education within the context of police officer performance is difficult. There is a lack of consensus in the literature on which personality traits can be understood as characteristics of a good police officer as well as on defining and measuring police officer performance according to these contested characteristics. This means that the empirical evidence on the added value of higher education does not provide clear and consistent empirical support for mandatory higher education for police officers to improve police performance.

Legitimacy

The findings from the previous section also impact upon police legitimacy through improvements in public confidence in the police. A key area of concern for all democratic countries involves the quality of the relationship that the police have with civil society. Indeed, Marenin (2005, 101) argues that the provision of effective and equitable policing services is a precondition of a democratic political structure. Ivkovic (2008) has demonstrated that public confidence in the police across jurisdictions is related to the quality of governance in each country as well as to the contact individuals have with the police. As outlined earlier, universities are in the best position to provide education in areas such as learning strategies, diversity, and the complexities of crime causation as well as enhancing police legitimacy through the accreditation of police training and education. Yet the strategic shift to service-oriented, community policing remains accompanied by an uneven shift in the provision of police officer training and education (Cox 2011).

A clear relationship has been identified between the way policing is carried out and experienced by the public and levels of public trust and confidence in the police (Hough et al. 2010). The introduction of higher education certificates in Australia led to increased public support for the police. Similarly, in the United States, Paoline and Terrill (2007) found that officers with higher levels of education received fewer complaints and worked in areas with higher citizen satisfaction. Public mistrust of the police in India provides a useful point of comparison here, with the low status and limited education of police officers being cited as two reasons for a lack of public confidence. This can be compared with the United Kingdom and the United States where more than three-quarters of respondents to public confidence surveys stated that they thought the police did a good job (Ivkovic 2008). The other area that influences public confidence is the representation of diverse communities. There remains concern that the inclusion of mandatory higher education could have a discriminatory impact upon the employment of minority groups (Decker and Huckabee 2002), although Roberg and Bonn (2004) contend that any potential discriminatory effects could be offset by an aggressive recruitment strategy.

Collaborative relations with higher education coupled with evidence-based policing provide a platform for agreement about what the core police mission is, how this mission can be achieved, and the values that the police should embrace (Sherman 2011). This agreement can be conveyed to police officers of all ranks and to the wider public. As Cox (2011) acknowledges, reform in police education and training requires a clear conceptualization of police "values" that can be operationalized across the different strata of police culture. Marenin's (2005, 109) requirements of democratic policing (professionalism, accountability, and legitimacy) provide a potential framework for understanding how a focus on police education can contribute to the learning and development of police officers at all levels of the police hierarchy and to an appreciation of the practical use of "values" as drivers of police reform. The final section brings together the findings of this literature review to identify three key policy implications: understanding the transnational context, the development of police training and education, and the role of government and other stakeholders.

Policy Implications

First, higher education adds value to the training and development of police officers and enhances the ability of officers to carry out their role. Therefore, degrees in criminal justice and police studies can be designed to incorporate a generic set of core skills and competencies and also to meet the demands of different police organizations. The broader benefit of other degrees must not be sidelined. Higher education promotes creativity and critical thinking ahead of control and the potential to counteract the cultural instincts of criminal justice institutions through flexible value systems that are more suited to the demands of community-oriented policing and an enhanced focus on ethical and professional behavior.

Second, Bradley and Nixon's "dialogue of the deaf" (2009) recognizes the problems that occur when taking research into the policy environment and the importance of acknowledging the different social, cultural, and political factors that feed into the complexity of the international policing mission. Research is but one component in a myriad of factors that influence policy. The lessons from the United States, the EU, Australia, and India emphasize the importance of governmental support in developing collaborative relationships among the police and higher education institutions. Organizational reform in the EU is most clearly embodied in the dual model of training and education and the recognition of police academies as equivalent to university standard that has been driven by the 1999 Bologna agreement. This highlights the importance of support for organizational reform from governing agencies at the local, national, and supra-national levels.

Finally, higher education provides police officers with an appreciation of the importance of global issues and their impact upon crime at the local level. The broad processes of globalization have impacted upon the nature of crime and the demands of policing, thus making a focus on transnational crimes and international cooperation increasingly important. These social changes have produced new demands for police officers, increasing the complexity of the police role and requiring a more advanced skill base. Higher education promotes international cooperation by enabling the transfer of knowledge on key global issues such as human rights and transnational crimes and fosters an appreciation of the transnational context in which police officers work.

Yet, within the academic sphere there remain contested perspectives on police and higher education collaborations. Across the United States, Europe, Australia, and India, criminological research has split into two schools of police research with *critical criminologists* questioning the role and function of the police within society and *police friendly* researchers focusing on policy, strategy, and performance (Manning 2005; Paterson and Pollock 2011). Both schools would claim to represent the wider public, yet their generation of knowledge and its subsequent use remain fiercely contested along different theoretical lines.

Conclusion

This chapter has pointed toward the benefits for the public, police officers, and the police institution in improving police professionalism, accountability, and legitimacy through collaborative relationships between the police and higher education. This involves the police identifying how higher education can help improve police learning through the construction of competencies and role profiles while universities identify the relevant teaching strategy to meet the police's identified objectives. A model that integrates training and education through a content focus on communication and conflict resolution as well as law and procedure and a method of delivery based on the theory of andragogy is supported by the educational literature. The added value of higher education involvement lies within the role of designing and implementing a learning strategy that is underpinned by a clear evidence base to meet identified targets.

References

Austin, T. & Hummer, D. (1994). Has a decade made a difference? Attitudes of male criminal justice majors toward female police officers. *Journal of Criminal Justice Education*, 5(2), 229–239.

Austin, T.L. & O'Neill, J.J. (1985). Authoritarianism and the criminal justice student: A test of the predispositional model. *Criminal Justice Review*, 10, 33–40.

Bayley, D. & Bittner, E. (1984). Learning the skills of policing. *Law and Contemporary Problems*, 47(4), 35–59.

Birzer, M. (2003). The theory of andragogy applied to police training. *Policing: An International Journal of Police Strategies and Management*, 26(1), 29–42.

Bittner, E. (1970). *The functions of the police in modern society.* Cambridge, MA: Oelgeschlager, Gunn and Hain.

Bjerregaard, B. and Lord, V.B. (2004). An examination of the ethical and value orientation of criminal justice students. *Police Quarterly*, 7, 262–284.

Bradley, D. and Nixon, C. (2009). Ending the dialogue of the deaf: Evidence and policing policies and practices. *Police Practice and Research: An International Journal*, 10(5), 423–435.

Bufkin, J. (2004). Criminology/criminal justice master's programs in the United States: Searching for commonalities. *Journal of Criminal Justice Education*, 15, 239–262.

Carlan, P. (2007). The criminal justice degree and policing: Conceptual development or occupational primer. *Policing: An International Journal of Police Strategies and Management*, 30(4), 608–619.

Chapman, C. (2012). Use of force in minority communities is related to police education, age, experience, and ethnicity. *Police Practice and Research*, 13(5), 421–436.

Chronister, J.L., Gansneder, B.M., LeDoux, J.C. and Tully, E.J. (1982). *A study of factors influencing the continuing education of law enforcement officers.* Washington, DC: DOJ.

Conti, N. and Nolan, J.J. (2005). Policing the platonic cave: Ethics and efficacy in police training. *Policing and Society*, 15(2), 166–186.

Cox, D. (2011). Educating police for uncertain times: The Australian experience and the case for a normative approach. *Journal of Policing, Intelligence and Counter-Terrorism*, 6(1), 3–22.

Decker, L.K. and Huckabee, R.G. (2002). Raising the age and education requirements for police officers: Will too many women and minority candidates be excluded? In *Policing: An International Journal of Police Strategies & Management*, 25(4), 789–802.

Ellis, R. (1991). Perceptions, attitudes and beliefs of police recruits. *Canadian Police College Journal*, 15(2), 95–117.

Farrell, B. and Koch, L. (1995). Criminal justice, sociology, and academia. *The American Sociologist*, 26, 52–61.

Feltes, T. (2002). Community-oriented policing in Germany. *Policing: An International Journal of Police Strategies and Management*, 25(1), 48–59.

Flanagan, T.J. (2000). Liberal education and the criminal justice major. *Journal of Criminal Justice Education*, 11, 1–13.

Guller, I. (1972). Higher education and policemen: Attitudinal differences between freshman and senior police college students. *The Journal of Criminal Law, Criminology and Police Science*, 63(3), 396–401.

Hays, K., Regoli, R. and Hewitt, J. (2007). Police chiefs, anomia and leadership. *Police Quarterly*, 10(1), 3–22.

Heslop, R. (2011). Reproducing police culture in a British university. *Police Practice and Research*, 12(4), 298–312.

Holland, B. (2007). The view from within. In Rowe, M. (Ed.), *Policing beyond MacPherson.* Cullompton: Willan, pp. 137–159.

Hough, M., Jackson, J., Bradford, B., Myhill, A. and Quinton, P. (2010). Procedural justice, trust and institutional legitimacy. *Policing: A Journal of Policy and Practice*, 4(3), 203–210.

Ivkovic, S. (2008). A comparative study of public support for the police. *International Criminal Justice Review*, 18(4), 406–434.

Jaschke, H. (2010). Knowledge-led policing and security. *Policing: A Journal of Policy and Practice*, 4(3), 302–309.

Jaschke, H. and Neidhart, K. (2007). A modern police science as an integrated academic discipline. *Policing and Society*, 17(4), 303–320.

Khan, M.Z. and Unnithan, N. (2008). Criminological and criminal justice education in India: A comparative note. *Journal of Criminal Justice Education*, 19(1), 97–109.

Lee, M. and Punch, M. (2004). Policing by degrees: Police officers' experience of university education. *Policing & Society*, 14(3), 233–249.

Lino, P. (2004). Police education and training in a global society: A Brazilian overview. *Police Practice and Research: An International Journal*, 5(2), 125–136.

Mahony, D. and Prenzler, T. (1996). Police studies, the university and the police service: An Australian study. *Journal of Criminal Justice Education*, 7(2), 283–304.

Manning, P. (2005). The study of policing. *Police Quarterly*, 8(1), 23–43.

Marenin, O. (2004). Police training for democracy. *Police Practice and Research: An International Journal*, 5(2), 107–123.

Marenin, O. (2005). Building a global police studies community. *Police Quarterly*, 8(1), 99–136.

Owen, S. (2005). The death of academic criminal justice. *ACJS Today*, 30(3), 10–12.

Owen, S. and Wagner, K. (2008). The specter of authoritarianism among criminal justice majors. *Journal of Criminal Justice Education*, 19(1), 30–53.

Pagon, M., Virjent-Novak, B., Djuric, M. and Lobnikar, B. (1996). *European systems of police education and training*. http://www.ncjrs.gov/policing/eur551.htm. Accessed May 30, 2014.

Palmiotto, M.J., Birzer, M.L. and Unnithan, N.P. (2000). Training in community policing: A suggested curriculum. *Policing: An International Journal of Police Strategies and Management*, 23(1), 8–21.

Paoline, E. and Terrill, W. (2007). Police education, experience and the use of force. *Criminal Justice and Behavior*, 34, 179–196.

Parker, L., Donnelly, M., Gerwitz, D., Marcus, J. and Kowalewski, V. (1976). Higher education: Its impact on police attitudes. *The Police Chief*, 43(7), 33–35.

Paterson, C. (2011). Adding value? A review of the international literature on the role of higher education in police training and education. *Police Practice and Research*, 12(4), 286–297.

Paterson, C. and Pollock, E. (2011). *Policing and criminology*. London: Sage.

Paterson, C. and Pollock, E. (2013). Developments in police education in England and Wales. In Cowburn, M., Duggan, M., Robinson, A. and Senior, P. (Eds.), *Values in criminology and criminal justice*. Bristol: Policy Press.

Peace, R. (2006). Probationer training for neighborhood policing in England and Wales. *Policing: An International Journal of Police Strategies and Management*, 29(2), 335–346.

Peeters, H. (2010). *Constructing comparative competency profiles*. Paper presented at the Inaugural Conference of the Higher Education Forum for Learning and Development in Policing, Preston, England.

Regoli, R.M. (1976). The effects of college education on the maintenance of police cynicism. *Journal of Police Science and Administration*, 4, 340–345.

Roberg, R. (1978). An analysis of the relationships among higher education, belief systems, and job performance of patrol officers. *Journal of Police Science and Administration*, 6, 336–344.

Roberg, R. and Bonn, S. (2004). Higher education and policing: Where are we now? *Policing: An International Journal of Police Strategies and Management*, 27(4), 469–486.

Schein, E. (1996). Culture: The missing concept in organization studies. *Administrative Science Quarterly*, 41(2), 229–240.

Scott, J., Evans, D. and Verma, A. (2009). Does higher education affect perceptions among police personnel: A response from India. *Journal of Contemporary Criminal Justice*, 25(2), 214–236.

Sherman, L. (1978). *The quality of police education: A critical review with recommendations for improving programs in higher education*. San Francisco, CA: Jossey-Bass.

Sherman, L. (2011). Professional policing and liberal democracy. *2011 Benjamin Franklin Medal Lecture*. http://www.crim.cam.ac.uk/research/experiments/franklinfinal2011.pdf. Accessed June 6, 2014.

Telep, C. (2011). The impact of higher education on police officer attitudes toward abuse of authority. *Police Practice and Research*, 22(3), 392–419.

Veic, P. and Mraovic, I. (2004). Police training and education: The Croatian perspective. *Police Practice and Research: An International Journal*, 5(2), 137–148.

Verma, A. (2005). *The Indian police: A critical evaluation*. New Delhi: Regency Publications.

Waddington, P.A.J. (1994). *Liberty and order: Public order policing in a capital city*. London: UCL Press.

White, D. and Heslop, R. (2012). Educating, legitimizing or accessorizing? Alternative conceptions of professional training in UK higher education. *Police Practice and Research*, 13(4), 342–356.

Williams, E.J. and Robinson, M. (2004). Ideology and criminal justice: Suggestions for a pedagogical model. *Journal of Criminal Justice Education*, 15, 373–392.

Wimhurst, K. and Ransley, J. (2007). Police education and the university sector: Contrasting models from the Austrian experience. *Journal of Criminal Justice Education*, 18(1), 106–122.

Justice Agencies
Academic Collaboration in Experiential Education

8

PETER C. KRATCOSKI
Kent State University
Kent, OH, USA

MAXIMILIAN EDELBACHER
Austrian Federal Police
Retired Security Advisor for ACUN
Vienna, Austria

JOHN A. ETERNO
Molloy College
Rockville Centre, New York

Contents

Introduction

The Association for Experiential Education (2014, 1) defines experiential education as "a philosophy and methodology in which educators purposefully engage with learners in direct experience and focused reflection in order to increase knowledge, develop skills, and clarify values." In Office of Experiential Education and Civic Engagement: Experiential Education Student Interest Form, experiential learning is defined as "engaged learning in which the learner experiences a visceral connection to the subject matter and combines direct, meaningful student experiences with guided reflection and analysis (Learn and Serve: America's National Service-Learning Clearinghouse)." This distinction between experiential education and experiential learning may be splitting hairs, but experiential learning focuses on the learning process of the individual while experiential education refers to much a broader concept, that is, the methods used in facilitating the experiential learning of the individual.[*] For example, a student can learn about the criminal justice system by being arrested, processed through the court, sentenced, and by being sent to prison. However, the same student can also learn about the criminal justice system by participating in a class in which students are given an opportunity to observe, or even participate in, the criminal justice process, as well as having an opportunity to reflect on the processing of individuals through the system. For example, a sociology–criminal justice course taught by the author required the students to spend an evening on patrol with police officers, observe court hearings, visit prisons, and even to spend one night in jail.[†] Obviously, the experience of the person who was processed through the system as a defendant is more profound and meaningful than that of the students who receive their information through observation and questioning of the participants in the process, while the experiential education experience provides opportunities for a more structured, focused, goal-oriented learning experience.

Experiential Learning Model

Kolb (1984) notes that obtaining knowledge on any subject matter is a continuous process. It can be obtained from many sources such as formal education or the mass media, as well as through personal experiences. Although formal (academic) learning and experiential learning are not separate entities, formal learning of a subject does not require direct experience. Formal learning

---

[*] Experiential Learning, Wikipedia accesses http://en.org/wiki/Experiential_learning Accessed March, 25, 2014.
[†] Kratcoski, Workshop Inside the Criminal Justice System Kent State University, 1975–1980.

tends to be more abstract and is provided through the typical classroom learning methods, such as lectures, discussions, examinations, and audio-visual aids. This is not to say that experiential learning cannot be achieved in the typical classroom setting. Efforts to approximate the real world in an artificial structure are often used by instructors in the social sciences through experiments, scenarios, demonstrations, role-playing, featured speakers, and other methods. Perhaps one of the better known experiments is the Zimbardo Prison Experiment (1971) in which a prison was constructed in the psychology building and students who volunteered for the experiment were randomly selected to take the roles of either guards or inmates.

Kolb's experiential learning model begins with the person engaging in active experimentation. This requires participation in concrete experiences, reflective observation, and abstract conceptualization. The knowledge obtained is then used as the basis for more active experimentation. For the learning experience to be fruitful, that is, for the learner to understand and retain the new knowledge.

- The learner must be willing to be actively involved in the experience.
- The learner must be able to reflect on the experience.
- The learner must possess and use analytical skills to conceptualize the experience.
- The learner must possess decision making and problem solving skills in order to use the new ideas gained from the experience.*

Experiential Learning in Criminology Justice

Some of the best known experiential education experiences in the United States were designed by sociologists. The sociology department at the University of Chicago is famous in this regard. For example, Thrasher's book, *The Gang* (1927), was the result of Thrasher's participation in gangs in Chicago while he was collecting data for his doctoral dissertation. Whyte wrote *Street Corner Society* (1955) after he had spent some time interacting with a gang in Boston. Many other examples can be given to illustrate the usefulness of experiential education. Kirkham (1975), a Florida State University professor, took a position as a Jacksonville police officer in order to obtain an experiential learning experience on police work. Murton (Murton and Hyams 1969), former superintendent of the Arkansas prison system, went into a prison impersonating an inmate in order to gain insight into inmate life and to be in apposition to discover the sources of corruption in that prison system.

---

* Experiential Learning, Wikipedia, 2.

The methodology textbooks may refer to the examples given here as one form of the participant–observation data collection technique.

The Law Enforcement Assistance Administration (LEAA), signed into law in 1967, provided major funding and served as a stimulant for colleges and universities to develop experiential education programs. Grants were available for co-op programs, internships, and for sponsoring workshops and symposiums for students enrolled in criminal justice degree programs as well as for police officers pursuing additional education or training. For example, during the 1980s, nearly every federal law enforcement agency offered a co-op or internship program for which those selected were paid. With the demise of LEAA, much of the funding disappeared, but most of the federal agencies continue to offer limited numbers of paid cooperative educational experiences or unpaid internships. The majority of the higher education institutions in the United States that offer one or more degrees in criminal justice feature an experiential learning component as either a requirement or as an optional course for receiving the degree.

Cooperative Educational Experiences and Internships in Criminal Justice

Cooperative education can take on many meanings, but for the purposes of this chapter it refers to a method for providing educational experiences in which classroom instruction is combined with a paid "on-the-job work" experience pertaining to the subject matter of the student's major. Several models are followed (Grubb and Villeneuve 1995) in the co-op programs established by agreements reached by higher education institutions and justice agencies in the United States. One model specifies that students who have completed a required portion of their degree program alternate completing a semester attending classes with a semester in the co-op program. Generally, on graduation, assuming the student's work has been satisfactory, the student is either offered a position with the agency or, if positions are not available, put on a waiting list. Another model has the student attending classes for part of a day and working at the co-op agency site for part of the day. Both of these models have strengths and limitations. For example, for the student who alternates semesters, the student is open to work at a site away from the educational institution for an entire semester and also can use the knowledge obtained during the co-op experience as a basis for developing a broader in-depth understanding of the subject matter after returning to the class room. On the negative side, the in-class semester/out-of-class co-op rotation may present a problem for students who have to find new living quarters each time they change positions, and the structuring may interfere with the normal progression toward their degrees. Another model requires the student to devote part of the day to attending classes and part of the day to working at the co-op site. This approach causes the least interference with the student's personal life and educational program. However, co-op positions may not be available in the city or state where the student lives. This is especially true for co-ops offered by federal justice agencies. Unless the student is willing to move to the site, such a co-op is not an option. Another type of co-op is a variation of the first model in which the student devotes only one semester to the co-op agency. Normally, students selected for this model will be in their senior year of study and thus will be eligible for employment immediately or soon after the completion of the co-op program. This third option is the model most often followed by federal and state justice agencies. Because the availability of co-op positions is quite limited, the one-semester co-op plan opens up more opportunities for new students.

Many universities in the United States that offer degrees in criminal justice emphasize the opportunities for students to participate in co-ops and internships in their brochures. For example, Northeastern University (2014, 1) claims to be "ranked # 1 in the nation for programs that combine classroom learning with real-world experience." John Jay College of Criminal Justice (The City University of New York Cooperative Education Cooperative Education:2) has established co-op arrangements with numerous federal and state justice agencies, including the Federal Bureau of Investigation (FBI), Secret Service, Drug Enforcement Administration, and the U.S. Marshals Service.

Internships

It is highly probable that a university in the Unites States that offers one or more degrees in criminal justice or a closely related field of study, such as paralegal studies, pre-law, or criminology, will offer an internship course as part of the program curriculum. The internship course may be a required course or an elective, and the number of credit hours received for completing the course may vary depending on the number of field hours completed. As with co-ops, some students are paid for their work; but in the majority of cases, the students are not paid. Generally, one or several professors will serve as internship coordinators. As with the cooperative educational program, the main objective of the internship is to provide an opportunity for the student to combine and integrate a practical educational experience with the academic in-class educational experience. For example, the objectives of the Justice Studies Internship Program at Kent State University are stated as:

- To expose the student to a holistic experience in a criminal justice agency to help the student develop an understanding of its philosophy, its relationship to its clients, and to the justice process, and its relationship to the immediate community

- To assist the student in developing the self-awareness, self-confidence, and self-discipline needed to undertake a professional role in a justice or closely related agency
- To familiarize the student with the specific skills needed in the day-to-day functioning of workers in the criminal justice field
- To assist students in developing career goals (Kratcoski 2014, 2)

There are two internship programs offered in the justice studies program at Kent State. One prepares students for positions in law enforcement, juvenile and adult corrections, law, court-related positions, and positions with agencies focusing on service, such as victim assistance and counseling. The second internship is a required course for students completing the paralegal degree (see Nasheri and Kratcoski 1996).

There are a few major differences between an internship and a co-op. First, the internship experience is generally completed during one semester. With the co-op, the students has an opportunity to devote the entire semester to the internship and not take any in-class courses during that semester, or the student can devote some of the time to the internship and also take classes. There are several factors that may determine which plan for completing the internship is followed, including the distance of the placement agency from the university, conditions for placement established by the agency, and the student's personal responsibilities. These factors are all considered when the intern coordinator, the supervisor of the placement agency, and the student communicate on the potential placement. A second major difference between internships and co-ops is the joint responsibility the academic supervisor of the internship and the agency supervisor of the internship have over the student throughout the entire internship. The internship supervisor will generally make one or several field visits during the course of the student's field placement to assure that the objectives of the internship experience are being met. Before the students begin the internships, they are instructed on the academic requirements for the course. The agency field supervisors are also informed of the academic requirements, and it is the joint responsibility of the academic and field supervisors to guide the students toward successfully completing both the academic and experiential learning objectives. Dinerstein (2008, 2), commenting on the legal internship program offered by Washington College of Law, American University, uses the concept "external programs" to refer to "the placement of law students who perform their legal field work under the supervision of a lawyer in practice who is not a full-time legal educator."

Kent State University has provided opportunities for students enrolled in undergraduate and graduate degree programs in sociology and justice studies to participate in co-op and intern programs since the 1960s. During these years, hundreds of students were placed with federal, state, and local justice agencies. A number of students interned in foreign countries, including those placed with U.S. agencies such as the Bureau of Diplomatic Security, the U.S. Department of State, and the American Embassy in Romania. Others were placed with law enforcement and corrections agencies of other countries, including those of the United Kingdom and Mexico. A number of these students who completed internships advanced to high level positions, such as police chiefs, superintendents and wardens of correctional facilities, court administrators, attorneys, judges, and educators. Although one cannot imply that the former Kent students' internship experiences were the sole factor, or even the major factor, contributing to their success, feedback from former students supports the claim that their internship experiences were powerful factors in helping to determine career goals and in opening up the opportunities to pursue such goals.

Service Learning in Criminal Justice Higher Education

Jacoby, B. and Associates (1996, 1) states, "Service-learning is a form of experiential education in which students engage in activities that address human and community needs together with structured opportunities for reflection designed to achieve desired learning outcomes." Service learning is similar to cooperative education, internships, and volunteer work, but there are also distinct differences. The distinctions are clearly spelled out in a publication, by the Colorado State University (2014). The document states that service-learning practitioners should emphasize a number of objectives when setting up in-service programs for students. Several of these objectives include:

- The experience of the student in providing service activities in the community should be applicable to the student's personal and academic development.
- There should be a balance between the service goals and the learning goals of the student.
- Service-learning academic courses are linked to community needs and are developed in cooperation with the community agencies receiving the service.
- The course/s used to prepare students for community service learning involve/s class room instruction before and during the time they are placed in the service program.

Before placement instruction involves teaching the students the terminology, theory, policies, and procedures for the activities in which they will be involved. During the course of the service-learning placement and after the experience has ended, students should have opportunities to meet in a classroom setting and discuss their experience and how they relate to their specific goals (Colorado State University 2014, 1, 2).

University Year in Action, Juvenile Justice Assistants Program, and Justice Volunteer Center

Several service-learning programs developed in the Kent State University departments of sociology and criminal justice directed by Peter C. Kratcoski include the University Year for Action, the Juvenile Justice Assistants Program, and the Justice Volunteer Center. These programs were initially funded through federal or state grants. The Justice Volunteer Center continued to be funded through the university until the retirement of the director.

The University Year for Action Program typified the service-learning approach. Candidates interested in the program were screened and interviewed by the director. The large majority of the students selected were majoring in sociology, psychology, social work, or criminal justice. The students selected for the program had to commit to three consecutive quarters of service learning. They enrolled in special topic courses designed for the program and were paid a stipend for their service. The students were placed with a variety of public and private agencies, including social work agencies, community organization programs for ex-offenders, delinquency prevention and diversion programs, halfway houses, probation departments, and with the courts. An attempt was made to place the students with agencies that would provide the best experience and preparation for obtaining their career goals. The initial training for placement was provided by University Year for Action staff, and in-service training was provided by the agency staff before the students assumed their service-learning positions. Generally, the students were expected to perform many of the same tasks as regular employees, with their work very closely monitored. As with many federally funded programs, the University Year for Action Program was discontinued once the federal grant funds were exhausted. (The program was funded for five years.) However, the director was able to maintain the basic structure of the program after new federal and state funding was acquired.

The Juvenile Justice Assistants Program (Kratcoski 1993) was developed under a grant from the Governor's Office of Criminal Justice Services in Ohio in 1990. Kent State University collaborated with 25 juvenile justice agencies located in eleven northeastern Ohio counties to operate the program. Qualified students were given the opportunity to participate and assist in the day-to-day functioning of a juvenile justice or victim service agency. The applicants were interviewed by agency staff to determine their education, prior experiences, interests, and career goals, so that those selected for the program were matched with the appropriate agencies. The students were given academic credit for their work. They did not receive payment for their work, but they were reimbursed for travel and other related expenses. Students selected for the program attended an initial training seminar prior to placement, and in-service training was provided by the agencies throughout the student's time of placement with the agencies. The students were required to commit to a minimum of 200 hours of training and community service.

The Justice Volunteer Center (1995) was created after the funds from other grants were depleted. The university administration provided funds to cover the costs of maintaining an office, supplies, and travel expenses for the director. The director did not receive a salary from the funds provided by the university but was compensated by a reduction in his teaching load. Compared to the Juvenile Justice Assistants Program, the geographical area covered by the Justice Volunteer Program was considerably smaller. For example, the juvenile justice assistants were placed in eleven counties, but justice volunteers were placed in a few of the counties surrounding the university. However, the scope of the Justice Volunteer Center was broader, and volunteers were placed in a wide variety of justice and victim service agencies, including policing, the courts, both juvenile and adult community corrections programs, and institutional correctional facilities. The students were not given stipends but, as with the juvenile justice assistants, they did receive academic credits for their volunteer service if they enrolled in the appropriate course and completed the required academic assignments. The Justice Volunteer Center is still a functioning program at Kent State. However, the large majority of students in the justice studies degree program wanting to obtain some form of experiential experience select the internship avenue rather than the service-learning experience offered through the Justice Volunteer Center.

Workshops, Practicums, Field Trips, Guest Speakers, and Team Teaching

Instructors of criminal justice and law-related subjects have used a variety of methods to provide experiential learning experiences to their students. The use of guest speakers is the most popular and is easy to arrange. Typically, the speaker will come in for a presentation for one class. Depending on the subject matter of the course, speakers have included police officers, probation and parole officers, judges, victim assistance advocates, prison administrators, and criminal offenders. Generally, the speaker will have visual aids and often puts on some type of demonstration, such as presenting the steps in a criminal investigation, demonstrating the use of a robot, and even bringing a dog used for detecting drugs or missing persons. A portion of the class period is used for questions. The students tend to be very satisfied with the presentations of these speakers, indicating that their input led to a better understanding of the subject matter.

The workshop provides an opportunity for students to leave the classroom and learn about the subject matter in the same settings that the practitioner performs. A workshop, by definition, involves providing opportunity to combine learning experiences obtained in the formal classroom experiential setting with learning experiences obtained through more direct, "hands-on" experiences.

Several workshops offered at Kent State in the past or presently can be used to illustrate the structure and process of the workshop course. A course offered by Peter Kratcoski was titled Inside the Criminal Justice System. This course, offered in the summer, was funded through an LEAA grant. The course was open to undergraduate and graduate students in sociology, political science, and criminal justice. Students were required to pay tuition for the course, but no extra fees were required because the costs of travel, meals, and accommodations were provided by the grants. The course was structured in the following manner:

- The first two weeks of the course were conducted in a classroom and were devoted to explaining and discussing the components of the criminal justice system.
- During the third week, Thursday and Friday were devoted to field experiences related to police work. Students visited local police stations, heard police officers explain their duties, and discussed issues relating to the police. On Friday evening, half of the class rode with police officers on patrol for the entire shift and the other half of the class rode with the police on Saturday evening.
- The fourth week was devoted to the judicial component of the justice system. On Thursday and Friday, students visited several courts, including municipal courts, common pleas, and juvenile courts. The students had an opportunity to interact with various practitioners, including judges, administrators, prosecutors, public defenders probation officers, and others who performed special functions. On Friday evening, the students were booked and required to spend the entire night in a city jail.
- The fifth week was devoted to the correctional component of the justice system. On Thursday and Friday, the students toured several state juvenile correctional facilities, including a minimum security facility, a maximum security facility, a facility for girls, and a facility for delinquents with mental health problems. On Friday, the entire day was devoted to touring correctional facilities housing adult criminals, again focusing on several categories of institutions—such as a classification center, a prison camp, a reformatory, a maximum security facility, and a facility for the mentally ill. Because many of the juvenile and adult correctional institutions in Ohio

are geographically close to each other, the travel time between institutions was not extensive, and rather than traveling back to the university at the close of Thursday, the class drove to the location of the first correctional facility on the list to be visited and spent the night in a nearby motel.

- The agenda for the sixth week was structured around touring federal correctional facilities. This necessitated traveling to West Virginia and Kentucky. Opportunities for interaction with the correctional staff as well as inmates enhanced the learning experience. In addition, the students were given the opportunity to purchase their lunches at the facility.

- The final week of the workshop was conducted back in the class-room. At this time, the students were given an opportunity to reflect on their experiences and to discuss how the experiential portion of the course connected with the academic portion of the course.

The students were required to write a short paper on their learning experiences for each week class was conducted in the field.

Mock Trial Competition

The intercollegiate mock trials held each year offer an opportunity for those students pursuing a career in law and law-related areas to engage in an experiential education experience. The American Mock Trial Association serves as the governing body for 25 regional tournaments, eight opening round championships tournaments, and a national tournament each year. Mock trial teams from 350 colleges and universities located in states throughout the country participate in the mock trial competitions each year. More than 5000 undergraduate students participate in the competitions each year (History: American Mock Trial Association 2014, 1). The competition is a good example of how formal classroom learning experiences can be integrated with out-of-class learning experiences.

Although the mock trial tournaments are held during February and March, the students' preparation for the competition begins early in the fall semester. Generally, the mock trial competition is integrated into one or more academic courses offered at the educational institution. For example, Kent State uses an upper division political science course titled Practicum in Trial Preparation. The students enrolled in the course are provided with materials pertaining to concepts, process, and procedures pertaining to pre-trials and trials, and they must demonstrate a comprehension of the material before any preparation of the case is commenced.

The intercollegiate competition process includes:

- A representative of the educational institution registers the team/s representing the institution.
- AMTA provides the standardized case (either criminal or civil) to the educational institution.
- Mock trial coaches and students study the case and prepare strategies.
- Team members are selected for either attorney or witness roles to prepare for either the prosecution or defense team.
- The team competes at a regional tournament. If the team advances, it will next compete at a national level competition.

Although the mock trial competition specifically focuses on the trial process, the students who enroll in the course and take part in the competition are given a much broader exposure to the entire criminal and civil justice systems. Information pertaining to constitutional law, civil rights, police procedures, evidence, objections, court cases, and lay and expert witnesses must be learned and used by the students as they play their roles during the trial.

Workshops Focusing on Comparisons of Criminal Justice Systems

Cordner and Shain (2011, 281) note that during the twenty-first century it is most probable that the education and training of police officers around the world will become more focused on the global matters pertaining to crime and on ways to prevent and control crime. This international focus has already been manifested in the number of international cooperative training and educational programs for police that have been developed in various parts of the world. According to Cordner and Shain (2011, 281), "In the international arena, police training has been used to upgrade technical police skills and as a vehicle to help export community policing, human rights, rule of law, and democratization in developing and post-Soviet nations."

We are beginning to see a similar shift in emphasis in higher education degree programs in criminal justice programs in the United States. Many degree programs offer one or several courses in comparative justice and in international crime and crime control. In addition, in many universities, criminal justice students have opportunities to study aboard or to travel abroad and take part in experiential learning experiences such as workshops.

Edelbacher (2009, 122) proposes a three-step process for teaching the theoretical and practical aspects of police work. The first step involves teaching legal framework, rule of law, and the field of expertise, always using specific examples to illustrate the material. The second step involves having the students break into work groups in which they plan strategies and engage in role-playing scenarios with some of the students playing the roles of police officers and others playing the roles of criminals. The third step is teaching the issues of practical police work, using examples of failures in past cases to illustrate what to avoid. Lehmann (2009, 43–45), a practitioner working with the United Nations Information Service (UNIS), notes that, when teaching of students who have an interest in international relations, she uses a variety of teaching tools beyond the traditional methods to provide the students with an experiential learning experience. She uses examples drawn from her own experiences and holds "mock press conferences" in which students take on the roles of journalists and the roles of "real-life spokespeople and their assistants." In addition, students write and present position papers on critical issues being discussed by the United Nations such as the UN International Criminal Tribunals. She also has speakers from the United Nations address the class on international matters being considered by the United Nations. Peintinger (2009) notes that teaching delinquents who are incarcerated in a youth prison helped broaden her knowledge of the laws and processes of the juvenile justice system.

There are many examples of international experiential educational programs in which the subject matter focuses on crime and on justice programs to illustrate how such programs function. A workshop course that the author developed with another Kent State professor was titled Comparing the Criminal Justice System of the United States with the Canadian Criminal Justice System. The workshop course was structured in a manner similar to the workshop, Inside the Criminal Justice System, described earlier in this chapter, with the exception that the students were required to pay a fee to cover the expenses connected with the course. Those enrolled in this course were junior and senior level students majoring in sociology and criminal justice and students enrolled in the criminal justice master's degree program. The students were required to attend several class sessions at the university during the first week of the course to review the U.S. criminal justice system, and during the weekend they traveled to Toronto, Canada. The entire following week was devoted to observing, listening to talks by criminal justice practitioners and law professors, touring police stations, riding with the police, and touring juvenile and adult correctional facilities. Each student was required to write a paper that focused on the similarities and differences in the U.S. and Canadian criminal justice systems.

Another internationally focused workshop that was taught at Kent State was titled International Prevention and Control of Crime. This course was rather unique, in that it was team taught. One of the instructors was a police practitioner serving as head of the major crimes bureau in Vienna, Austria, and the other was a Kent State professor of justice studies. Although the majority of the classes were conducted in a classroom setting, several techniques were used, including videos, guest speakers, and field trips, to demonstrate the differences in the legal and justice systems of the United States and those of most European countries, as well as to illustrate the numerous ways the countries of the world utilize the services of such international crime prevention organizations such as INTERPOL and the United Nations in their attempts to prevent and control international crime.

International Education in Criminal Justice: Case Exemplar, Molloy College

International experiential education is flourishing, relevant, and important. Future practitioners in the field of criminal justice in particular need to be exposed to a variety of cultures and languages. In modern democratic societies, justice practitioners need to be tolerant, understanding, and have the knowledge necessary to deal with people of many cultures. Students in criminal justice must not be ethnocentric. They must be open to different ideas that will improve the way they enforce the law.

Stereotyping by law enforcement officers is for the most part dangerous to democratic society. This can occur due to the influence of the police culture (Crank 2004; Manning 1977; Reuss-Ianni 1983) and/or management's influence (Eterno and Silverman 2010, 2012). When officers stereotype by categorizing an entire group of people through practices such as racial profiling, it can be disastrous and lead to racial/ethnic tension (*Floyd v. City of New York* 2013). Some examples of departments in the United States that were or are under consent decree for their racial/ethnic behaviors include the Baltimore Police, Los Angeles Police, the Maryland State Police, New Jersey State Troopers, New Orleans Police, and the Pittsburgh Police.

In this chapter, we use the international experiences of students in the criminal justice program at Molloy College as one example of learning about other cultures. Molloy College is a private institution for higher education located in Long Island, New York. It has approximately 4400 students with a little over 1000 of them being graduate students. Molloy College began international education in the 1990s. Nearly all of the college programs offer some opportunity to travel abroad. The college does offer some tuition reimbursement to students who take global courses, making the international educational experience more affordable. Global study is an integral part of the college's mission (Molloy College 2014). The mission statement (Molloy College 2014, 10) emphasizes the following:

> Molloy College, an independent, Catholic college rooted in the Dominican tradition of study, spirituality, service, and community, is committed to academic excellence with respect for each person. Through transformative education, Molloy promotes a lifelong search for truth and the development of ethical leadership.

The sentence in the mission statement pertaining to Molloy College being "… committed to academic excellence with respect for each person …" is particularly relevant. As Kathy Reba, Director, International Education writes, "Studying abroad is really a life-changing event, as well as a resume builder. Students who take advantage of our global-learning programs graduate from Molloy more aware of the world that we share—and more than ready to take their place in it" (Molloy College 2014, 2). The quest for truth in Molloy's mission statement also furthers these ideas. Expanding beyond one's own culture to more fully experience the world in which we live will ultimately better establish an understanding of truth and respect for various viewpoints.

Since Molloy launched the global-learning program about a decade ago, thousands of students have worked toward their degrees while spending time overseas. In fact, every one of the school's curricula offers students an opportunity to study abroad. There are a wide variety of programs available. Some are as short as eight days to fourteen days; others cover an entire semester or year (Molloy College 2014, 2).

In Molloy's Department of Criminal Justice, global experiences have generally been part of a larger trip overseas with approximately 50 students from various majors. The activity is conducted over the short term—usually about 10 days abroad. Criminal justice students enroll in a course entitled Cross Cultural Perspectives in Criminal Justice. The description reads:

> The criminal justice system in each country is informed by and responsive to a unique set of cultural imperatives. This course will introduce the student to the variety of criminal justice systems operating in advanced industrial democracies, totalitarian regimes, and developing countries. It will examine indigenous and imposed concepts of law and justice, the rights of the accused, general rules of procedure, and methods of punishment and rehabilitation in a cross-cultural perspective. (Molloy College Undergraduate Course Catalog 2013, 255)

In conjunction with the international education office, the criminal justice professor selects an overseas destination. The destination must fit with the goals of the class. Students need to be exposed to a locale that coincides with the range of countries that are being discussed that semester. Generally, every continent is covered. A recent text used in the class includes the following places: Austria, the Netherlands, Britain, Canada, Hong Kong, Ghana, Lesotho, Tanzania, Zambia, Argentina, Finland, Australia, and South Africa (Das and Jiao 2005).

Once a location for the trip is selected, the trip itself is carefully choreographed so that the time overseas is well spent. Although there are a variety of overseas programs including spending a semester abroad, the program that is most popular among the students and faculty alike spends spring break or some other short period of time abroad. During this time, the students and the professor spend about 10 to 14 days immersed in the foreign environment.

The international education office supplies guidance and assistance for the trips. They will provide transportation, lodging, and itinerary, and they will sometimes find pertinent side trips. Further, all professors who attend international trips are properly trained by the office in handling situations overseas and in being a responsible leader for the students. This involves workshops and interacting with seasoned professors. In fact, a seasoned professor is always designated as a leader for each trip. Generally, four professors or more will go on the trip with about 40 students. At least one male and one female chaperone are required as well. This is necessary in case something happens that requires the same gender chaperone to assist the student.

The key to making a truly focused criminal justice experience for the students is the professor of the course. The professor needs to be knowledgeable about the locale to be visited. It is also helpful if the professor has contacts in the countries where travel will take place. To that end, international organizations are very important. In this case, the criminal justice department is an institutional supporter of the International Police Executive Symposium (IPES). This is a registered not-for-profit educational institution. Their stated purpose is:

> The International Police Executive Symposium (IPES) brings police researchers and practitioners together to facilitate cross-cultural, international, and interdisciplinary exchanges for the enrichment of the policing profession. It encourages discussions and writing on challenging topics of contemporary importance through an array of initiatives including conferences and publications. (IPES 2014, 1)

At least two full-time professors from Molloy are involved in IPES. One has been extensively involved and has gone to at least four of its international meetings. At these meetings, numerous contacts are made with international researchers and practitioners. The professor was also managing editor for IPES's peer reviewed journal *Police Practice and Research: An International Journal*. As such, he has made contacts throughout the world. These contacts are an indispensable part of the global experience. The contacts act as liaisons with the country being visited, ensuring that the experience will be rewarding and pertinent to criminal justice students.

Two recent trips are excellent examples: (1) the Republic of Ireland and Northern Ireland from March 13–21, 2009, and (2) Austria and the Czech Republic, March 11–19, 2011.

The Ireland Experience

The trip to Ireland included both the Republic of Ireland to the south and Northern Ireland, a part of the United Kingdom. Everyone received a day-by-day itinerary. Before the trip, the professor contacted key personnel in Ireland who were in a position to assist with arranging pertinent events for the students in both the Republic of Ireland and Northern Ireland. For this trip, the local contact was Gwen Boniface. She was a former commissioner for the Ontario Provincial Police of Canada and the first female to hold that position. At the time of the trip, she was appointed by the Irish government as a Deputy Chief Inspector–Garda Siochana Inspectorate Republic of Ireland (2006–2009). In this position, she was an advisor to their police (An Garda Siochana) and their correctional services (*Ontario Press* 2006).

During the semester, various criminal justice systems and methods were discussed. As the departure neared for the trip to the United Kingdom and Ireland, the materials presented were more specifically focused on basic information that students needed for understanding policing in Ireland. The basic facts given to them before the trip cannot be repeated here. However, Deputy Chief Inspector Boniface supplied some materials, so that before they arrived the students had a good foundation of information about policing in the two countries they were visiting.

The professor was in direct communication (phone and e-mail) with the deputy chief inspector. As liaison to the college, she set up two key side trips for the criminal justice students. The first was in Dublin where they visited their historic Kevin Street station house. There, the commanding officer gave the students a personal tour. They went through the entire station and learned of its fantastic history. (For example, it was the residence of the Archbishop of Dublin when it was built at the end of the twelfth century.) The commander also explained how the police do their job in Dublin. Students found out that uniformed officers do not carry weapons, but plainclothes officers are armed with guns—among a host of other information they learned about policing in the Irish Republic.

The second excursion for criminal justice students was to the Police Service of Northern Ireland (PSNI). There they visited their memorial gardens and received a lecture on police operations. The memorial gardens are dedicated to those officers who lost their lives in the line of duty. There is a reflection pool of water with the names of the slain officers listed by decade of death. It was particularly revealing of the troubled history of Northern Ireland that the list of names was very long for some decades. The lecture too was very informative. Students were left with the impression that Americans can learn much from the PSNI, especially in the area of understanding and combating terrorism.

In the end, students were able to compare and contrast the two systems. Both were working under very different circumstances. In Dublin, the police were very service oriented and seemed to practice what is commonly termed community policing. Their presence as an unarmed force combined with an ability to maintain order was outstanding. The PSNI was clearly a more typical armed police force. They had obvious concerns with political issues, being part of the United Kingdom. However, their use of community-based strategies and compromise was a lesson for all. The lasting peace in both parts of Ireland is at least partially attributed to the brave men and women in their respective police forces.

The Vienna, Austria, and Prague, Czech Republic, Experiences

A second example of global education was the criminal justice program's trip to Austria and Prague. As was the case in the aforementioned Irish example, comparisons and contrasts can be made for Austria and the Czech Republic. Austria is a well-established democracy, while the Czech Republic is a comparatively new democracy. The Czech Republic was a satellite of the former Soviet Union until the late 1980s. For this trip, contact was made with Maximillian Edelbacher, a former chief of the Major Crime Bureau of the Austrian Federal Police (AFP). He worked with the AFP from 1972 to 2006.

For this excursion, the American students were treated to several events including a tour and discussion at Vienna police headquarters, a lecture on legal issues and the European Union at the University of Vienna, a tour and discussion at Prague police headquarters, and a tour of the Czech Police Museum. The trip took place from March 11–19, 2011.

At the Vienna police headquarters, students were allowed entry and escorted to a lecture room. They were given a basic understanding of the AFP. Additionally, they received a guided tour of the communications facilities, including a modern control center that rivals any in the world (see picture). Students were also treated to an in-depth lecture and tour of the University of Vienna. The lecture was given by Assessor Stefan Schumann. He spoke about some of the challenges law enforcement was facing in the new European Union including, but not limited to, extradition of felons who cross the borders into other countries. Since border control between countries no longer exists, extradition has become a major issue. The Molloy students and faculty entered into a discussion, talking about how the United States handles this issue. However, there are key differences because the European Union involves separate countries—not one country with 50 states working under one Constitution.

In Prague, we were also escorted by Jaromir Rada (a member of the International Police Association–a group of police that help other law enforcement personnel with international travel), who coordinated all activities there. He was kind and very informative – helping us with all our travel questions. His guidance made our experience simply outstanding. At Prague police headquarters, the students were given access to the communications center similar to the one in Vienna. Students viewed live CCTV images of the main square and were also shown some taped footage of various police-related events. In Prague, the criminal justice students also visited the Czech Republic Museum of the Police. The exhibits included the history of the police in the Czech Republic as well as some criminological displays. Interestingly, the building itself is located on the premises of a former Augustinian Monastery founded in 1350. Overall, the visits to Prague and Vienna were fascinating.

Reflecting on the International Educational Experience

When they return to the classroom the next week after the trip, students are asked to reflect on their experiences. Under the guidance of the professor, students talk about their expectations and their actual experiences. Students are not only able to compare and contrast the various criminal justice settings observed in various countries but also see similarities and differences between law enforcement in the United States and these other countries. Every student is enriched by the experience. There are no exceptions. For some it is a cultural awakening, for others it is a learning experience that they will never forget.

The law enforcement officers and contacts were very helpful in every country visited. Although differences in styles were noted, there was a commonality among all the officers and guides. In particular, students noted that democratic policing involves respect for visitors and, in general, all human life. Personnel at every one of the agencies visited were very professional. There were differences in rules, laws, weapons, and culture. However, the democratic principles of defending basic human rights were paramount to each and every department visited. Putting a human face to policing is important. Seeing these officers working up front and in their natural element made the experience all the more important. It was clear that every man and woman in law enforcement we observed in these democracies was well trained, polite, and professional. Students recognized this and developed a new appreciation for law enforcement in democratic society as well as a respect for other countries' police agencies and issues. Most importantly, being exposed to other countries helps students appreciate and respect different cultures and law enforcement officers.

References

American Mock Trial Association. (2014). *History of AMTA.* http://www. collegemocktrial.org/about-amta/history-/. Accessed March 29, 2014.

Association for Experiential Education. (2014). Theory and practice of experiential education. http://www.aee.org/theory-and-practice. Accessed June 15, 2014.

Colorado State University. (2014). *Definition of Service-Learning.* http://writing. colostate.edu/guides/teaching/service-learning/definition.cfm. Accessed July 20, 2015.

Cordner, G. and C. Shain. (2011). The changing landscape of police education and training. *Police Practice and Research,* 12(4): 281–285.

Crank, J. (2004). *Understanding police culture.* Waltham, MA: Anderson Publishing.

Das, D. and A. Jiao. 2005. *Public order: A global perspective.* Upper Saddle River, NJ: Pearson Prentice Hall.

Dinerstein, R. (2008). Methods of experiential education: Context, transferability and resources. Paper presented at the International Law Conference on Experiential Education in China: Curricular Reform, the Role of the Lawyer and the Rule of Law, University of the Pacific, McGeorge School of Lae, January 25–26, 2008.

Edelbacher, M. (2009). Critical issues of police work: the importance of practical "learned lessons" in police training. In *Can the United Nations be taught: proceedings of a colloquium on innovative approaches to teaching the U.N. system.* Diplomatic Academy of Vienna, ed., Vienna, Austria: Diplomatic Academy of Vienna, pp. 121–123.

Eterno, J.A. and E.B. Silverman. (2010). Understanding police management: A typology of the underside of compstat. *Professional Issues in Criminal Justice,* 5(2 & 3): 11–28.

Eterno, J.A. and E.B. Silverman. (2012). *The crime numbers game; Management by manipulation.* Boca Raton, FL: CRC Press.

Floyd v. City of New York order on liability. (2013). http://ccrjustice.org/files/Floyd-Liability-Opinion-8-12-13.pdf. Accessed June 16, 2014.

Grubb, N. and J.C. Villeneuve. (1995). *Cooperative education in Cincinnati,* Berkeley, CA: National Center for Research in Vocational Education.

International Police Executive Symposium (IPES). (2014). Mission statement. http:// ipes.info/organization/mission. Accessed June 28, 2014.

Jacoby, B. and Associates (1996). *Service learning in higher education: Concepts and practices.* San Francisco: Jones-Bass, Inc.

Justice Volunteer Center. (1995). Justice volunteer center, Kent State University, Kent web site: Centers. Accessed June 10, 2014.

Kirkham, G. (1975). Doc cop. *Human behavior,* 4: 16–23.

Kolb, D. (1984). *Experiential learning: Experience as the source of learning and development.* Englewood Cliffs, NJ: Prentice-Hall.

Kratcoski, P. (1993) Juvenile Justice Assistants Program. Unpublished paper presented at the Midwest Criminal Justice Association Annual Conference, September 1992, Chicago.

Kratcoski, P. (2014). Rules and procedures manual: Internship in justice. Unpublished Kent State Document.

Lehmann, I. (2009). What can UN practitioners bring to teaching about international organizations? In *Can the United Nations be taught? A compendium of innovative teaching techniques*. Diplomatic Academy of Vienna, ASO Ljubljana, Solvenia: diplomatische akademie wein, pp. 43–45.

Manning, P. (1977). *Police work*. Cambridge, MA: MIT Press.

Molloy College. (2014). http://www.molloy.edu/#. Accessed June 1, 2014.

Molloy College Undergraduate Course Catalog. (2013). Unpublished catalog. Rockville Centre, NY: Molloy College.

Murton, T. and J. Hyams. (1969). *Accomplices to the crime*. New York: Grove Press.

Nasheri, H. and P.C. Kratcoski. (1996). *A guide to a successful legal internship*. Cincinnati, OH: Anderson Publishing.

Northeastern University. (2014). *Experiential Education*. http://www.Northeastern. edu/sccj/experiential-education/. Accessed March 26, 2014.

Ontario Press. (2006). OPP Commissioner Gwen Boniface takes on new role in Ireland. http://news.ontario.ca/archive/en/2006/07/28/OPP-Commissioner-Gwen-Boniface-Takes-On-New-Role-In-Ireland.html. Accessed June 1, 2014.

Peintinger, T. (2009). Active learning: Field work experiences with UN guidelines. *Can the United Nations be taught? A compendium of innovative teaching techniques*. ASO Ljubljana, Solvenia: diplomatische akademie wein, pp. 125–126.

Reuss-Ianni, E. (1983). *Two cultures of policing*. New Brunswick, NJ: Transaction Books.

Thrasher, F. (1927). *The gang*. Chicago, IL: University of Chicago Press.

Whyte, W. (1955). *Street corner society*, 2nd ed. Chicago, IL: University of Chicago Press.

Reflections on Teaching Sociology to Austrian Police Officers

9

GILBERT NORDEN
University of Vienna
Wien, Austria

Contents

Introduction

In addition to my core work in teaching and research at the University of Vienna, as a sociologist concerned with police issues I was also involved in the education and training of police officers in Austria. As such, I lectured at advanced training seminars for department, district, and station commanders of the Gendarmerie (the law enforcement body in rural areas at the time) in Lower Austria. The training seminars, which were held three times a year with 15 participants each, were compulsory for these officers. Each time I spoke at these seminars, the topic of the lecture was "The Tasks of the Police Officer in Modern Society, Conflict Situations from the Sociologist's Perspective and Proposed Solutions." All in all, I presented and discussed this topic on approximately 30 occasions for three hours at a time, as my involvement in the training seminars lasted from 1991 to 2000, spanning a period of 10 years. For twice as long (i.e., for 20 years between 1983 and 2002), I worked as a lecturer at the Education Centre of the Gendarmerie (*Gendarmeriezentralschule*), later the "Security Academy" (*Sicherheitsakademie*, SIAK), first in Mödling, then in Traiskirchen (both of which are in Lower Austria). In my work there, I taught sociology in the basic training courses for commissioned officers (*leitende Beamte*, employment group W1, later E1) in the three law enforcement bodies in Austria at the time—the Gendarmerie previously mentioned, the Security Guards (the uniformed police working in the cities), and the Criminal Investigation Corps.* The basic training courses for these commissioned officers were only open to those who had qualified for entrance to "university"; however, they were also later open to noncommissioned officers (*dienstführende Beamte*, employment group W2, later E2a) without such qualifications. Candidates had to pass an entrance examination and a screening test for psychological prerequisites in order to be admitted to the courses.

The courses lasted for two years for those accepted. From 1989, as the first stage in the development of the Security Academy, the courses initially referred to as "W1 GAL (*Grundausbildungslehrgänge*, basic training courses) were designated as "Security Academy" courses, accompanied by the number of the corresponding year.† For courses that were held in parallel to one another, the numeral "I" or "II" was added alongside the year. In 1992–1993, a special course for district commanders of the Gendarmerie (*Bezirksgendarmeriekommandanten*, BGKdt.) was referred to as "Security Academy/BGKdt." With the exception of this special course, for which only 21 hours of sociology classes were scheduled, I was allocated 30 teaching hours for sociology in each course. In the mid-1990s, I appointed two colleagues from the discipline, Roland Girtler and Ralf Risser, to take on some of the teaching. This initially reduced the hours allocated to me personally to 26 and then to 20. At this time, I was also teaching the basic training courses for noncommissioned police officers (employment group W2 at the time), specifically the sociology of crime. Two hours were allocated for this subject in each course. All in all, I taught 673 hours of sociology classes at the Education Centre of the Gendarmerie and at the Security Academy. A total of more than 700 officers participated in my lessons. In this chapter, I would like to provide an account of my teaching work and some of the experiences I gained in the process. I will discuss the aims and content of the sociology lessons, the status of the subject in the curriculum for the training of commissioned police officers, and the reality of teaching the subject, including all of the positive and negative aspects of the work. I also will present further reflections. The temporal distance from which I can now look back at the occurrences under discussion here is advantageous in certain respects, but it also has its setbacks. The advantage is that I am now less fettered by emotions associated with the subject than I was in the period immediately after I stopped teaching at the Security Academy.

---

* Any unspecific references to the "police" in the following text mean these three law enforcement bodies.
† Further stages in the process of developing and expanding the Security Academy with a view to it becoming the central educational institution for the authority responsible for the police, the Federal Ministry of the Interior (*Bundesministerium für Inneres*), included establishing training courses for senior police officers in 1996 and the opening of the Academy building in Traiskirchen in early 2002. However, its expansion into a "higher education institution for security professions" never came to fruition as had originally been planned. The Academy remained what it had always been—an institution that was directly controlled by and dependent on the Federal Ministry of the Interior.

The disadvantage, of course, is that by this time certain memories of my work have faded somewhat. But this review not only draws upon what I can recall from my work but also the documents and records I collected and have since archived (with the intention of writing a review like this one someday) are also evaluated here. One important purpose of such a review is to help deepen and refine our insight into the present. To this end, this chapter concludes with a brief look at the present state of sociology instruction in the training of commissioned Austrian police officers. This is, however, only a somewhat fleeting glance. It is up to the reader to decide whether a report that only skims the surface of the present situation can still be useful in spite of its far greater emphasis on a portion of the history of the police education system.

Teaching Objectives and Program of Study

Originally, Professor Wolfgang Schulz was invited by the Federal Ministry of the Interior (*Bundesministerium für Inneres*) to develop a sociology program as part of the training of commissioned police officers; however, he delegated this task to me. At that time I was his assistant at the Institute of Sociology at the University of Vienna. This assignment greatly appealed to me because I was very interested in sociological police issues and was developing a major course on "Sociology for Law Students." I developed a program of study entitled "Sociology for Prospective Commissioned Police Officers," which included some ambitious aims and certain statements I would now classify as the kind of language used by a young academic trying to impress in order to gain recognition. Under the aegis of Wolfgang Schulz, this draft program was then presented to the Federal Ministry of the Interior where it was accepted in an appropriately abridged version: an introductory overview of the basic concepts, issues, and methods of sociology and the findings of sociological research. In addition to general sociological topics such as social stratification, social mobility, and social change, this overview would also place an emphasis on topics specifically relevant to the work of police officers. These included:

- Sociology of law: Creation and application of laws and regulations, sociology of legal professions, relationships between the law and social justice, and the effectiveness of law with regard to attitudes and behaviors
- Sociology of crime and deviance: Theories explaining deviant behavior, the development and incidence of criminality, dark and light areas of crime, and the sociological problems of the penal system
- Sociology of organizations/public administration: Organizational models, formal and informal organizations, the phenomenon of bureaucracy, and leadership problems in organizations

- Sociology of police: Police organizations, reasons for choosing the profession of police officer, occupational socialization, the social role of the police officer, interaction problems between officers and the population, working conditions and stress levels among officers, coping mechanisms, selectivity and efficacy of police actions, image of the police in society, and the sense of security among members of the population
- Sociology of disaster: Social conditionality of disasters, factors influencing behavior in disasters, and social consequences of disasters

The teaching hours allocated to these subjects were to be weighted in favor of the sociology of crime and deviance.

The aim of this choice of subject matter, the weighting of the subject areas and the teaching itself was to equip students with a broad knowledge of the current societies and, most importantly, to impart sociological knowledge that would enable prospective commissioned police officers to:

- View the problems arising during the course of their work from a sociological perspective, thus gaining a better understanding of such problems
- Understand that the problematic behavior demonstrated by individuals or groups is shaped by social processes and structures and—as a result of this understanding—to enable officers to deal with such behavior in a less emotional and less prejudiced manner
- Reconsider their own professional behavior from the perspective of the actions of the organization and their professional role
- Read and understand reports on sociological research, to evaluate and utilize the findings of research, and to suggest new research that could be carried out with regard to issues and problems relevant to the police

In addition to lecturing on the subjects of the course, group discussions and group work were to be carried out, individual student presentations were to be given, and role-playing organized. This was intended to facilitate autonomous learning and to provide a more practice-oriented learning process. The overall aim was to prioritize the practical aspects of police work within scientific completeness and systematics.

The Status of Sociology in the Curriculum

Sociology was one of 28 different subjects taught in the basic training courses for commissioned police officers. In this curriculum, a distinction was made between so-called "soft" and "hard" subjects. Thus, subjects with strict assessments of students' learning achievements were referred to as "hard subjects";

this was the case for the legal subjects and police methodology. Sociology, by contrast, was one of the "soft subjects." Together with psychology, pedagogics, rhetoric, politics, Austrian history, economic policy, and a few other subjects, it was regarded as a less important part of police training. This lack of appreciation for the subject was evident from certain students' repeated absences from lessons as well as from the examination system and the grading practices. According to the educational regulations of the Federal Ministry of the Interior (BGBI 1999, 3043), student performance was to be continuously assessed by means of oral or written tests, yet the final grades in the group of subjects to which sociology pertained—along with economic policy—were decided from the outset. AT the request of the directorate of training, all students were to be awarded the grade "excellent, outstanding performance" in this group of subjects (i.e., all students were to be awarded the highest mark in Austria's customary five-tier grading system).* The students were aware of this grading practice from the very beginning, which did not do much to improve sociology's marginal status within the curriculum. It was only when the educational reform of 1998–1999 was introduced that there was any significant change in this marginal status. At that time, the training of commissioned police officers underwent restructuring in a move toward becoming a University of Applied Sciences degree with a duration of three years. Although the original course duration of two years was initially maintained, there were fewer legal subjects, "pedagogical" training was extended, and a new form of service exam (*Dienstprüfung*, general examination) was introduced. In addition to sitting for a board examination, students now had to submit written course work at the end of the basic training course. The coursework was to be assessed by teachers at the Security Academy in order to ascertain "Whether or not the student was able to investigate a research question from his/her chosen subject (or a particular branch of this subject) in a methodologically correct, practice-oriented, and independent manner" (BGBI 1999, 3046, translated). In order to equip students with the skills required for this kind of work, the subject "Introduction to Empirical Social Research and Academic Method" was introduced. In addition to the techniques of research work and academic writing, this class delved into the methods of sociology in considerably greater detail than in previous sociology instruction. Two instructors and, eventually, two staff members from the Institute for the Sociology of Law and Criminology† took over the teaching of this new subject. These colleagues were responsible

---

* Given that more teaching hours were allocated to sociology than to economic policy, the marks in this group of subjects had to be signed by the sociology lecturer, so this was my responsibility.

† The Institute for the Sociology of Law and Criminology in Vienna ("Institut für Rechts- und Kriminalsoziologie," IRKS) has been dedicated to the critical analysis of law and enforcement since its inception in 1973. It is organized as a research institution outside the universities and outside the Federal Ministry of the Interior.

for most of the supervision of coursework, which included providing students with assistance when selecting a research topic (Garnitschnig et al. 1999). Only topics relating to the professional field could be selected and had to be approved by the course principal. As is plainly evident from the titles of the course work, sociological aspects played a part in many of the topics approved. As a result, relevant specialist information, further reading, and "reading aids" for sociological literature were in high demand, as was the students' desire to learn about sociological approaches and gain practical knowledge about sociological methods. This general increase in student interest made teaching a much easier task.

The Reality of Teaching

I would have liked for teaching to have been made easier when I started out because I found the first few years of teaching rather difficult. This was despite the several years of relevant experience I had gained not only working at the university but also at nursing schools. At the latter, sociology was taught through lectures and—just like in police training—did not involve any exams. I therefore assumed myself to be familiar with this form of teaching and thought I knew how the program of study for prospective commissioned police officers could be implemented appropriately. Nevertheless, problems that I had not anticipated started to appear early on when I was preparing to implement the program. For instance, after taking a closer look at the teaching aids I had used earlier in sociology lessons and trying to adapt some of them to police work, I found that they were not really suitable for police training. It is also important to bear in mind that, at this time, there was no sociology textbook similar to that by Frevel et al. (2002), which was developed specially for police officers and entitled, *Sociology: A Textbook for the Police*. There was also no handbook such as *Policing: Key Readings*, which brought together articles on "the core of policing studies" (Newburn 2005). Instead of being able to rely upon publications like these for support, I had to independently find and gather teaching materials that seemed suitable. The Federal Ministry of the Interior assisted me in my quest to find learning resources by subscribing to relevant professional journals such as *Police Studies* and *Disasters* and loaning these to me on a permanent basis.

Although I gradually managed to collect suitable journal articles and other materials to use, I soon learned that I only partly needed them because it was only possible to complete the full program of study in a small number of courses. The program was too densely structured, and I found myself having to sidetrack on too many occasions. Some of the deviations from the lesson program occurred during discussions that led me to go into greater depth on certain subjects and made me "digress" into other areas. Other deviations from the planned program of study were made at the express request of students, who were interested in specific sociological information due to certain events occurring in or outside of class. On one occasion, for instance, crowd riots at a football match on the previous day were the current topic of discussion, and I was asked how such riots could be explained in sociological terms. On yet another occasion, a political event was the hot topic of the day when students were interested in the somewhat surprising result of an election. I was asked why the election forecasts had been off the mark and the students were curious about the sociological interpretation of the election outcome.

I was also limited in my efforts to adapt the lessons to suit the students' different backgrounds in social sciences; in the vast majority of courses, the students ranged from those without any prior knowledge of the subject whatsoever to those who had successfully completed several semesters of a relevant course. I particularly found it difficult to explain the wide variety of sociological approaches to the former group, when these students were really asking for unambiguous points of view and clear answers. Another difficulty was in trying to provide a more practice-oriented approach in lessons, something the students repeatedly requested.[*] For instance, I found it difficult to increase the level of student participation and give the lessons a practical slant when it came to presenting the basic concepts and principles of general sociology. The best I could come up with in such cases was to think of a way of presenting the topic that made use of a number of examples from practical life and work. I tried using quizzes when presenting research findings carried out in special sociologies, inviting the students to try and guess the results before I told them the actual findings. Alternatively, I would present them with research findings that were the exact opposite of the actual results of the research. Given that the students almost always accepted these findings as plausible results, this enabled me to demonstrate the "I Knew It All Along" phenomenon and—as was the case with the quiz when the guesses made by students turned out to be off the mark—to explain that the findings of sociological research are not always as self-evident as people so often say they are.[†] Obviously, this kind of teaching approach did not work effectively when repeated; therefore, it only served as means of breaking up the lesson from time to time. Another way of breaking up a lesson was group work, during the course of which groups of students were told to interpret short

---

[*] The desire for a more practice-oriented approach not only applied to sociology lessons but to students' training as a whole. The educational reform of 1998–1999 attempted to take these concerns into account (Hödl 1999; Stangl and Hanak 1999).

[†] The "I Knew It All Along" phenomenon (or hindsight bias) is the tendency people have to assume that they already knew the results of a research study after reading these results (Lazarsfeld 1968).

texts or data and then give a brief presentation on the subject. Individual student presentations that required greater periods of preparation outside of teaching hours were only given on rare occasions—not surprisingly, in light of pressure to study for the "hard" subjects and the fact that the marks for sociology and economic policy subjects were predetermined.

Even providing the necessary documents and an offer of receiving books as an incentive (copies of my own publications that I still had on hand) did not really succeed in increasing students' willingness to give such presentations. My most successful experience, in terms of increasing the level of participation among students, came when I was teaching the methods of sociology, where I allowed students to try out techniques in order to learn them (something that was originally suggested to me by a student on one of my first courses). For instance, I would select certain students to conduct a qualitative or standardized interview in front of the class while the other members of the class had to observe the way in which the interview was carried out and subsequently report on their observations, paying particular attention to both the similarities and the differences between the interview and the police interrogation. Alternatively, I would ask four or five of the students to hold a discussion in front of the class, which the other class members in turn had to observe using a qualitative or standardized approach. This served as a way of demonstrating the procedures and problems of applying the methods of observation and the group discussion approach. I also attempted to demonstrate the procedure and problems arising when using the sociometric test, the approach for determining the dark area of crime,* the experimental approach, and techniques of content analysis by means of ad hoc demonstrations of these approaches.

In one course, these kinds of demonstrations led to the idea of carrying out an entire research project as part of the class in order to offer students the opportunity to be actively involved in all the stages of the empirical research process. I ran with the idea despite the reservations I had based on previous experiences with research projects while teaching at the university. One of the lessons I learned from such projects was that there is almost always too little time set aside for the projects to be carried out. This was also the case here. Although it was possible to plan the research project in the allocated timeframe and even collect the necessary data, there was not enough time to carry out a joint analysis of the data collected to interpret the results, or to write a report. Ultimately, all I could do was complete the project by myself, and this is obviously not the intention or purpose of teaching about

---

* In order to determine the dark figure of crime, self-report studies of criminal behavior or victimization are conducted. In these studies, respondents are asked to declare if they have committed criminal offenses or if they had been a victim of such offenses.

research projects. A report on this project, which dealt with police officers' and sociology students' opinions of one another, later appeared in a police journal (Norden 1989).

The opinion held by certain groups and the population as a whole regarding the police was one specific issue I addressed in detail in every course. This was not the least due to the fact that many students assumed that negative attitudes toward the police were rife among the population. Contrary to these assumptions, social surveys of the Austrian population in general showed that the police were quite popular and even held a positive ranking in the hierarchy of institutions, occupational groups, and services (Edelbacher and Norden 2000, 222–224). By reporting these findings to the students and, at the same time, asking them to circulate this positive news about the police among their work colleagues, I hoped I was able to make some contribution to reducing the sense of a lack of recognition that was fairly common among police officers at the time. This feeling of a lack of recognition often related not only to society as a whole but also in particular to the police officers' superiors. Police officers complained more than employees working in the private sector of a lack of appreciation from their superiors for their work (Meggeneder 1987, 6). This low level of appreciation was found to have repercussions on the officers' motivation to work, a phenomenon referred to as "mental resignation" (*innere Kündigung*, cf. Wolf and Korunka 1993, 242). In order to combat the processes involved in mental resignation, and with the aim of affecting cultural change in the police, I urged the prospective commissioned officers to praise lower level coworkers accordingly for their work achievements and to give them the recognition they deserve in the future.

It is difficult to ascertain whether or not the students actually went on to do this more markedly, and if so, how many of them did. This is definitely something that cannot be determined from course evaluations, which were limited to student surveys at the end of each session. These surveys asked students how satisfied they were with the class, how interested they were in the individual contents of the course, and what they felt they had gained from the program of study. The results showed that the majority of the students were reasonably satisfied with the sociology lessons and had gained something from the course, particularly in terms of their understanding of social and occupational problems, overcoming prejudices, forming a basic interest in the subject, and developing reading skills specific to the subject. This meant that I was able to maintain that, to a certain extent, I had been successful in achieving some of the learning objectives described above, even if this was not the case for all of the students taking the course.

For nearly every course, there was the occasional student who said they had not been able to gain anything from my style of teaching and the course content; such students, therefore, remained unreachable for me. And when these "unreachables" then began to occupy themselves with things that bore no relation whatsoever to the lesson and were only prepared to stop what they were doing when they were confronted about it, this was among the more unpleasant experiences I had in my work as a teacher. In the years prior to educational reform, this kind of experience lasted for whole lessons; this was particularly the case on the days before a legal exam because many of the students were only partially responsive on such days. For all the trouble I suffered in relation to this struggle, I was compensated with success stories in lessons on other days, particularly when discussions that had started in class continued on into the break over a cup of coffee. As a pleasant contrast to various debates at the university, which often forayed into specificities of the details, these discussions only lost their footing on very rare occasions. I myself learned a great deal in these discussions, including a little about the "inner workings" of the police. From time to time, I felt myself personally integrated into the police culture.

I have a short anecdote from one of my classes here: While we were discussing the subject of scientific objectivity in the course of a lesson, one of my students began to grumble about social scientists. To his mind, social scientists had an overly critical attitude toward the police and contributed to the dissemination of the image of the police as the enemy in the public sphere. I felt compelled to provide some kind of justification but found myself being interrupted by the student in the process: "No, I wasn't talking about you, you're one of us ..."

As "one of them" I really enjoyed fulfilling my teaching obligation to the students enrolled in my course—with the exception of the unpleasant situations I mentioned earlier. Admittedly, a small part of the attraction for me was the fact that a police car would pick me up from the university or from home and chauffeur me to and from class. This special service was provided to me by the Federal Ministry of the Interior with the aim of augmenting the rather modest fee paid for the teaching work. I enjoyed this service; the journeys were usually very pleasant, and the drivers were extremely friendly. I was generally fortunate to make a lot of interesting contacts within the police force, some of which went on to become friendships.

The Present State of Teaching Sociology to Police Officers in Austria

I taught my final lesson in the summer of 2002 because the training of commissioned police officers in Austria was provisionally suspended upon the completion of the Security Academy 2000/02 term. What had happened? Two years before, in February 2000, a new federal government had been formed by the Conservative Austrian People's Party (*Österreichische Volkspartei*, ÖVP) and the right-wing populist Freedom Party of Austria (*Freiheitliche Partei Österreichs*, FPÖ). This began with extensive police reforms, the most important aim of which (due to budgetary restrictions) was a reduction of costs and personnel. It was only natural that the training of commissioned police officers would be temporarily suspended as a result. The justification for this cessation was that there were "too many chiefs" in the police force, in order to reduce this number, the force was to be centralized. The centralization process, which was carried out with great speed, culminated in the consolidation of the Security Guards, the Gendarmerie, and the Criminal Investigation Corps into a single unit referred to as the Federal Police (*Bundespolizei*) in 2005. It was estimated, based on retirement data, that some 20 replacement commissioned officers per year would be needed for this Federal Police force (Brenner 2006, 113). In order to be able to meet these requirements, the training of commissioned police officers was resumed in 2006–2007; but this time—as had originally been planned at the end of the 1990s—the course was transformed into a University of Applied Sciences degree course (*Fachhochschulstudiengang*). The course is called "Police Leadership" and is also open to potential students working in private security companies. The course is offered at the University of Applied Sciences Wiener Neustadt (*Fachhochschule Wiener Neustadt*, Lower Austria), where two-thirds of the lectures are held. The other third of the course is held at training locations of the Security Academy. The course lasts for six semesters, with one semester credited to Federal Police officers because the course is primarily for training to become a noncommissioned police officer (employment group E2a) (Brenner 2006, 113). Students must complete two bachelor's theses during the course of the program, the topics of which are assigned by the course director. Following a positive assessment of the theses and after passing the final examination, students are awarded the academic degree "Bachelor of Arts in Police Leadership" (BMI 2009, 17). Bachelor graduates can also go on to complete a master's degree in "Security Management" at the University of Applied Sciences Wiener Neustadt. This course is intended for those officers hoping to qualify for top positions within the Federal Police. Its duration is four semesters. Graduates are awarded the academic degree "Master of Arts in Security–Management (M.A.)" (BMI 2009, 29). The "Security Management" master's course no longer includes a subject with that name. All that is provided is a lecture entitled "Security in the Course of Social Development." In the BA degree course "Police Leadership," a two-hour lecture on "Political Science and Sociology" is included. This means that, despite the fact that training as a whole has been extended, sociology has been reduced to a bare minimum in terms of the number of weekly hours (one hour per week in the second semester).

In comparison with the teaching hours I was allocated when at the Education Centre of the Gendarmerie and Security Academy, respectively, this means that the amount of sociology instruction has now been halved. Evidently, in keeping with the spirit of the times, the lessons freed up as a result of the reduction and the additional teaching hours introduced were used to develop a new teaching focal point in economics. Nowadays, it is apparently deemed more important for commissioned police officers to be able to think in an economic sense than it is for them to be able to view problems from a sociological perspective.

References

BGBl. (1999). Verordnung: Grundausbildungen für den Exekutivdienst und die Verwendungsgruppen E 2a und E 1 im Gendarmerie-, Sicherheitswach- und Kriminaldienst. *Bundesgesetzblatt für die Republik Österreich*, Teil II, 3041–3051.

BMI (Bundesministerium für Inneres). (2009). *Polizeiausbildung*. Wien. Retrieved February 26, 2012 from http://www.bmi.gv.at/cms/BMI_Service/Aus_dem_Inneren/Polizeiausbildung.pdf

Brenner, G. (2006). Studium Polizeiliche Führung. *Öffentliche Sicherheit*, 11–12/06: 112–113.

Edelbacher, M., and Norden, G. (2000). Challenges of policing democracies: The case of Austria. In Das, D. and Marenin, O. (Eds.), *Challenges of Policing Democracies. A World Perspective*. Amsterdam: Gordon and Breach Publishers, pp. 215–241.

Frevel, B., Asmus, H.-J., Groß, H., Lamers, J., and Liebl, K. (2002). *Soziologie: Studienbuch für die Polizei*. Hilden: Verlag Deutsche Polizeiliteratur.

Garnitschnig, K., Ribolits, E., and Stangl, W. (1999). Wie man vom Versuchskaninchen zum engagierten Forscher wird oder ausgezeichnete Hoffnungen für die zukünftige Fachhochschule. In Lang, G. (Ed.), *Festschrift der Sicherheitsakademie 1998/99*. Mödling: Bundesministerium für Inneres, Generaldirektion für die öffentliche Sicherheit, pp. 10–12.

Hödl, A. (1999). Überblick über die Ausbildungsreform 1998. In Lang, G. (Ed.), *Festschrift der Sicherheitsakademie 1998/99*. Mödling: Bundesministerium für Inneres, Generaldirektion für die öffentliche Sicherheit, pp. 4–7.

Lazarsfeld, P. F. (1968). *Am Puls der Gesellschaft. Zur Methodik der empirischen Soziologie*. Wien: Europa Verlag.

Meggeneder, O. (1987). *Arbeitsbedingungen von Polizisten und Gendarmen (Kurzfassung)*. Eine Untersuchung im Auftrag der Fraktion Sozialistischer Gewerkschafter der Gewerkschaft öffentlicher Dienst, Landesvorstand Oberösterreich. Linz: Landesvorstand Oberösterreich der Fraktion Sozialistischer Gewerkschafter der Gewerkschaft öffentlicher Dienst.

Newburn, T. (Ed.). (2005). *Policing. Key Readings*. Cullompton: Willan Publishing.

Norden, G. (1989). Autoritär und vorurteilhaft. Wie Polizisten und Soziologie-Studenten einander einschätzen. *Der kriminalbeamte*, Nr. 474, Oktober 11, 1989.

Stangl, W., and Hanak, G. (1999). *Theorie und praxis in der offiziersausbildung.* Forschungsbericht. Wien: Institut für Rechts- und Kriminalsoziologie.

Wolf, C., and Korunka, C. (1993): *Belastung und beanspruchung der österreichischen exekutive.* Forschungsbericht. Wien: Abteilung Allgemeinmedizin, Universitätsklinik Innere Medizin IV.

Collaboration among the Police, Professional Practitioners, and the Community in the Criminal Justice Process and in Crime Prevention Programs

II

The chapters selected for Section II illustrate the many ways professional practitioners—that is psychologists, doctors, attorneys, social workers, volunteers, and community organization leaders—assist the police and other justice personnel, as well as how they collaborate with the police in crime prevention programs.

In Chapter 10, Edelbacher traces the evolution of police training in Austria from its historical roots to the present time. He discusses how police experience on the part of the Instructor is important in the education and training of students interested in pursuing careers in police work and other justice-related occupations. The author draws on the different types of policing tasks he performed during his long career in police work to illustrate why both theoretical and practical information are important for the student preparing for a career in police work and other justice-related occupations.

In Chapter 11, Grekul and Thue demonstrate the methods used by the police and community residents to detect automobile drivers who are impaired and the effect such collaboration has had on reducing the amount of driving while impaired in the community.

In Chapter 12, Chafe, Eke, Collins, Cromer, and Brewster discuss how a multidisciplinary approach developed by academics and the police is used in the investigations of equivocal death (manner of death). The contributions of scientists have assisted police officers in making a better analysis of the causes and circumstances surrounding a death.

In Chapter 13, Rich presents a summary of a program in which police and victim advocates collaborate to assist the victims of rape. In addition, some areas in which communication and cooperation among police, advocates, and victims have *not* been very beneficial are considered, and suggestions for improving this collaboration are presented.

In Chapter 14, Kratcoski uses prior research findings and the information gleaned from extensive interviews of police investigators and professional practitioners to illustrate how professionals and law enforcement officials collaborate on investigations of homicide, rape, sexual assault of children, and other criminal offenses. In addition, special attention is given to the role of victim advocates and that of professional practitioners such as psychologists, social workers, attorneys, corrections workers, and scientists in assisting in criminal investigations and in providing expert testimony during the judicial process.

In Chapter 15, Kratcoski provides a summary of the ways police, academics, and professional practitioners have collaborated on education, training, and research and on the development and implementation of crime prevention programs. The expectations on how such cooperation will be expanded, particularly in terms of international collaboration, is also discussed in this chapter.

The Development of Austrian Police Education and Training

10

MAXIMILIAN EDELBACHER
Austrian Federal Police
Retired Security Advisor for ACUN
Vienna, Austria

Contents

Introduction

The education and training of police officers is a most important contribution to the fundamental understanding of democratic performance and control under the rule of law. The police act as a direct symbol of state power, and the duty of police officers is to check and balance state powers and individual rights. In Europe, the police served the king, the emperor, or the government for many centuries. Thus, the new role of policing—"to serve the community"—is fairly recent in Austria. It can be traced to the influence of the Anglo-Saxon understanding of policing, and the police role of serving the people was integrated into the police mandate in Austria on May 1, 1994, (CIA World Factbook: Austrian Police 2014, 1; "History of Austria" 2015). At this time, the duties and rights of the police were written into the Police-Security Law and the understanding that the police role must include service to the community was legalized (Austrian Parliament 1994).

History, Post-Napoleon Era, and Vienna Congress of 1815

In the early period of Austrian police history, after the Middle Ages, the police were not centrally organized. In Vienna, two police organizations were active. They were the *Stadtguardia* and the *Rumorwache* (Seyrl 2012). People did not trust them very much because they had a bad reputation for being lazy and corrupt. These organizations were abolished in the seventeenth century, and a "military police" structure was established. At this time, the minister of war commanded the military and the police. The reforms introduced led to a reduction in the laziness and corruption of the police and to greater efficiency. Thus, the people trusted police much more than before. Police were informed about crimes in the community more often than in the past. However, in the long run, the military system did not support with a democratic approach to police behavior toward the citizens or a more people-oriented approach.

After 1815 and the defeat of Napoleon, the Austrian emperor was very powerful. The Vienna Congress granted absolute power to the monarchy. Austria became aligned with the most powerful countries in the world (at that time): the United Kingdom, France, and Russia. The Austrian statesman, Metternich, was the mastermind of the treaty and the police organization in Austria. People were secretly observed by the police and all dubious activities of citizens were reported to the state authorities. People from countries all over Europe suffered under this concentration of powers, and individual rights were basically nonexistent. This situation resulted in a resurgence of the underlying of the ideas of the French Revolution of 1789; and, in fact, several revolutions were started in France, Germany, and Austria in 1848.

Police Management by the Ministry of War

Between the seventeenth century and 1848, the ministry of war managed both the military and the police. These absolute powers led to a powerful police organizational structure. The so-called Metternich information system established a massive spy system. All activities of Austrians were observed and reported to the authorities. People were under strict control, and personal freedom was nearly impossible.

Consequences of the Revolution of 1848

From 1789 to 1799, the French Revolution influenced European society, and the feudal-absolutistic status of the people that dominated the European populace was abolished. The goals of the French Revolution—guaranteeing fundamental ideas of human dignity and freedom—became the goals for other countries. The Revolution of 1848 continued the ideas of the French Revolution and, from this, different revolutions started in Germany and in the Austrian monarchy in 1848 and 1849. Although the Austrian emperor did have to leave the capital of Vienna in the beginning of 1848 because of the activities of and danger from the revolution, this upheaval was eventually stopped and its leaders defeated with the help of the Russian emperor. However, the ruling Austrian emperor was dismissed, and his 18-year-old son, Franz-Joseph, was crowned the new emperor in 1848. As emperor,

Franz-Joseph began reforming his country by establishing new regulations, implementing democratic reforms, and by granting constitutional rights to individual citizens.

Police Structure and Management in the Austrian–Hungarian Monarchy

The Austrian Empire was a multiethnic society. Although more than 52 million people lived in the Austrian Empire, only 12 million people had a German-speaking background. All others spoke different languages such as Hungarian or Slavic. The backbone of this multiethnic society was comprised of the military and the government. In these organizations, it was possible for those members of society coming from a "lower status" background to develop a career if they were clever enough to pass the required tests and if they showed support for the organization they served. In some ways, the Austrian–Hungarian monarchy served as a model for the present-day European Union (EU). The Habsburg dynasty was the connecting link that united the people regardless of their cultural diversity. (The emperor, especially Franz-Joseph, was a symbol of unification. As noted earlier, Franz-Joseph became emperor in 1848, and he reigned until 1916, while Europe was engulfed in World War I. His death, together with the enormous losses in the war, led to the breakdown of the Austrian-Hungarian monarchy.)

Establishment of the Austrian–Hungarian Monarchy in 1876

The outcome of the 1848 revolution was the *Ausgleich* (treaty) between Austria and Hungary in 1867. Ferenc Deák, a Hungarian who was deeply involved in the Freedom Fight against Austria, was successful in supporting an arrangement between the Austrian emperor and the Hungarians. Through his legal expertise as an "honor-prosecutor" in the Komitat Zala, he had considerable influence on the development of the Civil Law I the Monarchy. This treaty between Austria and Hungary supported the stability of power in the monarchy. However, one of the weaknesses of the treaty was that the human rights of other nationalities, such as the Slavic people, were neglected under the law (Wikipedia, History of Austria 2015, 12). (This weakness would eventually lead to the breakdown of the monarchy after World War I ended.) Under the *Ausgleich*, the Austrian emperor became the king of Hungary. A very important contributing factor leading up to this was the fact that the Hungarians liked Elisabeth, the Austrian empress, who in turn was very fond of Hungary. When she was murdered in Geneva, at the end of the nineteenth century, this event had a negative influence on the relationship between the Habsburgs and Hungary.

Constitutional Guaranties for Individuals

Once a constitutional government was established in Austria and a constitution was adopted, the citizens were provided with personal freedoms such as speech and the right to demonstrate, and the right to develop the sciences without interferences from the government. Several portions of the constitution pertained to individual- and organizational rights, such as personal freedom, freedom of speech, freedom to demonstrate, and freedom of sciences, and it provided a guarantee of these freedoms.

Institution of Legal Advisors

The institution of legal advisors became a guarantee for observing human rights and legal standards in the police organization. On the one hand, legal advisors should protect people against abuses of the law by the police; on the other, legal advisors also served as a free legal advice service for the people who could not afford lawyers. Every person living in Austria had daily access to legal advice at the Vienna Police Headquarters (*Polizei-Kommissariate*) or in the larger cities of Austria. Police legal advisors were responsible for communication among the police, the prosecutor's service, investigative judges, and trial judges.

Successful Reform of Police in 1858 and 1876

Another outcome of the Revolution of 1848 was the reform of the police structure in Austria (Seyrl 2012). However, crime increased dramatically during several periods. In Vienna after 1848, crime increased because the capital city was growing fast. At that time, Vienna was the sixth largest city in the world, with a population of 2.3 million people by the start of World War I. The Revolution of 1848 motivated the new emperor, Franz-Joseph, to change the police management and to create a people-oriented police organization. He sent an expert, Ritter Le Monnier, to London and Paris to study and learn about the best police organizations in Europe at that time. These were the London Metropolitan Police and the Sureté in Paris. As was previously mentioned, until 1848, the police in Austria were under the command of the minister of war. Police reforms by the Austrian–Hungarian monarchy in 1858 and in 1876 separated the police from the military, and the minister of the interior became head of all the police. The law enforcement agencies in the cities were referred to as the *sicherheitswache* (police); a different organizational model, the *gendarmerie*, was developed for the rural areas of Austria.

Uniformed Police—Sicherheitswache

When Ritter Le Monnier came back to Austria, the criminal police divisions were restructured following the French model, and the uniformed police divisions were restructured following the British model (Edelbacher 2008). The reform of the Criminal Police took place in 1858 and that of the Uniformed Police in 1876, but the police were only responsible for crime prevention in the cities; the gendarmerie policed the rural areas. As previously mentioned, it was very important to separate the police organizations from the military, and a minister of the interior became commander of police in Austria.

Sicherheitsbüro (Major Crime Bureau)

In 1858, the Vienna Criminal Investigation Department was established (the Sicherheitsbüro, or Major Crime Bureau) and, in 1876, the sicherheitswache (uniformed police) were structured similar to the metropolitan police (Lichem 1935). The men were given new uniforms, following the assumption that the new look would convince people that the police were more "people friendly" and community oriented because they no longer looked like the former military police. The main advantage of reforming the uniformed police was to separate them from the military so that they were no longer under the command of the ministry of war. This was very important because the minister of war had ordered police to shoot at revolutionists, students, and workers during the 1848 uprising. This action resulted in the general populace having a very negative opinion of them, which was still fairly pronounced.

Gendarmerie—Military Police in the Countryside

In rural areas, the gendarmerie—a rather militaristic organization—was responsible for all policing. The model of the gendarmerie had been brought to Austria by Napoleon. After the end of the revolution in 1848, the gendarmerie was separated from the military and, since 1876, the minister of the interior was responsible for the police and the gendarmerie.

Dr. Johann Schober, Police President, Police President Founder of INTERPOL in 1923

In 1916, the last emperor of the Austrian–Hungarian Empire, Kaiser Karl, appointed Dr. Johann Schober as police president in Vienna. All though the empire broke up in 1918, the police structure and its management remained intact (Deflem 2002). The Austrian police had such an excellent reputation at this time that it became known as the "world's best police organization." Police officers in the United States and China asked Austrian police to teach their officers either in Austria or in their home countries. Building on idea originally formulated by Prince Albert of Monaco (Fooner 1989), Schober announced that he wanted to found an international police organization that would be able to combat transnational crime and to improve police cooperation. His plans were interrupted by the start of World War I but, after the conflict ended, the idea was reactivated. In 1923, Dr. Schober invited representatives of neighboring countries and other important nations of the world (such as the United States and China) to Vienna to help create an international police organization. At this first meeting, the International Criminal Police Organization, later called INTERPOL, was founded. Between 1918 and 1938, INTERPOL's home was Vienna. Hitler transferred INTERPOL to Berlin. After the end of World War II, the organization moved to Paris. Then, in the 1980s, Lyon, France, became INTERPOL's new headquarters. Today, it is the largest police organization in the world.

Police Organization in the Austrian Republics

The Austrian police was recognized as the world's best police organization even after the breakup of the Austrian–Hungarian monarchy, and it continued as a leading model of policing worldwide during the 1920s and 1930s. This excellent reputation was built on the technical expertise of the police, who used the "Mulache technique" (a method for reconstructing bodies and faces of dead persons), and on the leadership and the personality of Dr. Johann Schober, who was an outstanding police leader.

The End of World War I

Although the structure of the police did not change during the First Republic of Austria at the end of World War I, the confidence in the police and their role was no longer accepted by the people of the Austrian–Hungarian Monarchy. The reason for this lack of confidence in the police and the people's reluctance to accept the authority of the police can be explained by the fact that the country had been divided into seven geographic areas and that the administrative structure was taken over by the authorities of the First Republic of Austria. The young republic was in a bad financial situation as a result of World War I and needed to rely on loans and other assistance from other countries to rebuild its economy. As a result, the *Volkerbund*, the international institution to support Austria, was given a high priority and the traditional internal institutions, such as the police, were given a lower priority, in terms of funding and being provided with other resources. However, the way the Austrian Police was structured, administered and operated was still considered to be of a high quality by other nations, such as China and the United States, who used the Austrian Police model when developing their police organizations. For example, the technical development of the Austrian Forensic Unit set a high standard that was used as a model by other countries all over the world (Seyrl 2012).

The Nazi Regime

The peace treaties after the end of World War I were very strict; so many remunerations had to be paid to the victors by the countries that were defeated that the consequence was an industrial collapse and a high unemployment rate in Germany and Austria. The people's hopelessness became the starting point for a new extremism. Hitler and his Nazi Party became more and more popular and eventually took over the German government. With the help of German industrialists, Hitler began production of war material and built a strong military system. It seemed to be clear from the beginning that he wanted to start a new war. One of the first countries he took over was Austria. Between 1938 and 1945, the period of the Nazi regime, the Austrian police structure and gendarmerie were abolished and the German Reich was established.

The End of World War II

After the end of World War II, the Second Republic of Austria was founded. The old system of policing was re-implemented. The police structure of the monarchy, which had continued in the First Republic was reactivated and worked quite well. As in the period before World War II, the police became responsible for law enforcement in the 14 large cities, and the gendarmerie was reestablished in the rural areas. The minister of the interior became the head of this hierarchic, federal system with the police and gendarmerie under his control.

Police Management, Education, and Training

The standard for police education and training was relatively high during the Austrian–Hungarian monarchy, especially when compared to other central European countries. However, the countries with the most developed police organizations at this time were Great Britain and France. The police force needed to become more modernized, especially after the experiences of 1848, in order to fulfill the expectations of the population who desired more people-oriented policing methods. Thus, the policing models of Great Britain and France were considered the best practices for improving the police system in the Austrian–Hungarian monarchy. The modernization of the police included improvements in the selection, education, and training of police officers. One of the main issues was reducing the military features of the police. Administration was the backbone of the Austrian–Hungarian monarchy with the police representing not only executive power but also administrative power. On the other hand, the military presented career opportunities for everyone, even if they came from a low social or economic background. If someone was talented and gifted, they could move up the socioeconomic ladder—even as far as the top—through advancement in either an administration position in the government or through a position in the military.

National Police Education System

Originally, education and training of police in Austria was based on a military model (Edelbacher and Norden 2000). Police officers started with two years of basic education and training (Oberhummer 1937). To become a high-ranking officer, one's education had to be continued following the completion of five years of service as a line officer. One of the important features of policing was that legal advisors were assigned to work within the police administration. These legal advisors had to provide free access to law materials and legal advice to people who requested it. A legal advisor was permanently on duty and, if any citizen requested legal advice, this would be provided without cost. Another responsibility of the legal advisor was to monitor police behavior and activities so that the actions of law enforcement personnel were based on sound legal grounds. Since this system remained in place during the two Austrian republics, police education and training did not change very much during that time. Line officers, leadership, criminal investigation officers, and legal advisors were the backbone of the police structure in large cities. The gendarmerie system differed from the police education system because the gendarmerie did not have legal advisors.

To give a personal example of the role of the legal advisor, I studied law at the Vienna University, Department of Law. After finishing these studies, I worked for a short period in a court in the justice system and then took a position in the private sector with a financial institution. After two years' experience in the private sector, in 1972, I obtained employment as a legal expert for the Federal Police of Austria. A young man or woman could choose to start as a line officer after reaching the age of 18 and after having served in the military. A young line officer had to pass two years of education and training at an Austrian police academy. In contrast, a legal expert candidate, at that time, had to start in a district and was trained for a period of six months in special courses. After passing the first tests, the candidate had to continue their studies for one year at a special administrative academy and then train further to study for the final examinations. This further training lasted for about four months. If the candidate passed all these tests, they started as a young *kommissär* (commissioner) (Kratcoski 2011).

Relationship between Researchers and Practitioners

Austria has had a long tradition of cooperation between scientists and the police organization. This type of cooperation with the science community is also very apparent in most other countries throughout the world. The assistance of scientists in analyzing evidence and clarifying the characteristics of crimes and criminal behavior is ongoing. In Austria, the first cooperation between the police and the scientific community started with the investigation of violent crimes—in particular, murders committed in Vienna. A fruitful relationship developed between Vienna University's Department of Medicine and the Vienna Police Headquarters. This collaboration mirrored similar experiences in France.

Positive Outcomes from a Relationship between Researchers and Practitioners

Based on the experiences that started in the beginning of the nineteenth century (especially after 1804 with the formation of the Forensic Unit at Vienna University's Department of Medicine), a successful cooperation between researchers and practitioners began. Their first case involved a murder. Researchers were successful in establishing proof that poison was used by the defendant. In 1858, the Major Crime Bureau was created, again following another French model, that of Sureté. Vienna was growing very fast, crime was increasing dramatically, and the emperor needed more efficiency and a higher success rate for solving crimes, especially those involving violence.

After 1858, researchers and practitioners began meeting together at crime scenes. For example, as chief of the murder crime unit, I would meet with the chief of the Forensic Unit. Until the police reforms of 2005, this was a standard practice. Professor Georg Bauer (Vienna University, Department of Medicine, Forensic Unit) and I are now retired but still are very good friends. This tradition of meeting stopped after the Police Reform Act was instituted. Currently, the chief of the Major Crime Bureau and the chief of the Forensic Unit do not show up together at the crime scene. The old traditional partnership has been abandoned and replaced with a more formalized procedure.

International Experiences

International police education and training becomes more and more important as the global society continues to develop. After the EU was founded and the European Police was created, the nature of international cooperation in the education and training of national police officers has changed significantly. Although national policing is still more important than international policing because of the understanding of the sovereignty of the single states, police agencies of various countries cooperate with each other more frequently today than ever before. Examples of international cooperative training of police are the Central European Police Academy (CEPOL), which offers many different special courses in all member countries in police academies inside and outside of the EU, and the Middle European Police Academy (MEPA).

The Middle European Police Academy

In 1989, after the fall of the Iron Curtain, Austria and central Europe were confronted with a dramatic increase in crime. In 1990, the Hungarian ambassador to Austria and Vienna's police president implemented an idea for fighting the new dimensions of crime (trafficking in weapons, drugs, humans, corruption, and smuggling), that were related to the breakup of the Soviet Union. This was the implementation of the Austrian–Hungarian Police Academy, which later was renamed the Middle European Police Academy. MEPA member nations are: Austria, Germany, Switzerland, Hungary, Slovakia, Slovenia, the Czech Republic, and Poland. Police officers are educated in each of the member countries for three months.

The Central European Police Academy

Currently, there are 28 member countries active in the EU. The question of how to structure police education and training among the member nations so that all their police forces would have comparable capacities for dealing with law enforcement matters facing the EU has been a concern ever since the EU's creation. The powerful member countries, such as the United Kingdom, France, Spain, Sweden, and Germany, each insisted that their own system was the best; thus, it was impossible to centralize police education and training at one location. The consequence was the founding of the Central European Police Academy (CEPA). In reality, it is a network of different police academies. Special courses are offered in Bramshile, United Kingdom; Münster, Germany; Encole in Paris, France; and in Stockholm, Sweden.

Cooperation with INTERPOL and EUROPOL

Although the MEPA and the CEPA are only administrative bodies, cooperation in the field of international contacts is necessary if the exchange of information and intelligence on international criminal activity is to take place.

INTERPOL with about 200 member countries, is the largest world-wide organization devoted to the exchange of information and intelligence relating to international criminal activity. Modern communication techniques allow fast information exchange. The tools used for analyzing information are sophisticated and efficient. The responses of these organizations, especially INTERPOL, in worldwide crisis situations have been very successful. Another development is the modern cybercrime unit that is based in Singapore.

EUROPOL, a representative law enforcement organization of the EU, offers the advantage of fast direct communication, because the system of liaison officers is structured in such a way that the problem of translating the different languages of the member nations is handled much more quickly than the way it works with INTERPOL. Each member country employs representatives of their own country; and, therefore, they can communicate with each other immediately and an answer can be provided very quickly. This system is much more efficient than that of INTERPOL.

Both organizations offer special training courses in different fields of expertise, such as organized crime, terrorism, cybercrime, smuggling of human beings, and combatting corruption. It is always very useful if experts have a chance to come together, to learn from each other, and to exchange knowledge.

International Cooperation with the Federal Bureau of Investigation, the Drug Enforcement Administration, and Others

In addition to INTERPOL and EUROPOL, there exists a long traditional cooperative relationship with American organizations such as the Federal Bureau of Investigation (FBI) and the Drug Enforcement Administration (DEA). Both are very much engaged in building international cooperation networks with other countries. Both also invest a lot of money to support and to educate national police organizations. The FBI and the DEA have a worldwide network of liaison officers, build ad hoc cooperation on special cases, and are involved with the police of many nations in fighting terrorism, organized crime, and drug trafficking. The international law enforcement academies and the training courses offered at the headquarters of the FBI and DEA are world famous and have attracted police officers and administrators from countries around the globe.

Faculty Exchanges: Teaching Experiences in the United States and Finland

My personal experience with teaching in foreign countries has led to many sources of new knowledge and to contacts with other professionals and academicians. Establishing these contacts would not have been possible without my being given the opportunity to teach at universities in other countries. In 1991, Professor Dilip K. Das traveled through Europe, including a visit to Austria; that was the first time that I learned about the new field of academic study and research referred to as criminal justice. In Austria, we did not know that academics were researching such questions as *What are people expecting of police organizations in modern democracies?* This was a new area for us, and we learned a great deal by comparing different police systems and the advantages and disadvantages of different models. At that time, our policing was very much influenced by and limited to a legal understanding of the law. We were only concerned about policing being based on the rule of law in our country. We were not much concerned about assuring that the social and psychological parameters of the peoples' needs were being fulfilled.

Today's Reality of Policing in Austria

Since 2005, daily police work has changed dramatically in Austria. Prior to that time, we had police in the cities and gendarmerie in the rural area. On July 1, 2005, both organizations were integrated into the National Police of Austria. The centralization of the administration was necessary because the number of officers employed in the two forces had dropped by more than 6000. In 2000, about 33,000 employees were working for the ministry of the interior. In 2014, the number was 27,000.

On an international level, Austria's police education and training has a high standard compared to other countries. The basic education starts with a two-year training course that each police officer must complete and pass. The selection procedure for joining the police force is rather strict. In Austria, police education and training is not an open system where everyone can start training and afterward the candidates are selected by police authorities. For example, in the Czech Republic, police education is open to all. The students can go to the police university, pass the tests, and then high level police officials decide who will be employed.

Police Reform in Austria

Austria is a rather small country with about 8.5 million inhabitants. Currently, there are approximately 27,000 individuals in the Austrian National Police, and about 6000 law enforcement officers work in Vienna. The Austrian capital has about 1.7 million inhabitants. The police system there is very efficient, in that it is still very militarily and hierarchically organized, but there is concern about a lack of emphasis on the part of the police when it comes to focusing on people's needs. However, the concern is not as pronounced as it might appear because the mentality of both the Austrian people and the Austrian police is rather mild and flexible.

With regard to police structure and organization, the top administrative position is the minister of the interior. Three units take care of the main issues. These are the Bureau for Protection of the Constitution and Fight against Terrorism (*Bundesamt für Verfassungsschutz* and *Terrorismusbekämpfung*); the Federal Bureau of Criminal Investigation, Austria (*Bundeskriminalamt Österreich*); and the Federal Bureau against Corruption (*Bundesamt zur Bekämpfung von Korruption*). Police education is managed by the ministry of interior and is supported by the Police Security Academy (*Sicherheitsakademie*). All these bureaus are under the minister of the interior, but each can act relatively independently.

Federal Bureau of Criminal Investigation of Austria

Since the structure of policing was so centralized, the Federal Office of Criminal Investigation, Austria, took over the registration and administration of all crime that happens within the country. Since Austria has nine provinces, a Regional Office of Criminal Investigation (*Landeskriminalamt*) is located in each providence, and it is responsible for fighting crime in that region. The central office for registration and administration is the Crime Analysis Unit established in the Federal Office for Criminal Investigation of Austria. The Security Monitor is the central instrument used for registering all crimes.

Police Education and Training at the SIAK Security Police Academy (Sicherheitsakademie)

During the past several years there has been an increase in the number of applicants for police positions in Austria. A number of young men and women try to pass the initial tests for becoming a police officer, but the dropout rate has been on the increase. The tests are not easy, and other factors such as psychological and/or physical conditions may disqualify them from becoming officers. As previously mentioned, candidates have to attend a two-year course that is a mixture of theoretical and practical modules. After candidates have successfully completed the final tests, they start working at a police station. Three years later, they can choose to go on and become police officers, or they can opt to complete an advanced training course in the police academy to become a police leader in lower management. If they have a matura, which indicates they have successfully completed secondary school and are qualified to attend a college or university, they can apply for a two-year course to be trained as a higher level police manager. The top police leadership positions are open to those applicants who have successfully completed the appropriate education for this management level. If accepted, they will complete this training at the *Fachhochschule Wiener Neustadt*. This training is comparable to a university degree and students receive a bachelor's or a master's degree upon graduation. The *Fachhochschule Wiener Neustadt* has a working relationship with different universities, primarily the Vienna University, and the police academy.

Development of Models of Partnerships: The Private Security Sector

In the 1990s, crime in Austria forced the ministry of the interior leadership to change its philosophy of only supporting security forces run by the state. The idea was to break this monopoly and to engage private business in the fields of safety and security.

During the first years of the twenty-first century, private security increased very rapidly in Austria. In 1989, the year the Iron Curtain fell, statistics revealed a dramatic increase in crime; the police could not handle the situation alone. This was the starting point for the growth of the private security industry in Austria. Today about 27,000 public police officers work in Austria along with about 14,000 employees of private security companies. Compared to Australia, the United States, or the United Kingdom, the number of private security officers is still rather small. The public police is still the major crime fighting force in Austria. However, it is very clear that private security is becoming more and more important. One of the main problems with private security is the quality of services. The technical developments in police work are changing to the extent that very fast and high-quality services can be delivered by private security agencies, if the organization requesting the service can pay for it. The problem lies with the employers and the employees, who serve in the field of private security. There is a high level of competition for private security contracts, and the market in Austria is fairly small. Thus, competition for the contracts is rather brutal. Since Austria is a member of the EU, competition for private security contracts may even come from outside the country.

Education in the Private Security Sector

More than 15 years ago, Danube University Krems, Lower Austria, started offering a university education in private safety and security. This is a high-quality program and is very well thought of throughout the German-speaking world such as in Germany, Switzerland, and—of course—in Austria. Therefore, many students from Germany and Switzerland come to Danube University to study safety and security management. This program was a success story from the beginning and is a pride of Austria. Other possibilities for private security study are at the *Fachhochschulen* in Vienna and at *Wiener Neustadt*. The latter cooperates with the Police Security Academy.

Vienna University's department of sociology has offered a seminar on the topic "Police–Sociology" for the past five years. This seminar is taught by Drs. Gilbert Norden and Josef Hörl. It is popular, and each winter semester more than 25 students attend. The advantage of this seminar is that issues of security are academically and critically discussed. Students have to prepare and present papers on topics connected to security and police issues.

Private Security Research in Austria

In 2009, private research projects in the field of safety and security were begun. One of these brought in Dr. Alexander Siedschlag from Munich. He started a study and research program at the Sigmund-Freud University, which is based in Paris and Vienna. This program is linked with the Austrian Research Center for Safety and Security. This Center sponsors (provides grant money to) research and other programs that are focused on public and private safety and security. Referred to as the KIRAS Program, it supports some 50 to 70 research projects each year.

Austrian Center for Law Enforcement Sciences

The Austrian Center for Law Enforcement Sciences (ALES) was founded in 2011 as an interdisciplinary institution, based in the Vienna University. This center focuses on all contents and procedures of law enforcement agencies and of the justice system. Here, research projects and proposals covering public security issues are drafted. The ministry of justice and the ministry of the interior are partners with this institution, which is headed by Dr. Susanne Reindl-Krauskopf and supported by Dr. Christian Grafl, head of the Institute of Criminology of the Vienna University Department of Law. Research content includes the following.

- Evaluation measures about:
  - Crime–political measures
  - Crime prevention
  - Measures of criminal law, security law, and administrative law
  - Law for employees and disciplinary law

- Organizational measures
- Data protection law, human rights standards
- Law pertaining to the media, public relations
- Procedural law and trial performance
- Prosecution service and criminal court
- Research on efficiency
- Optimization of crime statistics
  - Education and training:
    - Courses and seminars taught at the University of Vienna
    - Participating in training and education at the police academy
    - International cooperation
    - e-Learning
  - Symposia, meetings:
    - Kick meetings
    - Yearly meeting
    - Participation in other symposia
    - Cooperation meetings

All these activities are coordinated with the ministry of justice and the ministry of the interior.

Conclusion

Cooperation between researchers and practitioners has a long tradition even in Austria. However, many details had to be changed to make the cooperative efforts more efficient and more in line with the system of modern policing. The influence from the Anglo-American policing system was very helpful in the development of a new approach in police management and in the expansion of cooperation among academics, scientists, and police practitioners.

The understanding of public administration in Austria was very much based on a formal, law-driven approach. It was difficult to start a career as a simple police officer, to study at the university, and to change into the legal service, but not impossible. It was not possible however, to start as a practitioner and to end up as a professor of criminology as so frequently happens in the United States. This open relationship between the field of science and the practical job is still unusual in Europe. This may change in the future, but it was very astonishing for Austrians to find out that so many professors in criminal justice started their work experience as police practitioners and ended up in an academic career—either in research or teaching.

Presently, in Austria and throughout the world, there are extensive exchanges of information and experience between academics and practitioners. However, the career paths in Europe and the United States are different if someone starts as practitioner versus starting as an academic researcher. Since the creation of the EU and the large amount of national and international cooperation, much more flexibility came into the police systems. As a practitioner, I am very happy that I had the chance to learn about the different approaches in Europe and the United States. I would have missed a great deal of experience had I not had this opportunity. I like to teach our students at Vienna University and try to make them aware, to motivate them to learn about the different systems in place on both continents. This is an important step in understanding a globalized world. It is very clear that a large amount of cooperation and networking will drive the future development of justice systems. Cooperation between practitioners and researchers is a must. Modern science and modern policing have to learn from each other and have to find new ways of understanding and learning. High mobility and the flexibility to overcome all challenges of the future are a must in a society of growing and complex problems. The conclusion reached at a recent meeting at the Police Headquarters in Vienna was that the police officer of the future had to be gifted in languages to communicate with all people and must demonstrate the technical ability to handle all the new technology and tools used in modern policing.

References

Austrian Parliament. (1994). *Austrian Security Police Law, January 1, 1991*. Vienna, Austria.

CIA World Factbook. (2014). *Austrian police*. Washington, D.C. The Library of Congress Country Studies. http://www.photius.com/countyries/austrianational_security/austriapolice_html. Retrieved on June 30, 2014.

Deflem, M. (2002). *Policing world society: Historical foundations of international police cooperation*. N.Y. Clarendon Studies in Criminology.

Edelbacher, M. (2008). *Polzei Inside–Was lauft falsch – Analyse and die spektakularen Kriminalfalle*. Vienna: Amalthea Publisher.

Edelbacher, M. and Norden, G. (2000). Challenges of policing democracies: The case of Austria. In *Challenges of Policing Democracies—A World Perspective*, D. K. Das and O. Marenin, eds. Amsterdam: Gordon & Breach, pp. 215–241.

Fooner, M. (1989). *Interpol issues in world crime and international criminal justice*. N.Y.: Plenum Press.

"History of Austria," Wikipedia. https://en.wikipedia.org/wiki/History_of_Austria. Last modified June 21, 2015

Kratcoski, P. (2011). Interview with Mag. Maximilian Edelbacher (Ret.) Federal Police of Austria. In *Trends in Policing—Interviews with Police Leaders Across the Globe*, O. Marenin and D. K. Das, eds. Boca Raton: CRC Press, pp. 23–48.

Lichem, A. (1935). *Die Kriminalpolizei: Handbuck fur den Kriminellan Polizeidienst.* Lenkam: Verlag.

Oberhummer, H. (1937). *Die Wiener Polizei 2 Bande 200 Jahre Sicherheit in Osterreich.* Wien: Verlag Gerold.

Seyrl, H. (2012). Handout of the Vienna Museum of Crimes. Vienna, Austria: Museum of Crimes.

Curb the Danger
Six Years of Curbing Impaired Driving through Police–Community Collaboration

JANA GREKUL
University of Alberta
Edmonton, AB, Canada

LAURA THUE
City of Edmonton, Office of Traffic Safety
Edmonton, AB, Canada

Contents

Introduction

Drunk driving and, in its extreme form, impaired driving, is a major (albeit preventable) cause of collisions, injuries, and fatalities. Despite efforts to reduce drinking and driving, this problem persists on a global scale and is of concern to law enforcement officials, policy makers, and citizens alike. Among Canadians, drinking and driving consistently appears at or near the top of the list of societal concerns. In 2013, 70% of citizens reported that they were "concerned or very concerned about drinking and driving" (TIRF 2013, 4). In the United States, where more than one million people are arrested each year for driving under the influence of alcohol or drugs, 97% of people see drinking and driving by others as a threat to their own safety (Beck et al. 2009). Similarly, research in the European Union found that 94% of its citizens considered drinking drivers to be "a major safety problem" in their respective countries (Gallup Organization 2010, 5).

In 2006, the police service in Edmonton, Alberta, Canada, recognized a need to identify innovative processes for increasing enforcement in order to better address impaired driving (EPS 2008). The acknowledgment that patrolling city streets is labor intensive and presents challenges to police services led to an approach to traffic enforcement that augments police efforts by calling on the public to "act as the 'eyes' of the police by reporting suspicious driving behavior to authorities" (Fisher et al. 2014, 1). The result in Edmonton was the Curb the Danger (CTD) program. This program aims to improve communication with citizens, enhance community awareness of impaired driving, and to increase enforcement by encouraging citizens to call 9-1-1* if they suspect someone is driving while impaired. As such, it provides an example of how community policing applies to the problem of impaired driving.

Drawing on police-recorded data and a public opinion survey, this chapter provides an evaluation of the effectiveness of CTD.[†] Included is a detailed description of the CTD program as well as an evaluation of CTD in terms of its activities and organizational processes. Within the context of this evaluation, this research explores the capacity of CTD to deter individuals from driving impaired and to detect and intercept those that drive impaired despite the consequences. This chapter provides insight into the workings of community–police collaboration and exposes CTD as an example of an international best practice in dealing with drinking drivers and in promoting traffic safety.

The Problem of Impaired Driving

On average, about 20% of fatally injured drivers in high-income countries have excessive alcohol in their blood (i.e., their blood alcohol concentration [BAC] is above the legal limit) (Global Road Safety Partnership 2007).

---

* We use "9-1-1" to remain consistent with the CTD documents; however, as the reader will notice, other programs refer to these calls as "911" calls. We remain consistent in our use of these different terms depending on the source or program to which we are referring.
[†] An earlier version of this report appears in Grekul and Thue (2013a).

This percentage increases to between 33% and 69% for middle- and low-income countries. In 2007, Canada had the highest percentage of fatal crashes where alcohol was a factor, surpassing the United States, Great Britain, Australia, France, Ireland, and Austria (Global Road Safety Partnership 2007). In 2010, between 1000 and 1500 people were killed in alcohol-involved collisions in Canada (Fisher et al. 2014). Mayhew et al. (2010) report that, of drinking drivers who were fatally injured in collisions, 81% were found to have a BAC that surpassed the legal limit, which in Canada is .08% (80 mg. of alcohol per 100 ml of blood). Finally, Pitel and Solomon (2013) report that, in Canada, more than one in five of the almost 300,000 people seriously injured in motor vehicle crashes in 2010 were injured as a result of an impairment-related crash (Fisher et al. 2014, 1).

Although it appears that the problem of impaired driving experienced a significant decline in Canada during the 1990s, progress seems to have slowed considerably since 2000 (Vanlaar et al. 2009). For example, self-reported driving after consumption of *some* amount of alcohol steadily increased since 2005 when 14.7% reported such behavior (Vanlaar et al. 2009). Following a jump to 24.4% in 2010 (from 19% the year prior), 2011 and 2012 witnessed slight decreases (to 19.2% and 17.3%, respectively) in the proportion of Canadians who reported driving after consuming any amount of alcohol in the past 30 days. This was followed by a slight increase to 17.8% in 2013 (TIRF 2013). The decline in impaired driving during the 1990s could be explained by a number of factors including more effective educational campaigns, the establishment of dedicated organizations such as Mothers Against Drunk Driving (MADD), or changes in legislation and enforcement practices. Possible reasons for the apparent diminishing progress after the 1990s are discussed later in this chapter.

The enduring problem of impaired driving is not limited to any particular group, but research does find variation by age and gender. For example, young males are overrepresented among those killed in alcohol-related collisions in Canada; in 2007, 80% of those killed in alcohol-related collisions were male, and 43% were between 20 and 35 years of age (Mayhew et al. 2010). Research further finds a distinction between "social drinkers," those who drink moderately and may drive after drinking but almost never with a high BAC, and "heavy drinkers," who drink frequently and excessively. According to Simpson et al. (2004, 261), the majority of this latter group satisfies the clinical definition of alcohol dependence or alcohol abuse. They drink and drive at a high rate of frequency, often with a high BAC (Simpson et al. 2004, 261).

Recent research in the United States supports these findings, showing that a sample of convicted impaired drivers reported having driven impaired at a high rate of frequency, often daily or several times a week, for long periods of time prior to detection (ITSMR 2009). One estimate is that the typical impaired driver offends between 80 and 2000 times before being arrested (Stewart 2012). Further support for the existence of this group of repeat offenders is found in Canadian research, which suggests that a small group of drinking drivers is responsible for the majority of drinking and driving trips. One study estimates that 84% of all "impaired driving" trips are accounted for by less than 3% of licensed drivers (Beirness et al. 2005, 9). The implications are significant in terms of police resource allocation; increasing resources or deploying existing resources more strategically to effectively target and apprehend this high risk group of drivers should result in a reduction in collisions, fatalities, and injuries related to impaired driving.

Targeting so-called heavy drinkers who drive and who are now commonly referred to as "hard-core drinking drivers" (HCDD), Simpson et al. (2004, 261), have important implications for improving traffic safety in general. It is believed that this group represents as much as 50% of drinking driver arrests and collisions and could account for more than 35% of drivers involved in alcohol-related fatal collisions (Simpson et al. 2004, 264). Research also shows that it is typical for fatally injured drinking drivers to be involved in multiple risky behaviors at the time of their collision. A study by Transport Canada (2008) found that nearly 30% of fatally injured drinking drivers were also speeding at the time of their collision, approximately 60% were not wearing seatbelts, and almost 20% were both speeding and not wearing a seatbelt.

The existence of both social drinking drivers and the hard-core group should be taken into consideration by those working to reduce impaired driving and improve traffic safety. Simpson et al. (2004) explain that social drinkers are thought to be more responsive to general deterrence; if they believe they are likely to be detected, arrested, convicted, and punished, then social drinkers will be less likely to drink to excess and drive. They are also more likely to be responsive to specific deterrence in that contact with the police is incentive for them to avoid drinking and driving again. On the other hand, heavy drinkers continue their behavior despite the risk of detection and often despite repeated arrests and convictions (Simpson et al. 2004, 261).

The deterrence model of criminal behavior assumes that people participate in an action after considering the potential risks and rewards of such behavior (Goff 2008). Deterrence research has found that *certainty* of detection and punishment is the most important element of deterrence, overshadowing the other two key elements: severity and celerity (Sacco and Kennedy 2002). Deterrence theory also assumes a rational decision maker. In the case of impaired driving, however, the effects of alcohol on an individual's perceived ability to safely drive a vehicle as well as perceptions of certainty of detection require further investigation. Although these questions are beyond the scope of the current study, the impact of the effects of alcohol on decision making cannot be ignored.

Beirness et al. (2005, 9) suggest that persistent drinking drivers may now comprise the core of the drinking driver problem, which may help to explain why gains in the movement to reduce drinking and driving in recent years have been less dramatic. It is possible that many social drinkers have been deterred from drinking and driving by educational campaigns and other programs, leaving the HCDDs—perhaps less easily deterred by such measures—to make up a larger proportion of the drinking and driving population. If this is the case, then it follows that an effective approach to dealing with this latter group should yield more impressive declines in the magnitude of the problem. On the other hand, research by Gruenewald et al. (1996) into drinking patterns as they relate to drinking and driving, finds that social drinkers may actually comprise a larger portion of the drinking and driving problem. These researchers point out that

> Even though high level drinking provides a higher risk of alcohol-related harm, moderate level drinking constitutes the most likely level at which harm will be incurred simply because one drinks so much more often at that level ... if a drinker consumes alcohol more often at low levels with moderate risks, the contribution of moderate drinking to harmful outcomes may be considerably greater in the aggregate than the contributions made by heavier drinking. (Gruenewald et al. 1996, 1648)

Taken together, these research findings suggest that a more targeted approach for those HCDD who repeatedly engage in this behavior is essential but so too is consistent enforcement and activities designed to raise awareness among moderate or social drinkers.

The Program: Curb the Danger

With its emphasis on community-based collaboration and mobilization, and the recognition by police that enlisting the aid of citizens to deal with crime can be effective, CTD is fundamentally a citizen-driven program for reducing impaired driving. Launched by the Edmonton Police Service (EPS) in 2006, the goals of the CTD program are to: (1) increase enforcement of impaired driving, (2) improve communication with citizens regarding impaired driving, and (3) increase awareness of impaired driving in the community. This model of policing is not new and is in fact rooted in the writings of Sir Robert Peel, who inspired the concept of the modern police force maintaining that "... the police are the public and the public are the police ..." (Kelling and Coles 1996, 106). As Morabito (2010, 564) states, "In the 1980s and 1990s community policing was viewed by many as a radical innovation in the field of policing." Since that time, research on the topic has grown significantly, providing researchers and practitioners alike with studies that have investigated numerous aspects of community policing, including its implementation, successes with the practice, influence on crime rates, challenges faced by policing agencies, and the impact of community policing on communities (Trojanowicz and Bucqueroux 1990; Wycoff and Skogan 1994; Kennedy and Veitch 1997; Kerley and Benson 2000; McDonald 2002; Skogan 2004).

The CTD program relies on citizens to report suspected impaired drivers to the police—community awareness and involvement are critical to the success of the program. For that reason, in implementing this program, the EPS partnered with the city of Edmonton Office of Traffic Safety to provide highly visible signage for the program (EPS 2008). These signs encourage citizens to call 9-1-1 when they observe a possible impaired driver and are strategically positioned in key locations throughout Edmonton.

When a citizen calls 9-1-1 to report a suspected impaired driver, the call is received by a police dispatch 9-1-1 operator. Once it is determined that the caller is in view of the suspected impaired driver, the call is transferred to a call evaluator who gathers relevant information from the caller (e.g., license plate, the type and color of vehicle, driving pattern). If the caller cannot safely keep the suspected impaired driver in view (for example, if the driver is speeding), or if the caller is unable to provide the information necessary to dispatch a police vehicle, the call is terminated and the incident is broadcast to all police units as "Be On the Lookout For" (BOLF) (EPS 2009).

If the pertinent information is obtained, the call will be dispatched as a Priority One call, defined as "High Priority in Progress, Person at Risk"* and efforts at police interception begin. The call evaluator will keep the caller on the line and update the caller as needed until a police officer is able to intercept the suspected impaired driver. At that time, the call evaluator will request that the caller pull over and wait until the police officer can interview the witness. Where a successful interception occurs, the police officer(s) will determine whether or not the driver is impaired or if there is another explanation for the driving pattern. The caller will be informed of the results of the stop and, if charges are possible, they will be asked to provide a witness statement (EPS 2009). When no officers are available to intercept the vehicle, if enough information has been provided, the call evaluator will inform the caller that a follow-up letter

---

* Prior to 2006, a number of event types were automatically classified as Priority One, the highest dispatch priority. Since 2006, events have been prioritized by the evaluator based on the information provided by the caller. A Priority One call is defined as a "High Priority in Progress, Person at Risk." Impaired driving calls where the caller is following a suspected impaired driver are considered a Priority One calls.

will be sent to the registered owner of the vehicle and will then terminate the call. All event information is captured in the computer-aided dispatch (CAD) system.

At this stage, the CTD team becomes involved. This portion of the program is managed by two retired police officers and an analyst in the traffic section. Each business day, all CTD events for the past 24 hours are reviewed to determine whether or not there was a successful interception. As noted, if there was no interception but enough information was obtained from the caller, the CTD team sends a letter to the registered owner to inform them that their vehicle was observed driving in an unsafe manner and has been the subject of a CTD call. The letter is sent as information only and includes the date, time, and location of the report; information on the CTD program; and an invitation to contact the program coordinator should they have questions or concerns.

In addition to letters, to facilitate other methods of follow-up, license plate numbers are tracked to detect repeat calls to CTD. The subjects of these calls include drivers who are impaired by alcohol and/or drugs, those that are otherwise impaired (for example, medically at-risk drivers) and drivers who are not impaired but have been repeatedly observed and reported for driving in an erratic or dangerous manner. Repeat plates are reviewed and a report may be prepared and forwarded to traffic section, patrol, or—in cases involving suspected driver medical incidents—to the Driver Fitness and Monitoring Branch of the provincial government for follow-up. The CTD team records all call details in a separate database for tracking, analysis, and reporting.

In summary, this program works to increase enforcement of impaired driving by enhancing communication with citizens and by escalating real-time citizen detection and reporting of this activity. This increase in community participation and citizen–police cooperation should serve to elevate the level of deterrence in the community and to reduce the number of drinking drivers on the road.

This program has the potential to increase guardianship as described by Cohen and Felson (1979) in their routine activities theory (RAT). In turn, this should increase the perception of certainty of detection and apprehension on the part of potential offenders. Guardianship comes in the form of a citizen willing to make a CTD call and the capacity of the police to dispatch an officer to the event. Arguably, the stronger this collaborative effort or dual guardianship is, the greater the impact on drinking drivers. As noted, social drinkers may be more effectively deterred by programs such as CTD than HCDD who may be resistant to any form of deterrence. For that reason, increasing the odds of police contact through a program like CTD may be one of the more effective ways of dealing with this small population of drivers who repeatedly drive while under the influence and who are responsible for a disproportionate number of traffic collisions, injuries and fatalities. In short, social drinkers are more likely to be deterred by the *threat* of a citizen report to CTD while HCDD, who repeatedly drink and drive, may be more effectively dealt with through *actual* contact with the police as a result of a CTD call(s).

Methods

This study, made possible through the collaborative efforts of academic researchers, the City of Edmonton Office of Traffic Safety, and the EPS, aims to describe and evaluate the CTD program and its activities. Our research objectives were to provide a description of the CTD program and to evaluate the effectiveness of CTD in terms of activities and organization processes, using as a framework the goals of the program. These goals are to: (1) increase enforcement of impaired driving, (2) improve communication with citizens regarding impaired driving, and (3) increase awareness of impaired driving in the community (EPS 2008).

The data used in this study came from three sources. The first includes calls for service data from the EPS CAD system. These data include the details of all CTD calls including the date and time of the reports, dispatch priority, event type, and the final disposition. The time period for this analysis is 2007–2012, capturing six full years of data after the program began operating in October 2006.

The second source is data collected specific to the CTD program that tracks CTD calls and their outcomes. With the launch of the project in October 2006, the CTD team began tracking all impaired driving calls and identifying all repeat CTD calls for the same license plate, the number of calls intercepted by the police, the number of registered owners who received a follow-up letter, the number of 24-hour license suspensions and impaired charges resulting from CTD calls, and the number and types of other charges that may result from what was initially an impaired driving call.

The third source of data is taken from the results of the *2010 Edmonton Survey* (Werner-Leonard et al. 2010) conducted by the University of Alberta's Population Research Laboratory (PRL), which specializes in the gathering, analysis, and presentation of data about demographic, social, and public issues. Respondents were contacted by telephone using a random digit dialing (RDD) process, with each survey lasting an average of 15 minutes. If the respondent was on a cell phone and was not able to continue the call, they were invited to provide an additional phone number where they could be reached. The final sample consisted of 402 Edmontonians (201 males and 201 females), 18 years of age or older

(Lulu 1991; Werner-Leonard et al. 2010).* Among other topics, respondents were asked a series of questions about the CTD program.

The CAD and CTD data provide the basis for an analysis of the activities and organizational processes of the program, while the survey data allow for an examination of citizens' level of awareness, responsiveness, and participation in CTD.

CTD Program Activities

Analyses of CAD data reveal that subsequent to the implementation of the CTD program in late 2006, there was a significant increase in the number of calls received by the EPS that related to a complaint of suspected impaired driver. In 2006, the EPS received 6618 of these calls. In 2007, after CTD, impaired driving calls increased to 9559, 44% (2941) above the 2006 total. The number of impaired driving calls peaked in 2008 at 10,210, declined from 2009 to 2011 (9792 to 7895, respectively) and then remained stable in 2012 (7922).†

The number of dispatched calls related to impaired driving also increased significantly in 2007. In 2006, 2647 impaired driving calls were dispatched. In 2007, this number rose to 4361, an increase of 65% (1714) above the 2006 total. This was followed by decreases in 2008 and 2009, of 4% (156) and 11% (480), respectively. From 2007 to 2012, approximately 42% of impaired driving calls were dispatched on average. Impaired driving calls where the caller is following a suspected impaired driver are classified as a Priority One call or "High Priority in Progress, Person at Risk." In 2007, 32% of impaired driving calls were classified as Priority One calls. After 2007, this number fluctuated between 27% and 30%. The introduction of CTD in 2006, and the subsequent increase in the number of calls, clearly had an impact on the workload for the police service. By 2012, six years after the implementation of CTD, 39% of all Priority One events involved a report of impaired driving. This figure was almost two-and-a-half times that of 2007 (17%), a number that was already higher than in previous years.

---

* When determining the sample size, the PRL took into account the population the survey aims to represent. For a population aged 18+ in a metropolitan area (500,000+), assuming a 5% margin of error at 95% confidence under random sampling conditions and a population characteristic estimated at 0.5, it usually results in a suggested sample of 384. The PRL "rounded up" the sample size to an even 400 to allow for respondents who might withdraw from the study; they also tended to include a few more participants in case there were problems with the quality of responses. The result in this case was a sample size of 402. (For more information please see N. M. Lulu's 1991 "Determination of Sample Size for Surveys." *Population Research, Laboratory Research Discussion Series.* Paper Number 86.)

† These totals exclude reopened calls and are based on the original event type.

Notwithstanding the increase in calls and a resulting rise in dispatches, the majority of CTD calls are eventually cancelled (58% on average from 2007 to 2012). This occurs for a number of reasons including situations where the caller is not able to safely follow the suspect, the caller may not be able to provide enough information (e.g., license plate number), and/or no police vehicles are available for dispatch. If the focus is on Priority One calls only, in 2007, 22% of Priority One impaired driving calls were cancelled. This figure dropped to 19% in 2008, remained stable at 19% in 2009, dropped to 15% in 2010, to 13% in 2011, and then rose slightly to 14% in 2012.

Temporal Patterns

An informed approach to deterring impaired drivers requires an understanding of the patterns relating to this behavior. Temporal patterns of CTD calls received by the EPS provide insight into some of the activities of drivers suspected of drinking and the citizens who report them.

The pattern of impaired driving calls by day of week remained remarkably stable from 2007 to 2012 with the lowest number of calls received Monday through Thursday and the highest number received Friday through Sunday. The maximum frequency of calls occurred on Saturdays (23%), followed by Sunday (18%), and Friday (17%) (see Figure 11.1).

The pattern of calls by hour of day also remained remarkably stable from 2007 to 2012. Calls are lowest during the morning hours, but then begin to increase steadily throughout the afternoon and into the evening. On Friday night and into early Saturday morning and on Saturday night into early Sunday morning, calls increase steadily until midnight, level off until 0200 and then spike between 0200 and 0300.

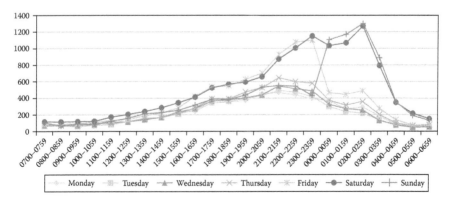

Figure 11.1 Impaired driving calls by hour of day and day of week, 2007–2012.

CTD Outcomes: Interceptions, Letters, Charges, and Repeat Offenders

Figure 11.2 presents the calls intercepted and the impaired outcomes of CTD calls as tracked by the CTD team. From 2007 to 2012, a total of 17,436 CTD calls were intercepted by police. On average, from 2007 to 2012, 34% of CTD calls were intercepted; the peak year was 2011 with 38% of calls successfully intercepted. When drivers are intercepted, an impaired charge, license suspension, other charges, or violation tickets are all possible outcomes. In Canada, a driver with a BAC of greater than .08% (80 mg. of alcohol per 100 ml of blood) is subject to a charge of impaired driving. The percentage of total CTD calls that result in the detection of an impaired driver has remained relatively constant over time at 9% to 10%. Between 2007 and 2012, almost 30% of intercepted CTD calls resulted in an impaired driving charge. This constituted almost 10% of all CTD calls made on a total of 5010 drivers.

Figure 11.3 presents the other types of outcomes that resulted from a CTD call. In 2007, nearly 30% (2407) of registered owners reported to the CTD program received a letter. However, gradual improvements to the process for identifying appropriate cases in which to send a letter has resulted in a decline in the number of letters issued over time, with only 7% (584) of registered owners being issued letters in 2012.*

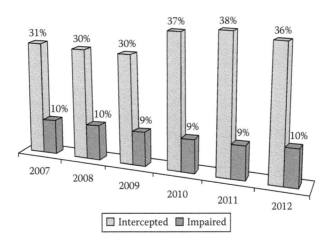

Figure 11.2 CTD calls intercepted that resulted in an impaired driving charge, 2007–2012.

---

* Improvements to the process include greater efforts to ensure the vehicle description provided by the caller matches that of the vehicle registered to the plate and requiring a more detailed description of the driving pattern.

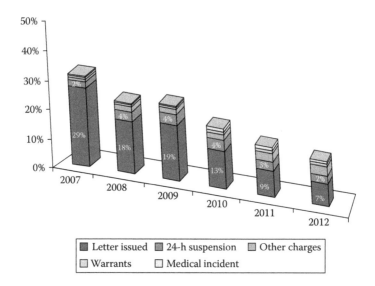

Figure 11.3 Other CTD outcomes, 2007–2012.

In several provinces, including Alberta, drivers with a BAC between .05% and .08% are subject to administrative penalties including immediate license suspensions.* Between 2007 and 2012, the number of 24-hour suspensions ranged between 2% and 4%. In addition to letters and suspensions, CTD calls often result in the issuance of tickets and in the execution of warrants. Although the manner in which these incidents are recorded precludes a precise accounting† these types of outcomes do occur with some frequency, pointing to the added benefits of the CTD program. For example, specific outcomes of calls have included, but are not limited to, tickets or arrests for the following: careless or dangerous driving; speeding; hit and run; suspended drivers, uninsured drivers, and drivers without a valid license; medically at risk drivers; and a variety of criminal charges involving assault, mischief, theft, drug and other alcohol-related offenses, stolen plates and stolen autos, firearms-related offenses, and breach of probation.

The CTD data shows that approximately 6–7% of CTD calls involve a repeat license plate. Although the driver and registered owner may not be the same person, this does provide a starting point for further police investigation of the repeat offender. In addition, although not all of these drivers are drinking drivers, it is possible that some of these plates belong to

---

* In Alberta, as of July 1, 2012, drivers with blood alcohol from .05% to .08% are subject to an immediate three-day license suspension and a three-day vehicle seizure. These penalties increase for repeat infractions.

† It is not possible to report on the exact number of other charges, warrants, and tickets based on these data because the information is not consistently provided to the CTD team, and it is difficult to estimate how much information is missing.

that group of persistent HCDDs. Most of these repeatedly reported plates have been called in at least twice and others have been reported as many as six or more times. For example, one license plate was reported to the program 35 times between October 2006 and December 2012, while another was reported 28 times. These statistics likely underestimate the number of repeat calls because a repeat call may only be tracked when the caller is able to provide sufficient information (i.e., the license plate).

Since 2007, the CTD program has become a major source of impaired driving offenses, accounting for 40% or more of these charges each year. However, survey results indicate that there is room for improvement in terms of encouraging the public to report drivers suspected of drinking.

Survey Results

In a survey of 402 citizens, using a representative sample, it was found that 66% (264) of Edmontonians were aware of the CTD program prior to being contacted as a survey respondent. Of those who were aware of the program, 40% (105) said they had seen the CTD signage on city roadways. Others said they had heard about the program on the radio (44%, 115), television (39%, 103), in the newspaper (25%, 65), from a friend (12%, 31), or the Internet (5%, 13), and three respondents said they were reported by a citizen to the CTD program (respondents were permitted to provide more than one response).

Despite the positive impact of the CTD program as gleaned from the police data, and the survey results showing that the majority of citizens are aware of the program, of the 39% of respondents who reported witnessing what they thought was an impaired driver in the past 12 months, 74% did *not* report the driver. Clearly, awareness of the program does not necessarily translate into action. The survey also questioned respondents about their perceptions of the likelihood that most adults in Edmonton would report an impaired driver. Only 26% (103) of respondents believe that it is extremely likely or likely that other city residents would call 9-1-1 to report an impaired driver.

With regard to deterrence, it is important to consider peoples' perceptions of the certainty of detection. Respondents were asked how likely they felt it was that someone would be stopped by the police while driving after having had too much to drink. Seventeen percent (66) of respondents believe that it is extremely likely or likely that an individual would be stopped by police. In sharp contrast, 50% (199) felt that it was not that likely or not at all likely that the individual would be stopped by the police.

Although the increase in calls from the public to report suspected impaired drivers following the introduction of CTD is very positive, the survey results expose a gap between awareness and action. Despite the increase in calls, a large majority of suspected impaired drivers are not being reported. However, the survey results indicate that the public is willing to participate in controlling drunk driving. If those respondents who *had* called 9-1-1 to report a suspected impaired driver in the past 12 months are excluded, 86% (305) of the remaining respondents said that if they *were* to see an impaired driver in the future they would call 9-1-1 to report the driver to the police. Thus, not only is there a gap between awareness and action but also between *intentions* and action.

The combination of citizen reluctance to report suspected impaired drivers and the finding that almost two-thirds of calls received by police are cancelled has important implications when considering increasing the impact of the CTD program and how to improve its impact.

Discussion

In this chapter, we have evaluated the CTD program, a community–police collaboration that aims to reduce impaired driving. The results of this study clearly point to the importance of community guardianship that translates into deterrence. In this case, guardianship takes the form of a citizen being willing to report a suspected impaired driver along with the capacity of the police to intercept that driver. If police capacity to detect and intercept impaired driving offenders is increased, or at a minimum, if there is a perception on the part of these offenders of an increased risk of being detected and intercepted by the police, this should increase deterrence. A number of cities in Canada have implemented 9-1-1 programs to empower citizens to assist police with the problem of impaired driving. For example, Calgary, Alberta initiated "Report Impaired Drivers" (RID) in 2009; Fredericton, New Brunswick, started a 9-1-1 call program in 2008, and York Region, Ontario, did so in 2006. MADD developed a nationwide campaign (Campaign 911) in 2007 in collaboration with its partner law enforcement organizations (e.g., the Canadian Police Association and the Canadian Association of Police Boards) (Fisher et al. 2014).

Evaluations of these programs show that citizens respond to media campaigns and especially road signage that encourage them to call 9-1-1 if they witness a suspected impaired driver (Fisher et al. 2014). The evaluation of the CTD program discussed in this chapter shows that an average of 34% of CTD calls from citizens are successfully intercepted by police each year, resulting in not only charges for impaired driving but also in numerous other charges and the execution of warrants. For those calls that do not result in interception by the police, the CTD program engages in a unique follow-up process by sending letters to registered owners to inform them that their vehicle was observed being driven erratically. Considering both interceptions and letters together, about 50% of calls resulted in official police attention. From a deterrence perspective, this translates into approximately 26,000 citizens over six years being subjected to what could be considered a form of specific deterrence.

On the other hand, this research has also identified opportunities to increase the effectiveness of the program. To begin, the processes and circumstances surrounding the high number of cancelled calls warrants further investigation. Each cancelled call translates into the failure to apprehend a potentially dangerous driver. Thus, there is a need to consider strategies for addressing existing challenges.

Survey data reveal that although the public is responding to the CTD campaign, this is not occurring to the extent initially expected. Of the proportion of survey respondents who observed a suspected driver in the past 12 months, only 26% called 9-1-1. This may be a reflection of the tendency for cognition and behavior to be disconnected under some conditions. People do not always do what they say or think they will do. The survey research indicates that the vast majority of respondents would call the police if they were to see a suspected impaired driver in the future, yet a much smaller percentage of the sample actually did so when the opportunity presented itself. Similarly, only 26% of respondents feel that it is extremely likely or likely that other city residents would call 9-1-1 to report an impaired driver and most feel that the likelihood of being stopped by police while driving after drinking too much is low. Future research should explore the factors that might impact the decision of whether or not to call 9-1-1 to report a suspected impaired driver. For example, attitudes may not always translate into action due in part to situational dynamics such as the effort and time required to make the call or feelings that the police will not be able to do anything about it. Along similar lines, survey data from an evaluation of the Calgary RID program shows that Calgarians experienced "little change in attitudes and intentions" regarding their willingness to call 911 to report a suspected impaired driver, yet, in that city, the volume of calls to police increased significantly (calls during the first year of implementation increased 80% compared to the year previous) (Fisher et al. 2014).

Another issue requiring further research concerns the police organization itself. It is evident that the community is responding to the police call for assistance in identifying impaired drivers, but this in turn has put greater pressure on the police to respond to these calls. With the implementation of CTD, it appears that more police resources are now being deployed to deal with suspected impaired drivers. This raises questions about resource allocation. Specifically, do the police have the necessary resources to respond, or are police resources being strained because of the greater community response to CTD?

One way of addressing this impact on resources may be to strategically deploy officers based on what is known about impaired driving call patterns and the drivers reported through the CTD program as identified in this evaluation. The most obvious implication is to consider strategic, supplementary deployment of resources during the peak times for calls identified in the temporal analysis. Future research could examine whether the dedication of additional police resources to impaired driving calls during this time frame is an achievable goal. Also, the spatial distribution of calls for service can be examined in conjunction with the location of CTD promotional signs.

It would be beneficial to explore the spatial distribution of impaired driving in terms of how this problem relates to the location of licensed premises. This raises interesting questions about neighborhoods, collective efficacy within neighborhoods, and the role of police in helping to build collective efficacy. Collective efficacy, which is related to lower rates of crime, refers to "the degree to which you trust your neighbors to provide [a] sense of safety, and to intervene if something problematic happens" (Uchida et al. 2013, 2). In neighborhoods with licensed drinking establishments that are identified as hot spots for impaired driving, programs such as CTD might help build collective efficacy among residents. If they follow the lead of some U.S. jurisdictions such as Montgomery County, Maryland, where "Citizen volunteers have been trained in the impaired driving detection cues and equipped with communication devices so that they can report suspected impaired drivers more directly and quickly to the police" (Fisher et al. 2014, 1), the community might increase its collective efficacy.

The data gathered by the CTD team supports the hypothesis that small groups of offenders repeatedly come to the attention of the EPS as a result of CTD calls. As noted, 6–7% of CTD calls are repeat calls in reference to the same license plate. Although not all of these plates will relate to an impaired driver, the implication is that greater efforts should be made to concentrate attention and resources on this group of drivers. Some of these drivers warrant the HCDD designation, while others could at the very least be identified as high risk drivers. Regardless, this is the group for whom general and specific deterrent efforts appear to be largely ineffective. In terms of enhancing the focus on these offenders, one option to consider is the feasibility of flagging plates that receive repeat CTD calls, either in CAD, the Canadian Police Information Centre (CPIC), and/or some other type of screening tool, which would allow for the real-time identification of these high risk drivers.* These calls could then be prioritized for dispatch. Again, this points to the need to consider dedicating resources for targeted dispatches to impaired driving calls. Focusing greater efforts on these repeat offenders, whether they are HCDDs or involved in other

---

* Currently, the CTD team will, on occasion, have a plate flagged in CPIC if a call analysis and subject profile indicates that this is worthwhile.

activities, could have significant cost benefit implications for any police service and ultimately for the community.

James Stewart, from the Saint John, New Brunswick Police Force, draws on a similar rationale in creating a method for providing a description of risky vehicles to assist officers with their enforcement efforts (Stewart 2012). Motivated by the observations that a high percentage of citizen-reported impaired driving calls involved vehicles that frequently appeared in their system, but that were never apprehended by the police, Stewart and his colleagues created a tool to assist officers. As part of their strategy, they selected "repeat target vehicle(s)" and created maps illustrating the location of all calls for service relating to each of the vehicles. The maps also included additional information that might assist enforcement officers in targeting the vehicles in question. In following the driving patterns of the Repeat Target Vehicles, Stewart reports that four of the seven vehicles were later involved in traffic collisions. When Stewart revisited records of alcohol-related motor vehicle accidents that resulted in injury or death since January 2000, he discovered that—of the 64 incidents—in 26 cases, the suspect vehicle had appeared in the police database prior to the accident (some appeared up to eight times). Stewart believes that his flagging instrument could have possibly resulted in police intervention with four of the suspect vehicles prior to their subsequent involvement in crashes (2012). These results validate the critical importance of citizen–police collaboration (such as CTD and other 9-1-1 campaigns) to crime prevention and the saving of lives.

A finding that emerged in this evaluation of CTD and one that appears in evaluations of other similar programs (Fisher et al. 2014) is the importance of provision of feedback to citizens regarding results of 9-1-1 programs in the community. As Fisher et al. (2014, 17) point out, "Publicizing the success of the public's efforts can be used to leverage further support from the public and will help increase perceptions that impaired drivers will be detected and apprehended." Quinton investigated the impact of information about crime and policing on public perceptions and reports that sharing crime and policing information with the public impacted positively on their perceptions of their neighborhood and the police. In the case of programs such as CTD, the ripple effects of such information sharing might be an increase in specific and general deterrence when it comes to drinking and driving, as well as the enhancement of police accountability.

Finally, research has shown that increased traffic enforcement can have the value added benefit of reducing other crime and disorder (Giacopassi and Forde 2000). Grekul and Thue (2013b) found that a small group of offenders, detected through the CTD program, are responsible for a disproportionate amount of traffic and other criminal offenses. A critical question to be addressed then is, what is the relationship among CTD, traffic enforcement, and crime reduction? Would an increase in traffic enforcement or a change in the deployment of resources, including those dedicated to CTD, contribute to a decrease in crime? By increasing the likelihood of interception and removing impaired drivers and/or other risky people from our roadways, the police could not only reduce impaired driving but likely also reduce other traffic violations, crime, and disorder as well. This deterrent effect and expected increase in the apprehension of repeat offenders translates into a decrease in calls for service and *less* demand on police resources and, therefore, costs to the police service. Also, these outcomes would likely result in an increased level of public satisfaction with the police.

Conclusion

The findings of this evaluation of the CTD program indicate that CTD has impacted the community in terms of its stated objectives of increasing communication, awareness, and enforcement. The introduction of the program in 2006 increased the number of impaired driving calls received from the public, and these calls have translated into results. CTD has now become a major source of impaired driving-related charges. This research further shows that CTD has the capacity to deter citizens from driving impaired and to increase the risk of detection and interception for those that do.

Although the increased number of calls to police indicates that the public is responding to the CTD campaign, survey results reveal that the response is not as strong as it could be. The survey research finds that the vast majority of respondents reported that they *would* call the police if they were to see a suspected impaired driver in the future, yet a much smaller percentage actually did so when the opportunity presented itself. In combination with the high number of cancelled calls, these findings suggest that there are many suspected impaired drivers that are not being reported, and of those that are reported, a large number are not being intercepted. The findings therefore have implications for both community responsiveness and for police resource deployment. Taken as a whole, while there is room to increase the effectiveness of CTD. This research has provided evidence that community–police collaboration can have an impact on impaired driving.

Acknowledgments

The authors extend their sincere appreciation to the Edmonton Police Service (EPS) for assistance with and use of their data and to the City of Edmonton, Office of Traffic Safety, for spearheading this research. The interpretations expressed herein are solely those of the authors and do not reflect the official positions of the city of Edmonton or of the EPS.

References

Beck, K. H., Yan, A. F., Wang, M. Q., Kerns, T. J., & Burch, C. A. (2009). The relationship between impaired driving collisions and beliefs about impaired driving: Do residents in high collision rate counties have greater concerns about impaired driving? *Traffic Injury Prevention, 10*, 127–133.

Beirness, D. J., Simpson, H. M., Mayhew, D. R., & Desmond, K. (2005). *The road safety monitor 2005: Drinking and driving*. Ottawa: Traffic Injury Research Foundation.

Cohen, L. E., & Felson, M. (1979). Social change and crime rate trends: A routine activity approach. *American Sociological Review, 44*, 588–608.

EPS (Edmonton Police Service). (2008). *Curb the danger—A process for curbing impaired driving through community involvement. IACP/Motorola Webber Seavey Award application*. Edmonton: Edmonton Police Service.

EPS (Edmonton Police Service). (2009). *Curb the danger: A process for curbing impaired driving through community involvement*. Edmonton: Edmonton Police Service.

Fisher, D. A., Michael, S., & Fell, J. C. (2014). *Call 911 programs for reporting suspected impaired driving: A preliminary investigation in four Canadian communities*. Beltsville, MD: Pacific Institute for Research and Evaluation.

Gallup Organization. (2010). *Road safety: Analytical report*. Flash Eurobarometer Series 301. Hungary: The Gallup Organization.

Giacopassi, D., & Forde, D. R. (2000). Broken windows, crumpled fenders, and crime. *Journal of Criminal Justice, 28*, 397–405.

Global Road Safety Partnership. (2007). *Drinking and driving: A road safety manual for decision-makers and practitioners*. Geneva: Global Road Safety Partnership.

Goff, C. (2008). *Criminal justice in Canada*. 4th ed. Toronto: Thomson Nelson.

Grekul, J., & Thue, L. (2013a). Curb the danger: A police-community collaboration to 'curb' impaired driving. *Police Practice & Research: An International Journal, 14*(5), 402–414.

Grekul, J., & Thue, L. (2013b). *Curb the danger phase II: Investigation of the relationship between impaired driving, other risky driving behaviours, and crime*. Edmonton, AB: Office of Traffic Safety.

Gruenewald, P. J., Mitchell, P. R., & Treno, A. J. (1996). Drinking patterns and their consequences: Report from an international meeting. *Addiction, 91*(11), 1637–1649.

ITSMR (Institute for Traffic Safety Management and Research). (2009). *A study on drinking and driving in New York State: A focus group approach*. ITSMR research note. Albany: University of Albany.

Kelling, G. L., & Coles, C. M. (1996). *Fixing broken windows: Restoring order and reducing crime in our communities*. New York: Simon and Schuster.

Kennedy, L. W., & Veitch, D. (1997). Why are crime rates going down? A case study in Edmonton. *Canadian Journal of Criminology, 39*, 51–69.

Kerley, K., & Benson, M. (2000). Does community-oriented policing help build stronger communities? *Police Quarterly, 3*, 46–69.

Lulu, N. M. (1991). Determination of sample size for surveys. In *Population Research, Laboratory Research Discussion Series*. Edmonton: Population Research Laboratory, University of Alberta, Canada. Paper no. 86.

Mayhew, D. R., Brown, S. W., & Simpson, H. M. (2010). *The alcohol-collision problem in Canada: 2007.* Ottawa: Traffic Injury Research Foundation.

McDonald, J. (2002). The effectiveness of community policing in reducing urban violence. *Crime & Delinquency, 48,* 592–618.

Morabito, M. S. (2010). Understanding community policing as an innovation: Patterns of adoption. *Crime and Delinquency, 56*(4), 564–587.

Pitel, S., & Solomon, R. (2013). *Estimating the Number and Cost of Impairment-Related Traffic Crashes in Canada: 1999-2010.* Oakville, ON: MADD Canada. Retrieved from http://www.madd.ca/english/research/estimating_presence.pdf.

Sacco, F. S., & Kennedy, L. W. (2002). *The criminal event. An introduction to criminology in Canada.* 3rd ed. Toronto: Nelson Thomson Learning.

Simpson, H. M., Beirness, D. J., Robertson, R. D., & Mayhew, D. R. (2004). Hard core drinking drivers. *Traffic Injury Research Prevention, 5,* 261–269.

Skogan, W. (2004). Community policing: Common impediments to success. In L. Fridell & M. A. Wycoff (Eds.), *Community policing: The past, present, and future* (pp. 159–167). Washington, DC: Annie E. Casey Foundation, Police Executive Research Forum.

Stewart, J. (2012). Reducing impaired driving through the identification of repeat target vehicles: A case study. *Journal of Safety Research, 43,* 39–47.

TIRF (Traffic Injury Research Foundation). (2013). *The road safety monitor 2013: Drinking and driving in Canada.* Ottawa, Ontario: TIRF.

Transport Canada. (2008). *Alcohol-related collisions in Canada: Driver characteristics and casualty trends.* Ottawa: Road Safety Directorate.

Trojanowicz, R., & Bucqueroux, B. (1990). *Community policing: A contemporary perspective.* Cincinnati, OH: Anderson.

Uchida, C. D., Swatt, M. L., Solomon, S. E., & Varano, S. (2013). *Data-driven crime prevention: New tools for community involvement and crime control.* Silver Spring, MD: Justice & Security Strategies.

Vanlaar, W., Marcoux, K. D., & Robertson, R. D. (2009). *The road safety monitor 2009: Drinking and driving in Canada.* Ottawa: Traffic Injury Research Foundation.

Werner-Leonard, A., Kennedy, T., & Brazil, J. (2010). *2010 Edmonton survey.* Edmonton: Population Research Laboratory, University of Alberta.

Wycoff, M. A., & Skogan, W. G. (1994). Community policing in Madison: An analysis of implementation and impact. In D. P. Rosenbaum (Ed.), *The challenge of community policing: Testing the promises* (pp. 75–91). Thousand Oaks, CA: Sage.

A Multidisciplinary Approach to Equivocal Death Analysis

12

EDWARD CHAFE AND
ANGELA WYATT EKE
Ontario Provincial Police
Orillia, Ontario, Canada

PETER I. COLLINS
Centre for Addiction and
Mental Health in Toronto
Ontario, Canada

JON D. CROMER
Virginia State Police
Appomattox, VA, USA

JOANNE BREWSTER
James Madison University
Harrisonburg, VA, USA

Contents

Introduction

It is estimated that there were 2.6 million deaths in 2013 (Centers for Disease Control and Prevention 2013), with other countries such as Canada reporting approximately a quarter million (Demography Division, Statistics Canada 2013). Common reasons for death vary based on factors such as age (e.g., in the United States, accidental deaths are most common for those aged 1–44 years, compared with death due to illness for those 45 years and older; Minino 2013). In most cases, the reason a person dies is well understood. There are, however, times where we may know the cause of death (e.g., subdural hemorrhage due to blunt trauma injury), but the manner of death (e.g., accident, homicide) is unknown or equivocal (e.g., ambiguous, uncertain, questionable). Some authors suggest that between 5 and 20% of deaths examined for certification by a coroner or medical examiner are equivocal (see Botello et al. 2013; Porter and Wrightsman 2014). In these instances, those investigating the death engage in a process to determine manner of death; we refer to this as an equivocal death analysis (EDA).

In this chapter, we define and describe EDA, and we examine the methodology used in these analyses. We discuss the roles that various professionals may play in an EDA and highlight the benefits of a multidisciplinary approach. Throughout this chapter, we also refer to the available peer-reviewed literature and provide examples to highlight key concepts and main points. It is important to know the true circumstances relating to a death for many reasons, such as to help us to better understand how to prevent such deaths in the future, to avoid a miscarriage of justice, and to help appropriately allocate criminal justice resources, to provide accurate information relevant to benefits and insurance policies, and to provide family and friends with closure.

Certification of Death

In some cases, a death is not unexpected. For example, someone has taken ill or is under the immediate care of a doctor. In these circumstances, the death will likely not involve a police investigation or any form of professional medical review. When a person dies outside of direct care (e.g., outside a hospital, hospice, or assisted living environment), or if there are questions relating to the care, a coroner, medical examiner, or similar professional (determined by the country, state, or provincial government) may be required to review the circumstances prior to providing certification of the death. For certification, the professional (we will refer to this person as a medical examiner throughout this chapter) provides an opinion relating to three specific areas or determinations: the mechanism, the cause, and the manner of death. Before continuing with the discussion of the process of conducting an EDA, it is important to note that, in most jurisdictions, it is the medical examiner, not the law enforcement professional, who has the absolute authority under statutory law to certify cause and manner of death. Nevertheless, as we shall describe here, there are occasions where an EDA conducted by a law enforcement professional is needed, but it cannot be successfully conducted without the information provided to the investigator by the medical examiner. Thus, all EDAs are by definition multidisciplinary, involving at the very least the participation of law enforcement professionals and the medical examiner; but in many cases, the assistance of mental health professionals and others will also be needed.

We are aware that not everyone uses the terms mechanism, cause, and manner of death in exactly the same way, but we will define what we consider to be common uses of these terms. The *mechanism* is generally defined as the physiological process or change that led to the medical cause of a death, such as the shutting down of an organ system (e.g., Froede 1990). The *cause* of death is the pathological condition that produced the death. For example, the medical examiner might specify that the cause of death was a subdural hemorrhage produced by blunt force trauma to the skull. The medical examiner does not need the assistance of police investigators to determine the cause of death; that is determined by the medical evidence based on the condition of the body. The trickier problem is to determine the *manner* of death (some refer to this as *mode*; e.g., Biffl 1996), which involves an explanation or judgment of the circumstances surrounding the death—that is, how the death came about. To answer this question, the information supplied by the police is almost always vital. Except in the case of a sudden natural death, such as a heart attack, the medical examiner may need additional information obtained through a police investigation to assist in determining manner of death.

Manner of Death

There are four main classifications of manner of death: natural, accident, suicide, or homicide. In addition, for some deaths, the manner is undetermined. Some investigators use the acronym NASH for the four determined categories of manner of death (see Shneidman 1981). Various government agencies have handbooks that detail their process for certifying a death in which they describe key components such as manner of death (Centers for Disease Control and Prevention 2003; Illinois Coroners and Medical Examiners Association 2007). The descriptions of the categories of manner of death are fairly standard. A natural death is generally one that is entirely, or mostly, due to a natural disease, including those due to old age. An accident is an injury caused in the absence of intent to do harm. A homicide involves the intent to do harm to another, and suicide is the intent to do harm to oneself. Sometimes the circumstances of death involve a combination of natural and other factors; in these cases, the manner may be determined by the unnatural circumstances using the "but-for" test (see the Illinois Coroners and Medical Examiners Association 2007). "But-for" a hostile environment, death would have been less likely. For example, the driver of a car has a heart attack (that may be survivable with treatment) that results in a car crash and his/her death. This might be ruled an accident using the "but-for" test (the car crash). Similarly, death due to cirrhosis of the liver from chronic alcohol use would likely be classified as a natural death (disease), whereas immediate intoxication involving purposefully ingesting an overdose of medications would be categorized a suicide. A death is undetermined or *equivocal* when there is no clear set of associated circumstances that allows the manner of death to be determined, even after a medicolegal investigation has been completed. At the heart of equivocal death investigations are often concerns of suicide versus accident or homicide. To assist in determining whether manner of death is associated with suicide, a psychological autopsy may be employed; this is described later in this chapter.

An Overview of EDA

The term equivocal death analysis (EDA) broadly refers to a methodology for determining manner of death. In theory, every objective and thorough death investigation thoughtfully considers each possible manner of death before arriving at a conclusion. A true EDA is done in those cases where, by definition, the circumstances of the death can be interpreted in more than one way.

Consider the following commonly cited hypothetical situation (originally Ebert 1987; also see Biffl 1996): An individual jumps from a plane wearing a parachute that does not open; he falls and dies from what appears to be multiple injuries. Did the parachutist jump and, being fully aware of the consequences, decide not to open his chute? If so, the manner of death would be suicide. Was the parachutist intentionally pushed from the plane before the chute was properly prepared for deployment? If so, the manner of death would be homicide. Did he accidentally fall from the plane, or did the chute malfunction? If so, it would be an accidental death. Or, did he have a heart attack that caused him to be unable to pull the cord? This would be a natural death. Even knowing what caused the parachutist's physical death (trauma), we cannot specify the circumstances that brought about the death without further information. In the vast majority of cases, a thorough police investigation will discover the manner of death. An EDA may be required in only a small number of cases (5–20%; see Botello et al. 2013) where the investigation does not result in a definitive opinion.

Genuine equivocal death cases are likely to be among the most difficult cases that any investigator will ever handle. By the time the equivocal death consultants become involved, these cases may have become quite problematic, with inconsistencies or biases in the way information has been gathered, handled, or shared. For example, a respected lawyer in a small town who often works with the police called 911 to report his wife's death from an apparent suicide. The dispatcher, who was acquainted with the lawyer, expressed condolences during the call and conveyed the idea to the responding officers that the death was a suicide. Bias has already been introduced into this investigation because the information conveyed by the husband may already have been accepted as the truth. The responding officers, working on the premise of a suicide, may inadvertently make quick work of the death scene and may fail to gather information and evidence that later becomes crucial when the question of homicide is eventually raised. An equivocal death consultant entering this situation may be facing a very difficult case. The investigator could be relying on inadequate information from the original investigation and decreased future cooperation from investigators who may have an unconscious bias. A very public and well-known example of the difficulties that can be faced in an EDA is reflected in the case of the explosion on the U.S.S. *Iowa* in 1989; investigations into the deaths of 47 crewmen focused in part on the actions of a specific sailor and questioned whether the explosion was accidental or an act of suicide or sabotage (e.g., see Thompson 1999).

The equivocal death analysis process reviews a wide variety of information with a focus on four pertinent areas: (1) the state of mind of the deceased, (2) the method or means of death, (3) the scene(s), and (4) the forensic science and medical evidence. Various professionals have developed checklists or guidelines to inform the investigation of each of these areas, and there are also specific tools for assessing potential suicides such as the empirical criteria for the determination of suicide (ECDS: Jobes et al. 1991), which will be briefly described later in this chapter. A review of these documents and a full discussion regarding the efficacy of various tools and guidelines is beyond the scope of this chapter; there are many examples available (see Ebert 1987; Shneidman 1981) and many discussions of the issues surrounding both EDA (e.g., see Ault et al. 1994) and psychological autopsies (see Biffl 1996; Ogloff and Otto 1993).

The State of Mind of the Deceased

A deceased's *state of mind* can be very difficult to understand or interpret. To further complicate this, people may apply their own personal logic or morality to explain why others engage in various behaviors, especially when examining uncommon actions (e.g., self-immolation or mutilation). Remaining committed to understanding how certain behaviors mattered to the deceased at the time of death is important. When examining the state of mind of a deceased, an analysis often requires a detailed time line of the last hours, days, weeks, or sometimes even years leading up to the death. During this stage of the EDA, collaboration with mental health professionals who can assist the investigator in interpreting the data can be very helpful.

Understanding the presence (or absence) of certain factors helps lead to the determination of the manner of death. When considering state of mind, these factors can range from usual behaviors for the individual to recent unusual or uncharacteristic factors. For example, had there been any recent stressors, such as occupational difficulties, familial crisis, or relationship breakdown? What were the person's typical reactions to stress; for example, did he or she become angry or withdrawn? Were there notable changes in habits or routines prior to death (hobbies, appetite, sexual patterns)? What leisure activities did he or she engage in—from yoga to extreme risk-taking behaviors? In considering the state of mind of the deceased, an EDA will examine and assess a variety of factors based on what is known about human psychology, using clinical and empirical or research-based knowledge. In developing hypotheses about the psychological state of mind of an individual, including factors associated with suicide, a mental health professional with expertise in the area is a valuable resource. This individual may carry out a psychological autopsy.

Psychological Autopsy

EDA and psychological autopsy (PA) are not interchangeable terms, although they are often used as such. The concept of PA was developed at the Los Angeles Suicide Prevention Center by Drs. Robert Litman, Norman Farebrow, and Edwin Shneidman (see Botello et al. 2013). The first documented PA was conducted at the request of Dr. Theodore Curphey of the Los Angeles County Medical Examiner's Office (Botello et al. 2003). Later, Curphey would write about the importance of a multidisciplinary approach to the medicolegal certification of suicide (see Curphey 1961). Based on this investigative procedure into the psychology of the deceased, Shneidman coined the term psychological autopsy (for a review of the work by Shneidman, see Leenaars 2010). Botello et al. (2013) describe the first high profile death that used a PA approach as being the death of Marilyn Monroe. It has been suggested that the PA is becoming a more common consultation for forensic psychiatrists, in collaboration with the medical examiner and other professionals (Botello et al. 2003).

The PA is an evaluation of, and retrospective investigation into, the deceased's psychological state at the time of death, including his or her intention to die (Botello et al. 2003). In a sense, it is an investigation through the lens of a mental health professional (e.g., psychiatrist or psychologist) or trained criminal profiler. As part of the state of mind component of an EDA, a PA should involve interviewing spouses, other family members, friends, witnesses, coworkers, family physicians, and so forth regarding the psychological characteristics and mental state of the deceased. An example of a PA was the evaluation of a homicide–suicide of a police inspector who murdered her boyfriend (a retired police superintendent) and then killed herself. The original PA report was more than 250 pages in length; the executive summary is available online through the London Police Service (report by Leenaars et al. 2008).

A concern with conducting psychological autopsies is that grieving family members and friends may find the process upsetting, or they may have difficulty coping with the emotions that the process invokes (see discussion in Wong et al. 2010). However, there may be fewer negative effects than might be expected, and participating in the PA may be viewed by many informants as beneficial (e.g., Wong et al. 2010).

The PA has some limitations (see review in Sher 2013). For example, there may be bias in the information recalled by interviewees, or they may underreport the major personal events of the deceased because they were unaware of them (e.g., unaware of a recent pregnancy, marital trouble, bullying, and so forth). As well, the interviewees' personal psychological reaction to the death, including what is believed about the events surrounding the death, may lead to incorrect reporting of events (e.g., exaggeration of drug use or risky behavior).

As stated earlier in this chapter, at the heart of an undetermined death are often concerns of suicide versus accident or homicide. Factors specific to suicide from both a clinical and empirical perspective are therefore important when considering state of mind. To minimize potential biases and limitations, it is helpful to have interview information from multiple sources and to use a team approach, with team discussions. Mental health professionals can often provide invaluable assistance to the lead investigator in evaluating the various factors, including the presence of a mental illness that may allow the investigators to discriminate among these possibilities. Information and research on suicide is available from multiple sources, including from the medical, psychological, and sociological fields.

Suicide is a leading cause of premature and preventable death in North America (see statistics from the Centers for Disease Control and Prevention at http://www.cdc.gov/; for Canada, see http://www.statcan.gc.ca/). There is a variety of research describing factors associated with suicide, suicide attempts, and the methods used in suicide. Suicide has been described as a multidimensional event that cannot be reduced to a single factor (Leenaars 2004). Knowledge of this type of information is valuable for the EDA and the PA; an expert in the area of suicide can help investigators in their consideration of various factors and how they may relate to the deceased. The risk of suicide is not the same for all members of a population, and a complex array of potential contributing factors exists, such as mental illness, social isolation, marital breakdown, physical illness, and substance abuse (Navaneelan 2012).

The Method or Means of Death

A key question to ask during the EDA process is why some people select or involve a specific instrument or means of death. With suicide or homicide, the type of weapon or injurious agent is often chosen because of access, but it may also be selected because of comfort level, skill, or familiarity. For example, in a suicide, a hunter may use his long gun, a police officer may use his issued firearm, or a doctor may use an anesthetic. In a homicide, someone who is proficient with knives may use an edged weapon, or a chemist may use poison.

Establishing the presence of lethal intent is an important consideration with regard to the means of death. For example, what defines death as a suicide, rather than an accident, is intention (Litman 1984). Evaluating whether there was lethal intent, and its extent, provides insight into the level of determination shown by the victim. For example, if a male drove his vehicle to a secluded location, poured gasoline over his entire body, and then lit a book of matches, that would be indicative of high lethality and high intent. If that same male decided instead that he was going to go to a busy city intersection and in plain view set his clothes on fire with one matchstick but without any combustibles, it would be indicative of low lethality and low intent. Again, if the same male decided that while on route to either of the locations he was now going to run his vehicle at a high speed into the rear of a parked car, it could be considered high intent but low lethality, given the safety equipment found in modern vehicles.

To assist in consideration of the means of death, investigators or equivocal death analysts (or a mental health professional conducting a PA) will sometimes utilize the ECDS (Jobes et al. 1991), which evaluates the two key components of suicide, self-infliction and intention. The ECDS helps to differentiate between suicide and accident, and although it is not intended to assess the likelihood of homicide, the absence of indicators of suicide may provide some insight into that manner of death.

The Scene(s)

The proper collection, documentation, and processing of evidence at a death scene (e.g., fiber, fingerprints, footwear impressions, biological samples) is of vital importance and is key to crime scene reconstruction (CSR). The collection of evidence for the purpose of the CSR is conducted by the investigative team and, depending on the jurisdiction, most often includes the assistance or guidance of forensic identification officers or forensic specialists. Many times, the manner of death is obvious to the investigators. For example, a male who was diagnosed with depression had barricaded himself inside his residence and had made several suicidal threats to his family members. Police were called to assist and upon arrival found the male deceased. Beside his body were a bloodied knife and an empty bottle of liquor. He had sustained numerous superficial incised wounds and two deep penetrating stab wounds to his chest. The blood flow on his clothing was patterned in one direction, indicative of no apparent resistance, struggle, or postmortem movement. This was ruled a suicide. However, every scene is different, and sometimes there are features of the scene that may initially go unnoticed or unrecognized by investigators, such as the presence of paraphilic behaviors. For this reason, it is important that all of the possible manners of death are deliberately considered, and the evidence for and against each possible manner of death is reviewed, before any is simply ruled out.

At any death scene, a concern for police is the possibility that the scene may have been changed in some way. Specifically, the concern may be the purposeful alteration of a scene to make the death appear to be something it is not. For example, an offender may engage in the physical manipulation of a murder scene or of the victim's body to divert suspicion away from himself or to disguise the manner of death. The offender may try to make the death appear to be a suicide or an accident, or he may attempt to make the death appear due to the actions of someone else (e.g., a serial killer, a break-and-enter offender). This is often referred to as *staging*. Staging is not a new concept and has been described in various crime scene investigation publications (Douglas and Munn 1992; Geberth 1996) including older texts describing "false" scenes (see Söderman and O'Connell 1962; Svensson and Wendel 1965).

Not all alterations to a crime scene are staging. This is part of the difficulty for an EDA. For example, some offenders alter a homicide scene for ritualistic purposes that have special meaning to them, such as posing the body in a specific position or adding items such as those with a personal, religious, or other symbolic theme. Other offenders may demonstrate empathy toward their victim after death, for example, by redressing them. There are also circumstances where a scene or a body may be physically manipulated by others to preserve the dignity of the deceased or to avoid embarrassment to the family. For example, a family member may alter an autoerotic fatality to look like a suicide.

There is limited research on staging in cases of homicide (e.g., Eke 2007; Hazelwood and Napier 2004; Schlesinger et al. 2014). Studies to date suggest that when there is a staged scene, most victims and offenders had some type of relationship (e.g., prior intimate, acquaintance, or family; see Eke 2007 as well as Hazelwood and Napier 2004). The existence of a relationship perhaps relates to the impetus to stage. Commonly staged scenes are break-and-enters and accidents. Scenes staged to look like suicides or natural causes were less frequent in the research (see Eke 2007; Schlesinger et al. 2014); however, these are perhaps the least likely to be detected as a murder.

The overall percentage of murders that are staged is unknown and some staging will be successful, leading to undetected or unsolved murders. Being familiar with and understanding staging (as well as recognizing scenes altered for other purposes) is an important role of investigators. To carry out their assessment of potential staging, investigators need solid forensic data collected at the scene, for which they often must rely on other law enforcement professionals, as well as observations and evaluations of behavioral inconsistencies at the scene. In this regard, the expertise of a mental health professional may be helpful.

The Forensic Science and Medical Evidence

With regard to the forensic and medical evidence, an autopsy can reveal many things about the deceased that family or friends were not aware of, such as substance abuse, sexual disorders, or even terminal illness. A medical examiner's findings are of paramount importance to the determination of cause, mechanism, and manner; but, unfortunately, there are occasions when investigators rely too heavily on the medical examiner to provide them with the manner of death based on the autopsy results, and that is unfair to the medical examiner. Depending on the jurisdiction, differences in crime scene procedures, lack of experience on the part of the personnel gathering the evidence, or lack of experience on the part of the investigator may result in medical examiners not being provided with accurate facts or circumstances of the scene; as a result, there may be misinterpretation of the evidence. What may appear during the postmortem examination as suspicious may actually be innocently explained. For example, a man was found deceased in his apartment with a ligature marking across his neck. Investigators initially believed that he had been murdered and died as a result of ligature strangulation; however, the postmortem examination revealed that the cause of death was not strangulation but was a heart attack. Upon review of the scene photographs, the male was observed to be lying across a computer cable that left the suspicious impression on his neck.

In many cases of ligature or manual strangulation, there will be petechiae in the eyes; however, the presence of these pinpoint hemorrhages does not necessarily indicate that death was due to strangulation. Petechiae can be seen in a number of other conditions, including natural disease. Sometimes there will be no evidence of petechiae in spite of strangulation because both external and internal injuries can vary with the intensity of the assault or the resistance of the victim. For example, if a victim is on drugs or unconscious, there may be less resistance and potentially fewer visible injuries. Some investigators believe that with strangulation there should also be evidence of a fractured hyoid; again, this is dependent on the force or type of force used. If an offender uses a soft ligature, there may be minimal or no damage to the internal neck structures. With regard to the death of a child, a forensic examination can conclude that there is a lacerated frenulum; however, it might be the result of a slap to the mouth, smothering, or an accidental fall. To reiterate, although an autopsy or forensic evidence may reveal a finding that is suspicious in nature, things may not always be as they appear. Or, something that initially appeared to be innocent may be revealed by the autopsy to be an indicator of homicide. The input of the medical examiner is critical to establishing an accurate manner of death.

Summary and Conclusion

Not all deaths are easily or quickly understood. In some cases, the manner of death—that is, how the death occurred—may be equivocal; in these instances, an EDA may be undertaken. Conducting an EDA can be time consuming and complex, and it is important to approach it from a multidisciplinary perspective rather than relying on the expertise of one individual. The type and nature of the expert advice needed and its role in the EDA may vary with each investigation. In some cases, experts will engage in a separate and specific assessment of their own, such as a PA, or they may use specific suicide checklists. In North America, it is common for the lead analyst to consult with medical examiners, psychiatrists, psychologists, forensic scientists, behavioral specialists, and others when their area of expertise is relevant to the death under investigation.

As complex or complicated as any death investigation can be, often the simplest solution to even the most difficult question is the correct one. However, there are those cases where, after the determination of the manner of death, the family or other individuals will dispute the accuracy of the finding. The fact that the death was deemed equivocal in the first place implies that there was more than one way to interpret the evidence. EDA is a process that identifies, evaluates, and analyzes four pertinent components: the state of mind of the deceased, the means or method of death, the scene, and the forensic science and medical evidence. A thorough examination of these four areas, in conjunction with the insight of experts and specialists from various disciplines, often creates a clearer picture of the manner of death.

References

Ault, R.L., Hazelwood, R.R., and Reboussin, R. (1994). Epistemological status of equivocal death analysis. *American Psychologist, 49,* 72–73. doi: 10.1037/0003-066X.49.1.72.

Biffl, E. (1996). Psychological autopsies: Do they belong in the courtroom? *American Journal of Criminal Law, 24,* 123–146.

Botello, T., Noguchi, T., Sathyavagiswaran, L., Weinberger, L.E., and Gross, B.H. (2013). Evolution of the psychological autopsies: Fifty years of experience at the Los Angeles County Chief Medical Examiners-Coroner's Office. *Journal of Forensic Sciences, 58,* 924–926. doi: 10.1111/1556-4029.12138.

Botello, T., Weinberger, L., and Gross, B. (2003). Psychological autopsy. In R. Rosner (Ed.), *Principles and Practice of Forensic Psychiatry,* 2nd Ed. London: Arnold, pp. 89–94.

Centers for Disease Control and Prevention. (2003). *Medical examiners' and coroners' handbook on death registration and fetal death reporting.* Hyattsville, MD: DHHS Publication.

Centers for Disease Control and Prevention. (2013). Detailed Tables for the National Vital Statistics Report (NVSR), *Deaths: Final Data for 2013.* http://www.cdc. gov/nchs/data/nvsr/nvsr64/nvsr64_02.pdf.

Curphey, T.J. (1961). The role of the social scientist in the medico-legal certification of death by suicide. In N.L. Farberow and E.S. Shneidman (Eds.), *The cry for help.* New York, NY: McGraw Hill, pp. 110–117.

Demography Division, Statistics Canada. (2013). Deaths, estimates, by province and territory. (Table 051-0004 and Catalogue no. 91-215-X.) Retrieved from http:// www.statcan.gc.ca/tables-tableaux/sum-som/l01/cst01/demo07a-eng.htm, June 20, 2014.

Douglas, J.E., and Munn, C. (1992). The detection of staging and personation at the crime scene. In J.E. Douglas, A.W. Burgess, A.G. Burgess, and R.K. Ressler (Eds.), *Crime classification manual.* New York, NY: Macmillan, pp. 249–258.

Ebert, B.W. (1987). Guide to conducting a psychological autopsy. *Professional Psychology Research and Practice, 18,* 52–56. doi: 10.1037/0735-7028.18.1.52.

Eke, A.W. (2007). *Staging in cases of homicide: Offender, victim, and offence characteristics.* Unpublished dissertation, York University, Toronto.

Froede, R.C. (1990). *The handbook of forensic pathology.* Northfield, IL: College of American Pathologists.

Geberth, V.J. (1996). *Practical homicide investigation: Tactics, procedures, and forensic techniques,* 3rd ed. Boca Raton, FL: CRC Press.

Hazelwood, R., and Napier, N. (2004). Crime scene staging and it's detection. *International Journal of Offender Therapy and Comparative Criminology,* 48(6), 744–59. doi: 10.1177/0306624X04268298.

Hoyert, D., and Xu, J. (2012). Deaths: Preliminary data for 2011. *National Vital Statistics Reports, 61.* Retrieved from http://dc242.4shared.com/doc/JEm3Zct7/preview.html, June 11, 2014.

Illinois Coroners and Medical Examiners Association. (2007). *Forensic autopsy guidelines.* Retrieved from http://www.coronersillinois.org/images/laws/20140703135013.pdf, July 24, 2014.

Jobes, D.A., Casey, J.O., Berman, A.L., and Wright, D.G. (1991). Empirical criteria for the determination of suicide manner of death. *Journal of Forensic Sciences, 1*, 244–256.

Leenaars, A. (2004). *Psychotherapy with suicidal people*. Chichester, UK: Wiley.

Leenaars, A. (2010). Edwin S. Shneidman on suicide. *Suicidology Online, 1*, 5–18.

Leenaars, A., Collins, P., and Sinclair, D. (2008). Report to the London Police Service and London Community on the deaths of David Lucio and Kelly Johnson. Retrieved from http://www.police.london.ca/Newsroom/PDFs/luciojohnson-report.pdf, July 10, 2014.

Litman, R.E. (1984). Psychological autopsies in court. *Suicide and Life Threatening Behavior, 14*, 88–95. doi: 10.1111/j.1943-278X.1984.tb00340.x.

Minino, A. (2013). Death in the United States. *Centers for Disease Control and Prevention, NCHS, No. 115*. Retrieved from http://www.cdc.gov/nchs/data/databriefs/db115.pdf, July 24, 2014.

Navaneelan, T. (2012). *Health at a glance: Suicide rates: An overview*. Statistics Canada, 82-624-X. Retrieved from http://www.statcan.gc.ca/pub/82-624-x/2012001/article/11696-eng.htm, July 23, 2014.

Ogloff, J., and Otto, R. (1993). Psychological autopsy: Clinical and legal perspectives. *Saint Louis University Law Journal, 37*, 607–646.

Porter, S., and Wrightsman, L.S. (2014). *Forensic psychology*, 2nd ed. Toronto, ON: Nelson Education.

Schlesinger, L.B., Gardenier, A., Jarvis, J., and Sheehan-Cook, J. (2014). Crime scene staging in homicide. *Journal of Police and Criminal Psychology, 29*, 44–51.

Sher, S. (2013). Psychological autopsy studies: Past, present and future. *Australian and New Zealand Journal of Psychiatry, 47*, 884. doi: 10.1177/0004867413479071.

Shneidman, E. (1981). The psychological autopsy. *Suicide and Life Threatening Behavior, 11*, 325–340.

Söderman, H., and O'Connell, J.J. (1962). *Modern criminal investigation*. New York, NY: Funk and Wagnall's Company.

Svensson, A., and Wendel, O. (1965). *Techniques of crime scene investigation*. New York, NY: American Elsevier Publishing Company.

Thompson, C.C. (1999). A glimpse of hell: The explosion on the U.S.S. Iowa and its cover-up. W.W. Norton, NY.

Wong, P., Chan, W., Beh, P., Yau, F., Yip, P., and Hawton, K. (2010). Research participation experiences of informants of suicide and control cases: Taken from a case-control psychological autopsy study of people who died by suicide. *Crisis, 31*, 238–246.

Best Practices for Addressing Rape
Police Collaboration with Victim Advocates

13

KAREN RICH
Marywood University
Scranton, PA, USA

Contents

Introduction

It is estimated that 19.3% of women and two percent of men in the U.S. have been raped at least once in their lives (Durando 2014, 1). Benjamin Pearson-Nelson (2009, 215) notes that rape is often not reported to the police because of its intimate nature, the stigma attached, the victim's belief that reporting will not result in police intervention, or the victim's wish to protect the offender. Male, adolescent, disabled, sex trafficked, intoxicated (at the time of the crime), non-white, and immigrant victims are among the least likely to make reports. This is unfortunate, in that many of these populations are at greatly increased risk of victimization. In addition, rape tends to be a recidivist crime, so nonreporting by victims places their communities at risk (Tjaden and Thoennes 2006).

Effects of Rape on Victims and the Police Interview

Sexual assault and rape can result in devastating sequelae for survivors, including anxiety, depression, sexual difficulties, sleep disorders, substance abuse, isolation, shame, and mistrust. In addition, a raped female is at heightened risk of developing posttraumatic stress disorder (Kaukinen and DeMaris 2009; Ullman et al. 2007). In the immediate aftermath of a rape, victims may fear men, enclosed spaces, weapons, reminders of sexual activity, physical proximity by an unknown person, raised voices, or demands of any kind (Tidmarch 2012). Because some of these "triggers" (or reminders of the assault) may be present during a police interview, the process of making a report can induce extreme anxiety in a victim (Epstein and Langenbahn 1994; Reid 2010). In conjunction with rape-induced posttraumatic stress, this can result in mental disorganization and difficulty constructing a clear and consistent narrative (Hardy et al. 2009). This can also cause an officer unfamiliar with psychological trauma to conclude that the crime reporter is lying. Thus the same emotional reactions that typify a rape victim may jeopardize her ability to deliver a persuasive official statement (Milne and Bull 2007).

Victims may feel unsafe, need reassurance, and require delicate emotional handling before they are capable of making a police report (Kaysen et al. 2005). They may need resources not typically provided by a police officer and may feel frustrated when these are not supplied (Skinner and Taylor 2009). For example, they may need accompaniment to forensic medical exams (which can last several hours) or assistance completing victim compensation forms (Zweig and Burt 2007). Repetition of key information, such as what will occur legally should the case progress, may be necessary in order to ensure it has been absorbed; however, officers may need to direct their attention away from the victim toward securing evidence and locating suspects (Martin 2005). Child and adolescent victims, especially those that have been trafficked, may be involuntary reporters and may require advanced skill in order to conduct a successful interview (Hershkowitz et al. 2013; Hodge 2008). Victims with disabilities and non-English speaking immigrants may require the services of a skilled translator (Kotria and Womack 2011). The role, skills, and training of some police officers can be at odds with the needs of rape reporters (Martin 2005), leading to assumptions by the public that police are not equipped to handle sex crimes. Although specialized units with trained sex crime detectives exist in some areas, they are not ubiquitous; in addition, even trained investigators may be unable to meet the needs of victims/witnesses in an ongoing capacity (Hazelwood and Burgess 2008).

Rape victims are faced with the dilemma of whether to report the crime at a time when decision making is particularly difficult. They may have had little contact with the police and may be unsure about what to expect, or their contacts in the past may have been negative (Campbell et al. 2009; Kotria and Womack 2011). Studies of nonreporting rape victims have indicated that fear of the police response is a key (though not sole) barrier (Tjaden and Thoennes 2006). Nonreporters may expect disbelief, harsh treatment, judgmental attitudes, and a lack of concerted police activity to bring perpetrators to justice. Many fear that their privacy and confidentiality will be violated, that they will be re-traumatized during the police interview, and that their cases will ultimately be dropped (Patterson et al. 2009). In fact, studies examining the mental health of victims have found that their anxiety and depression tend to increase as a case makes its way through the system (Kaukinen and DeMaris 2009; Parsons and Bergin 2010). This, however, is not inevitable, and some rape reporters experience positive interactions with police taking their statements. Positive treatment is not just helpful in a therapeutic sense; studies have shown that empathy and respect received during the police interview increases a victim's odds of having her case forwarded to the district attorney's office for prosecution (Maddox et al. 2011; Patterson 2011). Positive interactions with rape reporters may have elicited better quality statements; in addition, officers committed to combating rape (and engaging in the necessary investigations, arrests, and case referral for prosecution) may have invested more attention and effort on the key witness (the victim). This is significant given the discretion that police officers typically exercise when working on these cases.

A police officer's commitment to combating rape may be related to rape myth acceptance or to attitudes about rape and its victims that influence professional and personal behavior (Edwards et al. 2011; Suarez and Gadilla 2010). Studies examining attitudes among police officers toward rape victims have identified wide variability (Campbell 1997; Page 2008) with those receiving intensive training on rape dynamics (sometimes provided by victim advocates) showing better attitudes toward victims (Darwinkel et al. 2013; Kinney et al. 2008; Sleath and Bull 2012).

Attitudes about rape and attitudes about women may intersect because, according to research, women and girls are more likely to be sexually assaulted (Bureau of Justice Statistics 2006). In several studies, policewomen have reported sexual harassment (Shelley et al. 2011). Rich and Seffrin (2013) found that policewomen were more likely than policemen to hear disparaging comments about rape victims by their fellow officers. It has been posited that traditional police culture and goals are antithetical to the positive treatment of rape reporters by most officers (Martin 2005). This may be compounded by attitudes toward socially marginalized populations who are at high risk of repeated rape. For example, negative attitudes toward prostitutes may limit an officer's effectiveness with adolescents being sex trafficked (Hodge 2008; Reid 2010). Attitudes about persons with physical disabilities (for example, that they would not be raped because they deviate from norms of conventional attractiveness) (Plummer and Findley 2012) may impair the officer's effectiveness in processing their rape complaints. Rich and Seffrin (2012) found that officers with negative attitudes about rape victims were less inclined to follow best practice protocols when interviewing rape reporters. This may result in a lack of justice for some of the most vulnerable members of society.

Rape Victim Advocates and Police Officers

Victim advocacy organizations, often referred to as rape crisis centers, were developed in the 1960s and 1970s to improve institutional treatment of rape victims. They fall into two broad categories: community-based and system-based. Community-based organizations are freestanding, located in the community, and perform outreach and prevention activities in addition to offering individualized services. They are based on a philosophy that includes empowering survivors to make their own choices; thus they assist victims regardless of whether they make police reports. In addition, their communications with victims (and vice versa) are generally respected as confidential by the legal system. They may provide individual crisis counseling; accompany victims to criminal justice and medical appointments; help victims understand criminal justice procedures; inform victims of suspects' arrest and release from custody; accept anonymous reports; help victims file compensation claims; assist victims in relocating; and make referrals to other needed services such as psychotherapy, disability assistance, and legal aid (Lonsway and Archambault 2008; Macy et al. 2011). In addition, victim advocates are trained to work with secondary survivors: the friends and family members of victims who may affect a victim's recovery, motivation to lodge a police report, resolve to follow-through on criminal justice actions, and their safety following the assault. Such individuals can exert powerful influences on how a victim behaves and feels about accessing services (Ahrens and Campbell 2006; Christiansen et al. 2012; Smith 2005). For example, victims prefer participating in fewer interviews and receiving more coordinated services; they experience heightened distress when service professionals do not communicate about their cases (Zweig and Burt 2007). It is best when advocates are involved early in a case, before medical and police procedures have taken place; this reduces the likelihood of victims feeling re-victimized while undergoing difficult procedures (Macy et al. 2011; Westmarland and Alderson 2013). Victim advocates are particularly useful for rape reporters with special needs. They may assist child victims to overcome fear of the courtroom by bringing them to court when it is not in session, advocate for special services such as support animals or videotaped testimony, support nonoffending caretakers (who could substantially impact the case), and interface with child protective services and school personnel. With clients having disabilities they may interface with disability-specific agencies where the crime may have occurred or where the victim may need emergency services such as interpretation, alternative housing, and personal care providers. With victims of sex trafficking, they may assist in locating safe housing, legal aid, interpretation, and culturally specific counselors and programs (Hodge 2008; Reid 2010). The amount of nonpolice assistance many of these victims require is daunting; thus advocates are a tremendous potential benefit to victims (to the degree that rape crisis centers are sufficiently funded and utilized) (Maier 2011). In addition, they can benefit police officers working on rape cases, eliminating the need for the officers to locate these services themselves.

System-based advocates differ from community-based advocates, in that they are located within, or are arms of, specific police agencies. They may be members of the police force designated as special victim's assistants. These advocates work only with victims who are interested in lodging charges, and their purpose is to help move cases through the system. As a result, in contrast to community-based victim advocates, their communications with victims are not privileged—so victims cannot expect confidentiality (Lonsway and Archambault 2008). System-based advocates are relatively new to the criminal justice scene; some have argued that they have co-opted the profession of victim advocacy, which has always valued its independence from specific institutions (Simmonds 2013). However, police officials may trust system-based advocates to a greater degree, making interdisciplinary collaboration with them easier (Lonsway and Archambault 2008). Rape victims may be referred to either type of advocate or may utilize the services of either kind of agency.

Victim advocates can provide useful assistance to both rape victims and police officers. Listening to a rape survivor's narrative can be emotionally challenging, especially if the listener is not experienced or trained to do this (Salston and Figley 2003). Police training on sexual assault dynamics and victim interviewing is often elective and infrequently offered to patrol officers, who take most initial complaints (Milne and Bull 2007). At the level of detective or investigator, sexual-assault-related training may emphasize interrogation of suspects, securing crime scenes, and evidence collection rather than how to interact with traumatized crime reporters (Hazelwood and Burgess 2008). When challenged emotionally, police officers (as well as family, friends, and other professionals) may engage in behaviors that make survivors feel threatened. In the police context, these may include cutting off the flow of a victim's narrative, becoming excessively controlling, displaying an aggressive demeanor, or neglecting to record a victim's emotional reactions (Epstein and Langenbahn 1994). The resulting dynamics can compromise the quality of the sworn statement, an important document for decisions about the case (Milne and Bull 2007).

Victim advocates undergo intensive training about the emotional reactions and needs of victims. During victim interviews they can minimize tension between officers and rape reporters by attending to their clients' noncriminal justice-related needs, freeing officers to focus exclusively on their policing role. The advocates can also: (a) remind victims of criminal justice actions to be pursued, (b) keep victims informed about the progress of cases, (c) explain why certain (embarrassing or seemingly critical) questions may need to be asked, (d) cue officers when a victim may need a break from intense questioning, and (e) generally attend to their comfort throughout the process of making a statement. In addition, rape victim advocates may have knowledge of crime patterns and cases of which police are unaware (Lonsway and Archambault 2008).

Research has documented advocates' positive impact on the treatment of victims by formal authorities. For example, Campbell (2006) found that police officers responded more favorably (and engaged in fewer negative interactions) with victims when an advocate was present. They were more likely to take a report and follow up with an investigation. In addition, victims experience less distress when engaging with law enforcement. For these and other reasons, the utilization of advocates on rape cases is considered best practice by experts in the field (Hazelwood and Burgess 2008; Milne and Bull 2007). The importance of referring rape victims to advocates is enshrined in the Victims' Bill of Rights, both nationally and within state criminal justice guidelines. However, the Victims' Bill of Rights is a legislative law, subject to differing interpretations from state to state and across jurisdictions (Montegraff et al. 2006). This has resulted in inconsistent implementation, especially when police officers on rape cases exercise high levels of individual discretion. Some officers routinely involve victim advocates in rape cases, have excellent collegial relationships with specific practitioners, informally exchange knowledge with them about case trends and issues, and engage in cross-disciplinary training on a regular basis. Others do not utilize victim advocates in rape cases, are unaware of their existence, or avoid working with them directly by making referrals only after all police work has been completed (Carmody 2006; Lonsway and Archambault 2008; Shaina 2006).

Police Officers, Victim Advocates, and Gendered Institutions

Individual, institutional, and cultural resistance to collaboration with victim advocates can occur despite the advantages to police officers, victims, and the community. Individual officers may feel uncomfortable being observed (and potentially judged) by a third party, such as when an advocate is present during his or her interview of a rape victim. Experienced interviewers might feel an observer encroaches upon their personal style of forming a relationship with a victim. Some may view the incorporation of victim advocates as a "crutch" for inferior or insecure interviewers. Institutional norms may preclude collaboration with "outsiders" in order to preserve discretion in how cases are handled (Roberg et al. 2004). In organizations where sexual harassment is common, working with victim advocates may threaten to expose or alter internal norms (Kurtz 2008). Because victim advocacy has its roots in the feminist movement, an agency may feel that radical feminism is encroaching upon its territory (Nichols 2011). Traditional police culture has been described as hypermasculine (Roberg et al. 2004; Shelley et al. 2011) so collaborating with (largely female staffed) community advocacy organizations may seem antithetical to "real" police work (Martin 2005).

The percentage of females in police organizations can range from 0 to 27%, with an average of about 13% in the United States (Bureau of Justice Statistics 2006; Langton 2010); conversely, the percentage of women working in victim advocacy organizations ranges from 95–100% (Nichols 2011). In a gendered institution, members of the minority gender may be discredited or deemed less important (Kanter 1977; Shelley et al. 2011). In a police agency with few female officers, this might have an indirect effect on the perception of (primarily female) rape victims and cases. If rape cases are devalued within a given agency, even female officers may resent these assignments (Martin 2005).

Both police and victim advocacy organizations are gendered institutions, with gendered goals, roles, ways of relating to subordinates and clientele, language, traditions, and interpersonal norms. For example, in victim advocacy organizations, symmetrical power relationships, and emotional sharing are highly valued, whereas in police organizations emotional stoicism and hierarchical power relationships are the norm. In addition, rape crisis centers focus primarily on victims, while police agencies focus largely on criminal suspects (Martin 2007). Thus they can be said to occupy different universes even while addressing the same crimes. However, each can contribute an essential function to the successful prosecution of a rape.

The following are comments from victim advocates that illustrate difficulties they have experienced in working with police officers on rape cases:

> I sit and watch them interrogate the victims like criminals. Sometimes I want to yell at them, stop! Don't you see what you're doing? But instead I politely ask for a minute of their time … to step outside and explain that she's a person. Sometimes they decline, or pretend not to hear me. Then I'm as much of a victim as they are. I go home and binge on ice cream or horror movies, just to get it out of my system.

> He badgered her about going to [suspect's] house if she didn't want sex. He asked if she thought he was cute, and whether she had an orgasm. I told him she was getting upset by his line of questioning and needed a break. I could see it in her eyes and her voice … it was obvious. But he accused me of interfering; he said I didn't know how to do his job.

> We were in the E. R. with her. He told me to meet him at the station where he was planning to conduct the interview. I drove over there even though it was 20 minutes away. When I got there they told me he was gone for the evening, and had never come in with her. I was upset. He sent me on a wild goose chase so I couldn't be with her during the interview. As it turns out he did it at her house.

I finally gave him a piece of my mind. I let him know that he shouldn't stand over a victim with his gun at her eye level, it was very triggering. I never do that, I'm always soft spoken but this officer was over the top disrespectful. And you know what happened? He called my supervisor. And she said we need to be on good terms with the cops in order to get referrals. But how do I respect these guys and respect the victim at the same time?

These comments reflect similar qualitative findings from studies of victim advocates who interface with police officers on cases of violence against women. Those studies have identified secondary trauma, devaluation by others, compassion fatigue, powerlessness, rage, and fear (Carmody 2006; Kolb 2011; Maier 2008; Slattery and Goodman 2009; Sudderth 2006). In addition to these negative feelings, advocates have reported protectiveness, compassion, and spiritual satisfaction from assisting victims (Ullman 2010).

Police officers have reactions to working with victim advocates as well, but these have not been extensively studied. Rich and Seffrin (2013) researched this topic by administering an (author constructed) *Collaboration with Victim Advocates Index* to 442 police officers across the United States. The following is a sample of comments made by police officers regarding community-based victim advocates.

She's a great asset, females always seem more comfortable when she's around. That's what it's about, right? Having another gal in the room? She knows when to keep quiet, too. Not many like her though; I ask for her when I call the center.

I had a bad experience once or twice, and now I never use them. Who needs the negativity? It was written all over their faces. I think some of them need their own help.

They're out to get us. I'm not saying they're lesbians, but you can tell how much they don't like men. One false move and they'll be running to the papers.

I was encouraged to use the advocates, but when I look around nobody's doing it. So it's like a double message. Work with the advocates, make sure to contact them, it's best for the victim. But I why I should be the only one?

I felt sorry for her; she seemed like such a nice girl. But there was really no place for her in that room. She couldn't take notes, or talk, or do anything really. I mean, by law. I had it all under control and she was an unnecessary fixture.

Interviewing victims is an art and I take it very seriously. And over the years I've developed my own style. It's like a dance between the two of us; I advance, she pulls back, I pull back, and she advances. It's hard to describe. Anyway the last thing I need is some third wheel stepping in and standing all over my toes. It throws me off my game, upsets my balance, and the dance turns into a hockey match.

In 2013, Rich and Seffrin found that 69% of 442 officers reported at least some reluctance to work with victim advocates on rape cases. When asked why this reluctance exists, primary reasons given were (in order of decreasing frequency): (a) confusion about the role and purpose of victim advocates, (b) desire for complete control over victim interviews, (c) fear that advocates harbor negative attitudes about police, and (d) advocates' lack knowledge about police procedures. The previous quotations illustrate many of these themes. There is clearly a need for cross-disciplinary training to teach police officers what advocates do and teach advocates what police officers do. In addition, there is a need to decrease negative stereotyping and to develop trust among advocates and officers.

Rich and Seffrin (2013) evaluated relationships among a number of variables including gender, sexual-assault-related training, victim interviewing skill, and collaboration with advocates. Officer characteristics associated with collaboration included female gender, specialized training on sexual assault, and victim interviewing skill. The most skillful victim interviewers were most likely to involve advocates early, to know a specific advocate, and to invite their advocate to attend victim interviews (after securing the rape reporter's permission). These findings contradict the notion that unskilled officers utilize advocates as a "crutch" and suggest that skillful officers value the services victim advocates offer. Specialized sexual assault trainings may improve willingness to collaborate because they are often interdisciplinary (Hazelwood and Burgess 2008). Policewomen may have greater empathy for the emotional needs of crime victims (Lonsway et al. 2003) and therefore appreciate the availability of victim assistance specialists (Rich and Seffrin 2014).

Sexual Assault Response Teams

To improve victim services, multidisciplinary teams for sexual assault intervention (called SARTS) have been instituted in many jurisdictions. These teams are widely touted within professional policing literature as "best practice" interventions. They consist of forensic nurse examiners, social workers or psychologists, law enforcement, victim advocates, crime lab specialists, and prosecutors. Law enforcement participants may be local or federal officers, tribal, military, campus police, or deputy sheriffs. Some SARTs also include teachers, foster care workers, addiction or disability specialists, shelter employees, faith-based authorities, and college administrators. They problem solve and develop policies (such as memoranda of understanding) for handling sexual assault cases in a coordinated, efficient, and effective fashion. Often, cross training is involved; in addition, professional relationships may be strengthened. These are important for addressing issues within subcultures such as colleges, Native American reservations, or disability organizations, where differing legal standards or jurisdictions may overlap. Because each community is unique, no two SART teams are alike, and each is tailored to the specific needs of the local population. In order to be successful, SARTs must include frequent communication among members, regular meetings, and the development of specific protocols for handling sexual assault cases within the community (Hazelwood and Burgess 2008; Lonsway et al. 2012). An additional advantage of SARTS is the opportunity to develop and share resources, such as language interpreters, that may be useful in all aspects of sexual assault reporting and prosecution (Shah et al. 2007). Initial efforts to develop coordinated community responses to rape were instituted in the 1990s. Programs that made community members feel safer and that increased rape reporting shared three characteristics: a coordinated interdisciplinary team with a specific intervention protocol, interagency training, and efforts to change community attitudes through political action and education.

Current Model Programs

Research has shown SARTS to be effective when good teamwork and trust exist. Although each community has its own approach to handling sexual assault, model programs have been identified. For example, in the state of New Jersey, a standardized statewide protocol for handling sexual assault cases has been established. This ensures that in all towns, villages, and municipalities, victims have the same rights and are treated in accordance with best practice standards.

The Memphis Sexual Assault Resource Center has been handling rape cases since 1975 using an innovative protocol consisting of a centralized "one-stop" service portal where victims can access medical, forensic, counseling, and advocacy assistance. Law enforcement presents unique challenges because multiple jurisdictions are involved: northern Mississippi and Arkansas, a naval air base, and the city of Memphis. Despite these challenges, multidisciplinary collaboration ensures that victims receive high quality and coordinated services.

College campuses are fertile regions for implementing best practice interdisciplinary approaches to sexual assault; recent statistics show that one in four college women will be the victim of rape, that victims rarely disclose to authorities, and that victims are unlikely to contact police or community advocates (Kilpatrick et al. 2007). Montclair State University based its sexual assault protocol on the successful New Jersey model, with an interdisciplinary SART for the campus community. Coadministered by the chief of university police and the director of the health center, it includes residence life, the dean of students, community victim advocates, peer leaders, forensic nurses, and the campus counseling center. Studies following its implementation showed that rape reports increased and that female students felt safer. It also revealed the importance, within that community, of peer leaders as team members. It was these individuals to whom students were most likely to disclose and who were needed to "bridge" victims to other services. Without research informing the SART composition and protocols, the team may not have been as effective.

The following are quotations from professionals involved in SARTS within these communities. Their words capture some advantages of this approach:

> We know from prosecutors there are more pleas and more victims who are willing to talk to law enforcement. We used to have victims dropping out of the system, but now with all the different professionals checking in and making her feel important, they are more likely to commit to the process.
>
> **Systems Advocate, New Jersey**

> Some of us serve as law enforcement liaisons and spend a day a week at the [Police] Sex Crimes Unit. We don't violate anyone's confidentiality, but we do discuss cases. We indirectly help victims by forging better relationships. We familiarize the officers with victim issues and learn about what it takes to solidify a case. My staff feel respected, which is unusual in other parts of the country.
>
> **Supervisor, Victim Advocacy Agency, Memphis**

> I like going to the meetings because I never fail to learn something new about what the other professionals do. I have really gained an appreciation for their work, whereas I used to think I was the only one really invested in helping. Rape cases are hard and we all have a tough job, but part of the problem is being isolated.
>
> **Forensic Nurse, New Jersey**

> Advising a resident is tough when there's a campus judiciary, local police, campus cops, and a ton of laws about privacy and responsibility. We have a protocol so we know what steps to take and we're all on the same page. When I encourage a resident to take action, I'm doing it for her but also for the team.
>
> **Residence Advisor, Montclair University**

> Frankly, if there's no victim, there's no case. When the crime victim sees a collective of caring people who want to help her, it's beneficial for us as well as her. It means we can go forward without wasting a lot of time and energy.
>
> **Detective, New Jersey**

> We did some training with the residence directors and health services people. Also some of the Women's Center people from off campus. It's a real eye

opener, learning the counseling end, and it's amazing what they do. We got to tighten up some loose ends with the town police, since sometimes it seems like we step on each other's toes.

Campus Police, Montclair University

I couldn't get the girl to talk about what happened, so I was at a dead end. When I presented the case to the team, we developed a plan. The advocate started to work with the mother. The Sexual Assault Nurse Examiner (SANE) took four hours to examine the child, and the psychologist brought in a therapy dog. After a while, Kristen started to talk and we were able to move forward.

Child Sex Crimes Detective, Memphis

The attorney on the SART gave tips about evidence collection that were useful for the case. He suggested prosecution was a real possibility. I appreciated the input and it boosted everyone's morale.

Investigator, Sex Crimes Unit, New Jersey

I can better prosecute a case when I know I have all the pieces in place and working together: the SAFE nurse, the advocate, and the investigating officer. Things move quickly, the complainant is taken care of, and nobody passes the buck. If it takes a village to raise a child, it takes a well-functioning team to put a rapist in jail.

Assistant Prosecutor, New Jersey

Developing a Successful Sexual Assault Response Team

Despite the successes of many SARTS, there can be initial hurdles to surmount when people of differing philosophies, goals, protocols, language, and authority structures begin to collaborate (Greeson and Campbell 2013). Challenges faced by team members include, but are not necessarily limited to, each of the following: (a) concerns about how members are addressed, with some professional groups (often police officers) preferring formal titles and others (often victim advocates) preferring first names only; (b) questions about authority (for example, are all team members equal or are some of greater status on the team?); (c) issues concerning the primary goal of the team (for example, expanding the number of convictions, increasing community safety, improving experiences for survivors, and/or eliminating gaps in the helping systems); (d) conflicts over client confidentiality (for example, team members from other professions—often police officers—may want advocates to identify clients who wish to remain anonymous); (e) ideological clashes, particularly around the issue of victim blamelessness versus partial culpability; and (f) questions surrounding the allocation of police resources (for example, advocates tend to feel that police should investigate more cases than police officers feel is appropriate given limited resources) (Carmody 2006; Greeson and Campbell 2013; Maier 2008; Sudderth 2006).

Police officers associate primarily with other officers in both work and social settings; they rarely interact with members of the general public on an interpersonal level and are unlikely to seek out personal psychotherapy or counseling. As a result, they would not usually have informal social experiences with victim advocates. According to Sutherland's theory of differential socialization (1978), this exclusionary pattern of relationships is not uncommon among various professional groups. Police officers and victim advocates may encounter one another and develop positive working relationships at interdisciplinary conferences on violence against women or at cross-disciplinary trainings within their own communities. By developing personal relationships, they may be able to overcome myths and stereotypes about others from different occupations.

Some lessons have been learned as a result of both positive and negative experience with SARTs. One is that a community needs to invest the necessary resources to make these teams work; only by a full commitment of multiple professional groups can widespread change occur (Campbell and Ahrens 1998). An experienced task group leader should facilitate the meetings, even if that person does not specialize in issues pertinent to sexual assault. Diversity in membership should be encouraged; in that spirit, recovered victims, service providers of differing faiths, members of underrepresented communities, and as wide a variety of relevant helping professions should be invited to participate. Specific goals need to be clearly outlined, even if they change as they are accomplished. Rules about how to relate (i.e., interruption of expressions of frustration, the utilization of technical jargon, how persons shall be addressed, and other matters pertaining to interaction with victims) are important to establish before any discussion of issues begin. Some groups prefer *Robert's Rules*, while others endorse a less formal approach. Developing an atmosphere in which credit is given when someone makes a contribution is crucial. Turnover effects many SARTs, disrupting carefully constructed relationships that must then be recreated; therefore, only participants with a genuine commitment to the process (and the ability to remain engaged) should be included. Meetings should occur regularly rather than sporadically, with cross trainings on a regular basis that include some time for socialization. Case conferences are useful and may reveal previously unidentified gaps in the service system (Carmody 2006; Greeson and Campbell 2013; Hazelwood and Burgess 2008; Lonsway et al. 2012).

Police officers may collaborate with advocates on an individual basis; but the most effective way to establish the practice as a norm is through the efforts (modeling, sanctions, directives, and incentives) of administrators.

It is crucial that high ranking officers mentor their colleagues to expand the interdisciplinary approach to these cases (Hazelwood and Burgess 2008; Lonsway and Archambault 2012). The same teams developed for rape case coordination may later be invoked when addressing issues of domestic violence.

Summary

Police officers and victim advocates, in collaboration with other service providers, can greatly improve services to sexual assault victims. Interprofessional collaboration can improve the quality of evidence accessed and victim follow-through with criminal justice system requirements. Indirectly this may increase the number of rape reports from the general public—as well as from more vulnerable populations like immigrants, the elderly, persons with disabilities, children, and survivors of trafficking. Ostensibly, this can increase job satisfaction of involved professionals, aid in prosecution of offenders, and make communities safer. Several model programs have arisen and produced promising results; efforts such as these should be replicated and expanded upon in accordance with community needs.

References

Ahrens, C. and Campbell, R. (2006). Being silenced: The impact of negative social reactions on the disclosure of rape. *American Journal of Community Psychology*, 38(3), 263–274.

Bureau of Justice Statistics. (2006). *Local police departments: Law enforcement management and administrative statistics*. Washington, DC: Bureau of Justice Statistics.

Campbell, R. (1997). The role of work experience and individual beliefs in police officers' perceptions of date rape: An integration of quantitative and qualitative methods. *American Journal of Community Psychology*, 23(2), 249–277.

Campbell, R. (2006). Rape survivors' experiences with the legal and medical systems: Do rape victim advocates make a difference? *Violence Against Women*, 12(1), 30–45.

Campbell, R. and Ahrens, C. (1998). Innovative community services for rape victims: An application of multiple case study methodology. *American Journal of Community Psychology*, 26(4), 537–571.

Campbell, R., Dworkin, E. and Cabral, G. (2009). An ecological model of the impact of sexual assault on women. *Trauma Violence and Abuse*, 14(3), 116–138.

Carmody, D. (2006). Sexual assault victim advocates in Virginia: Challenges faced in the field. *Journal of Health and Human Services Administration*, 29(2), 191–208.

Christiansen, D., Bak, R. and Elklit, A. (2012). Secondary victims of rape. *Violence and Victims*, 27(2), 246–242.

Darwinkel, E., Powell, M. and Tidmarsh, P. (2013). Improving police officers perceptions of sexual offending through intensive training. *Criminal Justice and Behavior*, 40, 895–908.

Durando, J. (2014). Nearly 1 in 5 women raped. USA today network. http://usat.ly/1rS8LN. Accessed July 20, 1015.

Edwards, K., Turchik, J., Dardig, L., Reynolds, N. and Gidycx, C. (2011). Rape myths: History, individual and institutional level presence and implications for change. *Sex Roles*, 65, 761–773.

Epstein, J. and Langenbahn, S. (1994). *The criminal justice and community response to rape*. Issues and Practice in Criminal Justice Series. Washington, DC: National Institute of Justice.

Greeson, M. and Campbell, R. (2013). Sexual assault response teams: An empirical review of their effectiveness. *Trauma, Violence and Abuse*, 14(2), 83–95.

Hardy, A., Young, K. and Holmes, E. (2009). Does trauma memory play a role in the experience of reporting sexual assault during police interviews? *Memory*, 17, 783–788.

Hazelwood, R. and Burgess, A. (Eds.). (2008). *Practical aspects of rape investigation: A multidisciplinary approach* (4th ed.) New York: CRC Press.

Hershkowitz, R., Lamb, B. and Katz, A. (2013). Does enhanced rapport building alter the dynamics of investigative interviews of suspected victims of intrafamilial abuse? *Journal of Police and Criminal Psychology*, 28(5), 354–360.

Hodge, D. (2008). Sexual trafficking in the United States: A domestic problem with transnational dimensions. *Social Work*, 53(2), 143–152.

Kanter, R. M. (1977). Some effects of proportions on group life: Skewed sex rations and responses to token women. *American Journal of Sociology*, 82, 965–990.

Kaukinen, C. and De Maris, A. (2009). Sexual assault and current mental health: The role of help seeking and police response. *Violence Against Women*, 15(11), 1331–1357.

Kaysen, D., Morris, M., Rizvi, S. and Resick, P. (2005). Peritraumatic reactions and their relationship to perceptions of threat in female crime victims. *Violence Against Women*, 1, 1515–1535.

Kilpatrick, D., Resnick, H., Ruggiero, K., Concosenti, L. and McCauley, J. (2007). *Drug-facilitated, incapacitated and forcible rape: A national study*. Final Report (No. NCJRS 219181). Washington, DC: U. S. Department of Justice.

Kinney, L., Bruns, E., Bradley, P., Dantzler, J. and Weist, M. (2008). Sexual assault training of law enforcement officers: Results of a statewide survey. *Women and Criminal Justice*, 18(3), 81–100.

Kolb, K. (2011). Victim advocates' perception of legal work. *Violence Against Women*, 17(12), 1559–1575.

Kotria, K. and Womack, B. (2011). Domestic sex trafficking in the United States. Implications For policy, prevention and research. *Journal of Applied Research on Children*, 2(1), 5.

Kurtz, D. L. (2008). Controlled burn: The gendering of stress and burnout in modern policing. *Feminist Criminology*, 3(3), 216–238.

Langton, L. (2010). *Women in law enforcement, 1987–2008*, U.S. Department of Justice: Office of Justice Programs, Bureau of Justice Statistics, Washington DC, (NCJ Publication # 230521).

Lonsway, K. and Archambault, J. (2008). Advocates and law enforcement: Oil and water? *Sexual Assault Report*, 11(6), 81–82, 86–95. Civic Research Institute, Kingston NJ.

Lonsway, K., Archambault, J. and Little, K. (2012). *Sustaining a coordinated community response: Sexual assault response and research teams*. National Center on Women and Policing, Office of Violence Against Women, United States Department of Justice, Washington DC.

Lonsway, K., Carrington, S., Moore, M., Harrington, P., Smeal, E. and Spillar, K. (2003). *Hiring and retaining more women: The advantages to law enforcement agencies*. National Center on Women and Policing, Washington DC.

Macy, R., Johns, N., Rizo, C., Martin, S. and Giattina, M. (2011). Domestic violence and sexual assault service goal priorities. *Journal of Interpersonal Violence*, 26(16), 3361–3382.

Maddox, L., Lee, D. and Barker, C. (2011). Police empathy and victim PTSD as potential factors in rape case attrition. *Journal of Police and Criminal Psychology*, 26, 112–117.

Maier, S. (2008). Rape victims advocates' knowledge and insight on rape laws. *Women and Criminal Justice*, 18(4), 37–62.

Maier, S. (2011). Rape crisis centers: Doing amazing, wonderful things on peanuts. *Women and Criminal Justice*, 21(2), 141–169.

Martin, P.Y. (2005). *Rape work: Individual and organizational perspectives*. Routledge: London.

Martin, P.Y. (2007). Coordinated Community Services for Victims of Violence. In *Gender Violence: Interdisciplinary Perspectives, 2/e*. Laura L. O'Toole, Jessica R. Schiffman, and Margie L. Kiter Edwards (eds.), New York: New York University Press.

Milne, B. and Bull, R. (2007). Interviewing victims of crime, including children and people with intellectual disabilities. In Milne, B. and Bull, R. (Eds.), *Investigative interviewing: Psychology and practice*. New York: Wiley, pp. 9–24.

Montegraff, M., Garvin, B. and Beloof, G. (2006). *A review of the American bar association's guidelines for fair treatment of crime victims and witnesses*. Washington, DC: National Crime Victims, pp. 3–38.

Nichols, A. (2011). Gendered organizations: Challenges for domestic violence victim advocates and feminist advocacy. *Feminist Criminology*, 6(2), 111–131.

Page, A. D. (2008). Gateway to reform? Policy implications of police officers' attitudes toward rape. *American Journal of Criminal Justice*, 33, 44–51.

Parsons, J. and Bergin, T. (2010). The impact of criminal justice involvement on victims' mental health. *Journal of Traumatic Stress*, 23(2), 182–188.

Patterson, D. (2011). The linkage between secondary victimization by law enforcement and rape case outcomes. *Journal of Interpersonal Violence*, 26(2), 328–347.

Patterson, D., Greeson, M. and Campbell, C. (2009). Understanding rape survivors' decisions not to seek help from formal social systems. *Health and Social Work*, 14(2), 127–136.

Pearson-Nelson, B. (2009). Rape. In *The Praeger Handbook of Victimology*, Janet K. Wilson, (ed.) Santa Barbara, CA: Praeger.

Plummer, S. and Findley, P. (2012). Women with disabilities' experiences with physical and sexual abuse: A review of the literature and implications for the field. *Violence, Trauma and Abuse*, 13(1), 15–29.

Reid, J. A. (2010). Doors wide shut: Barriers to the successful delivery of victim services for domestically trafficked minors in a southeastern United States metropolitan area. *Women and Criminal Justice*, 20(2), 147–166.

Rich, K. and Seffrin, P. (2012). Police interviews of rape reporters: Do attitudes matter? *Violence and Victims*, 27(2), 160–176.

Rich, K. and Seffrin, P. (2013). Police officers' collaboration with victim advocates: Barriers and Facilitators. *Violence and Victims*, 28(4), 223–237.

Rich, K. and Seffrin, P. (2014). Birds of a feather or fish out of water? Policewomen taking rape complaints. *Feminist Criminology*, 32, 116–223.

Roberg, R., Crank, J. and Kuykendall, J. (2004). *Police and society*. Los Angeles, CA: Roxbury.

Salston, M. and Figley, R. (2003). Secondary traumatic stress: Effects of working with survivors of criminal victimization. *Journal of Traumatic Stress*, 16, 161–171.

Shah, S., Rahman, I. and Khashu, A. (2007). *Overcoming language barriers: Solutions for law enforcement*. Vera Institute of Justice, New York, NY.

Shaina, M. L. (2006). Rape advocates' perceptions of police re-victimization of rape victims. Paper presented at the annual meeting of the American Society of Criminology, CA.

Shelley, T., Morabito, M. and Tobin-Gurley, J. (2011). Gendered institutions and gender roles: Understanding experiences of women in policing. *Criminal Justice Studies*, 24(4), 351–367.

Simmonds, L. (2013). Secondary traumatic stress: Effects of working with survivors of criminal victimization. *Journal of Traumatic Stress*, 16(2), 167–174.

Skinner, T. and Taylor, H. (2009). "Being shut out in the dark:" Young survivors' experiences of reporting a sexual offence. *Feminist Criminology*, 4(2), 130–150.

Slattery, S. and Goodman, L. (2009). Secondary traumatic stress among domestic violence advocates: Work place risk and protective factors. *Violence Against Women*, 15(11), 1358–1379.

Sleath, E. and Bull, R. (2012). Comparing rape victim and perpetrator blaming in a police officer sample: Differences between police officers with and without special training. *Criminal Justice and Behavior*, 39(5), 646–665.

Smith, M. E. (2005). Female sexual assault: The impact on the male significant other. *Issues in Mental Health Nursing*, 26(2), 149–167.

Suarez, E. and Gadella, T. (2010). Stop blaming the victim: A meta-analysis on rape myths. *Journal of Interpersonal Violence*, 25(11), 2010–2035.

Sudderth, L. (2006). An uneasy alliance: Law enforcement and domestic violence victim advocates in a rural area. *Feminist Criminology*, 4(1), 329–353.

Sutherland, E. and Cressey, D. (1978). *Criminology* (10th ed.). Philadelphia, PA: J.B. Lippincott.

Tidmarch, P. (2012). *Working with sexual assault investigations*. Australian Institute of Family Studies, Australian Centre for the Study of Sexual Assault, Melbourne, Australia, pp. 1–8.

Tjaden, P. and Thoennes, N. (2006). *Extent, nature and consequences of rape victimization: Findings from the national violence against women survey* (Report No. NCJ 210346). Washington, DC: U.S. Department of Justice, National Institute of Justice.

Ullman, S. (2010). *Talking about sexual assault: Society's response to survivors*. American Psychological Association, Washington DC.

Ullman, S., Filipas, H., Townsend, S. and Starzynski, L. (2007). Psychosocial cor-relates of PTSD symptom severity in sexual assault survivors. *Journal of Traumatic Stress*, 20, 821–838.

Westmarland, N. and Alderson, S. (2013). The health, mental health and well- being benefits of rape crisis counseling. *Journal of Interpersonal Violence*, 28(17) 3265–3282.

Zweig, J. and Burt, M. (2007). Predicting women's perceptions of domestic violence and sexual assault agencies helpfulness: What matters to program clients? *Violence Against Women*, 13, 1149–1178.

Perspectives on the Professional Practitioner in Criminal Justice

14

PETER C. KRATCOSKI
Kent State University
Kent, OH, USA

Contents

Introduction: Professional Defined

Pavalko (1971, 18–26) stated that there are several factors that characterize professional occupations and distinguish them from other forms of work. These characteristics include that the profession is based on a systematic body of theory and abstract knowledge, the work is related to the realization of basic social values, and that a considerable amount of education and training is required to enter the profession. The training is ideational, symbolic, and specialized; those who enter the profession are motivated by a primary emphasis on service to clients and the public. Professional work requires that one has a considerable amount of autonomy; there is freedom to regulate one's own work behavior. Members of a profession have a common identity and a sense of community; and members of a profession adhere to a code of ethics that reinforces the concept of service and emphasizes the primary concern for the welfare of the client.

The professional characteristics listed here can easily be applied to doctors, lawyers, teachers, professors, psychologists, social workers, and various types of counselors. Although some professionals may at times place their own self-interests above those of their clients and the public, there are several mechanisms used to assure that the professional adheres to appropriate standards of behavior, including a professional organization that can censure the person for misconduct and provisions in the laws relating to licensing that require a license to practice be revoked for misconduct (Champion 2005, 206).

Justice Personnel as Professionals

When one considers the complexity of the criminal justice system, it is easy to understand why there is a need for a division of labor and for the personnel working in the system to have different educational and training backgrounds and skills. For example, within a policing agency, the minimum training for sworn officers is the completion of the basic police training. The nonsworn personnel, depending on the positions they hold, may have been educated and trained for work in a variety of occupations, including business, accounting, management, computer programming, clerical and secretarial work, communications, and counseling. Some of the work positions, such as janitor, may not require any prior formal education and training, while other positions, such as police psychologist, attorney, or police chaplain, require a considerable amount of prior education and training for an individual to be considered qualified for the position. In addition, to be hired for a professional position, education and training and obtaining credentials, such as licensing, must be completed before assuming the position. Those professionals assuming positions in justice agencies are subject to the rules and regulations of the agency as well as to the rules and regulations governing the profession. Tracing back to the development of formal police organizations in the United States, one can find evidence that although typical police officers were not trained in psychology, law, or social work, they were expected to provide many services to the community that are typically provided by professionals today. The mid-nineteenth century witnessed the development of formally organized municipal police departments in the large cities of the United States. Although there was no national plan to follow, the city police were typically modeled after London's Metropolitan Police. The officers were expected to provide public service, maintain self-control, and to gain the trust of the citizens, in addition to preventing crime and providing security (Kratcoski and Walker 1984, 100, 101).

A number of events that occurred during the course of U.S. policing history often resulted in changes in the focus of policing, from being service oriented to being more control oriented. These events included the Civil War, large-scale immigration, the industrialization of the nation, the prohibition of the sale of alcohol, and widespread poverty and unemployment during periods of economic recession (Kelly 1975, 3–10).

In the early development of U.S. police departments, the justice system, including the police, was predominately under the control of the power elite—those upper class industrial leaders who had considerable economic as well as political power. Gradually, political party bosses were able to gain control of city governments by offering patronage. Most government positions, including the police, were given to those who supported the political bosses. Although the credentials for being hired as a police officer were based on the number of votes that individual could guarantee city government officials during an election, officers were still expected to provide social services and security to the residents of the neighborhoods where they patrolled. The "political era" of the police fostered considerable graft, corruption, abuse of power, deviance, and improper conduct by police leaders as well as by officers on the street (Kratcoski and Kempf 1995, 609, 611). Nevertheless, the majority of large city police officers were honest and dedicated to their work. Numerous examples of their service to families in need, providing food, clothing, and shelter, and of assisting social workers in settlement houses, orphanages, and with homeless children have been recorded.

Police reform movements were generally started in the United States when the political graft, corruption, brutality, and incompetence could no longer be tolerated. Police reform in the 1950s resulted in the professionalization of the police. The attempt to become professional took the form of changes in administrative structure, including a more centralized police command and changes in policies. There was more emphasis on crime control, and the service function was deemphasized. According to Kratcoski and Kempf (1995, 611), "As the innovations gained acceptance, strides in the professionalization of law enforcement included a code of ethics; a clearly defined body of knowledge; uniform minimum standards of excellence for recruitment, education, and performance; and an emphasis on the development of specialists in law-enforcement technology."

Despite the reforms and overall improvements in the standards and performance of the police, there was still considerable dissatisfaction with police performance among some groups, predominately from lower income citizens and minority group members who resided in high crime areas. The movement toward community policing, starting in the 1970s, resulted in a new emphasis on the police providing service to the community and joining forces with the residents and community organizations in combatting crime and working toward improving quality of life in the community.

Social Service Professionals in the Justice System

The types of social service professionals who are either employed by police departments or who collaborate with the police and other justice agencies include those who work for child welfare agencies, juvenile courts, or as private independent service providers—such as child abuse investigators, caseworkers, social workers, psychologists, probation officers, foster/group home coordinators, family counselors, abuse and shelter and group home administrators, diversion counselors, and advocates for victims. The police and school administrators have cooperated and collaborated on educational programs such as Drug Abuse Resistance Education (DARE) and security programs, including the School Resource Officer program.

Programs for adults that require cooperation and collaboration between the police and social service providers include victim advocate programs; rape crisis services; alcohol, drug abuse, and mental health residential centers; and various types of community-based programs, such as neighborhood crime watch programs. The police also collaborate with the community in promoting recreational programs and sports-related events.

Police–Social Services Collaboration

With the beginning of the community policing orientation in the 1970s, many social service programs requiring collaboration between the police and social service agencies were implemented. The emphasis on police providing service to the community that stands as the cornerstone of community policing resulted in many changes in the way police tasks were performed. For example, many departments abandoned the standard method of using cars to patrol in selected neighborhoods and reverted to a foot patrol method. In the past, police were often indoctrinated with a belief that private citizens were "enemies" and not to be trusted. In addition, many social service providers were defined as "bleeding hearts" by the police, and agencies such as runaway shelters for youth were often viewed as contributing to delinquency because they were providing a safe haven for children who were law violators who should be punished. In contrast, the community policing philosophy encourages the development of trust between the police and the residents of the community and emphasizes cooperation and collaboration with service agencies.

The renewed emphasis on the service component of policing helped to stimulate changes in police training as well as the development of new ways to respond to police-related matters. A program (Bard and Shellow 1976) designed to train officers to handle family crisis intervention through the use of guest lectures by family counselors, role-playing, and discussions was shown to be effective, and it served as a model in cities for training officers in family crisis intervention. In several cities, police–social worker family crisis intervention teams were established (Coffey 1974).

The police–social worker team approach for family crisis intervention, particularly in cases involving children, is used by many police departments at the present time. The following excerpt from an interview of Crista J. Cross (Interview 14.1), forensic interviewer for Stark County Job and Family Services, illustrates the cooperative approach used by the police and a social service agency in a county in Ohio.

INTERVIEW 14.1

CRISTA CROSS
Forensic Interviewer
Stark County Job and Family Services

Q=QUESTION; A=ANSWER

Q: Crista, as an investigator of child abuse or neglect, please describe the typical procedure you followed in completing the investigation.

A: In the specialized investigations unit, I was assigned to specific jurisdictions and detectives throughout Stark County (Ohio). A report would come into Children's Services, I would contact my detective, and as a team we would conduct the entire case together. We would first speak to the reporter, if possible, then go to the alleged victim, and I typically would do the interview while the detective took notes. Then the detective or I would contact the alleged perpetrator and both the detective and I would interview the alleged perpetrator at the police department. Depending on the case, there may be other professionals who we would interview to gather information or evidence before coming to a conclusion. If the family needed any type of services (housing, medical, mental health, protection orders, court orders), it was my responsibility to provide it. My involvement with a case would last approximately 30 to 45 days. If the family was still in need of services, I would transfer the case to an ongoing worker, who then would work with the family for up to 12 to 24 months. The detective and I would present our case to the MDT (Multidisciplinary Team) and at that point it was decided whether or not criminal charges would go forward or the case would be closed.

Q: In your current position, describe how you set the stage and proceed with interviewing a child who allegedly was abused.

A: A report comes through the Child Protective Services (CPS) hotline and is assigned to an intake social worker and detective of the jurisdiction in which the alleged abuse occurred. Contact is made with the caregiver of the alleged victim, and the interview is scheduled for the child to come to my office, which is located at our Child Advocacy Center—The Children's Network. Typically, 15 minutes prior to the child interview we have a "pre-interview," where members of the MDT meet, along with the caretaker, and information is provided to me, the interviewer. I then show the caretaker the interview room and where my cameras are located in the walls with the microphone, and I advise the caretaker that I do not inform the children that they are being videotaped and give examples as to why I don't let them know.

There are children who come into my office where video-taping and/or porn is part of their abuse, and it would be a trigger to them by telling them that I too am going to video-tape them. We don't usually act like ourselves when we know someone is videotaping, and telling a child that prior to the interview could sway the way they talk or what they choose to say, and their body language would not be natural know-ing that they are on video. The family advocate then takes the caretaker into her office and explains the entire process to him or her, while I go and get the child for the inter-view. Usually with the smaller children I stop along the way and talk about all the jungle animals I have in my hallway, because it breaks the ice and gets them talking about regular things and I am able to observe their body language, eye con-tact, and just overall presence. I then take the child into the room, and as I walk in there is a switch on the outside wall that I flip and that starts the videotaping. During the inter-view, I ask general questions about everything to do with the child's life—family, friends, school, sports, hobbies—and then get into more sensitive issues such as fears, worries, secrets, and safe and unsafe body touches. I always advise the children that they are not in trouble nor will they get in trouble for anything that we talk about. I ask each child to only speak of the truth and that I will not lie to them and would ask that they not lie to me. During the interview, the MDT is in a big conference room watching the interview live. If there is anything I forgot to address or ask the child, I may get a knock at the door or a note slid under the door. After the interview, depending on what the child discloses, they would next see my nurse practitioner, I would advise the caretaker of what the child disclosed, and at that point I move on to the next family. I have no further involvement

> unless we go to court. I do burn the DVDs for the team and dictate a brief summary of what the child stated during the interview. (Kratcoski 2012, 100, 102, 103)

The Stark County Multi-Disciplinary Team consists of a nurse practitioner, detective, childcare social worker, family advocate, county prosecutor, and a child forensic interviewer. The team is charged with determining if the alleged abuse or neglect can be substantiated, if the child has sustained any serious bodily injury, and what course of legal action to take against the alleged offender.

Collaboration of Justice Agencies and Victim Services Programs

The justice agencies functioning within any municipal, county, or state political jurisdictions communicate and cooperate with numerous health and social service agencies on a daily basis. For example, on any given day, the police may have to assist in transporting emergency patients, victims of accidents, or of violent crimes to the hospitals; find shelter for homeless street people, domestic violence victims, or runaway children; and may assist in the investigation of alleged abuse of children and adults. In addition, they may transport alleged offenders to the county jail or correctional facility.

The police and other justice agencies collaborate with social service organizations that are either funded directly by the government and are under government auspices or that are privately administered and are funded through ongoing contracts with the government and grants. As a result of changes in the laws, and decisions by judicial bodies, the justice system in the United States and other countries of the world has become more concerned with the civil rights of the citizens and the needs of the victims of crime. For example, in the past, the police and prosecutors were more likely to perceive the victims of robbery, rape, and other types of violent crimes predominately in terms of being witnesses and thus assisting in the arrest and prosecution of the alleged offender (Tontodonato and Kratcoski 1995, 2). However, at the present time (Wilson 2009), the victim is considered one of the key components of the criminal justice system and plays a significant role in the entire process in terms of providing testimony during a trial and entering an impact statement during the sentencing phase. If the offender is sentenced to prison, the victim can provide testimony at the time the offender is being considered for release from prison. Kratcoski (2009, 118) reflecting on the reasons for changes of the treatment of victims in the criminal justice system in the 1960s noted,

> The civil rights movement had developed tools for grassroots movements to create change. The women's rights movement had brought to the surface the

mistreatment of women victims of violence by the criminal justice system and begun to develop a network to support those victims outside traditional channels. Child abuse was now recognized as a common event not confined to a pathological few. The criminal justice system was being challenged on its mistreatment of victims of crime in its focus on providing due process to defendants. These disparate elements would create new institutions in the coming decades.

According to Davis and Henley (1990), funds provided by federal, state, and local governments helped stimulate the implementation of programs serving victims of crime. In 1974 (Finn and Lee 1985), the Law Enforcement Assistance Administration provided funding to the National District Attorneys Association for the development of eight pilot programs to assist victims of crime. These original programs served as the model for thousands of programs that were implemented throughout the United States. Important federal legislation that helped to develop support for victim assistance programs included the Federal Victim and Witness Protection Act of 1982 and the Victims of Crime Act of 1984 (Gaboury 1992). These agencies, with titles such as victim services, victim advocates, and victim assistance, provided a variety of services to victims of crimes, including counseling and monetary stipends. In addition, hundreds of thousands of volunteers with civic organizations, churches, social work agencies, hospitals, and schools provide considerable assistance to victims of crime, particularly the elderly, children, and abused women (Kratcoski 1992, 94).

Victim Services Provided

Generally, the victim service providers will assist the victim of a crime throughout the entire criminal justice process. In addition, victim service agencies work closely with community agencies on crime prevention programs and also maintain crisis intervention "hot lines" for suicide prevention, victims of sex crimes, and victims of domestic violence. A study of victim service programs (Kratcoski and Tontodonato 1993, 21) revealed that the vast majority of the agencies included in the study provided such services as advocacy, court-related services, counseling, assistance in completing compensation claims, locating transitional housing for victims, notification of victims of court hearings, community education on crime prevention, training of volunteers, maintaining "hot lines," and crisis intervention.

Victim witness/assistance programs tend to be structured somewhat differently, depending on the auspices of the agency. For example, the Stark County Victim/Witness Program is located within the office of the prosecuting attorney. The victim/witness division is one of four divisions. The victim/witness administration has a great deal of autonomy in the development of policies, goals, and the day-to-day operations of the program as well as in the selection of personnel. However, the ultimate decision on certain matters, particularly policies, rests with the prosecuting attorney Stark County Prosecutor (2015). In contrast, the Victim Assistance Program in Akron, Ohio, is a private organization. The origins of this program can be traced to the late 1920s. During the Great Depression, the Reverend Bob Denton operated the Furnace Street Mission. It served as a halfway house for boys, established summer camps for youth, and provided food and clothing for the needy (Victim Assistance Program, *History* 2014).

In the 1960s, the mission was established as a halfway house for home-less men and as a halfway house for men under supervision in the criminal justice system. In the 1970s, the Furnace Street Mission, under the direction of Bob Denton, son of the founder, began to focus on providing services for victims of crime (Victim Assistance Program 2014). The Victim Assistance Program became incorporated as a nonprofit organization in 1994. Over the years and up to the present time, this program continued to expand and now offers a wider variety of services. The program gained nationwide recognition, and other victim service organizations have modeled their pro-grams after the Victim Assistance Program.

Leanne D. Graham (Interview 14.2) has served as the Executive Director of Victim Assistance since 2013. Before assuming the position, Graham had a wide range of work experience in victim advocacy (Victim Assistance Program 2014). She received a master's degree in justice studies from Kent State University, worked as a crisis intervention specialist in the Victim Assistance Program, served as Transitional Shelter Manager and Director of Grants Management for the Battered Women's Shelter in Akron, and as asso-ciate director of the Victim Assistance Program before assuming her current position as its executive director.[*]

INTERVIEW 14.2

LEANNE D. GRAHAM (LG)
Executive Director
Victim Assistance Program
Akron, Ohio

COMPLETED BY PETER KRATCOSKI (PK), JULY 10, 2014
Q=QUESTION; A=ANSWER

QPK: Please give the length of time you have held the executive director position. How many years have you been employed with the Victim Assistance Program?

ALG: One year and a half.

---

[*] Beginning with Interview 14.2, the interviews in this chapter are original to this book.

QPK: What are the major goals of the Victim Assistance Program?

ALG: I can divide the goals or programs into three categories: The first category is crisis intervention, the second is judicial/court advocacy, and the third is trauma therapy. We provide services to victims and family members in all three categories. In addition to crime victims, we have been asked by local law enforcement to provide crisis intervention to individuals and family members for situations such as infant deaths, traffic fatalities, suicides, and in any other traumatizing situation.

QPK: Have the goals (mission) changed since you became director? If so, how have they changed?

ALG: We have the same goals/programs, but I have perhaps changed some administrative focuses. Being fairly new as director, I assessed each program to ensure all staff had a clear understanding of their job role and reviewed procedures to ensure all were still warranted. In addition, we currently focus more on the training of the staff. It is important to find evidence-based practices and base our programs on these practices. In fact, I am attending a week-long training program sponsored by the attorney general pertaining to best practices for victim services intervention.

QPK: As executive director, what are your major responsibilities?

ALG: Predominately the same as any administrator. Funding, grant writing, budgeting, creating policies procedures, supervision of staff, and public relations. For example, I currently serve on 12 advisory boards or counsels.

QPK: Who determines what will be major goals of the program?

ALG: I do with input from the board of directors. However, in the final analysis, the community determines the goals. For example, the domestic relations court judges recognized that too many victims who were applying for protection orders from the court were not prepared, and they were misinformed about the petitioning process. We completed a study and found that in 71% of the cases, the victim did not have a victim advocate to help them through the process. Thus, we assigned an advocate to work directly with the clerk of courts. This advocate offers services to all domestic violence and stalking victims requesting information from the clerk about protection orders. This ensures each victim applying for an order has the opportunity to be guided and supported by the victim advocate. I use this example to illustrate that as the needs of the people in the community change, our goals and practices will also change.

QPK: As executive director, how much input do you have in the following?

ALG: Selection of staff: I have five staff who work in administrative roles, and I have 100% responsibility for selecting these individuals. The director of services is predominately responsible for the selection of the 11 advocates who provide the direct services to victims. We also have a volunteer/intern coordinator who solicits, trains, and provides the assignments to the interns and volunteers.

Assignment of victim advocates: The director of services is responsible for ensuring that the day-to-day assignments of the advocates are being met. The advocates are provided with biweekly supervision meetings and are provided with training opportunities to foster professional growth. I create the advocates' job descriptions, and the director of services ensures that the advocates are carrying them out.

Evaluation of staff performance: Again, I evaluate my direct staff, and the director of services evaluates the advocates. In addition, the director of services aggregates anonymous client surveys on a monthly basis to ensure our programs are advancing toward program objectives. These surveys also provide insight on the advocates' performance.

QPK: Briefly describe the duties of the advocates assigned to the following courts, if applicable:

ALG: Municipal courts: Each day, the court prints out a list of offenses that have a victim. The victim advocate obtains the docket and either contacts the victims in person if they appear in court or by phone for those who do not attend court. If the victim attends the arraignment, the advocate will inform the victim of the court process and provide assistance, information, and referrals.

Court of common pleas (felony): One advocate attends grand jury hearings on a daily basis. This advocate meets with the victims who are testifying and explains the criminal justice process. Crisis intervention and referrals are also provided to the victim based on their individual needs. If the grand jury deems the case to be a true billed and the case moves on for trial, the advocate will transition the client to an advocate in the Summit County Prosecutor's Office Victim Services Division. These advocates provide court-based advocacy and will act as a liaison between the victim and prosecutor. If the case is remanded and sent back to the municipal court, our advocate will support the victim through the municipal process. Secondly, we also assist victims who are petitioning the court for an anti-stalking protection order. We are very fortunate to be able to collaborate with other victim service agencies.

Juvenile court: The juvenile court has its own advocates who work directly for the court. However Victim Assistance Program provides assistance to victims during the sentencing (disposition) phase of their trials (hearings). As a neutral party, our advocates will meet with the victims whose juvenile offender is being sentenced for the crime (delinquent act). The victim advocate will help the victim complete a victim impact statement, which documents how the life of the victim or family has been affected by the victimization. The document is then read by the judge and taken into consideration when the appropriate disposition (sentence) is determined by the judge. The adult probation department assists in the writing of impact statements for the victims whose offenders are adults.

Domestic relations court: Our advocates are heavily involved in the domestic relations court. All of our advocates are cross-trained to help victims apply for civil protection orders. Advocates will guide them through the application process, the judicial process, and provide crisis intervention and support through both hearings.

QPK: Is Victim Assistance involved in community crime prevention? If so, explain.

ALG: As mentioned, I am on 12 or more advisory boards. Some, but not all, are related to crime prevention; some involve advocating for victims by being there to represent them. For example, I am on the steering committee for the Summit County Reentry Network. This program focuses on assisting ex-inmates [to] make an adjustment back into the community. I ensure this program remembers the victims while creating programming for the ex-offenders.

QPK: From the list below, check those services that are provided directly or indirectly to victims or the community by the Victim Assistance Program.

Directly	Indirectly (Referral of Victim to Service Agency)
__X__Crisis intervention counseling	____
_X__24-hour hotline services	____
____Mediation with offender	X____
X____Landlord intervention	____
X____Protection orders	____
_X__Legal advocacy	X (education about the law)
X____On crime scene support (assists at hospital, medical examiner's office, employment sites, crime scene at banks, gas stations, restaurants)	
_X__Medical care referral	____
_X__Financial assistance	____
____Food, clothing assistance	X (Make referrals to agencies providing such services)
_X____Compensation	____
_X____Restitution (rarely)	____
X____Emergency housing (occasionally)	X____(Make referrals to Battered Women's Shelter)
____Notification of prison release hearing	____(The Summit County Prosecutor's Office Victims Service Division provides this service
_X__Victim protection education	____
_X__Individual counseling	____
____Group counseling	X (Referrals to Battered Women's Shelter)
_X__Victim impact statements	(Juveniles)____
_X__Public education	____
_X__Domestic violence intervention	____
X____Legislative advocacy (For example, our agency was influential in the passing of the crime victim compensation law)	
X____Other (please identify) We provide neighborhood canvas to offer crisis intervention to anyone who may have heard about a significant crime in the neighborhood. We have established a partnership with the University of Akron to conduct canvasing on their campus as well. Finally, training about victim's rights is provided to new Akron police officers and trainings on providing death notifications are provided to the Summit County Sheriff's deputies.	

QPK: What credentials (education, experience) are required for an advocate position?

ALG: A degree in social work, counseling, criminal justice, or related field is preferred, but other degrees are acceptable, depending on other factors, such as prior experience and the degree to which the person has the other essential skills required for the position.

QPK: In your opinion, what type of personality traits should an advocate have to be effective?

ALG: Be empathic, open-minded, resourceful, patient, compassionate, logical in thinking, self-confident, and can take control of the situation and stay focused on the problem.

QPK: Does the victim/witness program do anything special with elderly victims, especially shut-ins? (Explain.)

ALG: No, nothing special, but we provide considerable service to the elderly who are abused. We also find identity theft of the elderly victims to be quite common, as well as assault. Domestic violence is the most common reason for us to become involved in cases of elderly victimization. Depending on the situation, we will visit the elderly victim in their homes.

QPK: To what extent and in what capacity do advocates regularly interact and cooperate with:

ALG: Police officers: We interact with the police departments who operate in Summit County every day. In fact we have an office in the Detective Bureau at the Akron Police Department and the administrative offices of the Summit County Sheriff's Department. Akron police and the Sheriff's Department provide us with daily incident reports, which allow us to make cold calls to each victim and offer services.

Assistant prosecutors: We interact with prosecutors every day. There are three municipal courts in the county and we have advocates in all three. We have an advocate assigned to the prosecutor's office in the Barberton Municipal Courts as well.

Defense attorneys: We have very limited contacts with defense attorneys. Occasionally we are summoned to testify, but we are generally successful in having it quashed.

Judges/magistrates: We are in court every day—in particular, the advocates in the municipal courts and the domestic relations courts—we have daily contact with the presiding judge or magistrates. In addition to contacting and interacting with the victim, there are times we are able to express the victim's safety concerns to the judge or magistrate who is issuing a bond.

Corrections personnel (probation, parole officers): We have very limited contact with correctional personnel. Occasionally, we will be contacted by a probation officer regarding some matter pertaining to one of the officer's cases, but rarely.

Defendants: Our only contact with the defendants is at the evidentiary hearing. However, we do not have any conversions with the defendants.

QPK: In general, when advocates interact with other justice personnel, what is the nature of the interaction?

ALG: Generally, very positive. It is professional and cordial. They tend to see us as an ally and more helpful than being a hindrance.

QPK: Are there any categories of justice personnel (police, prosecutors) who are more likely to be troublesome, uncooperative than others?

ALG: None of the justice personnel we interact with are troublesome. Victim Services over the years has developed very positive relationships with these agencies, based on being mutually beneficial to each other and trust. The only problem is that everyone is extremely busy, and it may take some time for some to respond to our requests for information.

QPK: What do you consider to be the major problems/concerns that will confront the victim/witness program in the future?

ALG: As with most private, nonprofit organizations, funding is a major concern. We depend on grants and contributions from foundations and individuals. We have two major fund-raising events each year and are constantly looking for new sources for additional funding. The requests for our services have increased, and we are going to need additional funding in order to be able to respond and assist all who requested services. We have to work hard to continue to have positive relations with the justice agencies and the community. A major change in an agency, such as a new police chief or a new judge, could result in our need to demonstrate our abilities again in order to maintain the cooperative relationship. A change in the sentiments of the people in the communities we serve could result in significant changes in our program. Currently, victim rights and providing services to victims of crime have a high priority in the justice system. This was not always the case in the past and the practices and sentiments could revert to those of the past, if we do not continue to work with the community by providing information about the importance of victims' rights and the needs of victims.

QPK: Are there any topics or areas that you would like to comment on or have not been covered in the interview? (If yes, please comment.)

ALG: We are fortunate that the justice system agencies in Summit County are so cooperative and collaborate with each other. Not many counties are as rich in victim services as we: Victim Assistance Program, Summit County Prosecutor's Office Victim Services Division, Rape Crisis Center, and Battered Women's Shelter are all here to meet a common goal of helping victims of crime. Having moved to Summit County from another state, I can personally say that the collaborative efforts of our community make it a great place to work and live.

PK: Thank you for your cooperation. Your comments will be most useful for those interested in learning about the services provided to victims of crime.

Shelters for Victims of Crime

Santana (2009, 254) notes that victims of stranger crimes often have little need for shelter away from home. It is the needs of victims of nonstranger violent crime that have led to the creation of shelters across the country and around the world. The establishment of shelters for victims of violent crime, including victims of rape, victims of domestic violence, child victims of physical and sexual abuse, runaway children, the homeless, and the elderly became widespread in the 1970s. It was at this time that the findings of research on domestic violence, child abuse, and elderly abuse, as well as the efforts of feminist activists, led to a better understanding of the extent of crimes against these groups and how little was being done to assist the victims of such crimes.

The first shelters established in the United States for women physically abused by their husbands were established to provide crisis intervention and short-term housing. A woman and, at times, her children would stay at the shelter for four to six weeks until alternative housing and other sources of assistance could be established (Santana 2009, 254). As the realization evolved that the needs of abused women extended beyond those of food and clothing, many of the shelters began offering long-term residency, at times extending several years; they expanded their services to include individual and group counseling and education on establishing independent living and the development of new skills. Private foundations and funding from federal and state agencies led to the establishment of shelter homes, group homes, and centers for many other categories of victims such as the elderly, the homeless, and abused children.

The Battered Women's Shelter of Summit and Medina Counties

The Battered Women's Shelter of Summit and Medina Counties, located in Ohio, focuses on victims of family violence by providing intervention and prevention programs. As mentioned in its mission statement, "The mission of the Battered Women's Shelter is to lead the community in the prevention of domestic abuse by providing emergency shelter, advocacy, and education throughout Summit and Medina County, and in an effort to break the cycle of abuse and help promote peace in every family" (Battered Women's Shelter of Summit & Median Counties 2014). In addition to providing emergency shelter for 50 female domestic violence victims and their children, the staff also provides crisis intervention and case management and assists the victims of domestic violence with legal, medical, and other matters related to making an adjustment in the community after the domestic violence incident. In 2012, the agency assisted more than 6000 individuals affected by domestic violence.

Police Agencies in the Schools

During the latter part of the twentieth century, the crime and disorder in U.S. schools became matters of great concern for parents, students, teachers, and school administrators. The fact that the large majority of schools are safe has not eased concerns over safety in the twenty-first century. How to provide maximum security is a major problem many administrators must contend with as part of their daily tasks. Several sensational disasters in the schools, such as children being murdered, have had the effect of making the entire citizenry fearful for the safety of those who attend school. The effect is especially huge if the shooting occurs in a school that has not had a problem with violence and crimes or in cases when the shooter turns out to be someone who would be least suspected of committing a violent act. A study relating to delinquency prevention and security in U.S. schools (Gottfredson et al. 2004) revealed that a typical school averaged 14 programs designed to prevent crime and improve security. A current trend toward enhancing school security that has been followed by school administrators is "Establishing cooperative relations with other agencies and community leaders, including the police, judicial officials, and those involved in service agencies" (Kratcoski 2012, 47).

Police officers have been assigned to some schools and have collaborated with school officials on various educational programs, such as DARE. This program originated with the Los Angeles Police Department in 1983 (Rosenbaum and Hanson 1998) and is used in all 50 United States and in several foreign countries. The program consists of uniformed officers teaching a drug prevention curriculum to elementary school children.

Another school-based program in which the school administration and the police collaborate is the Gang Resistance Education and Training (GREAT) program (Kratcoski 2012). This program, which originated in Phoenix, Arizona, has been utilized in schools throughout the country. It consists of police officers providing a school-based curriculum to middle school students with the goal of helping them resist peer pressure to become involved with gangs. The curriculum taught by the trained officers emphasizes taking personal responsibility for one's behavior, cultural awareness, resolving conflict without violence, and community responsibility. In addition to the in-school activities, the officers and students engage in out-of-school activities, such as sporting and community events. In recent years, there has been a steady increase in police involvement in the day-to-day operations of U.S. schools. Police officers who are specially trained to work with juveniles are assigned to the schools and serve in various capacities, including providing security, teaching highway and traffic safety, assisting in the disciplining of unruly or disorderly students, completing investigations of suspected criminal activities—such as possession of illegal drugs or weapons, helping coordinate crisis situations, and making arrests of students who have engaged in criminal or delinquent behavior.

The Student Resource Officer (SRO) Program (Kratcoski 2012, 154–155) has been adopted by school systems throughout the United States. SRO involves specially trained police officers being assigned to high schools and middle schools on a daily basis. In addition, SROs are generally expected to attend extracurricular school-related activities including sporting events and dances, as well as community events such as PTA meetings. The specific duties of SROs may vary, depending on the characteristics of the student population and the community. Generally, the school and police administrators work out the details together. The sources of funding for the programs might come from the police department, the school district, or be jointly shared by the schools and the police administration. Duties performed by SROs include providing physical protection for staff and students, prevention of delinquent acts—such as theft or destruction of school property, offering lecturers on all aspects of community life, mediating disputes between students, and providing mentoring for students who seek advice.

SROs generally have the discretion to work in uniform or in street clothing. Regardless of the dress code followed, an aim of SROs officers is to be as unobtrusive as possible and to become accepted by the school administrators, teachers, and students as regular staff members. The goal is to have students develop a positive image of the police so that the officer is seen as someone who is helpful rather than someone to be avoided. SROs have been known to be instrumental in developing links for improved relations among the police, faculty, parents, and students in the communities of which SRO programs are a part.

To be successful, the programs described here and many others require considerable cooperation and collaboration between the police and school officials. In the process, police gain an increased understanding and appreciation of the teachers' roles in young people's lives, and teachers and school administrators develop insights into the role of the police and the services they provide to families in the community as well as in the school setting.

Alternative Education Schools

Alternative schools are used for students who are low academic achievers, disruptive, expelled from regular schools, truant, or who have been adjudicated delinquent and are under court supervision. Alternative education schools are either under the administrative umbrella of the regular school system or are independent, privately owned and administered institutions. The curricula and programs offered in these schools are designed to work on the students' academic and behavior problems. Referrals to the alternative schools come from school administrators as well as the courts because a juvenile adjudicated delinquent who is given a disposition of probation may be required to attend the alternative school as a condition of probation.

For the alternative schools to be effective, their administrators must rely on the cooperation of numerous justice and social service agencies. Many of the students who attend these schools are under court supervision, separated from their families, and in need of consistent health care or counseling. Many of them are under the supervision of several professionals, including social workers, probation officers, and school administrators. Police officers who are not normally assigned to these schools on a regular basis may called in to the schools to curtail disturbances or to conduct an investigation of a crime.

Psychologists Working in Criminal Justice Agencies

Psychologists are employed with various criminal justice agencies, including police agencies, courts, and correctional agencies. The following interviews with Dr. Thomas Anuskiewicz (Interview 14.3), a private practitioner and Dr. Thomas Webb (Interview 14.4), employed by a public juvenile justice agency, illustrate the range of services professionals provide.

After obtaining an undergraduate degree, Thomas Anuskiewicz was employed at a school for delinquent and behavior problem youth. He later completed a master's degree in special education and obtained a license to teach special education. He taught at an alternative education school while completing a Ph.D. in counseling psychology. He received his degree and obtained a license in clinical psychology from the state of Ohio.

INTERVIEW 14.3

DR. THOMAS M. ANUSKIEWICZ (TA)
Clinical Psychologist
Forensic Sciences and Investigators

COMPLETED BY PETER KRATCOSKI (PK), JUNE 28, 2014
Q=QUESTION; A=ANSWER

QPK: Tom, during the earlier part of your career, you were employed by public and private nonprofit agencies; when did you started Marion Psychological, Inc.? What was your main motivation for starting your own business? Are other psychologists employed at Marion?

ATA: Marion Psychological, Inc. (MPI), became incorporated in 1987. I simply wanted to have my own business as a means of being able to do different things, advance my psychology resume, make more money, and have more job flexibility. I looked at it as a challenge, scary but exciting, something that none of my friends at the time were doing. There are no other psychologists employed by MPI at this time. I considered hiring a psychologist to assist me at the Stark County Jail. It is difficult to find a person with the correct attitude, who wants to work in a correctional setting and who is willing to take on the pressure and liability of decisions made in a correctional setting; finding someone who is not intimidated by the situations and the inmates of a correctional setting, as well as finding someone who can get the security clearance is difficult.

QPK: As a psychologist with Marion, what type of services do you provide that are related in some way to the justice system? Are you ever asked by police departments to provide professional service?

ATA: We work with jails, prisons, police and sheriff's departments, and the courts. We provide service to the inmates and staff at the correctional settings (i.e., crisis intervention, counseling, case management, 24-hour on-call, preemployment psychological evaluations, Ohio Police Officer Training Academy (OPOTA) training for corrections officers and sheriff deputies, as well as provide input on policy and program development). We also work with the courts, mainly by providing court-ordered forensic evaluations (NGRI, competency, sex-offender assessments, presentence evaluations, case mitigation/planning reports, risk assessments for violent offenders, and providing expert testimony). I have also provided discrete psychological evaluations for police departments who have high ranking officers get involved in "problematic situations" leading to possible reprimands (this included mental stability assessments, ability to safely carry a firearm, and return to work evaluations).

QPK: What subjects do you teach for the Ohio Peace Officers Training Academy?

ATA: I have taught such subjects as abnormal behavior, crisis intervention, suicide risk, stress reduction, and substance abuse. These are all related to my specialty in psychology.

QPK: Tom, can you recall a few cases in which you provided discrete psychological evaluations for police departments?

ATA: Generally, they were related to high level administration officers engaging in abnormal behavior. For example, one officer threatened his wife with a firearm, another showed signs of suicide tendencies. My evaluations pertained to their fitness to continue work.

QPK: Did you ever complete preemployment screening to police departments?

ATA: Yes, I did this for several departments, including the Stark County and Summit County Sheriff's Departments and the Stark County Park District and with isolated cases in the Cuyahoga County Sheriff's Department.

QPK: Do you ever serve as an expert witness? If so, provide a few examples and describe the process and procedure involved.

ATA: I have provided expert testimony a number of times for common pleas courts, juvenile and family courts, and for the U.S. Army. The court typically sends a subpoena. The army calls directly from either the lead prosecutor or defense attorney. Subpoenas can originate from either prosecution or defense. My job is to assess the client or defendant, generate a psychological report, distribute the report to the judge and attorneys, and, when called upon to do so, testify in court. This includes meeting with all relevant parties in the case to gather information for the final report. I have been involved with murder cases, assaults, kidnappings, arson cases, and family custody cases. I have also done

NGRI, that is restoration to competency, restoration to sanity, and risk assessments for reintegration or release back into the community reports and child custody reports. I have also provided evaluations for the Forensic Center of Northeast Ohio. This is one of eleven centers set up by the state of Ohio to provide court-ordered evaluations. The Northeast Center provides service to six counties in the area, including Cuyahoga County.

INTERVIEW 14.4

DR. THOMAS WEBB (TW)
Head Psychologist
Summit County Juvenile Court, Ohio

COMPLETED BY PETER KRATCOSKI (PK), JUNE 27, 2014

Q=QUESTION; A=ANSWER

Dr. Webb completed a bachelor's degree in psychology at Vanderbilt University and master's and doctoral degrees in clinical psychology at the University of Tennessee. In addition, he took advanced training at the Illinois State Research Hospital. He assumed a faculty position at the University of Pennsylvania and later became a research associate at the Northeastern Ohio Universities College of Medicine. His current position is forensic psychologist for the Summit County Juvenile Court in Ohio, a position he has held since 1997.

QPK: Dr. Webb, why did you become interested in pediatric/forensic psychology?

ATW: It relates back to an experience back in my early childhood. I had a close friend who committed suicide, and I often wondered why he would want to end his life. However, I did not make a decision to become a clinical psychologist until my senior year at Vanderbilt. After I decided to go to graduate school, one opportunity led to another, and I became fascinated with completing research. After completing my degrees and advanced training, I had an opportunity to teach clinical forensics in the graduate school at the University of Pennsylvania Hospital, and the experience made me realize teaching and working in clinical forensic psychology was my "cup of tea."

QPK: Dr. Webb, what do you consider the most challenging aspects of your present position as psychologist with the Summit County Juvenile Court?

ATW: The opportunity to try to understand how youth express their emotions and what motivates them toward their goals and how they adjust to the stresses in their lives. The children I see are often chronically ill, not in a physical sense, but psychologically. Nevertheless, they hide their dependency and helplessness. They put on a bravado act, that is, they tell you that they do not need anyone and that they can run their own lives. They often have an inflated self-image, particularly when they are with their peers. However, in a one-on-one situation, I can get them to communicate and talk about the things that are having a negative effect on their lives. They eventually develop a more realistic image of who they are and what to expect in the future once they approach adulthood.

QPK: Dr. Webb, what are the most difficult decisions you have to make in your position as chief psychologist?

ATW: Decisions on transferring youth to the criminal court are always difficult. The amenability proceeding is used to determine if a child will be responsive to treatments available in the juvenile justice system. Of course, the final decision on waiver to the adult system rests with the judge, and there are many factors that enter into the decision. However, my report is always an important factor. In cases of very young offenders, 14 and 15 years old, who are charged with very serious offenses, the community sentiments are often in favor of having the juvenile "bound over" to the adult criminal court; but after the youth's developmental and psychiatric history and other relevant factors are considered, I make my recommendations to the judge based on all of the factors. The judge makes the final decision.

QPK: Please outline the procedure you follow in testing a youth who is being considered for judicial waiver.

ATW: Under the Ohio Criminal Code, the court psychologist is allowed to give an expert opinion on the matter of the child's competence and on the child's amenability for treatment in the juvenile justice system. In regard to competence, if there is some question about the child's mental capacity to provide information to the defense attorney or understand the nature of the court proceedings, I am required to make an extensive assessment. I use standardized, scientifically validated tests and extensive personal interviews with the child to determine if the child is competent. I then write a report and submit it to the court. The question of competency comes up most often with younger children and those of borderline intelligence or those who have a history of mental health problems.

The matter of amenability to treatment in the juvenile justice system is complex and more difficult to determine. If a juvenile is charged with one or more serious offenses and the status of the youth, for example, meets the age requirement specified in the law, the prosecutor first recommends that the youth be transferred to the criminal court and be tried as an adult. At the probable cause hearing, evidence is presented to determine if it is sufficient to indicate that the child committed the act. If probable cause is established, I am asked to complete an amenability report before any additional action is taken on the case. It may take up to a month to complete the report. In the investigation, I consider: family history, early childhood development, school-related matters such as attendance, performance, peer associations and behavior, prior referrals to the juvenile court, [and] past and current involvement in psychiatric counseling and rehabilitative programs. These are weighed to make a determination of the youth's maturity with respect to emotional, cognitive, and physical status.

The youth's relationship with the family and siblings is very important. I look to determine if the youth receives support and guidance from the parents and how the youth is disturbing family relations, apart from other factors. If the family is being disrupted by conflict and violence, I look very closely at early childhood. The trauma of being abused or neglected can be very important in helping to explain present behavior. If available, I try to incorporate information about the child's behavior in preschool, kindergarten, and elementary school. At times, troublesome behavioral patterns will become manifest at a very early age.

The physical condition of the child is very important and is included in the amenability report. I collect information from various sources to determine if there are prenatal and perinatal issues along with medical conditions. A history of head traumas and other neurological disorders can have an effect on the youth's behavioral manifestations.

The youth's intelligence is a very important factor, but it is the pattern of relative weaknesses and strengths that is much more important than a single IQ score. Some children may have a high memory capacity but have a low reasoning capacity. For example, some children appear quite normal outwardly, but in ambiguous situations, they may have trouble abstracting what they have learned rotely and applying it to a new situation. The prior and present use of drugs may have an effect on behavior. Prior use of psychotropic medications and their effectiveness is included in my report.

I include information on interpersonal relations in the report. Such matters as the youth's daily routine, patterned behaviors regarding whom he/she interacts with, what he/she do for recreation, whether he/she is physically active such as being involved in sports or organizations, and whether his/her day-to-day behavior typically conforms to community expectations are weighed. Factors such as whether the youth is socially isolated, typically withdrawn, or aggressive and a bully are important and are included in the report.

I rely on the information obtained from standardized tests and gleaned from my personal interviews with the child to come up with an assessment of the youth's amenability for treatment in the juvenile justice system. After I write the report, it is sent to the judge and attorneys involved with the case. When the "bind over" hearing is actually held, I am generally summoned to appear at the hearing and provide testimony.

QPK: Dr. Webb, how many times during your years of experience have you served as an expert witness?

ATW: I have probably written about 60 competency reports, which generally do not require that I appear in court and testify and about 400 amenability reports, which do require my presence as an expert witness.

QPK: Have you testified in adult cases?

ATW: I have testified in custody cases where I evaluated the parents and made a recommendation on which parent should be awarded custody of the children.

QPK: When you testify as an expert, who initiates the process? Who decides if your service is needed?

ATW: When the youth comes into the court for the initial screening, the intake officer may determine that some psychological assessment of the youth is needed, and the intake department will make a request for a written psychological report. The intake officer will send such a request in writing for purposes of legal documentation. In regard to my appearance and testifying in court, the order comes from the judge.

QPK: Dr. Webb, how often in your daily work do you have contact with police officers?

ATW: Very rarely do I have direct contact.

QPK: How often do you interact with prosecutors?

ATW: Quite frequently. I contact them for information, particularly when such is needed for the amenability reports, I am questioned by the prosecutors during the hearings, and I can be subpoenaed to appear in court for other reasons as well.

QPK: Are you ever asked by the prosecutor's office to assist in preparing cases?

ATW: Yes, in connection with issues where a previously seen youth is now in an adult criminal court and information on childhood background is required.

QPK: Are the prosecutors helpful in any way when you are completing your work on a case?

ATW: Yes, the details in the prosecutor's investigation are very helpful. Details regarding the nature of the actual offense are not used, but social content from which the crime evolved is used.

QPK: Dr. Webb, how often do you interact with children services and other social service agencies?

ATW: Very frequently.

QPK: In what capacity?

ATW: Most often, our interaction is not with reference to a single child, although I am asked to consult on special cases such as those relating to mental health and drug abuse. More generally our interactions are with regard to collaborative programming, setting up conferences, and long-range planning.

QPK: Do you find the personnel of social service agencies to be supportive and cooperative?

ATW: Very much so. In particular, Summit County Children Services works very closely with the juvenile court. This is necessary to achieve the court's goals. There are a large number of children who are under the jurisdiction of the juvenile court but also need basic assistance in order to survive. The court and service agencies work together in a variety of ways to meet the best interests of the youth who fall under the jurisdiction of the court and outside agencies.

Criminal Investigator

The general occupational category of investigator encompasses a wide variety of specific occupations involving investigations (Mauet 2002, 317). For example, criminal investigators or detectives are employed by federal, state, and local government agencies as well as being privately employed. They investigate suspected violators of the laws. Investigators employed with the medical examiner's office collect facts on the circumstances and causes of death. Those attached to a prosecutor's office collect information pertaining to civil and criminal cases, and detectives or investigators with policing agencies complete various types of investigations related to criminal matters.

The expertise of several types of professionals may be used during the course of a criminal investigation. For example, forensic evidence will be collected by a police detective or investigator at the crime scene. The investigator will "take photographs and physical measurements of the scene, identify and collect forensic evidence, and maintain the proper chain of security of the evidence" (National Institute of Justice 2014). The evidence will then be sent to a laboratory and analyzed by a scientist. If the evidence is sufficient to bring charges against the person suspected of the crime, the police officer who gathered the evidence during the initial investigation and the scientist who analyzed the evidence may have to provide testimony in court if the case goes to a trial.

Although a common procedure is followed in all criminal investigations, the specific expertise required to investigate a crime scene and to analyze the evidence collected at a crime scene will vary, depending on the type of crime being investigated. For example, those investigating a death scene may need different skills than those investigating fire and arson cases. An expert on bombs and explosives requires a specific set of skills, as does an expert investigating missing persons.

An Occupational Employment and Wages Report (*Occupational Employment Statistics* 2013, 1) indicates that there are more than 100,000 criminal investigators employed by local, state, and federal governments. The highest number of investigators working for local governments is concentrated in the police agencies. Criminal investigators are used by state governments to investigate workers' compensation fraud, insurance fraud, medical fraud, crimes committed in state facilities such as state hospitals, consumer fraud, and violations of environmental protection laws. Generally, federal agencies will have an investigative component. The number of investigators employed with private enterprises such as corporations, the media, hospitals, insurance companies, and private educational institutions is also substantial. It is estimated that one-fifth of all investigators are privately employed (Occupational Outlook Handbook 2014, 1).

In the *Annual Report of the Ohio Bureau of Criminal Investigation* (Ohio Attorney General 2013), published by the Ohio Attorney General, it is reported that the Attorney General Special Prosecutors assist local and state law enforcement criminal investigators with a variety of different types of investigations. The Bureau of Criminal Investigation's Forensic Dive Team assists local law enforcement officials recover such evidence as human body parts and weapons that have to be retrieved from underwater sites. The dive team operates from a mobile command post, and all of the members are certified as public safety divers. They use equipment and technology that would be too expensive for most local enforcement agencies to purchase (4). The LINK Program uses special investigators from the Ohio Bureau of Criminal Investigation to assist local law enforcement agencies in finding persons who have been missing for many years and who are presumed to be dead. If the body is located, it helps bring closure to the family and to ease the anxiety and grief they experience in not knowing the fate of the missing person (5). The cases investigated by the LINK program are recorded in the Annual Report of the Ohio Bureau of Criminal Investigation (2013, 5).

Larry Hootman (Interview 14.5) has served as a field investigator with the Ohio Bureau of Criminal Investigation (BCI) since 2008. Prior to becoming employed by BCI, he worked as a patrol officer and detective with the New Philadelphia Police Department for 17 years. He has investigated a number of different types of crimes, including murder, rape, armed robbery, arson, corruption, and sexual assaults against children (*Akron Beacon Journal* 2014).

INTERVIEW 14.5

LARRY HOOTMAN (LH)
Crime Scene Investigator
Ohio Bureau of Criminal Investigation

COMPLETED BY PETER KRATCOSKI (PK), EMERITUS/ ADJUNCT PROFESSOR, KENT STATE UNIVERSITY JULY 31, 2014

Q=QUESTION; A=ANSWER

QPK: Larry, please tell me what motivated you to become a police officer and give a short review of your work history as a police officer.

ALH: I always wanted to become an officer, and I actually completed the Ohio Peace Officer's basic training before I was old enough to become an officer. Thus, I started as a police dispatcher for the New Philadelphia Police Department in 1991, and I worked in that capacity for 11 months. I was hired as a patrol officer and continued working as a patrol officer for the New Philadelphia

Police for 10 years. I became a detective after my patrol experience and held that position for another seven years until I was hired as a crime scene agent for the Ohio Bureau of Criminal Investigation [OBCI]. During the time I worked as a detective for the New Philadelphia Police, I investigated almost every type of major crime, including murder, rape, fraud, [and] drug trafficking; but the major crimes did not occur as frequently as is the case in the larger cities. I developed a sort of specialty in accident reconstruction.

QPK: How long and in what capacity have you been working for the OBCI?

ALH: I have been a crime scene agent for Ohio BCI for six years. I was hired as a crime scene agent and have never left that position. The Richfield District covers 22 counties in northeast Ohio. There are large cities, medium-sized cities, and many small cities and towns in the district, so we see a wide range of crimes and a diversity of people and cultures.

QPK: Please explain the process followed when you are assigned to an investigation. Who initiates the request; who makes the actual assignment?

ALH: The initial call is taken by the radio room at BCI Headquarters located in London, Ohio. The supervisor in charge of the district in which the request for assistance is located (there are several BCI district stations located in different sections of the state), as well as the supervisor of the unit from which the call originated will make a decision on which "crime scene" agent will be dispatched to the crime science.

QPK: What are your duties as a field investigator at the crime scene?

ALH: Detect, collect, and preserve physical evidence. We also provide courtroom testimony if needed. Each crime scene agent has a complete station (truck) that is driven to the crime scene. Depending on the severity and complexity of the crime scene, one or two agents are sent. In really complex cases, for example, a mass murder situation, as many as seven or eight agents may be dispatched.

QPK: From the crimes listed below, check those that you have directly investigated and those in which you may have been indirectly involved (perhaps referred the case to another agency/investigator).

ALH:

Directly Involved	In-Directly Involved
__X__Murder	_____
_X__Rape	_____
__X_Armed robbery	_____
_____Trafficking in drugs	__X__
_____Kidnapping	__X__
_____Identity theft	__X__
_____Trafficking in weapons	_____
__X__Arson	_____
__X__Child pornogophy	_____
__X__Sexual assaults against children	_____
_____Consumer fraud (Goods not delivered work not completed, etc.)	__X__
__X__Corruption	_____
__X__Receiving stolen property	_____
_____Money laundering	__X__
_____Counterfeiting (money, documents)	_____
_____Smuggling	_____
_____Bank, insurance fraud	_____
_____Other (identify)	_____

QPK: Could you elaborate somewhat on the investigation of corruption?

ALH: Someone will bring the suspicion of corruption to our attention. Depending on the source of the complaint and who is the subject of the suspicion, the investigation could take several different paths. For example, victims may go to the mayor or safety director of the community in question if the police are suspected, or they can go directly to the attorney general. We have investigated a number of public officials including judges, attorneys, police officials, and politicians. If an administrator of a police department is under suspicion, we are called in to assist because it is too close to home and the local officials want an outside investigation so that they can be assured that the finding of the investigation will be completely objective. We find on occasion that there is no basis for the allegations made against the accused and, since it was an outside investigation completed by professionals, no one can make a complaint about a cover-up.

QPK: Describe the process followed in investigating sexual assaults against children.

ALH: Generally, the local police contact us and ask for assistance. As mentioned, we have all of the latest equipment to make the tests needed. The investigation follows the general patterns of any investigation. We are trying to determine and obtain evidence on the who, what, where, when, and why factors related to the case. For example, if the alleged incident occurred in the bedroom of a home, we can collect the bedding and have it tested for traces of semen and DNA. The fact that we handle such cases regularly, plus having access to the latest equipment, provides an edge in assisting the local police departments, particularly the smaller ones that are not likely to have the equipment.

QPK: Do you investigate insurance fraud?

ALH: I have personally investigated insurance fraud while working with the New Philadelphia Police. It is a very complicated and time-consuming investigation. The case I recall was an auto body workshop. The owner was padding the cost of repairs and even would damage the auto more in order to get a larger settlement from the insurance company. Some of the owners of the autos being repaired were in on the fraud and received kickbacks. The insurance companies filed the complaint and were cooperative. We had to search all of the records [and] contact and interview the owners of the autos that were repaired until we had enough incriminating evidence to bring the case to court. The owner of the body shop was convicted but did not receive much of a penalty.

The Bureau of Criminal Investigation has specialists who work on insurance fraud cases. Most of their work is completed on the computer and in conjunction with investigative agents employed by the insurance companies.

QPK: When called on to complete a field investigation, what is your relationship with other police investigative agencies involved in the case? (Who is in command, determines the direction the investigation follows?)

ALH: We are called by the agency to complete a thorough crime scene investigation and recover whatever items of evidence are present. The agencies we deal with are very appreciative of what we do, and we work together very well. The requesting agency is still in charge of the investigation unless they request Ohio BCI conduct it.

QPK: Do you ever rely on private investigators for information/assistance?

ALH: I have not, and I [have] never heard of any other agent with BCI who has used private investigators to assist them in the completion of investigations. We do not need to rely on their assistance due to the number of resources we have.

QPK: In what type of cases would you rely on the expertise of other professionals such as scientists or technicians, photogrammetrists? (Give a few examples.)

ALH: The evidence collected from the crime scene is often sent to one of three laboratories operated by Ohio BCI. These laboratories have forensic scientists that work with agents and the agency to determine what needs testing and for what. We work with the scientists on a daily basis.

    We carry total stations in our crime scene trucks to document our scenes and where evidence was located in relation to that scene. We use images from the Internet on occasion to insert into our final product. Generally, two agents are sent to the crime scene, but as I indicated earlier, there may be as many as five or six if it is a complicated case or if there are several victims. If we have several investigators at the scene, we will break up into teams, and each team will complete a specified portion of the investigation.

QPK: Do you have access to all of the latest technical equipment needed to complete your work? What tools do you use most often?

ALH: We are on the leading edge of technology and strive to improve every day. I would say the items used most often are your brain, latent fingerprint kit, camera, and past experience.

QPK: How would you describe your relationship with other police/investigative agencies with whom you work?

ALH: We work as a cooperative agency to obtain a common goal. I think all the agents are accepted well with whom we work, and it becomes a team effort to find the person or persons responsible for whatever crime is being investigated to protect the citizens. BCI investigators will ask for assistance from other agencies, such as social service agencies, and federal law enforcement agencies when their assistance will help get the job done.

QPK: In your opinion, what are the skills a criminal investigator needs to be effective?

ALH: An open mind, common sense, and experience. As crime scene investigators, we do not have to test the evidence, but we have to have the ability to know what is potential evidence and how best to protect the scene from contamination. Every crime scene is different, and there may be some small thing that could be very valuable in the investigation that might be overlooked if the investigator did not have the experience. The investigator has to have the ability to get along with others and use their knowledge.

QPK: In your opinion, what is needed to enhance the effectiveness and efficiency of your operations?

ALH: We have the equipment to complete the initial field investigations and to get it ready to send to the lab. Of course, the technology is constantly being improved, and we are constantly being trained when new equipment is introduced. The number of investigations BCI handles has increased significantly each year; and thus, in order to handle the investigations, we need more crime scene investigators, more scientists, and specialists to complete the investigations.

QPK: How often are you called to testify as an expert witness in criminal court?

ALH: We testify on a regular basis, sometimes two or three times a month and then sometimes not for three or four months. Some are called to testify as an expert witness where others simply testify to the facts. To testify as an "expert" witness does not happen that often.

QPK: Briefly describe your role as an expert in court.

ALH: I have not been asked to testify as an expert witness.

QPK: In your opinion, what experiences (higher education, basic/ advanced training, on-the-job experience, mentoring by senior officers, etc.) best prepared you for investigative work?

ALH: I believe experience is second to none. Working with some of the people you do at Ohio BCI is the best experience you may ever obtain. Personally, the field training agent I worked with was exceptionally good. All of the trainers were the best of the best. We are required to do in-service training at least one time a year. We are fortunate to have some of the best instructors in the country come to Ohio BCI to train the agents; this includes basic and advanced training. Education is paramount.

QPK: Are there other areas related to your work as an investigator that have not been covered in this interview? (Explain.)

ALH: Well, thinking about my own career, I am very happy with my present position. I came up through the ranks, starting as a non-paid volunteer and even considered working in corrections before the position with the New Philadelphia Police became available. If I would have been able to complete my college education, more opportunities for advancement would be open for me. Perhaps the college education would have helped in broadening my view on the importance of cooperation and having respect for others who in some way or another contribute to the protection of society. In spite of the fact that we have the expertise and equipment to get the job done, we need that cooperation and input from others to get the job done.

PK: Thank you very much for your cooperation. I am sure the information you have provided will be very useful to those seeking careers in police work.

Professionals in Corrections

The types of offenders housed in jails, correctional institutions, and in community correctional facilities that often need special medical attention and/or psychological assessment and counseling are sex offenders (including rapists and child molesters), substance abusers, mentally ill or mentally handicapped offenders, those having HIV or AIDS, and elderly offenders. The proportion of all alleged and convicted offenders that are admitted to jails and correctional institutions who are suffering from some form of mental illness has increased significantly in recent years, especially in regard to those admitted to jails. For example, in the Cook County Jail (Chicago)—a facility holding 10,600 inmates, "On a Wednesday, 36 percent of all new arrivals report having a mental illness, on a Friday it's 54 percent" (Geller 2014, 1). Federal law requires that those being held in jails and other correctional facilities be provided physical and mental health care if needed; but in the case of the jails, a large proportion of the inmates may be housed for a few days or less and never get the proper assessment and treatment needed (Geller 2014, 4).

The professionals working in corrections will either be employed by private organizations or by federal, state, county, or local government agencies. They may be full-time employees, individuals hired under contract agreements to provide specified services, or they may be employed as consultants.

The nature of their work requires that they have special education and skills and that they be allowed to provide the type of service—be it counseling, physical therapy, or education—that is likely to produce the most desirable outcome. They are required to perform their duties in accordance with the professional and ethical standards of their profession. To do so requires a great deal of autonomy in decision making. At times, the requirements of the professional practice, such as private one-on-one counseling with "dangerous" inmates, may be in direct conflict with the security measures employed within the institution. Also, the inmates receiving the psychological counseling and other special services may be the same inmates who are the most troublesome and the most difficult to handle within their housing units. As a result, the correctional staff may resent having these inmates receive what appears to be special "privileges" when they meet with the professionals providing services. During an interview with Dr. Thomas Anuszkiewicz (Interview 14.6), a clinical psychologist who has worked as a psychologist in several types of correctional facilities including jails, prisons, and juvenile correctional facilities, he offered the following comments regarding the role of the professional working in a correctional facility.

INTERVIEW 14.6

DR. THOMAS M. ANUSKIEWICZ (TA)
Clinical Psychologist
Forensic Sciences and Investigators

COMPLETED BY PETER KRATCOSKI (PK), JUNE 28, 2014

Q=QUESTION; A=ANSWER

QPK: Tom, tell me about your experiences with the county sheriff's office. How many years have you been employed with this agency?

ATA: I have provided psychological services in the jail for more than 20 years.

QPK: Are you under a consulting contract or a salaried employee?

ATA: I am under contract with the Correctional Healthcare Group, which in turn contracts with the sheriff's department to provide medical and mental health services.

QPK: Are your assistants hired by you or by the sheriff?

ATA: My assistants are employees of Marion Psychological, Inc., my privately owned business.

QPK: Tom, describe some of the main duties you perform as the psychologist for the jail. Is a standard psychological evaluation given to all jail inmates? If not, how are those tested selected for evaluation? Do you have to appear before a committee to present the results of your evaluations?

ATA: Full comprehensive psychological evaluations are only completed when the court orders them. Otherwise, each inmate does receive a brief mental health screening upon entry into the jail. The same screening is used for every inmate. This screening, though, does not include involvement with the inmate's specific case. As mentioned, a full evaluation is completed only when the court orders a full psychological evaluation. I do participate from time to time on different policy and planning groups and have testified in court as an expert witness on numerous occasions.

QPK: In that you are a professional working within what is essentially a police organization, please tell me about the relationship you have with jail administrators, supervisors, and correctional personnel.

ATA: Relationships are kept on a strictly professional level. I focus on delivering the exact service requested, that is, providing high quality services that are industry standard or above. Relationships are characterized as honest, straightforward, trustworthy, confidential, productive, and with a touch of humor. Humor is essential in this type of setting.

QPK: Tom, reflecting on the past, do you feel as if you made a good career choice? Do you enjoy your work, or would you rather be doing something else?

ATA: Well yes and no. I enjoy the work sometimes, and the compensation can be good. I started my own business focused on getting contracts. It makes you feel good when you know your counseling or advice has helped a person get on the right track. However, there is a lot of liability, anxiety, and stress connected with [the] forensic and corrections psychological work I do. For example, I have been sued three times. In two of the cases, the persons committed suicide while in jail. It was not my fault and I won the cases, but there was a lot of anxiety because if I would have been found at fault, it could have possibly ended my career. Currently, I provide psychological services for the inmates housed in a maximum security prison. Many of these inmates are very hard to reach. They do not want to come and see me or communicate with me too much because they do not want the other inmates to think they are crazy. In summary, overall it is rewarding work, but there can be times when the work can get you down.

It is easy to understand why a professional working in a correctional setting may experience considerable stress and role conflict. While trying to adhere to the principles of the profession by providing the best service possible, the professional must also adhere to the rules and regulations of the correctional facility, particularly those pertaining to security, because they apply to all staff working in the facility.

Professional Input of Law Professors and Private Attorneys in Sentencing, Inmate Rights, and Wrongful Convictions

Many attorneys have devoted a large part of their careers to defending those they perceive as victims of the criminal justice system, persons who were arrested and convicted of crimes as a result of faulty evidence, biases in the system, or prejudices of the personnel in the justice system. In other cases, attorneys are involved in questioning or objecting to what is they perceive to be unjust or unconstitutional laws, such as the death penalty, and disparities in the sentencing laws. Numerous cases have been brought to the U.S. Supreme Court pertaining to conditions of confinement in prisons and jails. Those attorneys who devote considerable time and resources to these cases generally have a firm belief in the justness of their cause. They often work "pro bono" and, at times, the activity interferes with their personal lives.

The matter of wrongful conviction occurs when an innocent person either pleads guilty to a crime or is convicted of a crime that he or she did not commit. The Innocence Project and other groups have demonstrated that some people convicted of crimes were innocent. Ramsey and Frank (2007) questioned prosecutors, defense attorneys, judges, and police officers on the number of felony cases in which the accused was wrongfully convicted. They found that these professionals estimated as many as 1% in their jurisdiction and perhaps as many as 3% nationwide had been wrongfully convicted. Roman et al. (2012) estimated that up to 5% of all murder and sexual assault convictions may be wrongful convictions. These wrongful convictions may be attributed to misidentification of the person accused of the crime, false confessions, prejudices and biases of the jury, and to police investigators coming to conclusions regarding the perpetrator of the crime without having evidence to support their conclusions (Innocence Project 2013).

The contributions of scientists who developed the methods for DNA testing in regard to proving the innocence of hundreds, if not thousands, of convicted persons who were innocent cannot be overstated. According to the Innocence Project, as a result of DNA tests, 316 people convicted for serious crimes from 1989 to June 2014 were exonerated (Innocence Project 2014), and almost 14,000 convicted felons have been exonerated through DNA or other types of evidence (Michigan Law and Northwestern Law 2014). Of course, this did not occur automatically. It took the efforts of many dedicated attorneys and student volunteers to produce the evidence in court that was sufficient to convince the judges or juries that the original convictions were wrong.

The following interview with Dean Carro (Interview 14.7), professor emeritus of Akron University School of Law, illustrates how legal professionals have contributed to improving the criminal justice system in the United States. Dean Carro received a bachelor of arts degree in political science from the University College of New York at New Paltz in 1974 and his juris doctorate from the University of Akron School of Law in 1978. He practiced with a law firm for several years before accepting a position with the Akron University Law School in 1978. He served as a professor of clinical education and coordinator of the legal clinic offices from 1997 until his retirement in 2013. He is currently employed with a private law firm and also serves as an adjunct professor with the University of Akron School of Law.

INTERVIEW 14.7

DEAN CARRO (DC)
Emeritus Professor and Dean
Akron University School of Law

COMPLETED BY PETER KRATCOSKI (PK), JULY 25, 2014
Q=QUESTION; A=ANSWER

J. Dean Carro received his bachelor of science degree in political science from the State University College of New York at New Paltz in 1974 and his juris doctor degree from the University of Akron School of Law in 1978. He served as professor of clinical education and coordinator of the legal clinic offices at the University of Akron School of Law from 1978 until his retirement in 2013. He was granted emeritus professor status.

Currently, he is employed as "of counsel" with the law firm of Baker, Dublikar, Beck, Wiley, and Mathews. He also serves as an adjunct professor with the University of Akron School of Law.

QPK: Dean, tell me about what motivated you to seek a career in law.

ADC: I wanted to be an entomologist (study insects), but I was beginning to realize that science was not going to work for me. I had difficulty with math and hard sciences. My father was an attorney, but we rarely talked about the law or the legal profession. As a junior, I enrolled in a 15-credis course titled "Law and the Legal Profession." It was offered in the political science department. The professor integrated lectures with practical experience. We visited courts, jails, and had the opportunity to interact with several types of practitioners. I remember a highlight of the course was we travelled to Albany, New York, to watch an oral argument in the Court of Appeals (New York's highest court). This experience moved me toward law, and after taking a few other courses, in particular, constitutional law, I was hooked.

QPK: You have been providing community service (serving on advisory boards, etc.) throughout your career. Were there any particularly factors that had an influence on your decisions to provide assistance to those groups and organizations in need?

ADC: My personal view is that lawyers have an obligation to give back to the community. I agree with Thomas Jefferson who stated that lawyers have an obligation to be a public citizen. We are given great privileges by having a monopoly on the practice of law. With great privilege comes great obligation. There is a huge need for attorneys to represent poor people. In addition, we can be of service on many community issues. As a result of our education and training, we can be objective, identify problems, and offer a wide range of services.

QPK: Please give a brief overview of some of the programs/projects in which you played a significant role. What did you do?

ADC: I was the Akron Bar president. This is basically a three-year commitment. The first year you serve as president-elect, the second as president, and the third as immediate past president. I helped found and organize the Inn of Court in Summit County. This is a national movement, under the American Inns of Court, to replicate the English Inns of Court. An inn consists of lawyers, judges, and law students. We meet to discuss legal advocacy, ethics, and professionalism.

I was appointed to be the federal monitor of the Summit County jail by the United States District Court as a result of a class action lawsuit pertaining to conditions in the Summit County jail. This was a ten-year commitment. I had to visit the jail once a week, talk with the staff and inmates, and assure that conditions were up to constitutional standards.

I assisted the ACLU on several cases. For example, I co-represented the ACLU against the city of Stow, dealing with the placement of a Latin cross on the city seal.

I served on the Phoenix Alternative School Board of Directors for many years and served as legal advisor for various Mock Trial and Moot Court teams.

QPK: What factors did you consider when selecting the programs and projects for which you provided legal assistance?

ADC: For some, I was selected. For example, when I was asked to serve as the federal monitor. For others, it just seemed as if it was the right thing to do. I believed I could make a real contribution.

QPK: Correct me if I am wrong, but it appears as if you tend to assist those individuals, groups that are more or less the underdog. Is this correct?

ADC: It is easy to make a difference in Akron because of its small size. There are so many opportunities to help, and each person can make a real difference in others' lives. I enjoy helping individuals. I am sensitive to those who are underdogs. Often they just need a little advice.

There are enough lawyers representing the rich but not enough representing the poor.

QPK: When you served as a law professor and later as the dean of the law school, did you have any particular philosophy/message about the legal system that integrated into your lectures/administrative policies?

ADC: I was never the dean. My primary job was to teach courses and work in the legal clinic. The courses and seminars combined lectures on the criminal justice system, the criminal code, criminal law and procedures, and the development of skills such as interviewing, writing and research, mediation, litigation, and oral arguments. The students were also placed with government or nonprofit legal agencies. In short, we would lay the groundwork for students who wanted to become litigators. We would represent clients on civil rights cases, appeals, and other related cases.

QPK: Please provide some background on the first time you were involved in a matter pertaining to inmate rights/conditions in a prison or any matter pertaining to corrections. (How, why, when?)

ADC: I was appointed by a federal judge in a class action suit relating to conditions at the Ohio Correctional Facility in Lima, Ohio. This was originally the facility for those who were considered mentally ill. The conditions at the prison were far below minimum constitutional standards. I also was and continue to be involved in inmate assistance programs in Summit and Mahoney counties.

Our clinic engaged in conventional appeals and trials. In 1996, the Federal Prison Litigation Reform Act made it more difficult for inmates to litigate on prison conditions and other matters. Thus inmates housed in state correctional facilities who were seeking a hearing from the federal courts found it more difficult to prepare their case and had to rely more on professional help from attorneys than was the case before the Prison Reform Act became law.

QPK: While at Akron Law School, did you ever advise, help organize law students on projects pertaining to criminal justice matters (complete research, class action, legal advice)? If so explain.

ADC: Yes, as I explained earlier, the students in the clinic wrote briefs under my supervision. I would argue the felony appeals, and they would argue the misdemeanor appeals. We also represented clients at trial in prisoner civil rights cases and in federal and state criminal cases. They would visit the jail each week.

QPK: Were you an advisor to Mock Trial?

ADC: Yes, I was faculty legal advisor to the Mock Trial Team and the Moot Court Team. Moot Court focused on simulated appeals. The purpose of our Moot Court course was to train students to dissect and analyze a complex case, to anticipate the possible questions, and to present a comprehensive oral and written argument on behalf of the client. Mock Trial was simulated trial work.

QPK: When serving as an attorney for the defense in criminal matters, in general how were your relationships in terms of communications, cooperation, court room interactions with:

Judges: Throughout my experience, my relationships with judges has been very positive. It is a matter of mutual respect and professionalism.

Prosecuting attorneys: The same as above. We always were professional in our interactions.

Defendants: Again, No problem. Typically, they were thankful for the service we were providing.

Victims: In that I was representing defendants, I never had much contact with the victims.

QPK: Now that you are in private practice, are you involved in any projects, programs relating to the justice system? If yes, give some details.

ADC: I am working with the Ohio ACLU; coaching a high school Mock Trial team, and am developing a new program for expunging criminal records.

QPK: Do you occasionally teach a course at the Akron School of Law?

ADC: Yes, in fact I am scheduled to teach criminal procedure in the fall semester.

QPK: Is there any other subject you would like to address that was not covered?

ADC: No, I think we covered the topics.

PK: Thank you for your input. I am sure your responses will be most helpful to those interested in the law and justice system.

Summary

The materials presented and the interviews with professionals provided in this chapter were selected to illustrate how law enforcement officials, the judiciary, corrections agencies, social service agencies, professional practitioners (including private attorneys, educators, scientists, and technicians), and the community cooperate and collaborate in providing quality crime detection and prevention services to the community and assist those who have been victimized by crime. Throughout this chapter, it has been shown that, although some types of crime have not changed and the methods used to detect and prevent these crimes that have been found to be reliable in the past are useful today, many new types of crimes—such as Internet fraud, economic crimes, money laundering, consumer fraud, and various forms of trafficking in drugs, humans, and weapons—require the use of the latest technology and scientific methods in their investigation. In this regard, even many large police departments do not have the equipment and/or the personnel with the expertise to investigate and gather the evidence needed to prosecute those engaged in these criminal activities. Law enforcement officials and prosecutors seek assistance from scientists, educators, psychologists, economists, bankers, and administrators who have obtained considerable knowledge of a crime-related matter to qualify as expert witnesses.

Several sections of this chapter illustrate how the position of victims of crime has changed in recent years. In the past, victims were often chiefly regarded as witnesses that would provide testimony to assist in the conviction of a defendant. They are now given a central role in the criminal justice process. Their legal rights are considered, and law enforcement and prosecution officials are required to treat the victim with respect and dignity. In addition, numerous programs have been established to assist victims of crime, and a large number of human service professionals have focused their careers on being victim advocates and on administering victim service programs. In short, a fourth component of the criminal justice, the victim, has been added to the three traditional components—law enforcement, the judiciary, and corrections. The need for officials and professionals who work in all components of the system to cooperate and collaborate is critical if the goals of each component are to be achieved.

These interviews with professionals also illustrate how correctional personnel and professional practitioners collaborate to provide the medical, physical, educational, and social–psychological evaluations and care required by law for those remanded to jails, correctional institutions, and community correctional facilities.

Finally, the material in this chapter, coupled with the information provided by the professionals interviewed, illustrates how physical and social scientists, legal experts and attorneys, educators, students, judges, and community volunteers have collaborated in finding ways to improve the quality of justice, particularly in the trial and sentencing phases of the process. The Innocence Project and many other programs have used evidence obtained through scientific research to show that many innocent people have been wrongfully convicted and that the discoveries and innovations from scientific research and technology can lead to improvements in the "quality" of justice.

References

Akron Beacon Journal. (2014). Commentary: After DeWine Stepped Up. July 10, A9.

Bard, M. and Shellow, R. (1976). Neighborhood police teams. In *Issues in law enforcement*, Robert Shellow and Morton Bard (eds.) Reston, VA: Reston Publishing Company, pp. 171–182.

Battered Women's Shelter of Summit & Median Counties. (2014). Akron, OH: Nonprofit organization. http://www.scmcbws.org/. Accessed July 7, 2014.

Champion, D. (2005). *The American dictionary of criminal justice*, 3rd ed. Los Angeles, CA: Roxbury Publishing.

Coffey, A. (1974). *Police intervention into family crises.* Santa Cruz: CA: Davis.

Davis, R. and Henley, M. (1990). Victim service programs. In *Victims of crime: Problems, policies, and programs*, A. Lurigio, W. Skogan and R. Davis (eds.). Newbury Park: Sage, pp. 157–171.

Finn, P. and Lee, B. (1985). Working with victim/witness assistance programs: Benefits for law enforcement. *Police Chief*, June, pp. 54–58.

Gaboury, M. (1992). Implementation of federal legislation to aid victims of crime in the United States. In *Critical issues in victimology: International perspectives*, E. Viano (ed.). NY: Springer, NY, pp. 224–232.

Geller, A. (2014). Mental illness overwhelms U.S. jails. *Akron Beacon Journal*, Monday, July 14, 2014: A1, A 4.

Gottfredson, G.D., Gottfredson, C., Czeh, E.R., Cantor, E., Cross, S.B., and Hantman, J. (2004). Toward safe schools: the national study of delinquency prevention in schools. National Institute of Juvenile Research in Brief. Washington, DC: U.S. Department of Justice.

Innocence Project. (2013). *The causes of wrongful conviction*. http://www.innocenceproject.org/understand/, Accessed July 21, 2014.

Innocence Project. (2014). *Know the cases*. http//www.innocenceproject.org/know/, Accessed July 21, 2014.

Kelly, M. (1975). The first urban policeman. In *Issues in law enforcement*, G. Killinger and P. Cromwell, Jr. (eds.). Boston: Holbrook Press, pp. 3–10.

Kratcoski, P. (1992). An analysis of cases involving elderly homicide victims and offenders. In *Critical issues in victimology: International perspectives*, E. Viano (ed.). New York: Springer, pp. 86–95.

Kratcoski, P. (2009). History of victimology, 1960s. In *The Praeger handbook of victimology*, J. Wilson (ed.): Santa Barbara, CA; Praeger, pp. 116–118.

Kratcoski, P. (2012). *Juvenile justice administration*. Boca Rican, FL: CRC Press.

Kratcoski, P. and Kempf, K. (1995). Police reform. In *The encyclopedia of police science*, 2nd ed., W. Bailey (ed.). New York: Garland Publishing, pp. 609–614.

Kratcoski, P. and Tontodonato, P. (1993). Unpublished document printed by Kent State University, Kent, OH: Kent, OH: Kent State University.

Kratcoski, P. and Walker, D. (1984). *Criminal justice in America: Process and issues*, 2nd ed. New York: Random House.

Mauet, T. (2002). *Trial techniques*, 6th ed. New York: Aspen Publishers.

Michigan Law and Northwestern Law. (2014). The National Registry of Exonerations. http://www.law.umich.edu/special/exoneration/Pages/about.aspx, Accessed June 25, 2014.

National Institute of Justice. (2014). *Forensic sciences*. http://www.nij.gov/topics/forensics/welcome.aspx, Accessed July 8, 2014.

Occupational outlook handbook. Private detectives and investigators. (2014). *Bureau of labor statistics*. http//www.bis.gov/ooh/protective-service/private-detectives-and-investigators.htm. Retrieved June 6, 2014.

Ohio Attorney General. (2013). *Annual report 2013*. www.OhioAtorneyGeneral.gov/Pdf, Accessed July 8, 2015.

Pavalko, R. (1971). *Sociology of occupations and professions*. Itasca, IL: Peacock Publishers.

Ramsey, R. and Frank, J. (2007). Wrongful conviction: Perceptions of criminal justice professionals regarding the frequency of wrongful convictions and the extent of systematic errors in crime and delinquency. *Crime and Delinquency*, 53: 436–470.

Roman, J., Walsh, K., Lachman, P., and Yahner, J. (2012). *Post-conviction DNA testing and wrongful conviction*. Washington, DC: Urban Institute.

Rosenbaum, D. and Hanson, G. (1998). Assessing the effects of school-based drug education: a six year multi-level analysis of project D.A.R.E. *Journal of research in crime and delinquency*, 35(4): 381–412.

Santana, S. (2009). Shelters. In *The Praeger handbook of victimology*, J. Wilson (ed.). Santa Barbara, CA: Praeger, pp. 254–255.

Stark County Prosecutor. (2015). http://www.starkcountyohio.gov/prosecutor. Accessed July 1, 2015.

Tontodonato, P. and Kratcoski, P. (1995). *Crime victims' utilization of services: Final research report for the governor's office of criminal justice services*. Unpublished document printed by Kent State University, Kent, OH. Kent, OH: Kent State University.

Victim Assistance Program. (2014). *General Brochure:1.* http://www.victimassistan-ceprogram.org/eddia/1019/vap2014generalbrochure.pdf.page1. Accessed July 8, 2014.

Victim Assistance Program. (2014). *History.* http://www.victimassistanceprogram.org/who-we-are/history.aspx. Accessed July 7, 2014.

Wilson, J. (2009). *The Praeger handbook of victimology.* Janet K. Wilson, (ed.) Santa Barbara, CA: Praeger.

Police, Academic, Professional, Community Collaboration

15

Past, Present, and Future

PETER C. KRATCOSKI
Kent State University
Kent, OH, USA

Contents

Introduction

Many of the tasks of the police have not changed since the police became formally organized. The police still have the same functions of "protecting and serving." However, the recipients of the protection and service have changed as well as the manner in which the service and protection are provided. As nations move toward establishing democratic forms of government that are based on the rule of law, the citizens of these countries become the recipients of the protection and service provided by the police. While the nature of police work may not have changed, the types of training and skills needed to be effective changed tremendously. In addition, there has been a growing realization that, in our global society, the leaders of the components of the justice system must reach out for help from the leaders of other private and public agencies and institutions (Kratcoski 2013, 1). In response to a question posed by David Baker (2011, 7) to Mal Hyde, South Australia's Police Commissioner, regarding the most important changes he experienced in his policing career, Commissioner Hyde responded, "There have been enormous changes in policing. Policing is a profession where some things change and some things remain the same. The dynamics of policing, the problem of policing, the art of policing, what policing is all about don't change because it is a mixture of the behavior of people (innate human behavior that might vary because of different cultures) and then also the way authority interplays with that behavior." He continued by saying that, "There have been enormous changes within the communities … and modern technology, communications, and other factors have drastically changed the way police work is done."

Kratcoski (2010, 14) notes, "It has long been recognized by police administrators that police work is dependent on other agencies and organizations, both public and private, within the community. Police organizations in an open society are influenced by and often dependent on the national and state legislatures, the judiciary, the mass media, social service agencies, commercial enterprise, educational institutions, and the public." Several examples of how police and other institutions have collaborated include (14–15):

- Police organizations have adapted management models similar to those used in large corporations, government bureaucracies, and public service institutions.
- Police and academics have collaborated on community action programs, training and educational programs, and research.
- Civilians perform many of the police tasks, such as dispatching, record keeping, analysis of physical evidence, computer programming, and crime statistics analysis, that were completed by sworn police officers in the past. In addition, new positions have been created, such as psychologists, and these positions are generally held by civilians.
- Educational institutions offer academic degrees and even basic training in policing.
- Police academy administrators are relying on academics and professionals to provide instruction on specialized subjects such as the law, victim's rights, human relations, cultural awareness, and the use of new technology.
- Police administrators and line officers are receiving advanced degrees in administration, law, and criminal justice. In addition, the number of police officers or former police officers who hold either full-time or part-time academic positions has increased tremendously. In addition, police leaders have become involved in academic professional organizations, as well as academics becoming involved in professional policing organizations, such as the International Association of Police Chiefs.

- Private security agencies and auxiliary police now perform many of the tasks that were the responsibility of the public police in the past.
- Commercial enterprises provide police equipment such as computers and software, weapons, body armor, and various types of communications equipment.

These ways the police, educators, professional practitioners, and members of the community assist each other and collaborate on policing and justice matters are indicative of the trends in policing. As a result, one would expect that with the advances in science and technology and the renewed emphasis on providing service to the community, the amount and areas of cooperation and collaboration will expand significantly.

Reasons for Increased Collaboration in Education and Training

It was noted in Chapter 1 that police organizations and the functions the police perform are constantly changing, depending on changes in the laws under which they are governed, changes in the sentiments of the community, and the knowledge that police leaders and those in power positions have what enables them to make decisions on policy matter pertaining to police work. This knowledge comes from many sources, including personal experiences, parents, teachers, significant others, political and religious leaders, books, the Internet, friends, coworkers, work supervisors, and from many other areas. At times, the amount of information received may be so voluminous or technical that it overwhelms the person. In such situations, when the amount of information is so extensive and difficult to understand, the recipient either becomes selective and only tries to digest that information considered important to his/her well-being or turns for assistance to someone else who appears to be more knowledgeable about the subject matter and who can be trusted to provide a valid interpretation of the meaning and importance of the information.

The multifaceted functions the police perform leads to the development of an unusual relationship with the public. The tasks involved in the preventing and controlling of crime often lead to a fear of the police by the citizenry and the belief that interaction with the police should be avoided unless absolutely necessary. Kratcoski and Walker (1984, 98) note that, "When functioning as a representative of the criminal justice system, the police officer must assume a highly professional stance, making sure that he or she properly conducts all activities relating to serving citations or making arrests that will survive the scrutiny of judges, prosecutors, and defense attorneys." In regard to this function, a police culture sometimes is created in which the typical officer develops a "we against them" mindset that suggests that the only ones who can be trusted and turned to for providing accurate information are fellow officers. To some extent, even superior officers and other representatives of the justice systems, such as prosecutors and judges, are not to be trusted. On the other hand, the service function of the police role calls for an officer who is able to provide personal, compassionate assistance for those in need. The police are called to assist in medical emergencies, to intervene in family crisis situations, and to assist victims of crime, including child victims of physical and sexual abuse. In this role, the officer must be considerate and understanding and able to inspire trust. While performing the service function, the officer is not perceived by the people being served as the "enemy," and the officer welcomes any assistance or information from the victim or others that will be useful to ensure that the services needed are provided. Those who are receiving the assistance are likely to perceive the officer as a "friend," regardless of their perceptions of the police before they had the personal encounter in which the police officer provided assistance. The matter of the police accepting information and communicating, cooperating, and collaborating with the public as well as academics, professionals, and other justice agency functionaries is complicated and dependent on several factors. First, there is the matter of the usefulness of the information and the helpfulness of the assistance provided. Second, the question is whether the source of the information or the assistance provider can be trusted. The third factor is whether reliance on others outside the police organization is necessary to accomplish the task.

Considering the factors mentioned here, it is easy to understand why police administrators had many reservations about developing collaborative relations with academics and researchers on matters pertaining to police operations and administration. Feedback from police administrators and regular line officers revealed they were either not convinced that the finding of the scientific research completed by academics was useful, or that they did not have the background to be able to understand the methods used to complete the research and to interpret the results. Also, there was suspicion about the motives for completing the research. Many claimed the research was more likely to benefit the researcher than to benefit the police and the community. William Bratton, the former police commissioner of New York City, in response to a question on the importance the input of academics had on the day-to-day practice of managing a police agency answered:

> I really do not use, to any degree, the work of academics. There are several reasons. One, many academics write for each other, not for practitioners, and when you attempt to read many of their studies, they are literally not readable. Two, oftentimes their studies are dated. It always infuriates me that we're reading studies about events and issues of three or four years back. Policing is much more contemporary than that, and if there was one lesson in policing in the '90s it is (that) you need to be timely. (Henry 2000, 560–561)

The chapters written for this book and other sources sited throughout it reveal how administrators' views of the importance of academic research on effective policing have changed during the past several decades. Police leaders have become more progressive, better educated, and more willing to accept ideas and information from those outside police organizations. In addition, the "we against them" attitude, with "them" referring to anyone outside the police establishment, although not totally dissipated, has become far less pronounced. Knowledgeable police administrators are aware of their dependence on outsiders and how the police establishment is intricately intertwined with other justice agencies, the educational establishment, and the communities they serve. In addition, police work in general has become more internationally focused. This underlines the need for international cooperation and collaboration in the training of police officers because more emphasis is now given to combating international crime.

Collaboration in Education and Training

Chapter 4 in this book focuses on the organizational models of police agencies and the types of command and leadership abilities needed to successfully manage these organizations. Chan et al. (2011) noted that the concepts of command, leadership, and management are closely connected but are also different in meaning. Command is the authority that a person has, based on the position within the organization that person holds, while leadership involves the person's ability to influence people to act or perform willingly and ethically. Management refers to the planning, organizing, staffing, and controlling of organizational resources. Garner et al. (2012) defines command philosophy as the beliefs, values, and principles that influence and help a commander to focus on the type of leadership that will be used in the management of the organization. Thiagaraja et al. (2014) use the concept *command leader* to indicate a person who is successful in integrating and completing the command and management tasks and who possesses the leadership qualities that are needed to achieve the goals of the organization.

Although various countries may follow different models and have different command philosophies in the training and education of individuals who will eventually serve as line officers and police administrators, it is fairly certain that there will be a closer alliance between the higher education institutions and the police training academies in the future. Kratcoski (2007, 15) notes that, "Countries with a national force organized along the lines of the military tend to educate their officers in institutions staffed and controlled by the police rather than in colleges and universities." While in other countries, "Those seeking to become commissioned officers may pursue four-year degree programs at police academies or enter the police with degrees from domestic institutions after they receive some additional training."

In addition to the provider of police education, the matter of emphasis and content varies by countries. Das and Pino (2007, 127), in a comparative analysis of police training in four countries, found that, although historically the training of the police was militaristic, "The new philosophy includes more emphasis on public relations and working with community leaders." They note that, "Currently the use of psychology, citizen involvement, and developing good public relationships has been increasingly emphasized in the training." Although the acquisition of the knowledge and skills needed to perform the tasks related to police work was considered a necessary function of the training of the police in all four countries, the police leaders of each country also specified goals that they would like to achieve with the police training. For example, in Switzerland, there was an equal emphasis on learning the policing techniques and on understanding the emotions, needs, and sensibilities of the people with whom the police will likely come into contact in the different situations they will encounter. In Japan, they note that ethics and cultural understanding are emphasized within a community policing content in the training. And, in Germany, the aftermath of World War II has produced an emphasis on a training philosophy that teaches how democracy works and that the police must be trained to follow the rule of law. In France, there was more emphasis on training police to be generalists. Das and Pino (2007, 127) note that, "With generalization as the French civil service philosophy, training and education of civil servants in France are directed toward the objective of producing officials who can perform all of the required tasks associated with police work."

The number and variety of programs in which academics, police, and professional practitioners have collaborated is extensive. In this book, portions of Chapters 4, 5, and 7 pertain to specialized cooperative police training programs relating to Internet fraud, corruption, and trafficking in drugs, weapons, and humans, as well as other forms of organized crime and white collar crime. Other forms of collaboration between the police and the academic community can be found in the numerous variety of experience-based educational programs open to students interested in careers in justice studies, such as field trips, co-ops, internships, symposiums, workshops, and international travel to study justice systems in other countries.

International Collaboration in Police Education and Training

The International Law Enforcement Academy (ILEA), located in Budapest, Hungary, was established to provide advanced police training for Eastern European countries. The academy is jointly administered and funded by the U.S. Federal Bureau of Investigation (FBI) and the Hungarian government. The training is modeled after the training FBI agents receive at the National Training Academy in Quantico, Virginia (Kratcoski and Kratcoski 2010, 9). The International Criminal Investigative Training Assistance Program (ICITAP), under the auspices of the U.S. Department of State, offers training for the police in developing countries that have adopted democratic forms of government. Ducot (2008, 4) summarizes the mission of ICITAP: "To work with foreign governments to develop professional and transparent law enforcement institutions that protect human rights, combat corruption, and reduce the threat of transnational crime and terrorism." Cordner and Shane (2011, 281) give several examples of international collaboration in police training and research. They include the efforts of the European Police College (CEPOL) to develop and promote a common police training curricula on a number of important topics such as counterterrorism, response to domestic violence, and the management of crises. The Police Training and Development Branch of INTERPOL publishes the *International Police Training Journal* online. Edelbacher (2007) describes several international cooperative education and training programs connected with INTERPOL: the Middle European Police Academy, the FBI's International Law Enforcement Academy, and the European Police Academy.

Collaboration in Community Response to Natural Disasters

The police have always been expected to work closely with other service agencies in times of catastrophic events, such as when a huge fire threatens to destroy a city and when natural disasters such as floods, earthquakes, and hurricanes occur. In earlier times, before formally organized firefighting departments were established, the police were often expected to serve as firefighters. Thus, the tradition of collaborating with other community organizations and citizen volunteers in times of catastrophic events and disasters is well established.

The number and types of agencies that have responsibility for the safety and provision of relief to the victims of disasters has increased significantly. Many of the relief services that might have been performed by the police in the past, such as providing direct assistance in distributing basic life essentials such as food, clothing, and shelter, are now performed by formally organized agencies and volunteers; but the police contribution is still very significant in terms of coordination and communication, protecting the first responders, and protecting the area affected by the disaster from criminals. Yokohoma (2013) summarized the ways the police, community service agencies, the government, community volunteers, and the mass media worked together to provide relief and community security during the tsunami that hit Japan in 2011.

In the United States, the Department of Homeland Security's Disaster Section coordinates its relief and protection efforts with other federal, state, and local agencies, as well as with business establishments and community volunteers.

Police Collaboration with Professional Practitioners

The areas in which public police agencies have cooperated and collaborated with professional practitioners, such as psychologists, social workers, physical and social scientists, physicians, and other types of medical workers—including social workers, technicians, accountants, statisticians, and many other types of professionals, are numerous. Currently, professionals can be found working as employees of police departments or as consultants providing such services as:

- Developing and implementing standardized instruments used in the recruitment and selection of personnel
- Assessing stress, burnout, and job satisfaction among officers
- Providing direct counseling to officers experiencing post-traumatic stress, burnout, thoughts of suicide, alcohol or drug abuse problems, and other personal problems that have an effect on their performance
- Assisting in the investigations of crimes through crime scene and evidence analysis
- Providing medical reports on such matters as causes of death, types of wounds, and weapons used
- Assisting in specialized training in areas such as domestic violence, cultural diversity, community relations, and crime prevention
- Serving as advisory board members for various types of community organizations, commissions, and other agencies that are police–community related, such as civilian review boards, community crime prevention organizations, and victim protection agencies

Because there appears to be a significant increase in the proportion of inmates being held in jails and prisons who are suffering from some form of mental illness, the need to provide services to these individuals has resulted in more psychologists and drug and alcohol counselors being employed by these facilities. The types of offenders that are housed in jails, correctional institutions, and in community correctional facilities that often need special medical attention and/or psychological assessment and counseling are sex offenders (including rapists and child molesters), substance abusers, mentally ill or mentally handicapped individuals, offenders with HIV or AIDS, and elderly offenders. The professionals providing these services will either be employed by private, state, county, or local government agencies; they may be hired as consultants or may be under contract to provide specified services for these agencies.

The nature of their work requires that they have special education and skills and that they be allowed to provide the type of service, be it counseling, physical therapy, or education, that is likely to produce the most desirable outcome possible. Ethically, these professionals are required to perform their duties in accordance with the standards of their profession. To do so requires a great deal of autonomy in decision making. At times, the requirements of the professional practice (for example, private one-on-one counseling with "dangerous" inmates) may be in direct conflict with the security measures employed within the institution. The inmates receiving psychological counseling and other special services may be the same inmates who are the most troublesome and who are the most difficult to handle within their housing units. Thus, correctional staff may resent having these inmates receive what appear to be special "privileges" when they meet with psychological services. The professional may at times experience considerable role conflict in trying to adhere to the principles of the profession when providing the services and adhering to the rules and regulations that apply to the staff of the facility. It requires considerable cooperation and communication among the administration of the facility, the rank and file workers, and the professionals to avoid conflicts and to coordinate all their efforts to ensure that the goals of the institution are achieved.

Police–Justice Agencies' Collaboration with Advocates for Victims of Crimes

It is often stated that a victim of crime is twice victimized, first by the perpetrator of the crime and second by the criminal justice system. In the past, not much attention was given to the victims of crime, except that by using them to provide evidence, they could assist the police in making an arrest and later help the prosecutor in building a case that would lead to a conviction.

Sutherland was one of the first academics to develop an interest in the victims of crime in the United States. In his book, *Criminology* (1924), he classified victims into individualized (or direct) victims and societal (or indirect) victims. Direct victims were those who were murdered, robbed, assaulted, or who had property stolen from them. Indirect victimization was the costs that all citizens had to bear as a result of crime, such as paying higher taxes to support a larger criminal justice system, spending more on security, increasing fear of being victimized, and paying higher prices overall for goods.

Special categories of victims became the focal point of much of the research and activism during the 1950s and 1960s. Attention focused on the victimization of racial minority groups by discriminatory laws, discrimination in housing and employment practices, physical abuses such as beating or lynching, and educational discrimination by separate but equal policies in the schools. Physical abuse and victimization of women and children also gained attention. The mechanisms used to try and correct these evils included federal and state legislation (such as the Equal Opportunities Act and the Civil Rights Act) and court cases that challenged the discriminatory practices, such as *Brown vs the Board of Education of Topeka, Kansas* (Crowley 2009, 119–122; Kratcoski 2009, 113–116).

As the United States moved into the latter part of the twentieth century, the focus of the victim's rights movement changed somewhat with increased attention given to hate crimes, sexual abuse, and violence against women, through which both individuals and groups were victimized. During this time period, new federal and state legislation targeting these problems was passed by Congress and state legislatures. For example, the Federal Victim and Witness Protection Act (1982) granted victims of federal crimes several important rights, including the right to be notified of hearings, restitution, and fair treatment during the entire justice process. The Victims' Rights and Restitution Act, the Hate Crime Statistics Act, the Violence Against Women Act, the Federal Anti-Stalker Act, the Jacob Wetterling Crimes Against Children and Sexually Violent Offender Registration Act, the International Parental Kidnapping Crime Act, and other federal laws relating to the protection of victims were passed by Congress from 1990 to 1996 (Wilson 2009, xi). Many states also passed legislation similar to that enacted by the federal government.

International Development of Victimology

Viano (1992) noted that interest in the victims of crime developed in Europe during the 1970s for many of the same reasons as in the United States. European countries experienced significant increases in crime, particularly violent offenses. Research on the long-lasting economic and psychological effects victims of crime experience, as well as the "shoddy" treatment victims of crime often received from criminal justice agencies, helped to stimulate the victims' rights movement in Europe. Viano (1992, 3) notes that, "In European countries ... a strong central government has traditionally played a major role in providing extensive social services from 'cradle to grave.' Thus, the needs of the victims of crime have been addressed by appealing to the already existing responsibilities of the government for the social welfare of the citizenry." He also mentions that the victim service agencies in

European countries are not attached to a justice system component, such as the prosecutor's office, as they typically are in the United States.

As the world becomes a global society, there has been considerable movement toward standardizing laws, criminal codes, and international cooperation in establishing crime prevention and law enforcement mechanisms. The cooperation and collaboration among nations on security, legal, and justice-related matters can also be noticed, to some extent, in regard to the protection and servicing of the victims of crime. The World Society of Victimology was established in 1979 (Wilson 2009, x), and the United Nations has held several meetings pertaining to victims of crime. In 1985, it adopted the Declaration of Basic Principles of Justice for Victims of Crime and Abuse of Power (Wilson 2009, xi).

The Rise of the Professional Victims' Advocate

Concurrent with the victims' right movement in the United States, there was also a rapid increase in professionally trained social workers, counselors, psychologists, and various types of therapists (such as occupational therapists) who have developed careers in victim services. In the earlier development of the victim rights and services movement, these professionals often found that developing cooperative and collaborative relations with justice agencies was difficult or impossible. Phillips (2009, 197) noted that, "Prior to the 1980s, when the concept of community policing began to impact significantly not only the management of policing specifically but the entire criminal justice apparatus (CJA) generally, crime victims and others directly involved, such as witnesses, were treated more like objects than as 'real people' with real emotions, wants, and needs." He goes on, saying that victims and witnesses received very little feedback from the police and prosecutors about their cases until it was time for them to appear in court. Other researchers (Patterson 2011; Rich and Seffrin 2013) found that, even up to the present time, some police officers perceive victim advocates to be a "hindrance" and often that they interfere with the investigation of the crime.

Based on the research and case studies of victim service programs cited, it is reasonable to expect that communications, cooperation, and collaboration in training, program development, and implementation, and in other mutually beneficial endeavors between victim service agencies and justice agencies will not only continue, but will expand and be strengthened in the future. In addition, the scope of the concept of "victim" broadens. Victim service advocates will be expected to provide a range of services to victims, including to those victims of natural disasters—such as floods, earthquakes, and fires, and to victims of terrorist attacks.

One might expect that collaboration among justice agencies, the government, and victim service agencies will also expand in areas of indirect victimization, such as environmental crimes, financial crimes such as price fixing and banking fraud, and in various types of consumer fraud.

References

Baker, D. (2011). Interview with commissioner Mal Hyde. In *Trends in policing*, Vol. 3. O. Marenin and D. K. Das (eds.), Boca Raton, FL: CRC Press, pp. 1–22.

Chan, K., Soh, S. and Ramaya, R. (2011). *Military leadership in the 21st century: Science and practice.* Singapore: Cengage Learning Asia Pte Ltd.

Cordner, G. and Shane, C. (2011). The changing landscape of police education and training. *Police Practices and Research: An International Journal,* 4(12), 281–285.

Crowley, J. (2009). History of victimology, 1970s. In *The Praeger handbook of victimology.* Janet K. Wilson (ed.), Santa Barbara, CA: Praeger, pp. 119–122.

Das, D. and Pino, N. (2007). A comparative account of police training in four countries. In *Police education and training in a global society,* edited by P. Kratcoski and D. Das. Lanham, MD: Lexington Books, pp. 125–146.

Ducot, G. (2008). Democratic policing in an emerging democracy. *Panel Discussion at the 15th Annual Meeting of the International Police Executive Symposium,* Cincinnati, May, 2008.

Edelbacher, M. (2007). Police education and training: A perspective of Austria. In *Police education in a global society,* edited by P. Kratcoski and D. Das, Lanham, MD: Lexington Books, pp. 95–105.

Garner, H., Army, C. and Peterson, J. (2012). Developing an effective command philosophy. *Military Review,* 12, 75–81.

Henry, V. (2000). A conservation with William J. Bratton. *Police Practice and Research,* 1(4), 559–580.

Kratcoski, P. (2007). The challenges of police education and training in a global society. In *Police education and training in a global society,* edited by P. Kratcoski and D. Das. Lanham, MD: Lexington Books, pp. 3–21.

Kratcoski, P. (2009). History of victimology, 1950s. In *The Praeger handbook of victimology,* edited by J. Wilson. Santa Barbara, CA: Praeger, pp. 111–113.

Kratcoski, P. (2010). Police without borders: An overview. In *Police without borders: The fading distinction between local and global,* edited by C. Roberson, D. Das and J. Singer. Boca Raton, FL: CRC Press, pp. 1–26.

Kratcoski, P. (2013). Policing: Continuity and change. Unpublished paper presented at the 23rd Annual Meeting of the International Police executive Symposium, Budapest, Hungary.

Kratcoski, P. and Walker, D. (1984). *Criminal justice in America: Process and issues,* 2nd ed. New York: Random House.

Patterson, D. (2011). The linkage between secondary victimization by law enforcement and rape case outcomes. *Journal of Interpersonal Violence,* 26(2), 328–347.

Phillips, P. (2009). Police officers. In *The Praeger handbook of victimology*, edited by J. Wilson. Santa Barbara, CA: Praeger, pp. 197–199.

Rich, K. and Seffrin, P. (2013). Police officers' collaboration with victim advocates: Barriers and facilitators. *Violence and Victims*, 28(4), 223–237.

Thiagaraja, B., Khader, M., Ang, J., Maan, D., Tan, E. and Patrick, P. (2014). C5: A command leadership framework for law enforcement, safety and security commanders in Singapore. Unpublished paper presented at the Society for Police and criminal Psychology Conference, Las Vegas, Nevada.

Viano, E. (1992). Introduction. In *Critical issues in victimology*, edited by E. Viano. New York: Springer, pp. 1–12.

Yokohoma, M. (2013). Policing a catastrophe: Special policing after earthquake and tsunamie in Japan on March 11, 2011. Unpublished paper presented at the Annual Meeting of the International Police executive Symposium, Budapest Hungary, August, 2014.

Wilson, J. (2009). Chronology of selected victimology events. In *The Praeger handbook of victimology*. Janet K. Wilson (ed.), Santa Barbara, CA: Praeger, pp. x–xi.

Index

rns and Information please contact our EU
ylorandfrancis.com
imbH, Kaufingerstraße 24, 80331 München, Germany

A Call for Authors
Advances in Police Theory and Practice

AIMS AND SCOPE:

This cutting-edge series is designed to promote publication of books on contemporary advances in police theory and practice. We are especially interested in volumes that focus on the nexus between research and practice, with the end goal of disseminating innovations in policing. We will consider collections of expert contributions as well as individually authored works. Books in this series will be marketed internationally to both academic and professional audiences. This series also seeks to —

- Bridge the gap in knowledge about advances in theory and practice regarding who the police are, what they do, and how they maintain order, administer laws, and serve their communities
- Improve cooperation between those who are active in the field and those who are involved in academic research so as to facilitate the application of innovative advances in theory and practice

Police Reform in China

Mission-Based Policing

The International Trafficking of Human Organs

The series especially encourages the contribution of works coauthored by police practitioners and researchers. We are also interested in works comparing policing approaches and methods globally, examining such areas as the policing of transitional states, democratic policing, policing and minorities, preventive policing, investigation, patrolling and response, terrorism, organized crime and drug enforcement. In fact, every aspect of policing, public safety, and security, as well as public order is relevant for the series. Manuscripts should be between 300 and 600 printed pages. If you have a proposal for an original work or for a contributed volume, please be in touch.

Series Editor
Dilip Das, Ph.D., Ph: 802-598-3680
E-mail: dilipkd@aol.com

Dr. Das is a professor of criminal justice and Human Rights Consultant to the United Nations. He is a former chief of police, and founding president of the International Police Executive Symposium, IPES, www.ipes.info. He is also founding editor-in-chief of *Police Practice and Research: An International Journal* (PPR), (Routledge/Taylor & Francis), www.tandf.co.uk/journals. In addition to editing the *World Police Encyclopedia* (Taylor & Francis, 2006), Dr. Das has published numerous books and articles during his many years of involvement in police practice, research, writing, and education.

Proposals for the series may be submitted to the series editor or directly to –
Carolyn Spence
Senior Editor • CRC Press / Taylor & Francis Group
561-317-9574 • 561-997-7249 (fax)
carolyn.spence@taylorandfrancis.com • www.crcpress.com
6000 Broken Sound Parkway NW, Suite 300, Boca Raton, FL 33487

For Product Safety Conce
representative GPSR@ta
Taylor & Francis Verlag